A 50·YEAR ADVENTURE in the ADVERTISING BUSINESS

Ernest W. Baker

"Advertising nourishes the consuming power of men. It creates wants for a better standard of living. It sets up before a man the goal of a better home, better clothing, better food for himself and his family. It spurs greater production."
— *Winston Churchill*

THIS BOOK IS DEDICATED
TO MY GRANDCHILDREN

Matthew, Emily, Blaine, Bradley and Reid

I want my grandchildren and their children to know me. Not just as someone who was in the advertising business for half a century – but as someone who tried to make a difference.

In the eyes of my descendants I want to be remembered as someone who was dedicated to his craft, patient and community-minded. I consider myself most fortunate that I was able to work for 50 years at something that I truly enjoyed. I believe *we were not made to retire, but to work until we die if we are able, at a sensible pace, at something we enjoy.*

Hopefully, my grandchildren will learn from this book and find helpful information that will inspire them in their own business careers as well as in their lives.

To The Readers – An Introduction

My 50-some years in the advertising business began in mid-September 1948 when I became an employee of the Zimmer-Keller, Inc. advertising agency which was located on the 13th floor of the Stroh building (later renamed the Mutual Building) on Grand Circus Park in downtown Detroit. I had graduated from the University of Missouri School of Journalism in May of 1948 but immediately after graduation got a job selling automobile accessories (mainly car burglar alarms) for a company that was owned by an uncle of one of my Beta Theta Pi fraternity brothers at the University of Missouri. I took the sales job because it was imperative that I build some financial resources, as I was engaged to be married. That marriage took place on September 4, 1948 when Joan Elaine Bauman became my wife.

Joan and I met and fell in love at the beginning of my senior year in college. We were married 43 years when cancer took Joan's life in February of 1992. Without her support, concern and understanding I seriously doubt that I would have even completed the 43-plus years in advertising which I experienced while we were married. Over the years, as I progressed in the business, demands on my time increased. It was not unusual starting in the early 1950s that several times a month I worked at the office late into the evening and occasionally on a Saturday.

And, it became a routine matter nearly every evening to spend some time either reading various materials and trade publications or writing service reports or both. Joan's indulgence and encouragement greatly contributed to my career and she was a true partner in every sense of the word. I have known many men in the advertising business that did not have the support and understanding that I enjoyed which only makes me more appreciative and thankful for the partner that I had throughout most of my years in the business.

From the beginning of my career I have kept a daily diary. I used these diaries to record daily activities in order to do my time sheets (for cost accounting) and it's where I kept a record of expenses for my expense reports. To this information I added a brief description each day of business and social activities and having all this information readily available is what made it possible for me to write this book. It's amazing how reading a page from one of my diaries – although written 20, 30, or even 40 or more years ago – will bring back the events of a particular day almost as if they had happened a few days ago.

The advertising business and the world around us have changed tremendously over the past 50 years. Some of that change is reported as a part of this book but that's just one part of this story. I've included situations and events as well as the backgrounds of people and companies in order to try to make this book entertaining as well as informative. I hope you find it so.

A journey of a thousand miles must begin with the first step.
Chinese Philosopher Lao-Tzu
6th Century B.C.

A 50-Year Adventure in the Advertising Business 1948-1998
by Ernest W. Baker

Library of Congress Cataloging-in-Publication Data
Baker, Jr. Ernest W.   1926-
99   096494
ISBN   0-8143-2910-1
Includes Index

Distributed By:
Wayne State University Press
4809 Woodward Avenue
Detroit, MI 48201-1309

Manufactured in the United States of America by Sheridan Books,
100 North Staebler Road, Ann Arbor, Michigan 48103

Jacket design by Diane Schroeder of BBDO Detroit

CONTENTS

Chapter 1

The Beginning Of A 50-Year Career
In Advertising

*Advertising is the communication
of ideas for a company or product
designed to influence the minds
of people who buy.*

After a brief honeymoon following my marriage to Joan Elaine Bauman on September 4, 1948 – and a trip to St. Louis where I had been promised an advertising position that didn't materialize – Joan and I returned to Detroit where I started looking for a job with an agency. Fortunately, there were job opportunities in advertising for beginners and within a week I had three offers from which to make a selection. One offer was to become an assistant production manager at the Fred M. Randall advertising agency; another was to join a three year in-house training program at the Brooke, Smith, French and Dorrance agency; and the third was for a combination media/copy/production/office boy position with the Zimmer-Keller, Inc. advertising agency.

I selected the latter because I thought it offered me the possibility of getting more experience faster in various facets of the business. And I believe it did!

Walter Zimmer founded this agency in 1915. Like many Detroit agencies, throughout its early years it primarily served accounts related to the automotive industry. About a year after starting the agency, Zimmer met Ralph Keller at an auto show in New York and the pair teamed up to form Zimmer-Keller, Inc. Keller had worked as a copywriter for a Toledo agency that handled the Willys-Overland Automotive account prior to joining up with Walter Zimmer.

Some of the agency's early accounts included the Rickenbacker Motor Company in Detroit and Peerless Motors in Cleveland. The agency served the Stroh's Brewery for many years and the brewery eventually became one of its largest accounts. Harry Calvert joined the agency in 1945, coming from Cleveland, where he was an account executive on the Ford Dealers account. In 1952 (after I had left this agency) the agency's name was changed to Zimmer, Keller & Calvert, Inc. and in 1969 it was acquired by the Ross Roy advertising agency which was, at that time, headquartered in Detroit.

When I joined Zimmer-Keller in September 1948 there were about 30 employees. It operated as a copy/contact agency where the account executives not only contacted the clients but also wrote virtually all the copy for the accounts they serviced. The entire creative department consisted of just one art director. He only did rough layouts which were then sent to an art studio for execution.

My desk was next to the art director's so I had an opportunity to learn by watching him work. There were just a few private offices. Most employees sat at desks situated in one large open room. There were no partitioned "work stations" as we know them today.

My primary responsibility at Zimmer-Keller was to keep track of all the Stroh's Beer billboards. Stroh's Beer in 1948 was a regional brand. It was, at that time, a dark, bohemian-style beer with a heavy taste. It was popular primarily with people with an eastern European background. It was a regional beer with distribution throughout Michigan, Northern Ohio and Northern Indiana and the advertising budget was almost entirely dedicated to outdoor advertising. Television took America by storm in the 1950s and breweries quickly learned to take advantage of that medium. In the late '40s, however, most breweries still relied primarily on outdoor advertising to reach consumers.

Joe Keller, son of Ralph, had left the agency to join the Outdoor Advertising Bureau and it was his departure that created the job opening that I filled. Joe loved outdoor advertising, as I could readily tell by the detailed records and systems he had set up in order to keep track of more than a thousand Stroh's billboards. He had even developed his own rating system to determine the efficiency of each board. A single board with good visibility in a high traffic location received the highest score or rating while his system gave a very low rating where there were as many as four or more billboards clustered together with each fighting for viewers' attention. His criteria for each board also took into consideration other factors such as characteristics of board placement – was the panel angled, parallel to the line of traffic, or head on? Was it a left-hand or right-hand reader? Was the panel near a store where beer was sold? He then averaged these ratings for the showing in a market and it gave him a basis for bargaining for better locations.

It was also my responsibility to personally check every billboard location at least once a year to make sure each and every board was where it was supposed to be, that the paper was in good condition, that the board was well maintained and whether some obstacle (such as a tree, a shrub or a building) had materialized since the last review to impede visibility. I did not particularly enjoy field checking. Fortunately, when I joined Zimmer-Keller, Joe Keller had

recently gone to every outdoor plant in Michigan, Ohio and Indiana that the agency dealt with. He had checked every Stroh's billboard location. I got almost a year's reprieve before I had to hit the road doing the annual billboard checkup.

Field-checking billboards meant contacting the sales representative for the outdoor advertising plant assigned to the Stroh's account. Upon meeting this person, he drove you in his car from early morning until late in the day so you could check the board locations. I carried all my records in a large, heavy, black ledger along with a clip board on which to make notes. For instance, it took three or four days to check all the locations in Metropolitan Detroit. One day would suffice in Grand Rapids and a day or two to cover the tri-cities of Flint, Saginaw and Bay City. It required numerous days to cover the outstate and northern Ohio and northern Indiana areas. Every little town and village (except for a few dry counties) had one, two or more billboards depending on population. It was necessary to crisscross the states several times, past farms, orchards, fields and forests.

Lunch was absolutely the best part of the day. The sales representative for the outdoor advertising plant usually planned the day's itinerary so that we could have lunch at some "special" restaurant. Also, it was customary in those days to have one or two drinks before lunch, which helped make the day much more tolerable. On longer trips, I had to stay overnight.

One overnight stay will always be memorable. In 1949 there were very few motels so I stayed at the Bancroft Hotel in downtown Saginaw. I woke up in the middle of the night and thought I could see the outline of someone standing at the foot of my bed. After demanding "who's there?" several times and getting no answer – I slowly crawled to the end of the bed – then leaped at the mute intruder that I believed was standing there. What a surprise! It was a clothes tree on which I had hung my suit. I had put my suit coat on a hanger and with my hat on top of the clothes tree – everybody wore a fedora in those days – it looked just as if a person was lurking in the darkness.

Fortunately I suffered only a bump on my head, a split lip and a few bruises from my flying tackle but any hotel guests in the adjoining hotel rooms or on the floor below must have wondered "what in the hell was that crash?"

In the morning when I met the sales representative, his first question was, "Are you okay?" I said, "Sure!" I never explained what happened to my head and face as I was too embarrassed to tell him what I had done. He must have wondered what kind of a brawl I had gotten into the night before.

While my predecessor Joe Keller really *liked* outdoor advertising, the person who followed me at Zimmer-Keller must have *loved* it. I worked at Zimmer-Keller for 1-1/2 years. When I left, Jim Dingeman was hired as my replacement. Jim was so intrigued by billboard advertising that he bought an outdoor advertising business in Traverse City (Dingeman Advertising) and his plant eventually covered most of the upper part of Michigan's lower peninsula.

When I wasn't involved with my media duties for Stroh's I had plenty of other tasks. These included taking copy and layouts, keylines or proofs to various clients for approval in order to help out the account executives, running various errands for Walter Zimmer, proofreading, etc. But what I appreciated most was the occasional opportunity to write copy for an advertisement or a brochure. I was given some interesting copy challenges. One of our clients was the Larro Feeds Division of General Mills. Most of my copywriting assignments were for this account. Larro produced feeds for cows, horses, pigs, chickens, turkeys and even rabbits and pigeons. All their feeds were tested at a research farm located on Northwestern Highway, on the far northwest side of Detroit, and I either had to go to their research farm or to the Detroit Public Library whenever I needed reference or background information. It's hard to imagine a large farm on Northwestern Highway today as skyscrapers and the corporate headquarters of major companies now occupy both sides of the expressway.

I wrote a number of three and five minute scripts for radio bulletins that were distributed to stations throughout the country which carried

News Notes

FROM LARRO RESEARCH FARM

CAN YOU GUESS THIS COW'S AGE?

Eight experienced dairymen attempted to guess the age of this cow, "Grandma," pictured above with her owner, George Wilkinson, of Landenburg, Pennsylvania. Not one guess was even close to her *real* age.

"Grandma" is queen of Mr. Wilkinson's herd of 175 cows and heifers. She has produced 17 calves, 7 being heifers, and is due to calve again in July, 1949. She weighs around 1250 lbs., and has a strong back, a good head, and a nice udder.

"Grandma's" dam was Nancy of Goodview Farms, and she was sired by Naporeils Overseer of Breidablik. Official production records are not available but here is what she did during her last lactation . . . May, 1035 lbs., June, 985 lbs., July, 960 lbs., August, 935 lbs., September, 897 lbs. Fat runs about 4.8, which isn't bad for a 20-year-old cow. That's right, "Grandma" is actually *20 years old!*

Mr. Wilkinson started feeding LARRO about 30 years ago, and "Grandma" was raised on Larro 20% Dairy Feed. Mr. Wilkinson uses *Larro 20% Dairy Feed* as a milking ration, and as a dry feed as well.

NEW EMPHASIS ON PIGMENTATION

Broiler buyers today want rich, yellow pigmentation in the shanks. So broiler raisers too are giving more attention to growing birds with the desired shank color.

As an aid in measuring good shank color, Larro Research Farm has developed an ingenious device known as the Larro Pigmentation Meter. It is held over the back of a bird's shank as shown in the illustration. The degree of pigmentation color is determined by the number opposite the matching color. Birds raised on Larro Broiler Feed usually register a 40 to 50 score.

County Agents and Vo-Ag teachers can secure a Larro Pigmentation Meter without charge by addressing the nearest office of General Mills listed below.

•

General Mills
Larro Feeds
"Farm-tested"

Address Dept. OO at our nearest office

DETROIT 2, SAN FRANCISCO 6, CHICAGO 4

"Farm-tested" is a registered trademark of General Mills, Inc.

L-1872

This half page advertisement was adapted from a radio script that I wrote for use on stations that carried programming for farmers.

early morning programming directed at farmers. These scripts were sent to the attention of the Farm Editors of radio stations for possible inclusion in their news broadcasts. One script was about a cow that had produced a record amount of milk. Other scripts included "Once-a-Day Feeding for Dairy Cows," "Tips on Successful Turkey Raising," "How to Guess a Cow's Age," etc.

At Zimmer-Keller I had some really interesting experiences, most of them involving Walter Zimmer. Zimmer was a unique character. This was in direct contrast to his partner Harry Keller, who looked and acted like a banker or a lawyer. Short and portly, Zimmer wore custom tailored suits which had a western flair or style. Frequently he wore cowboy boots and a Stetson hat. He was definitely a colorful individual and he had some interesting quirks. For instance, he hated taxi cabs and any expense report that included a taxi fare was never approved. If you didn't have the use of your own car you either had to rent one or take a bus or streetcar. He wouldn't touch used currency – only new money – and he liked to play a "mind game" in which you tried to guess what the other person was thinking about. There was a barber shop on the first floor of the building and Zimmer's barber was his favorite "mind game" participant in spite of the fact that the barber always won – and won big!

My first involvement with Zimmer occurred in mid-November 1948 shortly after I joined the agency. He called me into his office and asked if I'd like to earn some extra money. I said of course I would and he then explained that at Thanksgiving he sent all the key contacts with the agency's clients a turkey. These were turkeys raised at the Larro Feeds Research Farm which had been dressed, frozen and packaged in a specially-designed and printed gift carton. Zimmer rented a large locker at a freezer plant and it was filled with these prize turkeys.

He explained that if I would deliver them, he'd not only pay mileage but also a bonus to get them all delivered promptly. It was a challenging task involving more than 50 deliveries throughout the entire Detroit metropolitan area. To get all the turkeys to their destination before Thanksgiving I first divided the city into sections and each afternoon and evening made all the deliveries. I had less than a week to get all the turkeys delivered, but managed to do so. As a side benefit I became quite familiar with the city and all the suburbs. Being new to Detroit I couldn't have found a better way to get to know the city that was to become my home.

After Thanksgiving, Zimmer complimented me on a job well done. My bonus was a two-week paid vacation at the end of December so Joan and I went to Missouri to spend our first Christmas and New Year's together with my mother and father. It couldn't have been a better bonus.

One particular assignment I really resented. Zimmer sent me to a small town in Canada to pick up two cases of a special 25-year-old scotch whiskey. He told me to put the scotch in the trunk of my car and to say nothing to customs when I came back across the border. I drove to Canada and picked up the scotch and fortunately returned through customs with no problem. Later, when I learned that my car could have been confiscated for not declaring the scotch and paying the necessary duty charges, I was "mad as hell" that I was ever sent on such a foolish and risky errand.

Over the years I have participated in a great many new business presentations. This is how advertising agencies win new clients. Inside the agency business presentations are known as "pitches." The first new business presentation – or "pitch" – in which I ever participated involved the Fruehauf Trailer Company.

Facing page: This full page advertisement for Larro rabbit feeds was the first copywriting assignment I was given at the Zimmer-Keller advertising agency. I felt quite proud when I saw this advertisement printed in *National Rabbit Raiser, California Rabbit News* **and** *California Rabbits.*

All of the men in the agency were notified by Zimmer by memo that they were to be available on a particular day early in 1949 for a meeting with Roy Fruehauf, the company's president. At the specified date and time all of us – about a dozen – went to Fruehauf's main office on Harper Avenue on Detroit's east side. Typical of the time, Fruehauf's office was large and wood paneled. We all stood in a group in front of Fruehauf's desk. Only Zimmer sat down opposite Fruehauf and he proceeded to tell him what a great agency Zimmer-Keller was and how the agency could help his business grow. Zimmer was a true character. He leaned back in his chair and put one of his western style boots on Fruehauf's desk and proceeded to "sell" the agency like a snake oil salesman. I was really impressed.

After ten minutes, Fruehauf suddenly said "Wait just a minute." He left his office and proceeded to round up a dozen of his men. The Fruehauf contingent was assembled in a line facing the Zimmer-Keller representatives and then Zimmer resumed "pitching" the agency. It was a strange scene. Two lines of men standing and staring at each other while the two bosses carried on a discussion about how the account would be handled.

Zimmer-Keller was officially awarded the business at that meeting. When it ended, we shook hands all around. Never since – nor do I ever expect in the future – to participate in as bizarre a new business meeting as that one. This was one of the industry's beauties. Later I learned that Zimmer and Fruehauf had been discussing a relationship for some time over lunches at the Detroit Athletic Club. The meeting at the company's headquarters was actually the culmination of those discussions.

In a conventional new business presentation, all of the agency representatives present are expected to participate in the presentation and have a specific subject or assignment that they cover in the meeting. Usually only three or four people make the "pitch."

My role at Zimmer-Keller changed

following the agency's acquisition of the Fruehauf Trailer account. I spent a considerable amount of time helping the account supervisor and the account executive handle the account, which involved a number of different divisions. I wrote a variety of trade advertisements which were directed at specific markets as Zimmer-Keller continued to function as a copy/contact agency for all their accounts – including the Fruehauf Trailer Company.

The agency also managed to get Fruehauf to sponsor a national radio program on the mutual network – a first for them and a feat I will never forget because the approval process was so unusual.

When the Zimmer-Keller agency got the Fruehauf account I was promoted to assistant account executive. My primary responsibility, though, was to write copy for trade advertisements like the ones shown here. The agency did not have a copywriter on the staff because of the way it was structured. Account supervisors and account executives wrote all the copy.

Al Ritter, the account supervisor, asked if I would help him make the presentation. My part consisted of hauling a heavy playback unit to the DAC (Detroit Athletic Club) where the presentation was made in a private room on one of the upper floors of this prestigious club, which was built in 1915. For several hours Al and I sat in a corner of the private dining room while six members of Fruehauf's top management drank and ate…mostly drank. Al and I patiently waited for them to finish dinner so we could present the radio program. The format for the program was essentially commentary by a fairly well known conservative personality who expressed his views and concerns about the free enterprise system, the economy, current events, the government, etc. The commercial messages which we proposed to run in the radio program would support the trucking industry by highlighting the issues and regulations that negatively affected the operation of trucking companies who were Fruehauf's customers. The goal was to build good will for the Fruehauf Trailer Company with its customers.

Finally, around 8:30 p.m. the client asked "What the #!*#!!@ do you want us to listen to?" Al then sprung into action describing the radio program and how it could be used for the benefit of the Fruehauf Trailer Company. When Al finished he turned to me and indicated that I should turn on the player and drop the needle on the record to play the program. I did…but nothing happened! I snapped the on/off switch back and forth several times but the turntable didn't move. One of the waiters walked over to us and asked if we had an adapter as the DAC's electrical system operated on DC current and an adapter was needed to run any appliance requiring AC current. I explained we didn't have an adapter and asked – "Where could we get one?" The waiter said he'd find us one and disappeared for what seemed like an eternity – although it was really only a few minutes.

Fortunately, the Fruehauf executives immediately returned to their drinks and were "certainly feeling no pain." Finally, the helpful waiter returned with an adapter and we played the half-hour program on the playback unit, which now worked. (You must remember this took place before tape playback units were available and sound was reproduced from records.) When the program ended Ritter made a few brief remarks and told them what it would cost to sponsor the program. One of the Fruehauf executives said "I think we should sponsor the #!*#!!@ thing." The others chimed in favorably and it was a done deal.

While Al and I were at the DAC all evening to make this presentation my wife was patiently waiting for us at a nearby restaurant on Woodward Avenue. It was after 10:00 p.m. before Al and I got to the restaurant where Joan was waiting. Al ordered Manhattans for the three of us and the biggest steaks the restaurant could find in their cooler. This was the first time my wife and I had ever tasted a Manhattan. The drink and the steak were a suitable reward for a successful presentation that almost didn't happen because the DAC still operated with DC current. Who would have guessed?

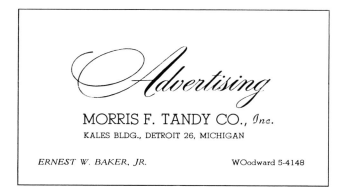

When I joined the Tandy agency I got my first business card, as I did not have one at Zimmer-Keller. Business cards were not prevalent in the '40s and '50s. Today, practically everyone has a business card.

My First Career Move

In late fall of 1949, shortly after my 23rd birthday, I left Zimmer-Keller and joined the Morris F. Tandy advertising agency in the Kale's Building which was on Grand Circus Park in the same block in which the Zimmer-Keller agency was located.

In 1949 Grand Circus Park was a bustling, important part of downtown Detroit. A large circular drive encloses Grand Circus Park and is bisected by Woodward Avenue – the main street of Detroit. Around this circular drive tall office buildings housed the city's leading medical professionals, advertising agencies, art studios and businesses of all kinds. The Statler Hotel, which was then THE HOTEL, dominated the south side of Grand Circus Park. Theaters, restaurants and clubs – such as the Detroit Athletic Club (DAC) and the Women's City Club were on streets running off the circular drive. Washington Boulevard, another one of the spokes off the wheel that was the core of the circle defining Grand Circus Park was Detroit's 5th Avenue. This area slowly and steadily declined for many years but recently has gone through a renaissance and once again is becoming a significant and vital part of downtown Detroit.

I had answered a "Help Wanted" advertisement that the Morris F. Tandy agency had run seeking an account executive. I thought I was ready to move from assistant account executive – the position I had reached at Zimmer-Keller – to a full-fledged account executive and was delighted to get the job with Tandy, which included a nice increase in pay.

Morris Tandy had been with the Kroger Company for more than 25 years but left Kroger's to start an advertising agency. He knew the grocery business inside out and his major client was the C.F. Smith Company – at that time the dominant food retailer in southeast Michigan. C.F. Smith had more than 300 stores which were essentially small neighborhood markets. Supermarkets were just starting to

Grand Circus Park as it appeared when I worked first in the Stroh Building (later renamed the Mutual Building) and, a few years later, in the Kales Building. Both buildings were located in the same block on the north side of Grand Circus Park which was a busy, eclectic area in the late 1940s and into the 1950s.

evolve and threatening the future of the neighborhood food markets. Tom's Markets, Big Bear, Wrigley, Packer, Kroger and A&P were the food chains in Detroit moving towards the supermarket concept with bigger and bigger floor space. C.F. Smith Company lagged behind their competition and it was eventually acquired by a Chicago food chain.

Morris Tandy assigned me to handle several accounts as well as work on the C.F. Smith food stores account. My accounts were:

Campbell-French Company –
Manufacturers of shopping carts for supermarkets.

Dorau-Owens, Inc. –
Manufacturers of grocery store fixtures and check-out units.

Both of these companies were in the "business to business" category and they advertised in the trade publications that reached the grocery chains – Progressive Grocer, Super Market News, Grocer's Spotlight as well as other publications that reached that market. I also was involved in some "point-of-sale" projects for Jiffy Biscuit Mixes, the Roman Cleanser Company and Aunt Jane's Pickles under Morris Tandy's direction.

Genevieve "Hap" Hazzard was the person I reported to at the Tandy agency. Working for Hap was a delight. She was a good teacher and her bright red hair matched her warm personality. When Hap left the Tandy Agency to join Campbell-Ewald she was the first woman ever to become a vice president of that agency.

In the early 1950s there were more than 300 C.F. Smith food markets in Southeastern Michigan. The market pictured above was built after World War II. Most though were built in the 1920s and 1930s and were essentially neighborhood convenience stores. Sanders' candy, ice cream and baked goods were featured in these food stores. Supermarkets, offering greater selection and lower prices, slowly eroded the sales volume of C.F. Smith stores and one by one they faded from the scene.

Life was good at the Tandy agency but it turned out to be a brief period in my career. I enjoyed what I was doing and kept busy. I not only contacted clients but also wrote copy for the accounts I handled plus the required service reports on every meeting. I was also learning a lot about the food business as I was involved with a sizable food retailer, grocery manufacturers and several companies that were suppliers to the food industry.

The C.F. Smith stores earned advertising allowances based either on purchases or other criteria and it was the agency's responsibility to see that the C.F. Smith stores not only received but properly used all the advertising dollars due them – a big and very detailed task as every company that provided C.F. Smith Stores with products had its own "co-op" advertising agreement. Many were based on a percentage of

goods purchased. Others were based on an allowance of so many dollars per column inch of advertising space that displayed the suppliers' products in C.F. Smith newspaper ads. There were other arrangements as well, all of which the agency had to be familiar with and handle on behalf of our client.

Hap Hazzard supervised the C.F. Smith stores account while John Mott – another account executive – and I assisted her. Mott was from Australia. His father owned the Leader Publishing Company in Melbourne, which published several newspapers. There were no professional journalism schools in Australia at that time so John had worked for the Windsor Star for several years as a reporter. When we met he was working as an account executive at the Tandy agency. His education thus consisted of on-the-job training in Canada and the U.S.A. We became good friends and corresponded for years after he returned to Australia.

Hap, John and I met with the buyers at the headquarters of the C.F. Smith stores on West Grand Boulevard every week to review purchases from all their major suppliers so we could determine how many "co-op" dollars could be applied towards their advertising. It was a lot of detail work because every manufacturer had its own specific advertising allowance agreement. Since this was prior to the age of computers all the record keeping, billing, etc. was done manually.

Every week the C.F. Smith stores ran a large space newspaper advertisement – sometimes a full page but usually slightly less than a full page – in nearly every daily newspaper in Southeast Michigan. At that time there were three daily papers in Detroit – *The Detroit News, Detroit Free Press* and *Detroit Times*. In addition, C.F. Smith placed its newspaper advertisement every week in newspapers in Ann Arbor, Mt. Clemens, Pontiac, Flint, etc. – around 15 to 20 publications – in order to cover all their stores.

One idea that Morris Tandy initiated for the C.F. Smith stores consisted of using 20% to 40% of its newspaper advertisements to feature just one basic food item at a very special low price. Morris Tandy claimed he originated this concept at Kroger's but most of the competition did – and still do – the same thing. The big difference with C.F. Smith was that the featured item was usually a frequently purchased food product available for less than 10¢ – such as a loaf of bread, box of crackers, apples or potatoes for 2 or 3 cents per pound, etc. I was astounded to learn how many tons of cottage cheese the C.F. Smith stores sold in one week when a carton of cottage cheese was advertised on sale for 9¢. The balance of the advertisement featured products that were covered by the manufacturers' advertising allowances.

The C.F. Smith specials sold in unbelievable quantities every week and the stores had to carry large stocks which nearly always had to be replenished during the week the item was on sale. This simple concept worked with great success because customers came in to take advantage of the low priced special and then usually purchased other groceries as well. Since there were more than 300 C.F. Smith stores in Southeast Michigan in 1950 and early 1951 it was convenient for thousands of customers to get to a store and take advantage of the weekly special offer.

Another concept that Morris Tandy initiated for the C.F. Smith stores consisted of full-page, full-color advertisements that ran in the Sunday Roto section of *The Detroit News*. In 1950, *The Detroit News* had the highest home delivery circulation of any newspaper in America and the full-color advertisements in the Sunday Roto really helped improve the image of the small neighborhood C.F. Smith store.

The Roto page was divided into quarters and the C.F. Smith logo appeared right in the center of the page. These pages had a specific theme and the four brand-name products, each of which were featured in a quarter of the page, then carried out the theme of the advertisement. For instance:

For a picnic theme:
Hot dogs, buns, mustard and pickles

For a lunch theme:
Bread, lunch meat, cheese and sandwich spread

For a breakfast theme:
Pancake mix, syrup, coffee and butter

For a spring clean-up theme:
Mops and brooms, cleanser, soap and furniture polish

These four-color advertisements were paid for by the co-op advertising dollars earned by C.F. Smith and it was an effective way to use the money. One of my tasks was to get the four-color materials from the various manufacturers (either photos, transparencies or art work) or else arrange for a photo to be taken of the product to be featured in the advertisement. I really "sweated out" a few insertions as we had several close calls making *The Detroit News* Sunday Roto production deadline.

Television was an entirely new advertising medium in the early 1950s and the C.F. Smith stores sponsored two programs on WWJ-TV. The station's studio was crammed into a small area in the back of *The Detroit News* building. This was a time when everyone – the station, the advertisers and the advertising agencies – were learning about TV production. I remember how dreadful beautiful cuts of roasts and steaks looked on live TV as they actually turned black when the camera panned them. Baked goods and ice cream either burned into mush or quickly melted away under the hot lights – lights so harsh and strong that you couldn't touch anything that had been under them for several minutes due to the heat. After a burn or two, you learned to be very careful what you touched.

In the early 1950s, newspapers were printed from metal – not by the offset method as they are today. Agencies sent newspapers a matte of an advertisement and that's how the C.F. Smith advertisements were reproduced. The mattes were produced from the metal engraving and shipped from an engraver while the insertion order, a proof of the advertisement and special instructions regarding any changes in copy, etc. were sent from the agency. The Morris F. Tandy agency offices were on the tenth floor of the Kale's Building. Next to the elevators on each floor was a mail chute and the envelopes containing the agency's materials were regularly dropped in the chute and ended up in a mail bag on the first floor.

One week all of the agency's mail got caught in this mail chute and none of the newspapers received their insertion order, proof, and special instructions. We rushed to redo everything and then John Mott and I hit the road. We divided up the 20 papers and personally delivered the new materials. There were no expressways then so it took all night to get to all the papers. To this day I will not drop an envelope down a mail chute in an office building and fortunately new office buildings have eliminated them.

Surprise! Surprise!

Ruth Brewster was the office manager at the Morris F. Tandy agency. The Morris F. Tandy agency had a staff of 18 and was humming with work and growing. To my great surprise – after I had been with the agency about six months – Ruth called me into her office, closed the door and told me I would be well advised to look for another job. In great confidence she told me that Mr. Tandy – who was married and had a family – was "keeping" a woman in another city. Paying for this secret love life was "bleeding the agency to death."

This was quite a shock but I took Ruth's advice and started checking the "Help Wanted" ads in the newspapers and *The Adcrafter* (which is the newsletter for the Adcraft Club of Detroit) as well as talking with various suppliers to see if they knew of an opening. Through one of these sources I found another job – with the Denman & Betteridge agency in the Buhl Building in downtown Detroit.

Denman & Betteridge, Inc.
Becomes My Third Career Move

Bill Denman's career in advertising included a number of years as a type salesman, followed by a stint as production manager of the Fred M. Randall Agency in Detroit and later as an account executive for Young & Rubicam, Inc. On September 1, 1947 Bill Denman and Harry Betteridge started an advertising agency in the Penobscot Building in downtown Detroit named William I. Denman, Inc.

Harry Betteridge was the sales manager of WWJ radio and for several years an inactive silent partner in the agency until he resigned his WWJ position and joined the agency full time. When that occurred, the agency's name was changed from William I. Denman, Inc. to Denman & Betteridge, Inc. and Bill and Harry moved the agency's offices to the Buhl Building – across the street from the Penobscot Building.

Unfortunately, Bill and Harry, who had become close friends while students at Albion College, didn't agree on a lot of things when they had to work together on a daily basis. Soon after I joined the agency in the spring of 1950, they split up. Betteridge left to form his own agency. I decided to stay with Denman but the name of the agency remained Denman & Betteridge, Inc.

Just prior to my joining Denman & Betteridge, three members of the staff had left to start their own agency. Rudd Otto, Jerry Abbs and Don Fox opened the Otto & Abbs, Inc. agency in the Guardian Building taking with them the Mutual Liability Insurance Company, New Era Potato Chips and several other accounts. Otto, whose father was president of Mutual Liability, was chairman of the agency; Abbs was president and Fox was production and office manager. Otto & Abbs operated very successfully and eventually became Behr, Otto, Abbs & Austin, Inc. Many years later the principals dissolved the agency. Abbs eventually joined me as part of Baker, Abbs, Cunningham & Klepinger, Inc.

The staff of Denman & Betteridge, consisted of eight people. So I'd gone from Zimmer-Keller with a staff of 30, to Morris Tandy with 18, to an agency consisting of only eight people. I wasn't sure if that was progress or not. I was an account executive as well as the production manager of the agency. I was assigned to handle the Standard Federal Savings and Loan Association account – new to the agency – and also helped Bill Denman service the Buhl Sons Company account, a large wholesale distributor for Philco Appliances, Columbia Records, Mohawk Carpets, ABC Washers and Dryers and Coleman Products. Buhl Sons Company distributed these lines – along with hardware and other products – to appliance, hardware and department stores throughout Michigan, Northern Ohio and Northern Indiana.

Sure enough, a few months after I joined Bill Denman, the Morris F. Tandy Agency declared bankruptcy. So I quickly met with the accounts that I had handled at the Tandy agency – the Campbell-French Company and Dorau-Owens, Inc. – and brought them to Denman & Betteridge and continued to service their businesses. This was an unexpected bonus for Bill Denman's hiring me and I was successful in adding several other accounts, which led to my being named a vice president along with some welcome increases in pay.

Sunshine Chicks Became An Interesting and Challenging Client

The Sunshine Chick Hatchery was one of the new accounts that I recruited and I handled it for eight years. This was one of the most challenging accounts that I was ever involved with in my career because it was **entirely direct response**. When you run advertising for a direct response business you immediately know the results of the campaign. The success or failure of the business depends entirely on the advertising.

George Kalman, who owned the business, operated it from his home in Zeeland, Michigan. He owned a hatchery in Zeeland but his main business was selling baby chicks by mail order for $3.95 per 100 plus shipping costs all paid for C.O.D. Radio advertising was the medium used to sell the chicks.

George had agreements with hatcheries all across the country to sell him their surplus production for $1.00 per 100 chicks. If hatcheries didn't sell all the chicks they hatched each week, they had to dispose of the surplus and would either drown or burn the chicks to get rid of them. George Kalman offered a solution to that problem by purchasing the surplus production at a very low price.

Sunshine chicks were ordered by people who either lived in the country or the suburbs of the city where they could raise chickens in the backyard. In the one-minute radio commercials, we emphasized that not only was raising 100 or 200 chicks easy and fun, but you could also enjoy a lot of chicken dinners at a super bargain price.

We advertised Sunshine chicks on radio stations starting in early January in the deep South. Then we moved North as the weather got warmer, ending the advertising in early June in the northern states. The advertising message used to sell Sunshine chicks consisted of a one minute "live read" commercial and the copy was never changed during all the years that I handled this account.

The planning and negotiating for radio time began in late October for the next selling season. I personally bought all the radio time on several hundred stations. It was necessary for every radio station to inform me weekly as soon as we were on the air exactly how many orders they had received. Listeners sent their orders to the radio station, where they were counted, and the station then sent them in bulk to Zeeland, Michigan for processing.

The advertising budget was based on $1.00 per order. So for every dollar we spent on a radio station we needed one order to recoup the investment. I increased or reduced advertising schedules weekly based on how a station pulled orders.

This is how the business was basically structured by George Kalman:

100 chicks	**$1.00**
Advertising per order	**$1.00**
Cost of shipping box, out-of-pocket expenses and other overhead	**$1.00**
Profit Goal	.95
Total	**$3.95**

Shipping was included in the C.O.D. charges – $3.95 per hundred chicks plus the cost of shipping, which was by rail.

Kalman, his wife and two daughters lived in a nice ranch house which had a full basement. He had rows of desks in his large basement where women sat and typed the C.O.D. order forms. These orders were then sorted and bulk-shipped to a hatchery nearest to the person who ordered the baby chicks. We sold millions of chicks and, in fact, had several 50,000 watt clear channel radio stations on our schedule that produced as many as 25,000 orders. 25,000 orders represents 2,500,000 chicks!

The growth of television, which steadily eroded the radio audience, plus the rapid development of the broiler business in the South, had a big impact on selling baby chicks by mail order on radio stations. By 1957 chicken was so inexpensive in the grocery store that you really couldn't save much money, if any, raising chickens in your backyard. Kalman saw the handwriting on the wall as orders dropped year after year even on the most productive radio stations. He got out of the mail order business in 1958 and opened a large fruit market between Holland and Zeeland where he did quite well. The chicken by radio business taught me a lot. To this day, I know the call letters of a great many radio stations in cities all across the country as a result of this experience.

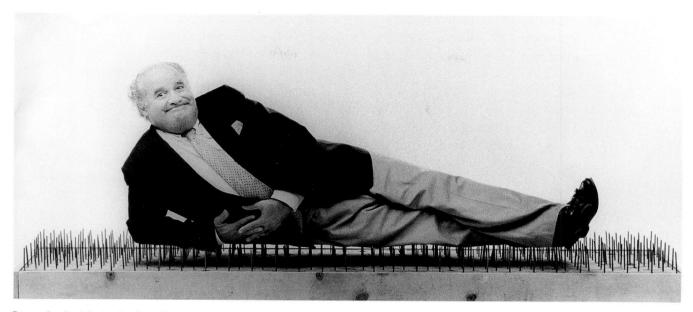

Steve had this bed of nails made to prove a point with clients who wanted to put too much information in an advertisement. "If you try to make too many points in a headline you'll never penetrate (the audience)," and he demonstrated this by lying on his bed of nails. Then, he would pull out a block of wood with a single nail and slam another board down on top of it. The nail would go right through the block proving his point in a dramatic way – "make one point and watch it penetrate."

Steve Cosmopulos' Career In Advertising Began In Detroit

The art director at Denman & Betteridge, Inc. was Steve Cosmopulos. During his advertising career, Steve helped found six advertising agencies and five of the six agencies still bear his name:

HILL, HOLLIDAY, CONNORS, COSMOPULOS, INC.
– BOSTON, MASSACHUSETTS

COSMOPULOS, CROWLEY, DALY, INC.
– BOSTON, MASSACHUSETTS

PALMER, COSMOPULOS, PALMER
– ELMIRA HEIGHTS, NEW YORK

CAHILL, COSMOPULOS, INC.
– MERIDEN, CONNECTICUT

COSMOPULOS, ANTHONY & PARTNERS
– BOSTON, MASSACHUSETTS

Steve served as chairman of the board and creative director for the various agencies he helped launch. Along the way he also worked for BBDO Boston and Kenyon & Eckhardt.

At Denman & Betteridge, Steve's title was – "Head Art Director" – an impressive title except he was the agency's **only** art director. When I was successful in bringing in the two former clients I had handled at the Tandy agency, plus several other accounts, Steve then inherited my production manager responsibilities as I had to devote all my time to servicing accounts.

Steve was a highly talented creative person with tremendous dedication and energy. He regularly arrived for work by 4 a.m. – a habit he never changed throughout his very successful career in the advertising business.

Steve's artistic talents cover a variety of outlets – computer, oil, watercolor, acrylic, sewing, sculpture, carving and furniture making. He holds four U.S. patents for toys he has invented. He has been honored by many prestigious organizations, including the New York Art Directors Club. He was elected into the New England Advertising Hall of Fame in 1989 and has been the subject of a profile by *The Wall Street Journal*, for whom he still serves as a panelist for their <u>Meeting of the Minds</u> series. Quite a guy!

There were three account executives at Denman & Betteridge – Bill Denman, Bill Botsford and me. Not long after I joined the agency it was down to Denman and me. Botsford left after a disagreement on an expense account.

George Black Joins the Denman & Betteridge, Inc. Agency

George Black was one of the most talented and well-liked ad guys that I have ever known. We were neighbors in Grosse Pointe and slightly acquainted but I really didn't get to know him well until after he joined the agency. Being neighbors, we sometimes car pooled together downtown. Being stuck in rush hour traffic never mattered because he was such an entertaining conversationalist.

Rising young advertising executive George Black, Jr. (right) affects a striking pose with his client from Altes Brewing Company. Black handled the Detroit brewery's account while working for the Grace & Bement agency in the 1930s.

There were endless tales of his experiences – stories about his fraternity days and as an English major at the University of Michigan; of his travels after graduation with a band that played on ocean liners; of his apprenticeship as an advertising copy writer for a large Detroit printer which led to account executive positions with the Grace & Bement advertising agency, and later with MacManus, John & Adams. After a stint with the U.S. Office of War Information during World War II, Black joined Young & Rubicam. Before arriving in Detroit, he worked in New York and Chicago.

Black seemed to know everyone, including a host of celebrities, who enjoyed his charming manner. He had a razor sharp memory for names and was hailed constantly on the street by the people he knew, whether it was a cab driver, a shoe shine boy or a bartender.

He had a terrific "ear for music." A band he had organized after college was booked to play on the grand ocean liners of the day. He spent over a year crisscrossing the Atlantic. Once when his ship stopped for several days in Bermuda, George and his band were hired by Howard Hughes to play for a party on his yacht. Hughes was apparently so impressed that he insisted that the group stay to work for him. In fact, he was very adamant, to the point of "refusing" to allow the band to go back to the cruise ship on which they were working. During the night, Black said he and his band "escaped" in a dinghy from the clutches of bodyguards of the eccentric Hughes and returned to their cruise liner.

It was during this period that Black met many of the famous people with whom he later corresponded. His meticulously organized files contained handwritten letters from such notables as Louis "Satchmo" Armstrong, Bing Crosby, Eddie Duchin, Norman Rockwell, Albert Schweitzer, and many other celebrities. His background in English literature was the basis for a collection of leather-bound first editions by some of America's best-known authors.

He played nine instruments without reading

George Black, Jr.

music, and while working for Young & Rubicam in Chicago and commuting to his home in Detroit for the weekend, he'd sit at the piano in the lounge car of the Twilight Limited and get everyone singing all the way home.

Black played as hard as he worked. In the late '40s, it caught up with him. He suffered a heart attack and had to quit his job with Young & Rubicam in Chicago to rest for a year at home. But he was resilient. Soon he contacted Bill Denman for some part-time work to keep him busy. He and Denman had worked together at Young & Rubicam in Detroit.

Once advertisers in Detroit heard that Black was back in circulation, they brought more than $1 million in billings to the agency in just one year's time! In those days, that was quite an accomplishment.

His major account was McLouth Steel, which was heavily advertising its high-ticket stainless steel. When producing a new campaign,

Black would talk to the client, sit down at the typewriter, bang out the copy in the first draft, and most amazing of all to me, sell the concept to the client without their changing a single word! His clients trusted his judgment implicitly.

I envied the trips that George used to take with various friends. For example, he and his friend Ted Buhl would annually travel for a week or more with the Ringling Brothers, Barnum & Bailey Circus. George and Ted would live on the circus train traveling from city to city; and when George returned, he had great stories to tell. George and Ted also loved to hunt, and they would go to Louisiana for duck hunting, to South Dakota for pheasant hunting and to Turtle Lake in northern Michigan for deer hunting. When it came to deer hunting, though, George went just for the fun of playing poker – he never shot a deer.

Accounts that George Black Handled

At Young & Rubicam, Inc.
Pullman Corporation
Borden's
Northern Tissue
Stinson Aircraft
Parke Davis

At Denman & Betteridge, Inc.
McLouth Steel
First of Michigan Corporation
National Bank of Detroit (*PR project*)
Inland Plastic Tile
Sheller Corp. (later Sheller-Globe, Inc.)
Wyandotte Chemicals

One of the accounts that Black brought to the agency was the Wyandotte Chemicals Company which produced various chemicals for industry. Their advertising was in business-to-business publications. One of their industrial products was a cleaner similar to Bon Ami and they asked the agency to design a consumer package and come up with a name for the product. Steve Cosmopulos designed the package and named it WISK. The client didn't like the name WISK and decided it should be called Beaver Cleaner so that it could be advertised as the cleaner that "works like a beaver." Beaver Cleaner was a failure as a consumer product. Wonder what might have happened if they had gone with the name WISK?

Political Advertising Made 1952 a Banner Year For the Agency

Early in 1952 Denman & Betteridge was appointed as the agency for the Michigan Republican State Central Committee. We had competed with several agencies – all much larger than our shop – and were elated when we won the account which we anticipated would possibly bill about $500,000. Little did we know when we got the account that Dwight D. Eisenhower would head the ticket and win by a landslide carrying a lot of other candidates on the Republican ticket into office as well. In addition to the Michigan Republican State Central Committee account, we also handled United States Senator Charles E. Potter's campaign – a victory – as well as several other candidates for state and county offices.

Bill Denman was the account supervisor for all the political advertising we handled and we added Joe Bracken from Young & Rubicam to assist Bill in handling the business. Bracken was very capable and a good choice. A few years later he went to New York where he became president of Ogilvy & Mather Direct. George Black and I assisted Bill and Joe whenever we were able to do so but our task – and a crucial one – was to handle all the other clients of the agency until the election was over.

I specifically remember helping to put together an advertisement one evening using the floor of the bathroom for our work surface which was in a suite rented by the Michigan Republican State Central Committee at the Statler Hilton Hotel. Several of us were on our hands and knees with a big layout pad creating an advertisement that had to go into production that night. The bathroom was the only quiet place to work in the hectic headquarters offices.

Political advertising must be paid for in advance and due to the popularity of General Eisenhower it was incredible to me how much money poured in from all over the state to underwrite the advertising for the presidential campaign in Michigan as well as for other candidates. After the election, when we totaled up all the political advertising we handled, it exceeded $2,000,000 – a big surge in billings for our little agency. Everyone received a well deserved year-end bonus for we put in many long days and weekends, particularly the last six weeks before the election.

This was my one and only experience with political advertising and it left lasting memories. Political advertising has become a very specialized business and today is a far cry from the kind of advertising we created, produced and placed in 1952. Negative advertising – which is so common in political advertising today – didn't exist back then, nor had we even heard of the "rule of six," which maintains that you must expose each voter to your message six times before it is committed to memory.

Denman & Betteridge, Inc. Is Renamed Denman & Baker, Inc.

In the late fall of 1953 Bill Denman invited George Black and me to a lunch meeting at the Savoyard Club which was on the 27th floor of the Buhl Building. At the luncheon Denman announced that he would like to rename the agency Denman, Black & Baker, Inc. and offered us the opportunity to buy stock in the agency. I was 27 years old and had been in the advertising business just six years so I felt tremendously flattered to receive this recognition.

Black reluctantly decided that because of his and his wife's health problems that he had better pass on having his name included in the new name for the agency. He explained that he was thinking seriously of retiring in about two years and moving to Arizona. Thus the agency's name became Denman & Baker, Inc.

George and I took equity positions in the agency and became members of the board of directors. In addition to Denman, Black & Baker, the board also included an attorney and Dick Wilson, who was a Cadillac dealer, and friend of Denman's. The directors met only twice a year, at which time we received a silver dollar and a free lunch.

For the first two and a half years of our marriage my wife and I both worked and managed to save $3,000. Joan's parents matched that sum which enabled us to buy our first home – a three bedroom colonial in Grosse Pointe Farms for $22,500 – in February, 1953. Our son Robert was born February 1, 1951 and Michael on May 19, 1953.

With a family of four, we had a comfortable home and the future looked bright and promising. In 1953 the nation's economy was not only exploding but also employing the nation's human and physical resources at a high degree of efficiency.

From 1950 to 1970 it was the rule rather than exception that an ordinary family – without higher education – could sustain itself decently on the income of a single bread winner.

In 1953 a good suit cost $30 and 75¢ was worth today's $7.50 before and after taxes. Members of Congress were paid $12,500 and did what needed to be done in less time with less than half the staff. The difference between then and now, though, goes beyond the time warp of inflation. Forty-five years ago a much smaller percentage of the work force was made up of lawyers, accountants, regulators, social workers and bureaucrats. There were less than 100,000 people employed in the advertising agency business in the United States in 1953. During the '50s the automobile manufacturers hit their stride with 12 million car buying booms. More than $400 million was spent on auto advertising and a new manufacturer, Kaiser-Frasier, was promoting the Henry J sedan at $1,299. The concept of a smaller American car was pioneered by George Romney of American Motors in his vitriolic attack on "gas guzzlers."

Heavy appliances were much in demand throughout the decade. Thor, Westinghouse, Philco, Bendix, Mullins, Hotpoint, Borg-Warner, Maytag, Frigidaire…these and other manufacturers kept bringing out new models with new features, and advertised in all media, including direct mail. At the retail level, the discount chains, such as Korvette in New York and Polk Bros. in Chicago, brought the prices down and bombarded the public with carload sales and better values. It was a $40 billion market. Cheesecake and nudity were reaching full flower in advertising as photographic techniques improved and full color, both in newspapers and magazines, came into greater use.

At the end of the decade, there were 85 million TV sets in the world, of which 52 million were in the U.S. The battle for the Government-approved color system was bitterly fought between RCA and CBS. Color was rapidly replacing black and white in television.

Suits and countersuits were the order of the day. P&G sued Lever for bringing out Swan soap as an "imitation" of Ivory. Zenith sued RCA for so-called infringement of TV color tube patents. The soft drink makers were constantly in the courts. Schenley was sued by Park & Tilford for their $25 million "loss" in sales. Du Pont was sued for $53 million. And, of course, the Federal Trade Commission and the Food and Drug Administration brought scores of lawsuits.

There were crippling newspaper strikes in Detroit, Philadelphia and other cities, as the unions fought for higher pay and continued feather-bedding in the face of inevitably increased automation. Added to this were periodic newsprint and paper shortages that created additional problems for all print media which were pushing aggressively for increased circulations.

The Decade of the '50s

Here are a few highlights in marketing and advertising during the decade:

- Multi-million mailings of advertising and product samples due to relatively low third class mail rate.

- U.S. population neared 160 million.

- Thirty-one million families owned cars in 1951.

- Revenues of TV networks and stations crossed the $1 billion mark.

- The Post Office was constantly pushing for higher mail rates. First class mail was still 4¢ in 1954.

- The cereal makers bought up leading toy companies as an adjunct to their marketing and advertising programs to children.

- Vending machines took an increasing share of the retail business. Sales exceeded $2 billion by the end of the decade.

- Ford and Chevy fought for the No. 1 sales position in the auto field, Schlitz and Anheuser Busch waged a furious battle for predominance in beer sales. Hertz and Avis had it out in the car rental field.

- Agencies assumed a large role in the marketing and public relations programs of their clients.

The decade had its peaks and valleys but it was overall a period of booming sales, new product introductions and marketing innovation. Advertising volume exceeded $10 billion, with an increasing share going to larger, multi-office, multi-national agencies. Media competition intensified as more ad dollars went into television. It was a decade of massive post-war adjustment in every segment of the economy.

Chapter 2

From 1954 Through 1958
Our Lifestyle Changed Significantly

Lifestyle: How we spend time and money.

Playing poker became a most pleasant and regular activity starting in 1954. George Black loved to play poker. He initiated and arranged a once-a-month ritual that continued until he passed away from a heart attack in 1963. We never met again to play poker after we lost George.

The "regulars," besides George, included Bill Denman, Don Brown, Ray Krohl and me. I've already introduced George and Bill. Don Brown was the public relations director and Ray Krohl was the production manager of Denman & Baker, Inc. Steve Cosmopulous had left the agency and moved to Florida.

Usually one or two of George's friends were invited to play with us and Bill Hamilton, who was president of the William R. Hamilton Funeral Homes, was a frequent participant. Occasionally, Bob McLoughlin of McLouth Steel joined us. Both Bill Hamilton and Bob McLoughlin were clients. There were a lot of others who played with us including, on one occasion, Henry Ford II, at the Country Club of Detroit in Grosse Pointe when George Black was the host. "The Deuce," as Henry Ford II, was called, was having dinner at the club and afterwards came over and watched us play. George invited him to join us. Which he did! Henry and George had known each other for years starting when they were teenagers. Another time, several years later, when we were once again at the Country Club of Detroit, Henry Ford II pulled up a chair and sat and just watched us play. Later, his wife Cristina came over and sat on his lap with her arm around

her husband's shoulder. It was the only time that we ever had an audience and it was a most interesting conversation because Henry Ford's vocabulary was liberally sprinkled with some very crude and sometimes vulgar words. The one time that he participated in our poker game it really didn't seem at all significant because he simply sat down at the table and joined the game for a while. But now, years later, I think "Gee whiz – that was really neat" playing poker with Henry Ford II.

We always played our poker games on Friday nights starting right after work, usually at someone's house. We also played at the University Club which was on East Jefferson near downtown Detroit, at the Pine Lake Country Club in Birmingham or at the Country Club of Detroit in Grosse Pointe. Bill Denman was a member of the University Club and Pine Lake while George was also a member of the University Club as well as the Country Club of Detroit. The evening started with cocktails and dinner and if there was a piano (and there usually was) George would entertain us for awhile playing any requests we made. The two hours of socializing and dining that preceded our poker games gave us an opportunity to relax and talk about things that we never had the time to discuss during the day.

George always provided the poker chips. He had a mahogany chest filled with white, red and blue chips which he had inherited from his father. (George's father, by the way, was one of the founders of the Packard Motor Car Company and The Detroit Club in downtown Detroit).

The white chips were a nickel, reds a dime, and blues a quarter. The stakes were kept low because we played for enjoyment and if you went home with an extra $10.00 you were a "big winner." Over the years George and I were the consistent winners while Bill Denman, Don Brown and Ray Krohl usually lost a few bucks. The games were serious though as we basically played 5 card draw, 5 or 7 card stud with a few other games mixed in but the suggestion of more than one wild card was always met with a chorus of boos. The game usually started around 8:30 and we always stopped at 11 pm. Coffee and cold cuts for sandwiches were available if you wanted a snack before heading home.

When we played on the east side of Detroit I would be home before midnight. If we played in Birmingham it was much later because it was an hour and a half drive to Grosse Pointe. Once – sometimes twice a year – we played at Don Brown's home on Grosse Isle and were guests at Don Brown's parents' home on the island on two occasions. Don's father had been treasurer of Great Lakes Steel and was credited with developing the Quonset hut. The senior Brown's large home reflected his former position with the Steel Company. It was an impressive place in which to play cards but the drive home was a bear because it took more than two hours. There were no expressways in those days. But in spite of the driving distance to and from Grosse Isle or Birmingham, the evenings were most enjoyable and worthwhile due to the camaraderie and friendships they developed.

Bill Hamilton lived near George Black in Grosse Pointe and the Friday night poker games at Bill's home were among our most memorable. Bill Hamilton had a den with a game table specifically for playing poker. It had a green felt top with a recessed area around the perimeter to hold your chips. But what made the games particularly memorable was Taylor, Bill Hamilton's ugly, fat, old bulldog. In the corner of the den was a large comfortable leather chair and Taylor always took possession of this chair. First he would just sit there watching us play cards and when he got bored doing that, he would roll over and lie on his back and go to sleep. Everything was fine until Taylor passed gas – emitting the most horrible odor you can imagine. Two, three, sometimes four times during the evening Taylor would let go and we had to quickly get out of the room and wait for the air to clear. In spite of the complaints we always had a good laugh.

Vernor's Ginger Ale Becomes a Client

Denman & Baker, Inc. was the first advertising agency that Vernor's Ginger Ale ever employed. In 1954 Vernor's did not have an agency but committed for a half sponsorship of a half-hour syndicated television program called "Meet Corliss Archer," which was produced by Ziv Studios in Hollywood. The show aired on WWJ-TV in Detroit. Standard Federal was the other sponsor. In 1954 the sales manager of Vernor's called to ask if Denman & Baker would handle their advertising and create and produce their television commercials.

Standard Federal was already a sponsor of television programs in the Detroit market starting with "Victory At Sea." This series was followed by the Edward R. Murrow "Person To Person" program and year after year they were the sponsor of the "New Year's Eve with Guy Lombardo" shows until the demise of Guy Lombardo. In future years Standard Federal sponsored "Sing Along With Mitch," the election returns, plus various other specials and then for many years the "World Adventure Series with George Pierrot." The sponsorship of these shows did much to build the Standard Federal "brand" and George Pierrot contributed to the image and recognition of Standard Federal by appearing at branch office openings. He also spoke to Realtor groups and attended various meetings on behalf of Standard Federal.

In the early 1950s when an advertiser sponsored a television program, the station made available, free of charge, production time equal

Signing the contract to commit to the sponsorship of the "Meet Corliss Archer" TV show involved (seated left to right): Walter J.L. Ray, president of Standard Federal Savings and James Vernor Davis, president of the James Vernor Company. Standing left to right: Robert Hutton, treasurer of Standard Federal Savings, Ernie Baker of Denman & Baker, Inc., Edwin K. Wheeler, general manager of WWJ-TV and R.J. Wojeiehowski, advertising manager of the James Vernor Company.

to the length of the television program. For every half-hour or hour of programming time that the advertiser sponsored, the station provided equal time for the production of commercials. This was in lieu of doing commercials "live" during the program, which could have been the advertiser's option – ridiculous as this would be. The "earned time" was accumulated. When it was necessary to produce commercials, there were up to four hours or more of production time available to do them. Commercials were produced at the television station on a two-inch video tape. They usually consisted of a "blending" together of film, color slides, graphics and super-imposed images with a voice-over or someone on camera serving as a spokesperson. Music and/or sound effects were included if the agency producer decided to do so.

As television production companies developed and proliferated, most television stations phased out of commercial production. In the early years, however, it was absolutely necessary for stations to serve the production needs of advertisers in order to sell air time. Today, unless it's an infomercial, stations rarely sell a full program sponsorship to one advertiser. They earn far more revenue by selling commercial breaks in the programs to a variety of advertisers. Hollywood's Ziv Studios produced a number of syndicated television programs. They frequently included in the cost of the program package the opportunity of using the talent in their programs to do local commercials without having to pay talent fees or any residuals.

Thus, with the "Meet Corliss Archer" program – a popular family sitcom – Corliss, her boyfriend and her mother and father, were all available to do commercials for sponsors of the show in the various markets in which it was sold. This special benefit helped to sell the program but also meant a lot of extra work for the talent.

"Meet Corliss Archer" was originally a Broadway play written by F. Hugh Herbert called "Kiss and Tell." The play featured a teen-aged snip of a female named Corliss Archer. Corliss was first played on Broadway by an unknown actress named Joan Caulfield, who went on to become a Paramount star. In the television program Corliss was played by Ann Baker, her boyfriend by Bobby Ellis, the mother by Mary Brian, and the father by John Eldridge. The latter three were all successful actors. We prepared commercial scripts for all four principals for both Standard Federal and Vernor's. I went to Hollywood to supervise the production of the eight commercials – each commercial one minute in length.

With Joan accompanying me, we flew to Hollywood on November 15, 1954 for an assignment that was an exciting adventure. We stayed at the Hollywood Knickerbocker Hotel, which was close to the Ziv Studios in the heart of Hollywood. Early Tuesday morning we went to Ziv Studios to meet with Herb Gordon, the head of production.

I already knew the commercials would be worked into the shooting schedule for the TV shows. They were done while sets were being changed. The props for all the spots were all accounted for, including a case of Vernor's Ginger Ale. Before leaving Detroit, I had asked Ralph David, the sales manager of Vernor's, if I should take a case of Vernor's with me. He said that wasn't necessary because there was a bottler in Los Angeles who would drop off a case at Ziv Studios. When I checked the case of Vernor's that had been delivered to the studio the bottles didn't look exactly like the ones that were used in Detroit. I called the sales manager in Detroit to express my concern but he assured me that the bottles had to be the same because it was specified in their franchise agreement with the bottler.

Ann Baker was a very successful model and appeared on many magazine covers prior to winning the role of Corliss in the television program "Meet Corliss Archer." She played the role of a teenager in this family show.

We went to the stage in the studios where the "Meet Corliss Archer" series of programs was being produced. Herb Gordon introduced us to Bobby Ellis, Mary Brian, and John Eldridge. Ann Baker, who played Corliss, hadn't arrived on the set yet. While we stood in a group talking about the schedule for producing the commercials, I heard someone shout, "Ernie Baker, what are you doing here?" It was Ann Baker, who then ran up and threw her arms around me and gave me a big kiss. I thought it was a joke because I didn't know Ann Baker. She could see I was bewildered, so she said, "Don't you remember me?"

I didn't recognize her, so she explained that she was Buster Baker's sister. When I was a senior at Smith-Cotton high school in Sedalia, Missouri, Buster and I sat next to each other in several classes. Buster had a little sister named Ann, who was then a sophomore – the same Ann now playing the role of Corliss. My grandmother Baker lived in Sedalia and frequently I went to her home for lunch as it was near the high school. Buster and Ann also lived near the high school, so they regularly went home for lunch. Buster and I walked together with his little sister, Ann, following behind. I didn't know that Ann had gone to Hollywood after she graduated from high school and had enjoyed a very successful career as a model. She had appeared on more than 50 magazine covers and had won the role of Corliss by beating out several hundred competitors. Buster had moved to California, too, so that evening Joan and I had dinner with them.

During our week in Hollywood Joan and I met a number of actors and actresses. At the Ziv Studios we had an opportunity to talk with Eddie Cantor, John Cameron, Thomas Mitchell, Charles Laughton, Richard Carlson, Tristan Crawford and Gertrude Michaels – all well-known at that time. Herb Gordon arranged a tour of Paramount Studios where we watched Diana Lynn and Jerry Lewis film a scene for the movie "You're Never Too Young."

Soon after returning to Detroit, I met with the Vernor's management to show them the four commercials utilizing the leading characters in the "Meet Corliss Archer" program. Their immediate reaction upon seeing the spot was "That's not the same bottle we use in Detroit." Although hardly noticeable, the neck of the bottle had a slightly different configuration. Fortunately, I had noticed the difference and had called the sales manager to alert him of this possibility. Ziv Studios reshot the scenes where the bottle appeared using new bottles sent from Detroit.

Ziv Studios made the correction in the commercials for a minimum charge. Except for that slight hitch, both Vernor's and Standard Federal were quite pleased with their commercials.

The "Meet Corliss Archer" program ran for 26 weeks and the series ended after one season because Ziv Studios decided not to continue its production.

Vernor's, however, continued as a client of Denman & Baker, Inc., and we had become their agency at the point in time when they had decided to initiate an aggressive expansion program. The company experienced significant growth and the advertising budget steadily rose while we were their agency.

Vernor's is a unique and versatile soft drink and it's made like no other beverage. To start with, the Vernor's extract combines ginger, vanilla, citrus and other natural flavors in the exact formulation set down by James Vernor over 130 years ago. This formula has historically been known only to the presidents of The James Vernor Company. It is kept in a locked bank vault to ensure its secrecy.

The extract is aged in oak barrels for four years to give it a robust flavor. After aging, the Vernor's extract is combined with pure water and sweetener. Then it's carbonated for a zippy, tingly, tangy taste.

As people discover Vernor's, they usually find lots of enticing new ways to enjoy it…to spice up gelatin deserts…to baste flavor into hams and turkeys...and to add a deliciously different flavor to their holiday recipes and other dishes. Over the years a whole collection of Vernor's cold drink concoctions have been created. Favorites include the Boston Cooler (Vernor's and vanilla ice cream) and the White Cow (Vernor's and milk). Of course, some like it hot, too. Hot Vernor's served with a cinnamon stick or a wedge of lemon has taken the chill out of more cold winter mornings than any other soft drink.

This photo of the Vernor's Ginger Ale Company plant on Woodward near the Detroit River courtesy of Archives of Labor and Urban Affairs, Wayne State University.

Without the Civil War, there might never have been a Vernor's. Before the war started, James Vernor, a Detroit pharmacist, had been concocting a new drink. It was a secret mix of 19 ingredients, including ginger, vanilla and natural flavorings.

When Vernor was called off to the War in 1862, he stored the secret mixture in an oak cask in his pharmacy. Four years later he returned from battle. As he opened his secret keg, he found his drink inside had been deliciously transformed by aging in the wood. It had taken on a zippy, zesty, gingery flavor. It was like nothing else he had ever tasted.

For years, the only place you could get a Vernor's was from the fountain in James Vernor's original pharmacy at 233 Woodward Avenue in downtown Detroit. But demand for the drink kept growing. Soon, soda fountains throughout Detroit began selling cold, carbonated Vernor's.

In time, The James Vernor Company would open a landmark bottling operation in downtown Detroit to handle its expanding business. This riverfront headquarters became a favorite stopping place for "locals" and tourists in the 1940s. It was where you could sip a fresh Vernor's for a nickel and watch its making through big plate glass windows.

This downtown site is where the Vernor's main office and plant was located when Denman & Baker, Inc. became their agency, and it was only two-and-a-half blocks away from our offices in the Buhl Building. A few years later, though, Vernor's was forced to move their business several miles north into the old Convention Hall further up Woodward Avenue as the site of the original plant became part of the Detroit Civic Center along the Detroit River.

Denman & Baker, Inc., lost the Vernor's account to Zimmer, Keller & Calvert, Inc., in 1961. Don Graves, president of the Zimmer, Keller & Calvert agency, had a power boat that he moored near the *White Cloud*, a sailboat owned by Vernor Davis, then the president of Vernor's. They became friends and Don Graves came up with the phrase "Va Va Voom Vernor's." Zimmer, Keller & Calvert developed it into a campaign that Vernor Davis liked, so we lost the account.

Don Graves then changed the name of his boat to *Va Va Voom*. Unfortunately, however, the boat developed a gas leak and blew up. A picture of the aft (rear) end, with the name *Va Va Voom* just above the water line went out over the newswires and appeared in newspapers all over the country with the photo caption "The *Va Va Voom* Goes Boom."

Huron Cement Becomes a Client In 1956 – A Relationship That's Maintained For More Than 40 Years

In the 1950s the Beta Theta Pi Alumni Association started meeting for lunch every month at the Savoyard Club, which was on the top floor of the Buhl Building. Since my office was in the Buhl Building, it was easy for me to attend these luncheons. I met a lot of brother Betas that I would never have known had I not attended these luncheons. This included Stanley Kresge and Harvey Kresge (the latter also a Beta at my alma mater, the University of Missouri), and Charles Wilson, who married the widow Matilda Dodge (wife of Horace Dodge), and together they built Meadowbrook Hall (now a part of Oakland University). Another frequent attendee was Edward Hartwick, who donated to the state of Michigan the property that is now Hartwick Pines State Park.

Another Beta who frequently came to these luncheons was John B. Ford III (a Beta from Yale). John was the assistant treasurer of the Huron Portland Cement Company, which at the time was headquartered in the Ford Building in downtown Detroit. As a result of our regular attendance, John became the president of the Alumni Association while I served as secretary for a number of years. John and I became friends, which led to discussions during 1955 about the 50th anniversary of Huron Portland Cement Company, which would be celebrated in 1957. As a result of these meetings and the ideas we proposed, Denman & Baker was hired in early 1956 to help promote Huron Cement's upcoming 50th anniversary. The Huron Portland Cement Company was principally owned by the John Ford family – not as well-known in Detroit as the Henry Ford family – but another Ford family that also had a tremendous influence in the development of Michigan, as well as the nation.

Detroit's first skyscraper was the Majestic Building and this is where the Huron Portland Cement Company came into being in 1907.

Captain John B. Ford, the first in the John Ford line, had a long exciting career which is recorded in a book by historian Arthur Pound ("Salt of the Earth," 1940). Capt. Ford was the father of the plate glass industry in America. He and his son Edward established the first plate glass manufacturing plant in America at New Albany, Indiana. The family later opened glass plants in Louisville, Kentucky and Jeffersonville, Indiana. Unfortunately, these ventures failed due to their inability to effectively compete with established European glass makers.

Undaunted, Edward Ford and sons Edward and Emory L. organized a new company in 1880 in Creighton, Pennsylvania (the forerunner of PPG Industries).

Aerial view above of the Huron Portland Cement Company's plant at Alpena, Michigan which was the largest in the world in 1957. In the far background can be seen the stepped ledges of the limestone quarry which is more than a mile across. Another view below in 1998 of the plant, showing the modernization that has taken place to prepare the plant for the next century.

Edward Ford served as president and general manager of the new venture for 10 years before moving to Ohio to found the Edward Ford Plate Glass Company. Ford purchased 173 acres of undeveloped land along the Maumee River, just south of Toledo, and in 1898 began construction of the largest plate glass manufacturing plant under one roof in the United States.

Libbey-Owens Sheet Glass Company and Edward Ford Plate Glass Company merged in 1930 to form a powerful new force in the American flat glass industry. In later years, Libbey-Owens-Ford Glass Company pioneered many new concepts in glass manufacturing, including Thermopane® insulating glass units for commercial and residential construction; laminated safety glass windshields for automobiles; E-2-Eye® automotive tinted safety glass and the curved windshield.

In the 1890s, Edward Ford built a plant in Wyandotte, Michigan, for the production of soda ash, an essential material in the manufacture of glass. That plant was named the Michigan Alkali Company and in 1943 was renamed Wyandotte Chemicals Company. Today, Wyandotte Chemicals is part of BASF, a German conglomerate.

Capt. John B. Ford was the great-grandfather of John B. Ford III. On January 26, 1907, John's grandfather, John B. Ford II, and his uncle, Emory L. Ford, founded the Huron Portland Cement Company with the help of three other men. It was the Ford family, however, that provided most of the capital and consequently owned most of the stock in the company.

When Denman & Baker became Huron Cement's agency, the chairman of the company was Emory M. Ford (son of Emory L. Ford and grandson of Capt. Ford). Paul H. Townsend was the president. The company operated what was then the largest cement plant in the world in Alpena, Michigan, with most of the cement transported by ship to 13 distributing plants around the Great Lakes. There were more than 1500 employees in 1957 but over the next decade that number swelled considerably as production of cement expanded, then dropped dramatically through plant automation.

The plans for the 50th anniversary celebration included the writing and printing of a hard-bound book that was a history of the company. I took the primary responsibility for doing this, without realizing what a challenge it would be. I gathered all the background and historical information I could find. John B. Ford III and I made a number of trips to Alpena early in 1956, meeting with the plant management, retirees and anyone else who could help us. The first superintendent of the Alpena Mill, W.P. Harris, had kept a daily diary for many years of the plant operation and these diaries became a valuable resource. Old photos, ledgers and all kinds of reference material were accumulated until finally I ran out of room in my office to house all of it. I took the material home and used our spare bedroom as a place to read, sort and organize. I prepared a comprehensive outline and rough layout of the book, catalogued and wrote captions for all the photos, and wrote some

John B. Ford III and I at a press check for the book "The Huron Heritage" published to celebrate the 50th anniversary of the Huron Portland Cement Company.

of the text. Don Brown, public relations director of Denman & Baker, Inc., assisted me with the text and our draft was then edited and expanded by Paul Townsend, the company president. It was then decided to have George W. Stark, a columnist for *The Detroit News* (who was known as the historiographer of the city of Detroit), add colorful events that had taken place in Detroit early in this century that were pertinent to the history and development of the Huron Portland Cement Company. This 94-page history, "The Huron Heritage," was published with a green cloth cover with gold lettering. A copy of the book was presented to all employees, customers, and suppliers, and also sent to libraries in cities around the Great Lakes, to government officials, and members of the press.

In addition to this printed history, a substantial and interesting exhibit was designed and built by the W.B. Ford Design Company which graphically described and presented the 50-year history of the company. This exhibit was displayed in Detroit, Alpena, Cleveland, and a number of other cities during 1957 and 1958. Later, sections of it were utilized for sales promotion purposes at sales meetings and conventions, making it overall a very worthwhile investment. This is when I first met George Pisani, an artist at W.B. Ford Design Company who helped design the Huron exhibit. More than 30 years later our paths would cross again and we would work together every day for a number of years.

During 1957, an aggressive public relations program was also carried out to promote Huron Cement's anniversary and its products. One of their ships was docked in downtown Detroit for a weekend during Michigan Week and thousands of people toured the ship. A new distributing plant at St. Joseph, Michigan, was also opened during the year, and again a ship was docked at the new plant and made available for tours. The number of visitors was far beyond what was anticipated.

There was actually a very good reason for using the 50th anniversary as a vehicle to raise the awareness and image of the Huron Portland Cement Company. Cement had been in short supply for years, but with the expansion of cement production plants following World War II, there was then – in the late 1950s – a buyer's market. This would become an even greater and more serious factor, resulting years later in the closing of cement plants and a consolidation of cement manufacturers.

The Huron Portland Cement Company eventually was purchased by National Gypsum Company and I was present the day the exchange of stock took place. National Gypsum Company was a public company; thus, there was no secrecy about the transaction. The Huron stockholders received $72,000,000 in National Gypsum Company stock, which was reported in the business press.

Handling the 50th anniversary celebration provided Denman & Baker an opportunity to learn a great deal about the company, the cement business, its competitors and its communications needs. Huron published a monthly magazine for the employees with an editorial emphasis on safety. Following the 50th anniversary assignment the writing and publishing of this house organ became the agency's responsibility. Don Brown and I alternated for years going to Alpena every month to gather news and information for this publication. In addition to this project, the agency created and produced Huron Cement's trade advertising, a calendar, wrote and issued news releases on numerous subjects, helped introduce several new products, and created and produced a wide variety of brochures and catalogues.

Interestingly, one of the biggest challenges each year was selecting the illustration for the next year's calendar. The calendar consisted of one large illustration which was visible all year long with a big pad of the months below it. Only one month of the year was displayed at a time on the pad with each day of the month in a box in which important notes could be written. Even though the calendars took a lot of wall space, customers liked them because they were "working" calendars with the boxes for their notes. The sales force distributed the calendar during their sales calls, but I also spotted them in barber shops and a few other interesting places. More time, thought, and energy went into selecting the illustration for the next year's calendar than nearly any other project. Over the years, we used photos or paintings of all six of the Huron ships, significant structures built of Huron Cement, and even some hunting scenes. There was a great collective sigh of relief when the decision was made and the calendar went into final production. This project was usually initiated in July, with a goal of having the calendar on press by early November. Calendars and Christmas cards remain among the most challenging assignments that any advertising agency can handle, because the selection of the cover design or illustration is so subjective.

Of all the accounts that I have handled or serviced over the years, I learned more from being involved with the cement business than any other because it involved mining; manufacturing on a colossal scale; transportation of products by truck, train, and ship; and environmental issues, as well as the distribution and marketing of various kinds of cement. Then, there's the use of the product in the construction of skyscrapers, highways, driveways and sidewalks, and structures of all kinds, including stadiums, parking decks, dams, airports, and houses. In addition, there are specialized concrete products, such as pipes, blocks, and pre-stressed beams. Over the years, I was involved in every facet of the business, principally because I always considered that I was in the communications business – not just the advertising business – and therefore willing to participate in any assignment involving communications.

Cement and the concrete that is made from it has become so integrated into our lives that we have become indifferent to it. It is basic to our very being, yet we are so accustomed to it that we no longer think of it as a material. The Coliseum, the Forum, the Roman Baths…these and other famous structures of antiquity attest to the fact that concrete is a centuries-old building material. They also prove that cement, which is the binding agent of concrete, was originally invented by the Romans. They used a natural cement which was formed by mixing slaked lime and sand with volcanic ash from Mt. Vesuvius. Yet, simple as the formula was, the art of mixing cement was lost in the Dark Ages. It was not until the scientific spirit of inquiry revived in the eighteenth century that men rediscovered the secret of cement that would harden when water was mixed with it. Cement as we know it today was first discovered by an English stone mason named Joseph Aspdin. He called his discovery Portland Cement. A man by the name of David O. Saylor pioneered the production of Portland Cement in this country when he started a small plant in 1871. Today, cement manufacturing is one of the world's great and vital industries.

When I started handling the Huron Portland Cement Company account in early 1956, Emory M. Ford was chairman of the board. He was also chairman of Wyandotte Chemicals' board of directors, and served on the boards of a number of other companies, as well as that of a major Detroit hospital. Emory graduated from Princeton in 1928, and joined Michigan Alkali, where he worked his way up through the ranks. He was a very impressive individual.

Paul Townsend succeeded Emory M. Ford as president and was the first to hold that position outside the circle of the Ford family. Paul was well qualified by inclination, character, and experience, as he first served as a Captain of field artillery in World War I (soon after he graduated from Yale). I worked closely with Paul Townsend for a number of years, and respected his keen intelligence and knowledge of many subjects outside the cement business. My wife and I and our sons were guests every summer at his home on a lake near Dryden, Michigan, where he enjoyed his own trout stream. When his wife died suddenly, he called me to help prepare her obituary – as difficult a task as I ever faced – because she was an outstanding lady.

Following Paul Townsend as the president of the Huron Cement Company was H. Ripley

Schemm, a graduate of the University of Michigan Engineering School. Rip, as everyone called him, was a warm, pleasant individual with a brilliant mind. He invented the Airslide Cement Conveying System, which was patented in 1950 and is employed the world over for the conveyance of finely divided materials. Cement, by the way, is finer than face powder. Rip also invented a number of devices used for measuring bulk dry and liquid materials in large tanks, bins, or silos, and these products were manufactured and sold by the Bin-Dicator Company, which was owned by Rip and his brother George. The manufacturing plant was on the east side of Detroit for many years, but moved to Port Huron in 1970. The Bin-Dicator Company also became an agency client, but I'll address that experience later in this story.

During the 40 years that I was involved with Huron Cement and its successors, I worked with a number of exceptionally nice, competent people – Peter Herguth and Mike McCormick in marketing, Bruce Wideman in the technical sales department, and a number of other men who served as presidents after Paul Townsend and Rip Schemm retired.

As previously reported, National Gypsum Company acquired the Huron Portland Cement Company in 1959. Two years later, in 1961, they also acquired Allentown Cement in Allentown, Pennsylvania, which also became an agency client. Huron and Allentown were merged in 1976 and became the Cement Division of National Gypsum Company.

The cement industry went through some very difficult years in the 1960s, '70s, and '80s, due to the greatly expanded production capacity resulting in keener competition. This brought about more consolidation, with some cement plants even closing down. Lafarge Corporation is a big international company headquartered in Paris that is the second-largest producer of cement in the world. A Swiss conglomerate is slightly larger.

Lafarge acquired the assets of the Huron Cement portion of the Cement Division of National Gypsum Company as of January 1, 1987. Over the next few years, Lafarge added several other cement manufacturers in the United States and Canada and for some time continued the product names of the various companies they acquired. They gradually phased them out by reducing the size of the names on the bags of cement and increasing the Lafarge name. Today, all products are sold under the Lafarge brand name, and the Huron Cement brand no longer exists.

A 25-year relationship was celebrated with a luncheon at Machus Red Fox Restaurant at which I presented John Piecuch a special plaque to recognize the many years the agency had served Huron Cement as its marketing partner.

John Piecuch was first hired by the Cement Division of National Gypsum as a consultant in the late 1970s, but he eventually joined the company as its controller. John became president of the Cement Division in February 1982, and remained in that position until the company was acquired by Lafarge. He then became president of the Great Lakes Region of Lafarge in January 1987, and two years later moved to Reston, Virginia, when he became president of the Cement Group of Lafarge, which included all of the United States and Canada. John has since moved on from that position to higher responsibilities with Lafarge, which confirms his outstanding management and leadership abilities. I really enjoyed and appreciated the years that I was fortunate enough to work for and with him when he was in Detroit.

At one of our meetings, John insisted that I take a trip on one of the company's ships. I had been offered the opportunity of taking such a trip several times, but had not done so because I was not eager to take a week's time sailing around the Great Lakes on a ship hauling cement. John prevailed.

So, on Monday, July 26, 1982, Joan and I, along with my mother and Joan's dad, left Alpena on the Str. Iglehart bound for Superior, Wisconsin. We sailed north in Lake Huron into the North Channel passing through the locks at Sault Ste. Marie into Whitefish Bay, then across Lake Superior to the distributing plant at Superior, Wisconsin, where half the ship's cargo of cement was unloaded. Then we moved to Duluth, Minnesota, where the rest of the cargo was discharged into the storage silos at the distributing plant. We had ample time to explore both Superior and Duluth (a car was provided) before re-boarding the ship for our return back across Lake Superior through the locks to Alpena. It was a relaxing, memorable week and the four

Joan Baker pointing out the Mackinac Bridge, which we passed under on our Great Lakes cruise on the Str. J.A.W. Iglehart.

of us each put on a few pounds enjoying the delicious meals. Warm, freshly baked cookies were available in the galley 24 hours a day for the crew and they shared them with us. It was a great experience and I'll always be grateful and indebted to John Piecuch for insisting that I take a trip on one of the company's ships. The guest accommodations were outstanding because the use of these trips is for the entertainment of customers.

In 1995, my 40-year relationship with the cement industry ended. There was a significantly reduced level of activity and as a result there was no longer a need for Lafarge to use the services of a large advertising agency.

In 1956, American Community Builders Also Became An Agency Client

Philco was a major manufacturer of household appliances in the 1950s and its products were distributed in Michigan by our client, Buhl Sons Company. A Detroit builder decided to feature Philco appliances exclusively in a major housing development in Southfield, south of 10 Mile Road and east of Southfield

My mother, Sara Elizabeth Baker, steering the Str. J.A.W. Iglehart – a self-unloading cement carrier – across Lake Superior. This ship is 500 feet long, has a capacity of 12,000 tons and is powered by a steam turbine that produces 4,400 horsepower.

Road in an area that was largely undeveloped in 1956. Bill Denman and I met with Lester Taubman and Arnold Levin, the principals of American Community Builders, and they assigned us the advertising for this project, consisting of several hundred tri-level "American Beauty" homes.

Philco was, at that time, also a major sponsor of the Miss America Beauty Pageant held each year in Atlantic City. Lee Meriwether was the reigning Miss America, having won the title in 1955. For the grand opening of the American Beauty homes, arrangements were made through Philco to have Lee Meriwether come to Detroit to participate in a parade from downtown Detroit to the project site, and then cut the ribbon for the grand opening of the model homes. Through the Oldsmobile Division of General Motors, I was able to arrange for five white Olds convertibles to lead the parade. We festooned the cars with ribbons and balloons and I – along with three other people from the office and my brother Joe (who happened to be in town from California) – drove the five cars to the subdivision. Lee Meriwether rode in the first car, followed by the mayors of Detroit and Southfield. Les Taubman and Arnie Levin completed the list of occupants of the five cars.

Following the five white Olds convertibles was a conglomeration of cars and trucks (mostly the company's subcontractors) to help make our parade an impressive one. We even had a readi-mix cement truck – empty, of course. It really worked, because the grand opening got extensive news coverage in newspapers, on radio, and in television newscasts.

Over the years, I have driven through Southfield many times where these homes were built. It's now totally developed with homes and businesses. In my mind's eye though, I can still picture how remote it looked in 1956 when we staged that parade from downtown Detroit on a drizzly and misty Saturday morning.

This project in Southfield was quickly sold out and American Community Builders then started housing developments in Midland,

Flint, Bay City, and Mansfield, Ohio. On April 30, 1957, Les and Arnie asked me to accompany them on a tour of the four projects as we were now handling the advertising for these developments. We met at Willow Run Airport early in the morning, where we were picked up in a four-passenger Cessna. The pilot and Les sat in the front seat, while Arnie and I sat in the back. We first flew to the Tri-City Airport in mid-Michigan where we were met by the project superintendent. He drove us to the three projects in Flint, Bay City, and Midland, and returned us to the airport in the afternoon. We flew to Mansfield, Ohio and left there after dinner. It was quite dark and bumpy as we flew back to Willow Run. Arnie, unfortunately, became airsick and the only thing available to throw up in was his hat. Thank goodness he had a hat that he could use for that purpose! When Arnie finished "up-chucking" his dinner, he slid the side window open and threw his hat (and contents) out of the plane somewhere over Lake Erie. That was one long day with a ragged ending!

While the American Beauty Home project in Southfield was a big success, the other ones outstate and in Ohio were not. American Community Builders ended up declaring bankruptcy. Fortunately, Denman & Baker, Inc. had already parted company with them when it happened, as we saw the handwriting on the wall, and thus managed to avoid any loss.

Chapter 3

The Events Of The Next Five Years (1959-1963) Proved To Be Both Challenging And Traumatic

As we grow better, we meet better people.

St. James Lutheran Church of Grosse Pointe Farms, Michigan, began as a mission congregation in 1940. Anita and Edward Bauman, Joan's mother and father, along with Joan and her sister Barbara, were part of this small mission group. Eight years later, on December 5, 1948, a beautiful church of pure Georgian Colonial design was dedicated. Ed Bauman headed the building committee.

For the next 25 years, starting soon after our marriage in 1948, St. James was a very important part of our lives. Joan and I sang in the choir, she taught Sunday school, and I served on the vestry and frequently ushered. Joan and some 20 other young women in the church became members of the Abigail Division of the Women's Guild. Social activities were frequently planned and initiated by the Abigails, such as progressive dinners, hay rides, costume parties, square dances and special projects. These resulted in a lot of close friendships being made among the couples whose wives were "Abigails."

Not only did we have a lot of fun socializing, but we also raised funds for our church through pancake suppers and white elephant auctions. The husbands of the Abigails even put on a minstrel show in the church basement auditorium. The show was a sellout for two nights running. I was an "End Man."

All the couples in the Abigails Group in 1959 were under 35 years of age, with young children, and struggling to get ahead. A guild division for young married women was really a good idea, for it gave them a way to work for the church as well as providing them with what turned out to be an important social outlet.

Doug Graham, whose wife was an Abigail, was a young attorney in 1959 and he became a lifelong friend and confidante. Doug was my personal attorney for 45 years until he retired, and he also served for 26 years as the secretary and a member of the board of directors of the agency that I started in 1964. He ultimately became a partner in a large, prestigious Detroit law firm, Butzel, Keidan, Simon, Myers & Graham. Doug was twice elected president of the St. James Lutheran Church congregation. He was also a member of the Grosse Pointe City Council for many years serving as the mayor from 1981 to 1983. Doug passed away on May 24, 1997 of lymphoma and I said goodbye to a very special friend.

Another couple, Harriet and Marvin Asmus, Jr., also became our close friends. They were the godparents of our son Bob when he was baptized, and Joan and I were the godparents for one of their daughters. Marv was with Asmus Spices & Seasonings and his father, Marvin Sr., was president of the company. Asmus Spices & Seasonings was started by Marv Jr.'s grandfather and the company had been in business since the early 1900s providing spices and producing seasonings for meat processors and bakeries. The company's plant was a delight to visit, as the aroma of all the various spices being processed and blended was a pleasant experience. They appointed Denman & Baker

St. James Lutheran Church of Grosse Pointe Farms, Michigan.

in 1952 to handle their advertising, which ran in the national meat packing and baking publications. The relationship continued for many years, until the company was sold to the A.E. Staley Company, which is headquartered in Decatur, Illinois.

Another business relationship that evolved from participation in the Abigails was with Fred Schriever. Fred and his wife Pat were another couple who became good friends. Fred was a graduate of the University of Michigan School of Engineering and was a manufacturer's representative for foundries. He became very successful, and in time acquired a foundry and a machine shop, as well as several other businesses including the J.P. Bell Company. He was also a successful inventor of products that are used on boats, a fire safety system for commercial buildings, and a leveling device used under machines and missiles. A missile obviously won't hit its target unless it's launched from a perfectly level base and because Fred's device would do that, thousands of them were purchased by the U.S. Military. Fred's patented machine leveling device performed better than any other leveler then available. It was manufactured and marketed by the J.P. Bell Company, which became our client in 1968.

E.W. Baker, Inc. carried out an advertising and publicity program that generated lots of sales leads for the leveler which worked on the principle of a convex spherical radius which aligned and adjusted itself in the saucer-shaped top of a lifting wedge to find true self-alignment. This was a simple solution for a complicated problem. Over the years I handled a variety of communications assignments for Fred, consisting of advertising, public relations, and collateral materials for his various companies.

In 1959, Fred Schriever bought his first power boat, and on July 11 of that year, he invited several couples who were all friends through Abigails to go for a cruise on Lake St. Clair. We crossed the lake in Fred and Pat's new boat to Canada, where we ate dinner, and on the way home we went around the south end of Peche Island. It was a hot evening and a man was cooling off in the lake, with only his head sticking out of the water. Suddenly, the boat's propeller started hitting rocks and Fred quickly stopped his boat. We were in extremely shallow water with a badly damaged propeller. The man in the water then stood up – as he had been sitting down in the lake. We had assumed he was standing – not sitting – in the water. The Coast Guard had to tow the boat in and it was the wee hours of the morning before we got to our homes. Fred learned well from the experience because he became an expert in navigation, an instructor and commander for the Grosse Pointe Power Squadron, and the Commodore of the Grosse Pointe Yacht Club.

When I joined St. James Church, I never ever expected any of this to happen. All of the accounts that I just described developed as a result of friendships that were made in a church group made up of young couples. However, more and bigger business would follow from other members of the church. The president of the C.M. Hall Lamp Company was a member of St. James. His name was Leonard Zick. Leonard called me one day to offer the agency an opportunity to plan and create a trade advertising campaign for his company. C.M. Hall was an original equipment manufacturer of headlights and other lighting equipment for the automotive and trucking industries and a public company. Denman & Baker got the business, then handled the advertising for this company for several years, until Leonard resigned to become president of a much larger company in Grand Rapids, Michigan.

Two of Leonard Zick's married daughters were also members of the Abigail Women's Guild. Rowene (and Art) Niedow and Arlene (and Tom) Anton. Tom Anton retired in 1994 as executive vice president of Kelly Services but during his successful career with Kelly, he tried several times to direct the Kelly Services advertising account to me. It never happened, but I certainly appreciated his efforts. Tom died in 1995, shortly after he retired, while he was on a safari in Africa.

...And Then Came Howard Johnson's

Al Sherman and his younger brother Jack owned the popular Howard Johnson's restaurant on Mack Avenue in Grosse Pointe. Both Shermans were members of St. James. Jack sang in the choir with Joan and me.

Al invited me to his home one evening in 1959 to discuss a problem they had with their restaurant. From Memorial Day through Labor Day, they did a tremendous volume of business. The fall, winter, and spring months however, were not near capacity. The second problem was that they did not get a lot of new customers.

At that time, I knew very little about the food service business, but it seemed to me that one way to change this situation was to offer a special meal at a very low price every month during the slow season. This would hopefully solve both problems – increase business and bring in new customers. We put together a series of low-price specials consisting of a complete lunch or dinner which would be available for a two-week period during the off-season months. They were essentially as follows:

September . . . . Fried Claims
October . . . . Fried Chicken
November . . . . Roast Turkey
December . . . . Spaghetti
January . . . . Baked Chicken
February . . . . Fried Claims
March . . . . Baked Ham
April . . . . Fried Fish

For $1.19, diners could enjoy a cup of soup, the entree, and a single scoop of Howard Johnson's ice cream for dessert. The special was priced to cover just the food cost. We reasoned that when several people came in together for the special, not everyone would order it. Some would order from the regular menu. The monthly specials would be available for both lunch and dinner.

The agency then put together the advertising and promotional materials. The strategy was to advertise the specials on radio and in newspapers. Each participating restaurant was provided posters, danglers, table tents, and menu tabs for each promotion. There were more than 30 Howard Johnson's restaurants in Southeast Michigan in 1960, the year we launched the program. To get the campaign started, Al Sherman invited all the owners to a meeting at his restaurant at which this program was presented. They all enthusiastically agreed to support it and an organization was formed with Al Sherman as president.

That first year the campaign ran – September 1960 through April 1961 – it was an incredible success. Some members of the association had questioned offering a roast turkey dinner the two weeks immediately prior to Thanksgiving but this turned out to be the biggest volume producer of any of the monthly specials. Fried clams were a Howard Johnson's specialty but proved to be the least popular special. However, it pushed the check average higher because those who didn't order fried clams ordered something else off the menu at the regular price, just as we had anticipated.

Word of the success of this Southeastern Michigan Howard Johnson's promotion spread quickly to other cities. In the years to follow, the monthly specials were utilized by Howard Johnson's advertising associations in Toledo, Cleveland, Chicago, Milwaukee, St. Louis, and Atlanta and Marietta, Georgia. The restaurants in Marietta were also owned and operated by Al and Jack Sherman. Jack moved to Georgia to manage the restaurants he and his brother owned there. Al stayed in Michigan to supervise their operations there. Al and his wife bought one of the homes on Mackinac Island up the drive a few doors from the Grand Hotel. It was then painted in the distinctive Howard Johnson's colors and you couldn't miss it when you crossed over to the island either from Mackinac City or St. Ignace. Unfortunately, Al and his wife lost their summer home to a fire and there's now a vacant lot where this colorful Victorian-style summer home once stood.

The Howard Johnson's advertising account for promoting these monthly specials didn't exist prior to September 1960. Funds were collected year-round from the franchise owners and some company-owned operators of the Howard Johnson's restaurants and expended during an eight-month period. The price of the monthly specials increased every year by at least 10¢ going from $1.19 (where we started) to $1.29, to $1.39, to $1.49, to $1.69, until they finally reached $2.29. The original intent of the promotions, to increase monthly business during the slow seasons, and to bring in new customers was simply ignored or objected to by a number of the operators after a few years because as competition grew they decided that these promotions were to be used to generate more profits. Meetings of the associations became heated, to say the least, because some owners wanted to increase the price by more than 10¢ each year, eliminate the dessert or reduce the portions.

The national advertising agency for Howard Johnson's in the 1960s was the Cabot Agency in Boston. They were well aware of the success of these midwest promotions and convinced the corporate management in Boston that they should be carried out on a national basis which they, of course, would handle. They succeeded! We lost the business to the Cabot Agency in 1969, but the great satisfaction is that we started from Ground Zero and built an account in nine years that was billing nearly a million dollars when it departed. This is not all that unusual in the advertising business, but it is very satisfying when it happens to you.

Throughout the 1950s and into the 1960s, Howard Johnson's was the leading restaurant chain in the United States. However, McDonald's, Burger King, and the other fast food chains, plus pizza operators and many other franchised food restaurants significantly eroded Howard Johnson's business as they spread across America. Howard Johnson's restaurants, unfortunately, became inconsistent in food, service, and even cleanliness...so they faded away. The familiar red roofs are nearly all gone as most former Howard Johnson's are now either used for some other venue or the buildings have been totally replaced with something else. We served this restaurant chain's needs at an opportune time and the experience and knowledge gained would serve us well in the future.

The friends I made at St. James Lutheran Church taught me that *few people are successful operating a business unless a lot of other people want them to be.*

– 1962 –

Standard Federal Savings and Loan Association was founded in Detroit in 1893. It became an agency client in 1952, and Robert Hutton was vice president in charge of everything except the mortgage department. Standard Federal's headquarters building was located at Griswold and Jefferson in downtown Detroit and occupied the site where Sainte Anne's Catholic Church had been built in July 1701 – a log structure that was the first building ever constructed in Detroit. However, it wasn't until after World War II that Standard

Federal started to achieve significant growth. This was due primarily to Bob Hutton, who pushed hard for adding branch offices in the rapidly-growing outlying areas of the city and suburbs. For every four locations for branches he submitted to the board, he was able to get one approved.

By early 1962, Standard Federal had opened seven branch offices and we had carried out some successful promotions to attract savings. At that time, the only product that S and Ls could offer was a passbook savings account and every savings and loan association paid the same interest rate, and invested the funds they attracted in loans for single-family homes. Savings and loans in California had started offering premiums to attract savings accounts and we followed this lead.

Our most successful promotion prior to 1962 consisted of offering a Philco AM-FM clock radio for opening – or adding to a present savings account – $5,000 or more. The Philco clock radios were purchased from our client, Buhl Sons Company, for just over $20 each. The initial order was for 100 clock radios with the stipulation that any not used in the promotion could be returned. The response to the advertising was overwhelming! More than 1000 Philco clock radios were given away during the promotion and a sales executive from the Philco factory in Philadelphia came to Detroit to see what was going on here. He was so impressed with our promotion that Philco opened a premium division specifically to encourage the sale of their products for incentive purposes.

As the Standard Federal account grew, Bob Hutton and I talked frequently on the phone. We met almost daily. In a service business, relationships are critical because the road you travel together is not always smooth. Getting over bumps and making sure that the work is done well and delivered on time is a challenge every single day. In advertising, **it's not what you did for me yesterday but what you do for me today that counts.** What also counts are the people you work with and Bob

The Auto-Teller window makes it easier to save at STANDARD FEDERAL SAVINGS

Here we are at the window.

Good morning, the teller greets you through a two-way communication system.

A drawer slides out toward your car.

Please put your money, your savings passbook and addition slip in the drawer.

The drawer slides quickly back to the teller. Now watch how fast the teller completes the transaction and returns the drawer with your passbook, some more addition slips and your change.

Thank you, says the teller.

You're welcome. Goodby.

Yes, you can even talk to the teller! Easy, isn't it? And it didn't take more than a few minutes—much less time, in fact, than it takes to park and walk in.

You can use the auto-teller window for making mortgage payments, cashing checks, paying utility bills and, of course, for adding to your account.

SAVE BEFORE NOVEMBER 10 AND GET A FULL TWO MONTHS' EARNINGS ON OUR NEXT DIVIDEND DATE, DECEMBER 31. MONEY RECEIVED BY NOVEMBER 10TH EARNS FROM THE 1ST.

STANDARD FEDERAL SAVINGS

MAIN OFFICE:
GRISWOLD AND JEFFERSON
WOodward 5-4774

BRANCH OFFICES:
17540 **GRAND RIVER** near Southfield
25712 **GRAND RIVER** at Beech Road
16841 **SCHAEFER ROAD** S. of McNichols
10641 **JOY ROAD** 1 block E. of Meyers
16530 **EAST WARREN** at Outer Drive
11600 **KELLY ROAD** and Whittier
1406 **N. WOODWARD** 1 block S. 12 Mile Rd.

Visit unusual and interesting places by watching "The Standard Federal George Pierrot Show," Mondays at 7:00 PM. A full hour in color on WWJ-TV, Channel 4.

OFFICE HOURS	Main Office: Monday thru Thursday 9:00 AM—4:00 PM, and Friday 9:00 AM—6:00 PM
	Branches: Monday thru Thursday 10:00 AM—5:00 PM, and Friday 10:00 AM—8:00 PM

Standard Federal Savings started sponsoring the "George Pierrot Show" in 1961. This popular one-hour program was telecast in Detroit on Channel 4, 7 p.m. to 8 p.m. on Mondays. The contract for the 1962-1963 season was signed by, left to right: Frank Sisson, WWJ-TV station manager; John Albert, WWJ-TV sales representative; Thomas R. Ricketts, vice president of Standard Federal; and Ernest W. Baker, executive vice president of Denman & Baker advertising agency.

Hutton was one of the most pleasant and delightful individuals that I was privileged to work with in my lengthy career.

On January 16, 1962, Bob Hutton was elected president of Standard Federal and the primary responsibility for the advertising was then delegated to Tom Ricketts. This was the start of a new and long-lasting personal relationship because Ricketts followed Hutton as president of Standard Federal in 1973, and became chairman of the board, president, and chief executive officer in 1981. In time, Ricketts would become recognized as one of the nation's top executives as Standard Federal Bank grew to become one of the country's largest, strongest, and healthiest banks. Tom and I had frequent phone contact and met several times a week

Facing page: My wife Joan and our sons Robert and Michael are in the car in this advertisement promoting the Standard Federal auto-teller window service.

during the 15 years that he was directly responsible for the bank's advertising.

Lee Crooks and Tony Franco Join Denman & Baker, Inc.

The dissolution of the Fred M. Randall advertising agency in 1962 had a big impact on Denman & Baker. Lee Crooks, the president, informed us that the Randall agency was going to be dissolved, as the chairman and principal owner had decided to retire. Lee and a number of other members of the staff were interested in moving to our agency, where they could continue to service the accounts they were handling at Randall.

In early March 1962, Crooks, Tony Franco, and several other members of the Randall staff joined us to more than double the size of the agency. Franco, who had headed the public relations division of Randall, continued that role at Denman & Baker. Shortly after the amalgamation, on April 6, Franco and I made a presentation to the John Henry Company in Lansing, Michigan, and we won the account. Franco was assigned its public relations and I took charge of its advertising. John Henry was then, and continues to be, the world leader in providing florists and garden centers with virtually all the products needed to operate their businesses.

The influx of people and accounts made it necessary to move the agency's offices from the 10th floor of the Buhl Building to much larger quarters on the 13th floor. The mood in the agency was positively upbeat all through the spring and summer of 1962 because we thought we had no place to go but up!

Suddenly fortunes changed. George Black died of a heart attack on September 14, while driving to the office. We not only lost a key to our success, I had also lost one hell of a friend. George's death also marked the turning point for the Denman & Baker advertising agency. We didn't know it at the time, but the agency had

Lee Crooks   **George Black**   **Ernie Baker**   **Bill Denman**

reached its peak. After George's death, we lost clients and momentum.

Bill Denman immediately took on the management of the McLouth Steel account, which was the agency's largest client, as well as several other accounts that George had handled. Bill was in a position to do this because Buhl Sons Company had stopped distributing major appliances and no longer did any advertising. Vernor's had been lost to Zimmer, Keller & Calvert in 1961. I had phased out of the Vernor's account in 1958 because I had a very heavy account load to handle at the time and Bill Denman did not. After Bill became responsible for managing the Vernor's account, he and Ralph

David, Vernor's sales manager developed a very good working relationship. The advertising expenditures had increased considerably, because Vernor's had grown significantly by adding bottlers in a number of cities outside Detroit. Thus, the loss of this account in 1961 to Zimmer, Keller & Calvert and their "VA VA VOOM" concept had been a real blow to Bill's ego, as well as to the agency.

The addition of the accounts that Lee Crooks and Tony Franco brought to Denman & Baker was exciting. But for Bill Denman it was offset by a number of serious setbacks in his personal and business life. In 1960, Bill's wife Phyllis had been diagnosed with multiple sclerosis.

Then, just prior to George Black's death, a close personal and business friend of Bill's had died suddenly. His friend, Tom Lytle, owned several businesses, including Proof Products, which distributed a foot powder, toiletries, and vitamins through a number of retail drug chains. Advertising for these products had been handled by Bill. After Tom's death, the businesses were sold and the billings ended.

In late November 1962, McLouth Steel notified the agency that it had decided to move its account to Young & Rubicam. This was another tough blow for Bill. The stress caused him to be severely afflicted with psoriasis (a skin disease consisting of red patches covered with white scales). It covered his entire body and made it necessary for him to sleep at night in a plastic bag. Bill became very discouraged and told several of us that the "heat in the kitchen was getting too hot – more than he could bear" and that if the right offer was made he'd consider selling the agency. Lee Crooks, Tony Franco, and I had several meetings with Bill in December 1962 to discuss this possibility.

– 1963 –

When Lee Crooks and Tony Franco joined Denman & Baker, they also brought with them the membership in the National Advertising Agency Network (NAAN). This network of advertising agencies had been represented by the Fred M. Randall agency in Detroit but the franchise was transferred to Denman & Baker, Inc. For me personally, NAAN would become a very valuable asset in the future, as I learned many things about agency operation and client service at regional and national meetings of this network.

The first NAAN meeting I attended was held at the Peabody Hotel in Memphis, February 7-10, 1963. This was a regional meeting, but representatives from nearly every network member from across the U.S. attended. In addition to an annual national meeting, which all members were required to attend, there were usually a couple of regionals held each year, covering specific subjects, at which attendance was optional.

The Peabody Hotel was one of America's great hotels, and staying there for several days was a real treat. The Peabody Hotel had a number of traditions, including the famous duck walk: every morning at a precise time, a flock of ducks that were housed on the roof of the hotel came down to the lobby in an elevator. The ducks then waddled in a line on a red carpet from the elevator to a large pool of water in the lobby where they spent the day. Late in the afternoon, the procedure was repeated, with the ducks going to the penthouse for the night. Years later, the Peabody burned but it was rebuilt.

At this NAAN meeting, I met for the first time principals of agencies from all over the country. According to the organization's charter, there could only be one agency member from a city, so none of your local competitors could participate in this network. The interchange of information and ideas, therefore, was generous because the intent of the network was to help each other grow and prosper. I was able to fraternize and learn from Howard Swink, who headed the famous Howard Swink agency in Marion, Ohio. Howard is referred to in the book "The Advertising Agency Business" by Kenneth Grosbeck more than any other agency manager in this "bible" on how advertising agencies should operate. Other participants included Harry Hoffman of Hoffman & York (Milwaukee); Ray Milici from the Milici agency (Honolulu); Jim Henderson of Henderson Advertising (Charlotte); Hal Shoup of Carr Liggett (Cleveland); Henry Kaufman of Henry J. Kaufman & Associates (Washington, DC); and Bob Luckie of Luckie & Forney (Birmingham, Alabama), as well as many other successful agency managers of that decade.

While much of NAAN's value was derived from the information, systems or procedures that members made available to one another to help each other function better as an advertising agency, they also provided a variety of services that benefited clients of agencies that were network members. NAAN represented more than 1000 advertising people working in 40 agencies across the nation, handling more than 700 different accounts, so there was a great amount of expertise available in a number of fields for clients to draw upon if and when they needed to do so. In addition, there were specific services available to clients of NAAN agencies at a minimal charge for such activities as the following:

FIELD SURVEYS

OBTAINING CASE HISTORIES
AND TESTIMONIALS

DISTRIBUTION CHECKS AND
TRADE CONTACTS

SCOUTING COMPETITION

MAKING LOCAL MEDIA BUYS

SUPERVISING LOCAL PRODUCTION
AND PHOTOGRAPHY

MONITORING RADIO AND
TV ADVERTISING

PR CONTACTS AND PROMOTIONS

CHECKING STORE DISPLAYS
AND PRESENTATIONS

SUPERVISING INTERVIEWS FOR
RADIO AND TV SHOW PRODUCTION

SPECIALIZED MARKET INFORMATION

ARRANGING TIE-INS WITH DEALERS

In effect, membership in NAAN gave Denman & Baker a network of branch offices and enhanced our stature as an agency. We fulfilled many requests for services from member agencies and our clients also utilized the network for a wide variety of services that were well-executed at a minimal cost.

Joe Gallagher Becomes Agency Creative Director

In February of 1963, Joe Gallagher was hired to be the creative director of Denman & Baker, Inc. Joe, a charming, red-headed Irishman, was very bright and a gifted writer. He also had the Irish curse – a love of Irish whiskey – which had led to his forced departure from key positions at several agencies, including Campbell-Ewald and Howard Swink. Joe was in his mid-40s when he joined Denman & Baker, and had gotten his life under control. During his career, he had created many award-winning campaigns and had an uncanny sense about what a client would – or would not – accept. This is an attribute many creative people lack.

Joe Gallagher

His influence on the creative work done by the agency was immediate and positive, as there was a noticeable improvement in everything the agency turned out – from collateral material to posters, radio and television commercials, print advertisements, as well as special projects such as annual reports and corporate brochures.

Orderly Transition of Agency Ownership and Management Becomes a Key Issue

In the spring and summer months of 1963, Lee Crooks, Tony Franco, and I met with Bill Denman on a number of occasions to discuss his expressed interest in getting out of the business. In addition to the psoriasis, he had several severe attacks of gout which kept him out of the office for weeks at a time. Lee, Tony and I met with an accounting firm and an attorney who helped us put together a buy-out plan. We took these steps with Bill's full knowledge and approval.

On September 23, Lee Crooks met with Bill Denman to present an extremely fair arrangement which would have enabled Bill to phase out of the business. Tony and I were not present at this meeting, but it ended with Bill angrily firing Crooks. Lee subsequently joined the Grey & Kilgore agency. Inevitably, the clients he handled moved their accounts to that agency.

Firing Lee Crooks was a terrible mistake, but something must have been said that caused Bill Denman to lash out in anger – I'm sure due or related to the stress he was under at the time. The stress was evident in his personal appearance and the fact that he had become a chain smoker after having stopped smoking for a number of years. In any event, Bill forfeited a lot of money that we had proposed paying to redeem his stock and for counseling services after he left the agency.

Tony Franco decided to resign in late September to start the Anthony M. Franco Public Relations Agency which became, in time, the largest public relations firm in Michigan. He eventually sold his company to Ross Roy Communications and became a director of that agency. After Omnicom purchased Ross Roy in 1995, several executives of the Anthony M. Franco Public Relations firm purchased the business, but Tony retired from the PR business and pursued other interests. Tony and I have been friends for lo these many years since we first worked together in 1963, and I have felt a personal pride in the success that he achieved in the public relations field.

Bill Denman Announces His Retirement

On October 1, 1963, Bill Denman informed me that he had decided to retire at the end of the year. He said he hoped I would keep the business going and would work with me to help make that happen. Bill had told me on a number of occasions that if I would just "stick with him" he would turn the agency over to me someday, though there was nothing in writing. That "someday" had now suddenly arrived. However, he said if I wanted to join some other agency and take the agency's remaining accounts there, or pursue some other opportunity, he would support my decision.

In the book "Alice In Wonderland," Alice comes to a fork in the road where she sees a Cheshire cat sitting on a bough of a tree a few yards off. "Cheshire Puss," she asks, "Would you tell me, please, which way I ought to go from here?"

"That depends a good deal in where you want to get to," said the cat.

"I don't much care where –," said Alice.

"Then it doesn't matter which way you go" said the cat.[1]

Unlike Alice, my fork in the road offered several different paths to consider, and it mattered greatly on which direction I decided.

In October and early November, I met with five advertising agencies, all eager to absorb the business remaining at Denman & Baker. I met several times with Maxon, Inc., as Art Wiebold, an executive with the agency, was particularly eager to have us join. Art lived directly in back of Bob Hutton, the president of Standard Federal, and shared the backyard fence. My concern, though, was that the strong leader of that agency – Lou Maxon – had suffered a stroke and the Maxon agency was having major account losses.

By early November, I had determined that I wanted to keep the agency going. Offers from

---

1 "Alice's Adventures in Wonderland" by Lewis Carroll (1832-1898). From Chapter 6, "Pig and Pepper."

other agencies had been tempting, but I wanted the opportunity to be captain of my own ship. While I appreciated all the opportunities that were presented, I was particularly grateful for the support that Bob Anthony, an account executive at Denman & Baker, offered. Bob and his wife Leona were then in their fifties. They had never had children and were quite well off financially. Leona had a successful decorating business and they owned two movie theaters – the Shores Madrid in St. Clair Shores and The Main in Royal Oak. Bob offered to invest $15,000 in the agency – more if needed. His offer pushed aside any doubts that I had about keeping the business going.

I then refinanced our home, taking $15,000 of the equity to invest in E.W. Baker, Inc. My $15,000, combined with Bob Anthony's $15,000, constituted our working capital. We knew that we would essentially have 12 months of overhead in 1964 with only 11 months of income because the January 1964 billings (including commissions and fees) would belong to the Denman & Baker, Inc. agency, having been placed or handled in the prior month.

Bill Denman sold us all the furniture, fixtures, and equipment for twelve offices, plus the lobby and a conference room for $4,103.00. Also, he sold us the contents of a large storeroom – steel shelving and storage cabinets, all the typewriters and various kinds of projection equipment – as well as the carpeting, drapes, window air conditioners and a safe. Denman was delighted that the agency was going to continue as a new entity, as he would have had to pay off a lease with the Buhl Building that extended for several more years. For that reason, Bill was glad to sell all the office furniture, equipment, and furnishings at this bargain price in exchange for what he saved by transferring the lease to E.W. Baker, Inc.

If we had purchased all this furniture and equipment new it would have cost far more than the $30,000 we had for working capital. In terms of buying power, $30,000 would be equivalent to $120,000 in 1999. The lease for the 13th floor office space in the Buhl Building occupied by Denman & Baker, Inc. was transferred to E.W. Baker, Inc., effective January 1, 1964. It called for a monthly payment of $1,035.00. Fortunately, we had clients, 22 to be exact, that confirmed that they would be represented by the E.W. Baker, Inc. advertising and public relations agency.

THE E. W. BAKER, INC. ADVERTISING AGENCY CLIENT LIST

American Annuity Life Insurance Co. . . . . Life insurance policies

Asmus Brothers, Inc. . . . . Spice importer and seasoning manufacturer

The Borden Company . . . . Fluid milk and ice cream products – Michigan only

Cleary College . . . . Collegiate school of business

Detroit and Canada Tunnel Corporation . . . . Travel facility

Glidorama Division, Whizzer Industries, Inc. . . . . Horizontal gliding aluminum windows, window walls, curtain walls

Howard Johnson's . . . . Midwest restaurant associations

Huron Portland Cement Company . . . . Portland and masonry cements

Modern Materials Corporation . . . . Aluminum siding and accessories

Panel Clip Company . . . . Truss fasteners, builders' hardware

R.E.T.S. . . . . Electronic training schools – U.S.A. and Canada

H. M. Robins Company . . . . Export management

Red Barns of Michigan, Inc. . . . . Fast food chain

Rose Exterminator Company . . . . Pest control service

Semmler Corporation . . . . Distributor of Coleman heating and air conditioning for Michigan and Ohio

Sheller-Globe, Inc. . . . . Automotive parts supplier

Sparton Corporation . . . . Marine and automotive accessories, electronics, and railway equipment

Springaire Floors . . . . Gymnasium floor systems

Standard Federal Savings and Loan Association . . . Savings accounts and home mortgage loans

St. Julian Wine Company . . . . Wines and champagne

Tradco, Inc. . . . . Importers and distributors of lighting fixtures

Williams Equipment and Supply Co., Inc. . . . . Seals, gaskets, waterstops, sealing compounds

(The John Henry Company had consolidated its advertising and public relations accounts with the Anthony M. Franco Agency when Tony Franco started his public relations business in the fall of 1963.)

ROBERT J. HUTTON
PRESIDENT

STANDARD FEDERAL
SAVINGS AND LOAN ASSOCIATION

STANDARD SAVINGS BUILDING
GRISWOLD AT JEFFERSON

DETROIT 31, MICHIGAN

WOodward 5-4774

December 20, 1963

Mr. Ernest W. Baker, Jr., President
E. W. Baker, Inc.
1330 Buhl Building
Detroit 26, Michigan

Dear Ernie:

Under date of December 11 you informed us of the creation of
E. W. Baker, Inc. Naturally we were thrilled with this new
venture and delighted that Standard Federal could look forward
to a continuation of an aggressive and superior program of advertising and public relations.

As we approach the end of the present year we want to express
our confidence in your new venture, assure you of our continued association, and wish you and your associates a wonderful
Holiday Season with the New Year bringing you exciting
challenges that will bring out the very best in your Agency.

Sincerely,

Robert J. Hutton
President

RJH:lh

S I N C E   1 8 9 3   -   S A F E T Y   F O R   S A V I N G S
MEMBER FEDERAL HOME LOAN BANK SYSTEM
MEMBER FEDERAL SAVINGS AND LOAN INSURANCE CORPORATION

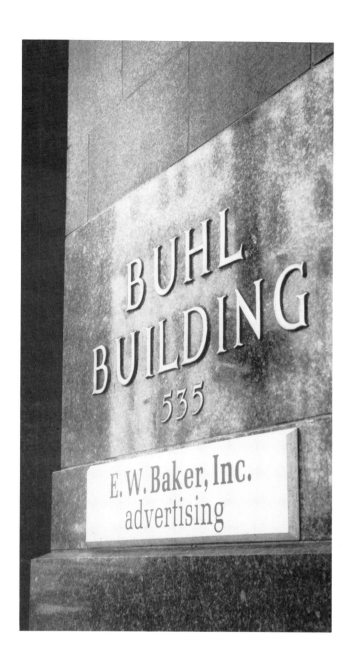

Dotting the I's and Crossing the T's Necessary In Starting a New Business

E.W. Baker, Inc., had the good fortune of being launched from a solid base of diversified clients, with attractive offices in a major downtown Detroit building, a staff of 11 people, and a lot of enthusiasm. From mid-November until the end of December all the details relating to starting a new business were taken care of including the critical issue of establishing credit with the media.

Bob Hutton, John B. Ford III, and several other clients wrote letters confirming that they were assigning their accounts to E.W. Baker, Inc. I then met with the credit managers of all major media in Detroit and presented these letters and other information necessary to establish agency recognition. The head of the Media Credit Managers Association in 1963 was Don Parker, the credit manager of *The Detroit News*, and I recall how relieved I was when Don gave his blessing to E.W. Baker, Inc. by extending credit recognition. The rest of the media in Detroit then followed suit. E.W. Baker, Inc., was organized and ready to go starting January 6, 1964. The last day of operation for Denman & Baker, Inc. would be Friday, January 3, 1964.

Early in 1964, the affairs of Denman & Baker were settled with the stockholders (including me) sharing the equity remaining when the business was closed. The Denmans sold their home and moved to Warm Springs, Georgia, never to return to Michigan. Bill died of cancer in 1966, and Phyllis outlived him by ten years.

President John F. Kennedy's Assassination

No one forgets where they were on November 22, 1963 – the day President Kennedy was assassinated. I was having lunch at the Detroit Press Club with Joe Gallagher, Don Brown, and Bill Stephenson. Bill was leaving to join J. Walter Thompson's production department.

In 1963, the Detroit Press Club had a large membership and was a very popular place in downtown Detroit. The Press Club had its own building, the former Knife and Fork restaurant at 516 Howard Street at the corner of First. Just as we started to eat, someone ran into the dining room shouting "President Kennedy's been shot." With that, virtually everyone having lunch ran out of the restaurant, as most of the diners were members of the press. Joe, Don, Bill and I sat there stunned and waited for additional news. Following lunch, we walked over to St. Aloysius Church on Washington Boulevard which was near the Press Club. We sat in the back of the church – each of us silently praying and thinking about this terrible tragedy. When we returned to the office, everything had stopped…our office… as well as the rest of the nation. Later in the day it was announced that President John F. Kennedy was dead. For the next three days the entire nation was totally absorbed in the events surrounding the assassination and the president's funeral on Monday, November 25, 1964.

There Was Trauma In the Baker Family, Too, During 1963

While watching fireworks on Thursday, July 4, Joan was stung on her ankle by a bee. It was sore on Friday and worse on Saturday. She called our family doctor, who told her he'd look at it on Monday morning. By Monday morning, the infection had spread and an area of skin approximately 4" x 4" and 1/8" deep had to be removed, leaving a gaping wound. It was slow to heal, and the first skin graft didn't take. The second skin graft was done on Monday, November 18, so Joan was in the hospital when President Kennedy was assassinated. We watched the events of Saturday and Sunday on the television in Joan's hospital room as well as the funeral service on Monday, November 25. She left the hospital the next day; fortunately, the second graft was a success and the wound healed.

In the spring of 1963, our son Michael signed up to play Little League baseball. He played shortstop and unfortunately a hard-hit grounder took a bad hop, hitting him in the eye. He had to have surgery to relieve the pressure that built up in the eye and sadly lost all sight in the eye. Mike overcame this handicap to become a very successful dentist and orthodontist.

1963 had many up days as well as its share of down days. It was a year of transition for my family, my career, and for the nation.

Chapter 4

E.W. Baker, Inc. Opens With High Hopes

Success is never final, and failure is never fatal – it's trying that counts.

On January 6, 1964, the front page of *The Detroit News* informed its readers that: Pope Paul VI was continuing a successful visit to the Holy Land; American Tobacco Company became the first to print tar and nicotine contents on its Carlton brand cigarette packs; Senator Barry Goldwater said he would renounce the nuclear test-ban treaty if necessary; Michigan's teachers averaged $6,503 in pay; and the Greyhound bus strike had ended after only twenty-two hours.

In the business news section that day, there was a notice that a new advertising and public relations agency – E.W. Baker, Inc. – had opened in the Buhl Building in downtown Detroit.

I remember the day distinctly. I nervously called the staff together to talk about the challenges facing us. When the meeting ended several hours later, there was no doubt that this was a *new* business with a *new* direction. A high priority was acquiring additional business, as we needed more income just to maintain the existing staff.

At that time, Bob Hutton was president of Standard Federal, and Tom Ricketts was vice president in charge of advertising. Their encouragement contributed greatly to the confidence needed to start a new business.

Also, two phone calls I received that first day are etched in my memory. One call was from Ed Tweedle of Tweedle Litho, a printing company that was one of our suppliers. Ed called to wish us well and offered to extend as much credit as we needed to help us get started. That offer and the confidence he showed in our future

meant a great deal. The other call was from Harlem Ives, chairman of the board of the Rose Exterminating Company, one of our clients. Harlem told me that he had said a special prayer for our success in church the day before. Such consideration was truly appreciated. These were people who really cared.

We Win Five Out of the Seven New Business Presentations That We Made During 1964

During 1964 the E.W. Baker, Inc. advertising agency was invited to make seven presentations to companies seeking a new advertising agency and, **incredibly, we won five out of the seven**. We never came close to matching that record again.

If there was one key reason for this unusual success I believe the answer would be **enthusiasm**. We worked extremely hard putting the presentations together and our creative director, Joe Gallagher, and the senior art director, Don Koelzer, crafted outstanding speculative work. What came through **loud and clear**, according to the feedback I received at the time, was the eagerness we exhibited to handle the prospective accounts. This eagerness fed and enhanced our **enthusiasm** and, because the prospects obviously wanted an agency that they thought would work hard in their behalf, **we won the business**. We were "hungry" for their business and it showed.

Here's our score card for wins and losses:

Prospective Account	Won	Lost
Buhr Machine Tool Co.	√	
CKLW AM/FM-TV	√	
M. P. Pumps	√	
Richard C. Rich and Assoc.	√	
Fred Sanders Company		√
Claude B. Schneible Co.	√	
Jervis C. Webb Co.		√

Buhr Machine Tool Company

The Buhr Machine Tool Company was located in Ann Arbor and its agency was Zimmer, Keller & Calvert, Inc. Buhr designed and built huge dial and transfer machines that were primarily used to produce parts in high volume for the automotive industry. Zimmer, Keller & Calvert had created a clever campaign calling these huge machines "Buhr Babies." The illustrations for their advertisements showed a stork with an extra large diaper in its beak carrying one of these Buhr machines cradled in the diaper. The ads got attention and were well read because they were unusual in the rather "staid" machine tool field. At a National Machine Tool Builders Show in 1964 – as a joke – the top executives of all the companies that competed with Buhr showed up for the opening session with huge diapers pinned around their waists over their suits. All of them sat in the front row to show off their diapers and Joe Buhr, the president, was so embarrassed and angry that he fired the advertising agency.

We won the account in the review they held to select a new advertising agency. The "Buhr Baby" concept was never brought up again. Buhr regularly ran four color, two page spreads in the machine tool trade publications and we created and produced a lot of collateral materials, including a catalog that was printed in English, German and French. We won a very active, profitable and worthwhile account and the advertising manager, Bill Windhovel, was a delight to work with because he really understood the machine tool business and provided the agency with all the right and necessary information that we needed to do our job.

The agency was also invited on occasion to participate in Buhr's customer entertainment activities. The Buhr Machine Tool Company's manufacturing and assembly plant was in Ann Arbor, a few blocks from the University of Michigan football stadium. In the fall Buhr regularly invited representatives of its customers to attend U of M football games. First they served an elaborate lunch at the manufacturing plant and then everyone attended the football game. After the game, all the guests returned to the plant for refreshments, followed by dinner either at a private club or restaurant. Everything was done first rate and it was really considerate of the company to occasionally include representatives of its advertising agency. Unfortunately, we only had the account for five years, as the Bendix Company acquired the Buhr Machine Tool Company and it was merged into Bendix' operations. Buhr was a great account while it lasted.

The CKLW AM, FM and TV Stations

In 1964 the CKLW stations were incorporated as Essex Broadcasters and were owned by RKO-General. The stations operated under Canadian license and while the station's facilities were located in Windsor, across the river from Detroit, the ownership and programming was by an American company. The CKLW AM radio station had a significant share of the listening audience in Ontario, Canada and Southeastern Michigan because it offered news and popular music beamed over a big geographical area with its strong 50,000 watts of power.

CKLW-TV (channel 9) at this time was the leading independent television station and in many time segments had the highest ratings of any television station in its two nation coverage area. Bill Kennedy, a former movie actor, hosted afternoon movies and was a popular Detroit celebrity. On Saturday mornings the station owned the kid show audience with Captain Jolly (Toby David) and other personalities. It was a major medium in a large metropolitan U.S. market even though it was a Canadian station.

In the spring of 1964 we received a letter from Essex Broadcasters informing us that it had decided to change advertising agencies and inquired as to whether we would be interested in soliciting its business. We immediately replied "affirmative" and started working on our "pitch."

CKLW's offices for the television and radio stations were in the Guardian Building in downtown Detroit directly across the street from the Buhl Building. To start our formal presentation when we solicited their account, we put together a fast moving slide presentation showing members of our staff rushing from our offices in the Buhl Building, down an elevator, across the street into the Guardian building and up to their offices. If the corner traffic light was green we claimed we could be in their offices in less than four minutes. If the light was red it would take us up to five minutes to get there. It was a lighthearted and humorous way to start our "pitch," which then led into all the speculative creative work that we had prepared. They liked this attitude and even though E. W. Baker, Inc. was the smallest advertising agency competing for the account, **we won**. On August 17 we were officially informed that we had been selected to handle the advertising for the CKLW AM/FM-TV stations. They also wanted to use most of the speculative creative work that we had designed for our presentation, which enabled us to recover our investment of time and money involved in soliciting the business.

Our financial arrangement with CKLW provided for a $5,000 a month fee to cover account service and agency overhead ($4,000 to be paid by the television station and $1,000 by the radio stations). In addition to the fee, we also billed them for the creation and production of all advertising and promotional materials, charging for our creative and production time. In 1965 we produced over 750 advertisements and

promotion pieces – many were small "tune-in" type ads for TV magazines – but there were also a number of elaborate promotion packages which amounted to a lot of activity and volume. The agency's income from CKLW in 1965 was well in excess of $150,000.00. The 15% commission that a million dollar advertising expenditure generates for an advertising agency amounts to $150,000.00 so the Essex Broadcasting account was a big win for a small agency with ambitious growth goals.

Acquiring the Buhr and CKLW accounts made it necessary to add ten more people to the staff for account management, traffic and production, layout artists and keyliners as well as support people for secretarial and accounting.

Wynne Garlow

In November, 1964 Wynne Garlow was hired to be my secretary/assistant. She became a valued employee. In addition to handling many tasks for me, she functioned as the office manager. In time, Wynne advanced to account manager and did an excellent job servicing several of our largest accounts.

In 1969 the Canadian government decided that radio and television stations licensed by that nation could not be owned by an American Company. Thus, RKO General was forced to sell Essex Broadcasters, Ltd. to Baton Broadcasting, Ltd. and we were notified early in 1970 that our contract and relationship with the CKLW AM, FM and TV stations would be ended.

M.P. Pumps

F.O. Fernstrum, formerly the general manager of the Gray Marine Engine Company, founded M.P. Pumps in 1942. He designed a unique pump which was used extensively in landing crafts, PT boats and other vessels in World War II. Following World War II the U.S. government's Defense Department singled out 50 special people and recognized them for their leadership in helping the country go from a peacetime to wartime production. F.O. Fernstrum was one of the 50.

When we won the account in 1964, there were several members of the Fernstrum family active in the business. The founder was chairman of the board and his son, Richard Fernstrum, was president. It was an industrial manufacturing company serving specific niches and very successful – with the distinction of being one of the first companies in America to offer an employee profit sharing program. The company was **sales driven**. It manufactured a variety of pumps that were sold nationally for specific markets as well as export. OEM sales also accounted for a significant part of its volume of business. Its sales representatives were particularly well trained, highly motivated and well compensated. Sales territories consisted of sizable geographical areas.

At the end of the day, the sales representatives dictated a "report of call" for each contact made that day which included who they had called on as well as the results of the sales call. Every salesman carried a binder of specially prepared letters concerning nearly every conceivable subject that a customer or prospect could ask about during a sales call. In his report the salesman would specify the appropriate letter to go to the customer or prospect, if any changes needed to be made in the letter, what literature to include, etc. Then a few days after every sales call, a customer or prospect received a comprehensive letter as a follow-up to what was covered in the sales call, which demonstrated that M.P. Pumps was a well organized, efficient company with which to do business.

M.P. Pumps advertised in a number of trade publications covering its various markets and the agency carefully tracked the leads generated by each publication. We also produced fact sheets and folders on its products and assisted with the design and production of exhibits, as M.P. Pumps participated in a number of trade shows.

Everything ran smoothly for several years until a decision was made to "fix something that wasn't broken." A young MBA was hired to make the company **marketing driven rather than sales driven**. Joint ventures in Canada and Mexico were initiated which took considerable company resources as well as manpower. Then the economy began to slip and soon found itself in considerable trouble.

After a couple of rough years, in 1975 the company was sold to Tecumseh Products. We parted company in 1971 as it no longer needed the services of an advertising agency. The company is now located in Fraser, Michigan in a large modern plant and continues to serve the market niches that it knows best.

Richard C. Rich and Associates

Find a need and fill it. That's precisely what Dick Rich did by specializing in the design and construction of parking decks for automobiles. His firm designed and built hundreds of parking decks in the United States, Canada and overseas. Or, if it wasn't the primary contractor, it was hired as a consultant because of its specialized experience and knowledge of designing and building parking decks.

Richard C. Rich and Associates was founded in the early 1950s just as the growth and expansion of the U.S. economy took off. By 1964 the company had grown to the point where it occupied several floors of a downtown Detroit office building. Advertising and public relations services were needed to provide the fuel necessary to maintain the volume of business required to support a large staff of architects, engineers, planners and project managers. It decided to hire an advertising and public relations firm and we won the business. The fact that we already had several clients either in or related to the construction field undoubtedly gave us an edge over our competitors. For our client Huron Cement we were writing and producing a monthly house organ and as soon as we went to work for Richard C. Rich and Associates we initiated a newsletter for them that was sent to its clients and prospects.

In addition to this informative, interesting and well designed newsletter, we produced a variety of collateral materials and case history report sheets. We also created and produced advertisements that ran in selected trade publications, which generated a lot of inquiries and solid leads that resulted in specific jobs or projects. Eventually, Don Brown, our public relations director, who handled the account, was hired by Richard C. Rich & Associates. That was really the end of the account although we continued to place advertising in a few publications for several years after all the other activity ended.

Fred Sanders Company

The front page of the Detroit Free Press for Thursday, June 17, 1875, carried the following notice announcing the start of a new business in downtown Detroit.

"A New Establishment— Mr. F. Sanders late of Philadelphia will this morning open a confectionery and ice cream establishment in the new store, No. 166 Woodward Avenue, corner of State Street. He is a practical confectioner, has a handsome place, and will devote his entire attention to customers. He will keep a large stock of fine candies and make a specialty of pure confections."

Photo Courtesy of the Burton Historical Collection, Detroit Public Library

The famous Sanders "Pavilion of Sweets" was located at Michigan and Woodward at the turn of the century. This busy northwest corner in downtown Detroit was an ideal location and this store did a high volume of business. There's quite a crowd in front of Sanders. The people in the picture are interesting, wearing the latest fashions of the "Gay '90s."

In 1965 Sanders started opening stores in Detroit area shopping malls. The first two stores were in the Livonia Mall and the Macomb Mall. These units were smaller versions of the Sanders neighborhood stores that offered food and fountain service.

From the modest start described in this newspaper notice, the Fred Sanders organization had grown into a unique business by 1964 and had become a local institution. Through its 58 stores and 104 supermarket departments in the metropolitan Detroit area, Sanders sold a tremendous variety of baked goods, candy and ice cream. Fifty-six of these stores had fountain counters serving light lunches, sodas, and sundaes.

Sanders also did a substantial mail order business for practically all of its products, processing as many as 150,000 packages a year.

The foundation of the success of the Sanders business was the courage and experience of the "Mr. F. Sanders" of the Free Press notice. A native of Biehl, Baden, Germany, he spent much of his early life in the United States. He was an ambitious young man, though, and returned to Germany at the age of 17 to learn the confectionery trade from the finest masters of his day.

Returning to America in 1870, he eventually moved to Detroit, and in 1875 he and his young wife opened their first store at Woodward and State.

Frederick Sanders attempted to establish himself as close to Detroit's business hub as possible and in the early days moved his business to several different downtown Detroit locations. It was in one of these first stores, around 1875, that Frederick Sanders served the **first** ice cream soda. The popular drink at that time was the sweet cream soda, but one warm summer evening, with his store packed with thirsty customers, he discovered that all of his sweet cream had soured.

Since ice cream was readily at hand, the confectioner decided to try it as a substitute for the sweet cream. His customers were delighted with the new drink, the idea caught on, and it wasn't long before every soda fountain in the country was serving the new ice cream soda.

Finally in the 1890s, Frederick Sanders established himself at the corner of Michigan and Woodward, in the store that became known as "The Pavilion of Sweets." With its familiar striped awnings and mosque-like roof design, it was one of the city's landmarks as well as a favorite rendezvous for busy Detroiters.

Along the back wall of the Pavilion ran the glamorous "World's Fair Fountain" from the Chicago Fair of 1893, which had been installed in the store at the close of the Fair. With its three large, bas-relief panels, its stately fluted columns, and its dozens of gleaming flavor-taps, it was worth going a long way to see.

Also in the Pavilion, Frederick Sanders installed one of the city's first electric motors, but much to his annoyance, it continually broke down. He was about to discard it when the electric company asked for one more chance and sent over a young electrician. The slender young man fixed it, and it stayed fixed – his name was Henry Ford.

Through the years Sanders was a family-run enterprise and in 1963 John M. Sanders, great-grandson of the founder, was named president. Jack – as everyone called him – initiated an agency review in 1964 as he believed they needed to improve their advertising. The individual in charge of Sanders advertising, Fred Pantillon, had worked closely with the advertising agency that had represented them for many years and was a strong advocate of loyalty. Signs on his desk and in his office stressed the virtue of loyalty. Fred did not want to change agencies and he managed to prevail. The company did not change advertising agencies in 1964. They held agency reviews in 1968 and in 1969 and still did not change.

In 1970 a fourth review was held and again we participated. This time we won the account. In the six years that had elapsed since the first presentation was made Sanders had lost a lot of ground to competitors. Business had slipped to the point where a change in advertising agencies had to be made to help them survive.

Claude B. Schneible Company

Since 1935 the Schneible Company has designed and manufactured air pollution control equipment used throughout the world. The industries served include metal casting, foundry, chemical, industrial, waste treatment, automotive, utility, paper and plating, plus others.

It designs, engineers, manufactures and installs equipment that reduces or eliminates pollution while also reducing energy costs. This equipment tends to be quite large, technical and, while very essential, not very glamorous.

When we won the account it was assigned to Bob Anthony and there couldn't have been a better marriage between a client and an agency. Bob found its products – consisting of scrubbers and collectors, condensers, absorbers, evaporative coolers and quenchers – really fascinating. Bob and Al Lundy, the vice president of engineering, got along famously and this led to a long-term relationship between agency and client.

Bob loved film-making and was in his element with this client, supervising the filming of the installation of Schneible air pollution control systems. These films were edited into sales presentations and were essential to sales efforts. A case history or technical product bulletin was also prepared to describe each particular installation.

The Schneible Company was sold to CMI International in 1990 and now operates under the name CMI-Schneible Company. It is located in Holly, Michigan a small town located halfway between Pontiac and Flint in southeastern Michigan. In 1996, I was surprised to learn that the films that Bob Anthony had produced for

Robert Anthony

this company in the 1960s and 1970s were still being used in sales presentations. They had been converted to video. Bob Anthony died of cancer in 1982, but I was pleased to learn that some of the work he had done for Schneible had lived on and was still serving a worthwhile purpose.

1964... A Break-Even Year!

The first year of operation for the E.W. Baker, Inc. advertising agency was a good one. We had doubled in size and were moving a lot faster down the track. We didn't expect to make a profit our first year of operation with only 11 months of income to cover 12 months of overhead plus all the costs involved with starting a new business. Actually, we did better than our forecast. When the board of directors met in late December we decided to distribute the anticipated profit of $4,000 among the employees to reward them for their efforts. With all the new business we had added in 1964 the outlook for 1965 was truly bright.

It's Onward and Upward In 1965 For E.W. Baker, Inc.

January 6, 1965 was the agency's first anniversary and we celebrated that milestone with a buffet dinner for our entire staff – including our spouses and/or significant others – at Lee and Bob Anthony's home. Dinner was followed by a theater party as Bob had a home theater in the basement of his St. Clair Shores home with a 35 mm projector – the same size and type used in regular full-size movie theaters. All the seats in Bob's basement theater were recliners, each with a little table next to it for your refreshments and snacks. Hot, buttered, freshly-popped popcorn was provided as well as a well-stocked bar. It was just like going to a neighborhood movie theater except a whole lot more comfortable.

When Bob dimmed the lights the curtain in front of the floor-to-ceiling screen would open and immediately you watched a Movietone News® feature. Several *cartoons* would follow as well as some unusual and very funny *theater advertisements,* of which Bob had a sizable collection. A few choice *coming attractions* would then lead into the movie – usually a current feature film that was being shown at one of the two commercial theaters which Bob owned and operated in St. Clair Shores and Royal Oak. It was a lot of fun and we also entertained our clients occasionally using this unusual venue. It made for a delightful evening.

The aggressive new business effort initiated in 1964 was maintained right into 1965. On January 7 we made our first presentation of our second year in business to Briggs Manufacturing Company. Briggs manufactured ceramic fixtures – Briggs Beautyware toilets, tubs and sinks. We did not win this account but in the next several months we added the S.J. Tutag Pharmaceutical Company, Better Heating and Cooling Bureau and the Budget Rent-A-Car franchise for Southeast Michigan. We made several other new business presentations in early 1965 to Vineyard Homes (a large home builder), Little Caesar's Enterprises (pizza) and the

Metropolitan Detroit Honda Dealers (motorcycles and other vehicles). We did not win the latter three accounts in 1965 but before the end of 1966 all three became clients of the agency.

During 1965 I attended a number of interesting advertising meetings all over the country. On January 24, I flew to New York with Ed Metcalfe, general manager of CKLW-TV and George Sperry, the station's promotion director. It was a stormy, wintry day and we sat around Detroit Metro airport for hours waiting for our departure time to be announced. Finally, late in the day our flight was called and while our flight to New York was routine – our landing was not. When we landed the plane skidded the length of the runway, even doing some fishtailing before coming to a complete stop. A very scary landing. Later, we learned that the airport had been closed most of the day due to bad weather conditions. I have done a lot of traveling by airplane but that was the worst landing I ever experienced.

The next two days I attended sales presentations that our client made to media planners and buyers with New York advertising agencies. In the fall of 1964 we had produced the presentation that our client CKLW-TV was using in New York so it was really interesting to observe the reaction of the mostly young men and women who made up the audience. The presentation took place at noon in a large private dining room of a major hotel. First, lunch was served and the presentation followed. The theme of the presentation, which was written by Joe Gallagher, was "Rediscovering Detroit" and featured an actor playing the part of Le Sieur Antoine de la Mothe Cadillac, the French explorer who established Detroit in the early 18th century.

Early in his career Ed Metcalfe was a member of the Spike Jones band and he enjoyed being on stage. This particular presentation took advantage of Ed's ability to perform as there were a number of places in the combination film and slide portions of the presentations where he interacted carrying on a dialog with the actor in the film or in the sound/slide portions. The

audience found this fascinating and I've never seen this technique utilized as effectively as we did in this production utilizing a movie projector as well as several slide projectors with sound on film. Following exposure in New York our client took this show on the road to Chicago, Los Angeles, San Francisco and Dallas – and it was of course shown in Detroit – with great results for CKLW-TV.

From January 28 through January 31 I attended the National Advertising Agency Network meeting held in Birmingham, Alabama where it was hosted by the Robert Luckie & Company advertising agency – the local NAAN Network member. It was always interesting to visit advertising agencies in other cities because every agency has a personality or uniqueness of its own. The basic purpose of NAAN was to provide support for one another. There was an openness and a sharing of information which could never occur in your own market as your competitors were not about to reveal anything that they considered a competitive advantage. In NAAN we shared everything. Many of the forms, systems, and techniques that the E.W. Baker, Inc. advertising agency used were copied or adapted from information that we received at these meetings.

Bob Luckie started the Robert E. Luckie advertising agency in 1948 and in 1956 the name was changed to Luckie & Forney. In 1988 they merged with Tucker Wayne of Atlanta. Following a "friendly" divorce in 1996, they returned to the Luckie & Company name. At the time of the merger with Tucker Wayne, Luckie & Company had nearly 100 employees and billed more than $50 million. Since then Bob has retired but the agency is doing quite well with two of his sons at the helm.

In June I attended another NAAN meeting at Whiteface Inn in Northern New York state which was hosted by the Conklin, Labs and Beebe advertising agency of Syracuse. I flew from Detroit to New York and took a commuter plane from New York to Plattsburg. On the commuter plane were seven other people representing NAAN agencies including Henry Kaufman and his wife from the Henry J. Kaufman & Associates, Inc. agency in Washington, D.C. None of our baggage was on the plane when we landed and we were requested to wait for its arrival as there was another commuter plane on the way. We waited at the tiny Plattsburg airport for hours and when our bags finally arrived it was late afternoon and almost dark. We boarded the Whiteface Inn van with our bags and headed for the Inn which was more than 25 miles away. The Kaufmans had not had anything to eat since breakfast and they were starving. At Henry Kaufman's insistence the van driver stopped at a small roadside tavern which was just ready to close for business. The tavern owner explained that the kitchen was closed and the only thing he could do was make us some ham sandwiches. The driver said, "That's all he could offer." Henry Kaufman and his wife took a long look at each other, shrugged and then he turned to the tavern owner and said "bring us each a ham sandwich and a bottle of beer." Henry took some kidding during the meeting with comments like "was that ham really kosher?"

In 1965 my two sons were members of a large and very active boy scout troop. In late September the entire scout troop, along with a number of dads, were transported by three large sailboats from the Grosse Pointe Yacht Club to the grounds of the Old Club on Harsen's Island. Vernor Davis, president of Vernor's Ginger Ale, had a son in the troop and he arranged for the sailboats and permission to camp on the grounds of this prestigious private club, which is open from Memorial Day through Labor Day. The Old Club and most of the cottages were closed for the season but there was a very large yacht owned by Benson Ford anchored in front of the club. The big meal for this campout was planned for Saturday night and Keith Evans (another scout dad) and I were in charge of preparing the food. There were more than 80 scouts and dads to be fed. Saturday afternoon after lunch we had scouts peel potatoes, carrots and onions. The main meal was going to be pot roast cooked in dutch ovens with the potatoes, carrots and onions nestled on top of the roast in the dutch ovens. We also had about a dozen large whole chickens wrapped in aluminum foil and hanging over charcoal from a cross bar just in case we ran out of pot roast – or for those who preferred having roast chicken for dinner instead of pot roast.

A middle aged couple stood off to the side for some time watching all the activity, apparently fascinated with how the meal was being prepared. They finally came closer but they didn't introduce themselves so I didn't know who they were. The man finally asked if they might be able to join us for dinner. I should have said "**of course**" but thought about all the hungry boys we had to feed. My reaction was something like – "Well, we've got a bunch of famished boys to feed…" – but before I could finish what I wanted to say, he became embarrassed and said--"Oh, no, no, that's quite all right"--and they walked away. A short time later, Vernor Davis – who had noticed the couple watching the meal being prepared – came over and asked me, "What did Benson Ford and his wife want?" I replied that "they were interested in joining us for dinner. However, I didn't know who they were and because I was concerned that we might not have enough food to feed all the scouts and the dads, I didn't invite them." Vernor didn't say anything – he didn't have to – but I was embarrassed and regretted not inviting Benson Ford and his wife to join us for dinner.

In late October I attended the annual meeting of the Bank Public Relations Marketing Association in New York City – and Joan accompanied me – the first time that we'd ever been to the Big Apple together. We saw the musical "Funny Girl," attended a Tijuana Brass Band concert and heard Jack Jones sing at the Plaza.

One night when we returned to our hotel, Pearl Bailey entered the lobby just ahead of us. Joan recognized her and excitedly exclaimed, "Pearl!" With that Pearl Bailey turned to Joan and said, "Gisell!," mistaking Joan for Gisell

McKenzie, a popular singer in 1965. It was a funny incident but Pearl gave Joan an 8"x10" photo of herself autographed: "To my new friend Joan – from Pearl."

1965 ended with a big flurry of activity for several clients and especially for Standard Federal as the interest rate paid on savings accounts was increased to 4-1/4% on December 15. This required changing all their advertising and collateral materials.

It was a successful year as the agency experienced significant growth as a result of new accounts added in 1964 and 1965. We became a real tax paying corporation as we made a decent profit and were able to begin the process of building a financial reserve.

1966...Year Three For E. W. Baker, Inc.

Early in 1966 we acquired the Little Caesars Pizza business which was a small account at that time. In the fall of 1965 I had hired a very personable, young account executive who was formerly a sales representative for a radio station. He played hockey on a team sponsored by Little Caesars and through this activity had become acquainted with the owner, Mike Ilitch. We were appointed the agency for Little Caesars and were, quite possibly, its first advertising agency.

Unfortunately, we only had the Little Caesars account for a year as I had to terminate the young account executive who helped us get the business. In the agency business it is essential that a service report (SR) be written after every client meeting which details what was discussed and the decisions that were made. Copies of the SR are distributed to all the appropriate people in the agency who then must execute the decisions made in the client meeting. Copies are also sent to the client to verify that all the information in the service report is correct.

This particular account executive was extremely remiss in writing service reports.

He tried to operate by issuing instructions verbally but things frequently fell through the cracks. A number of mistakes were made and there was a chorus of complaints from clients and members of the staff. In spite of repeated warnings the situation did not improve – which resulted in termination. Single-handedly, he managed to lose several of our clients.

For example, Little Caesars ran a half-page advertisement in the Detroit Red Wings program which listed locations of all its restaurants. Addresses were consistently wrong in this advertisement and some store locations were missing. Ilitch called several times to complain because he had given the correct information to the account executive. Finally, Ilitch had enough. He called to inform me that he was changing agencies. We lost an account that in time would become a huge company with a big advertising budget. This loss was in addition to the Honda Dealers account, which the same account executive also mishandled simply by not writing service reports.

The story of Little Caesars Pizza's growth is a phenomenal one. Founded in 1959 by Mike and Marian Ilitch, what began as one neighborhood pizza restaurant has today grown into one of the top three international pizza chains.

The decision in the 1960s to franchise has been an important element in the story of Little Caesars' success. Although franchising was a relatively new idea at the time, Mike Ilitch saw its potential for his restaurants, and it was the key to Little Caesars' growth in the 1960s.

Franchising began in 1962 with the opening of the fourth Little Caesars restaurant. By the end of 1965, there were 16 restaurants and sales had reached $1.5 million. By 1966, Little Caesars expanded into Ohio, and by the end of the decade, the chain had become an international one with its first restaurant in Canada, along with units in Michigan, Ohio and Illinois.

The 1980s were a period of enormous growth for Little Caesars, and during that time the company made the commitment to expand from a regional to a national chain. From 1981 to 1986, the pizza chain's landscape changed dramatically. Little Caesars restaurants were located in 48 states and the chain moved from the position of 10th largest pizza chain to the number three slot. It also was widely recognized as the number one carryout pizza chain.

While the 1,000th restaurant opened in 1986, only two years later the 2,000th restaurant opened. Little Caesars had doubled its size in that short time. And by 1989, Little Caesars passed the $1 billion sales mark.

And the growth continues. Little Caesars is aggressively pursuing expansion in both the domestic and international marketplace, and is increasing its presence in the nontraditional segment.

In addition to Little Caesars, we also added a large home builder's advertising account early in 1966 – Vineyard Homes – and in May we were offered the Sparton of Canada, Ltd. advertising account. The Sparton Corporation was a client of Denman & Baker, Inc. and had continued its relationship in 1964 as a client of E.W. Baker, Inc. Sparton was a very interesting company as it consisted of various divisions when we handled the account, serving different markets as follows:

SPARTON CORPORATION

Sparton Electronics:
    Sonobuoys (Purchased by the U.S. Navy and used to locate enemy submarines)

Steger Furniture:
    Cabinets (Primarily for radio and TV sets)

Sparton Manufacturing:
    Automotive and marine horns

Allied Steel and Conveyors:
    Conveyor Systems

Sparton Southwest, Inc.:
    Weapon control equipment and products for the aerospace industry

Sparton Railway Equipment Division:
    Easy Loader System (ELS) for loading railway cars

Sparton Corporation was founded in 1900 in Jackson, Michigan and early in the history of the company it made parts for agricultural implements. In 1909, it started making automotive stampings and in 1911 it developed and introduced the first all-electric horn for automobiles and trucks. In 1925, Sparton manufactured battery powered radios and the next year introduced the first all-electric radio, known as "Radio's Radiant Voice." Other firsts include the first push-button-tuned radio and the first electric eye tuner.

In 1938, it started working on television receivers but this was put on hold until after World War II. During World War II it made bomb hoists and a wide range of military products. Following the war, it renewed its production of television sets and launched a line of outstanding color sets in 1953. Their distribution was primarily through TV repair shops because Sparton did not believe it could go head-to-head against RCA, Philco, GE, Motorola, Sylvania and Zenith, which dominated the market and sold their sets through retailers. Also, because of Sparton's insistence on high quality, the price range for Sparton TV sets was not competitive enough to provide the company with a sufficient profit margin. Thus, in 1956, Spartan's production of television and stereos in the United States was discontinued.

However, it continued to produce televisions and stereos in Canada at its plant in London, Ontario as it did have a number of appliance dealers in that country that carried the Sparton line. However, Sparton was steadily losing its share of market and when the advertising account was offered to us in early 1966 it was really a last ditch effort to try and save its television and stereo business in Canada. We did the best we could with the budget we had to work with and did come up with several innovative sales promotions but it was really too little, too late. In 1967 Sparton discontinued production of televisions and stereos in Canada and instead concentrated on manufacturing and marketing electronics and other specialized material components.

The Sparton Corporation is alive and well today and its stock is listed on the New York Stock Exchange. Sparton's chairman and CEO, John J. Smith, flew his own plane for many years even though he had lost his right arm. I flew with John once to a meeting in Canada and was impressed with how capably he managed to pilot the plane with one arm.

Throughout 1967 we were extremely busy serving all our clients. There was lots of activity especially for Standard Federal. I met with Tom Ricketts, vice president in charge of advertising, three or four times a week. We talked on the phone at least once a day. In August the government authorized savings and loans to increase the interest rate paid on savings accounts to 5%. No sooner did we get all the advertising changed to offer this new rate when the government decided in mid-September to roll back the interest rate to 4-3/4% – making it necessary to revise all the advertising again. Then, on October 17 the government increased the insurance for savings accounts to $15,000 which meant that all the advertising had to be revised again to reflect this change. If I had all the money that it has cost savings and loans, banks and credit unions to revise their advertising over the years due to either a change in interest rate, the amount of insurance available to protect savings or for a new lending policy, I'd probably be the richest person in the world.

We also initiated a newsletter for the agency early in 1966 called "Baker's Dozen." It contained 13 unusual news items about business and our goal was to produce and mail 13 issues a year – a challenging task – because we wanted to make it a unique, talked about publication that would get read. One of the recipients of "Baker's Dozen" was Hal Middlesworth, public relations director for the Detroit Tigers. In November, Middlesworth called me to ask if we would be interested in handling the Detroit Tigers' advertising as they did not have an agency. I met with Hal and at our first meeting he awarded us the account. We immediately started planning the

Detroit Tigers advertising for 1967 and the production of a brochure to promote the sale of season tickets. This was the start of a relationship that would last 26 years – long after Hal retired and was replaced by Dan Ewald. I've had the pleasure of working with a lot of wonderful, good people in my 50 years in the advertising business and Hal Middlesworth belongs among those at the very top of the list. He was a kind, quiet, nice man who was well-organized and highly respected for his honesty and fair dealings, particularly with the press. Hal retired in 1979 and, unfortunately, died of cancer shortly after.

There was an increasing amount of turmoil in the country throughout the year with more and more demonstrations against the bloody war in Vietnam, including student riots at Berkeley, widespread burning of draft cards in spite of severe penalties and bloody riots in Chicago where the National Guard had to be called out. 1966 was another successful year for E.W. Baker, Inc. with significantly increased billings, added business and a higher year-end profit than the preceding year. However, more turmoil – nationally, in Detroit, and for the agency – lie ahead in 1967.

1967... A Year of Great Turmoil

Gerald Warren, who was vice president for public and community relations for the National Bank of Detroit, called me in January and requested I meet with him. In the early 1960s Denman & Baker, Inc. had handled a special public relations project for NBD involving the construction and grand opening of the bank's new headquarters building at 611 Woodward in downtown Detroit. George Black had secured this assignment for the agency. When he suffered a heart attack in 1962, the agency subcontracted the project with the Ken Drake Public Relations firm, which was also located in the Buhl Building. Jerry Warren was the Ken Drake account executive assigned to handle the project. As a result of Jerry's many contacts with top NBD executives, he was offered, and accepted, the position as the bank's vice president for public and community relations upon the completion of this special project. Campbell Ewald was NBD's advertising agency in 1967 and Jerry told me in great confidence when we met that the bank was planning to change advertising agencies. He said the bank had decided that it would be wiser to work with a smaller agency, preferably one located in the downtown Detroit area. Jerry further explained that NBD liked what E.W. Baker, Inc. was doing for Standard Federal and would have no objection to our continuing to handle that account along with NBD's advertising. Howard Baldwin, who was chairman of the board for Standard Federal, was also on the board of directors of the National Bank of Detroit so I didn't expect that Standard Federal would object to this arrangement.

When I returned to the office after meeting with Jerry I was ecstatic. I believed the NBD account was virtually ours. I called two key people of the agency together to report to them in strictest confidence the subject of my meeting with Jerry Warren. Joe Gallagher, our creative director, had advanced to the position of vice president, executive creative director and essentially also functioned as our client service director. Joe participated in all important meetings with clients where strategic planning or campaign development were concerned. The day-to-day management of the creative department had been assigned to a new creative director in April 1965.

When I described my meeting with Jerry Warren to Gallagher and our creative director they both became very enthused – particularly the new creative director, because NBD was, by far, the biggest bank in Detroit at that time – and he immediately recognized that this would be a special opportunity to showcase his talent.

We had taken something of a gamble in hiring this individual. He was then in his late 50s and had once held a top creative position in New York with a large, well known advertising agency. He unfortunately became an alcoholic and had lost his job, as well as any future in New York. Returning to Detroit he joined AA and, to his credit, got his life under control. Managing our creative department was a challenging position in 1967 as we now served more than 30 active clients, which were generating a substantial work load every day for the creative department to handle. Thus far our new creative director (whose name I won't reveal) had done an outstanding job and we had won a great many creative awards. The walls of our offices were covered with plaques. There were trophies everywhere. Nobody in the advertising business thinks much of awards **unless you win them**. And we had won lots of them.

A few days later I met with Bob Hutton and Tom Ricketts at Standard Federal to tell them about the meeting I had with NBD. I was quite surprised at Bob Hutton's reaction – it was not what I expected. But when I listened to all he had to say, his position was understandable. He explained that Howard Baldwin, being a director of both Standard Federal and NBD, was – he believed – a factor in restricting the growth of Standard Federal. For every four possible branch office locations he submitted to Standard Federal's board for approval, he was fortunate to get one approved. It was also his belief that savings and loans and banks would become arch rivals in the future as the competition for business would become much more intense. Bob's prediction about the latter came true even quicker than he expected.

Hutton said they would certainly understand if we decided to resign from Standard Federal's business in order to take on the much larger NBD account. I replied that we would not do that, as we had a very good working relationship and I was confident that Standard Federal would continue to grow and prosper in the years ahead.

I then notified Jerry Warren that we were going to continue our relationship with Standard

Federal and that we would not be available to handle NBD's advertising because Standard Federal considered it a conflict. When I told Joe and our creative director of my decision, Joe took it in stride and accepted it. Our creative director was flabbergasted and disgusted. He lost all confidence in me and his attitude about his job and the agency changed dramatically. By early June, his negative, hostile attitude was affecting the operation of our creative department and he was terminated. We then turned to several competent freelance writers to get the workload caught up and this proved to be an excellent solution because the level of our creative output actually improved. Sid Houghton, a vice president and creative director at the Ross Roy advertising agency, took on various, challenging assignments and continued to do freelance work for the agency, for many years. Sid had the same instinct that Joe Gallagher had in recognizing and understanding the culture of a company and consequently was able to create advertising that was not only outstanding but also readily accepted by the client.

Abbot Gibney, a writer with J. Walter Thompson, also came to our rescue and eventually ended up as a member of our creative staff. After several years though, J. Walter Thompson wanted him back and made Abbot an offer that we couldn't match. Bob Paklaian, another very talented writer, also handled some freelance assignments and he became our creative director in 1968. Bob left the agency a year later to join another agency as a principal but ultimately joined Young & Rubicam, where he has worked for many years as a creative director.

Other outstanding people who joined the agency in the spring of 1967 include: Carole Trzos as production traffic manager. After several years, Carole left the agency to join Grey Advertising as an account executive on the *Detroit Free Press* and Knight-Ridder Newspapers accounts. She moved to a similar position at D'Arcy, MacManus and Masius,

then to the Chicago office of McCann-Erickson. Recruited to join Motorola, Inc. in the early 1980s, she became the electronics giant's first director of corporate advertising and launched corporate image and product-oriented campaigns to introduce cellular telephones and micro-computers to business audiences in the U.S., Europe and Japan. Two other good choices were George Walcott as an account manager and Bob Nelson as a writer.

In late June, Joe Gallagher informed me that he felt tired and burned out. He took a leave of absence. However, Joe never returned to the agency. His health deteriorated and he died less than a year later. He was one of those special unassuming people capable of doing extraordinary work. As long as I live, I will remember Joe with fondness, respect and gratitude.

Carole (Trzos) Book when she was production manager of E.W. Baker, Inc. Carole joined the agency in 1967 and in 1969 became the first female member of the Advertising Agency Production's Men's Club of Detroit. This organization was then renamed the Advertising Production Club of Detroit.

In the spring of 1967 we remodeled our offices and also added more space in the Buhl Building as the agency grew. This activity contributed to turmoil in the office. In May we won a lawsuit filed earlier in the year against the Udylite Corporation. This company had invited us to solicit its account when it held an agency review. We were scheduled to be the last agency to make a presentation. The director of marketing made his choice, selecting Gray & Kilgore – the agency that preceded us in making presentations. Udylite then cancelled our scheduled presentation, saying it had made a decision and it would be a waste of everybody's time to have us make our presentation. I explained to the advertising manager that we had expended considerable time and money preparing our presentation. I sued for $5,000 to recover primarily our out-of-pocket costs and the court agreed that Udylite had caused us damage and awarded us our entire claim. We didn't win the business but it was a victory of sorts.

The Detroit Riots

On Sunday, July 23, Detroit was rocked by civil rioting. It was a scary, terrible situation even though we lived in the suburbs. Standing in our yard we could hear gunfire and sirens. Disturbing rumors flew around. Downtown Detroit was off limits to the public. Our staff members living on the east side of Detroit met Monday morning at my home. We spent the day sitting around the picnic table on our patio. This picnic table was to be our office for the next several days but little was accomplished. On Tuesday morning, I attended a meeting of the Southeastern Michigan Howard Johnson's restaurants in Belleville. To get there, I drove across Detroit from the east side to the far west side on the I-94 expressway. There was still some sporadic rioting and looting but I attended the meeting without any problem, even though I was very apprehensive about driving across the city.

On Wednesday, July 25, we again met at my house and on Thursday we returned to the office. Three of our black employees never returned. The riots fortunately ended Thursday, July 27.

Our receptionist at the time of the riot was an attractive young woman who had a beautiful voice. Her parents were originally from Jamaica and had emigrated to Windsor, Canada. When our receptionist didn't show up for work after several days I called her mother in Windsor and learned that her daughter (our receptionist) and her boyfriend had eloped to Toronto where they planned to live. Two other employees – a secretary and a traffic manager – left Michigan along with their families. One returned to Arkansas and the other to Georgia – and we had to find replacements for these employees as well.

Our clients were keeping us quite busy and to that volume we added two new clients – Bin-Dicator and Comp-U-Check. The Howard Johnson's account was expanding in the midwest and we also handled the advertising and public relations for two Howard Johnson's Hotels that opened in Detroit – one downtown at Michigan Avenue and Washington Boulevard and the other in the New Center area near the Fisher Building. Both no longer exist as hotels. Huron Cement, Buhr Machine Tool, the CKLW stations were all very active and, late in the year, we started planning a 75th anniversary celebration for Standard Federal, which took place in April 1968.

Major Events That Occurred In 1967

During 1967, the Israeli army defeated Egyptian and other Arab armies in a stunning six-day war. Astronauts Grissom, White and Chaffee burned to death in an Apollo space capsule on the launch pad. The two longest ocean liners, the Queen Elizabeth and the Queen Mary, were retired from service, while mini-skirts reached an all-time high in popularity.

The award for the "Best Comprehensive Presentation" in the 1967 annual "Best of the Year" awards of the Public Relations Society of Savings Associations went to Standard Federal Savings of Detroit. Tom Ricketts, vice president in charge of advertising of Standard Federal, right, and Ernie Baker, president of E.W. Baker, Inc. hold the award which was presented at the Association's annual meeting at the Conrad Hilton hotel in Chicago.

– 1968 –

In January 1968, Tom Ricketts and I attended the Savings Institutions Marketing Society of America (SIMSA) meeting in Palm Springs, California. This was a new organization sponsored by the United States Savings and Loan League. The competition between banks and S&Ls was intensifying and the banks now had their association – the Bank Public Relations and Marketing Association (BPRMA) and the S&Ls had formed their own marketing association. At this meeting in Palm Springs, Tom Ricketts was elected president of SIMSA. Following the meeting I flew to Cincinnati for a four-day regional meeting of the National Advertising Agency Network (NAAN).

That spring, serious merger discussions were held with Reilly Bird of the Reilly Bird Advertising Agency. Reilly was formerly the advertising director for Hudson's and now his agency handled that account along with several others, and he was ready to retire. In the midst of our talks Hudson's named a new president who then announced that he was going to select a new agency. He appointed Wells, Rich & Green and our merger discussions with Reilly were for naught.

On June 19 we made another full-scale presentation to the Fred Sanders Company at its invitation and again did not win the account. Sanders stayed with the agency it had worked with for many years. During the last half of the year, though, we added four new accounts – two savings and loans and two industrial clients:

Saginaw Savings
First Federal of Hollywood

Koebel Diamond Tool
The J.P. Bell Company

In August I flew to California to meet with First Federal of Hollywood, where my brother was an executive vice president. We were given a number of assignments and, based on our performance, we were officially appointed as its advertising agency in October. From that time on, I flew to Los Angeles nearly every month for two or three days of intense meetings to plan and carry out First Federal's advertising. First Federal expanded, merged with Santa Fe Federal and ultimately became Pacific Savings Bank and a large advertising account.

In September, Justin Way, the marketing director of Saginaw Savings, called to ask if we'd be interested in handling their account. Way, the S&L's president, Fred Theurer, and I met and we were appointed as its agency. Saginaw Savings had branch offices throughout the middle of the state and in many towns in the northern portion of the lower peninsula. Our relationship continued for many years long after

Photo Courtesy of the Burton Historical Collection, Detroit Public Library

Tiger Stadium as it appeared in 1968 when the Tigers finished the regular season in first place, 12 games ahead – winning 103 games. Detroit won the world series, beating the St. Louis Cardinals, coming back after being down three games to one. Downtown Detroit and the Detroit River are in the background.

Way retired. Unfortunately, Standard Federal and Saginaw Savings eventually overlapped with competing offices in Flint and we had to resign the Saginaw Savings account.

The Impossible Can Really Happen

On October 5 a most unusual event occurred. On the preceding Friday, I attended the World Series Game between the Detroit Tigers and St. Louis Cardinals as a guest of WWJ-TV. It was the first World Series I'd ever attended. The box seats we sat in were right behind home plate and there were dignitaries all around us. In the next box sat United States Senator Hubert Humphrey and UAW President Walter Reuther. Since it was an afternoon game I was able to be home in time for dinner.

I described my excitement to my family. My sons, Bob and Mike, wanted to go to Saturday's game. I said there was no chance to

68

get tickets. The next morning they were just as insistent. "Dad, we gotta go. This may never happen again in Detroit." I finally relented, insisting that it was going to be a wasted effort. We left the house before 10 a.m. and Bob – then a high school senior – said we had to pick up his girl friend Vivian. "She has never seen a World Series game," Bob said, and I replied; "Well she's not going to see one today either." We picked up Vivian, drove downtown and found a place to park the car several blocks south of the stadium. We walked up Trumbull where hundreds of people were milling around outside the Detroit Tigers ticket office.

If you were caught selling or buying a ticket from a scalper you faced a big fine and jail time. Because of all the local publicity about this possibility, there were probably a great many more people than usual gathered around the stadium trying to buy a ticket at face value.

Realizing that remaining with this mob of people wouldn't offer any possibility of getting tickets I directed Bob, Vivian and Mike to a quiet place about 100 feet down Michigan Avenue. I told them to stay out of the crowd while I tried to find tickets in one of the bars in the area.

Hoot Robinson's Bar on Trumbull was jammed with people. Pushing my way through the crowd I kept calling out "Anybody got extra tickets?" No response – except one man sitting at the bar turned as if to say something to me – but he didn't. I left Hoot Robinson's and was standing out front when that same man tapped me on the shoulder and said, "I've got two tickets – what'll you give me for them?" I said, "I'll pay face value because for all I know you could be a cop." He said, "OK – I was hoping to get something extra – but I don't want to take a chance on getting caught scalping tickets either." I bought the two tickets then hustled back to give them to Bob and Vivian. I told Mike to stay put and I then started walking around Tiger Stadium. Just as I was about to cross the street to try my luck in another bar, a taxi pulled up to the curb. I said to a couple that got out "Do you have any extra tickets?"

"Yes, we have one," was the reply. I bought that ticket and took it to Mike. That left just me on the outside of the stadium. I walked around the ball park several times calling out to anyone who would listen – "Do you have an extra ticket?" All I heard were "No's." By 2:00 p.m. the pre-game activities had taken place and the game had started. An hour earlier there were thousands of people on the streets around the ballpark, but now you could count the people on two hands. All the action was inside.

When I came around the north side of the stadium near the entrance to the bleachers I saw a young man running up Trumbull Avenue in the middle of the street. I yelled – "Do you have an extra ticket?" He stopped and said, "Yes!" He had one extra ticket because his girlfriend was sick and couldn't attend the game. I bought the ticket and sat with him in the bleachers. This was the one and only time I ever sat with the **real** baseball fans. It was a great day – the Tigers won and went on to win the World Series. It was a day my sons and I will never forget. *I learned that what you think is impossible can actually happen but only if you try to make it happen.*

Highlights of 1968

The year 1968 was marked by two political assassinations and the televised riots at the Democratic Convention in Chicago. Martin Luther King, Jr., was shot by James Earl Ray in Memphis in April and Detroit was under an alert for several days expecting another riot. A curfew was declared and the tension passed. Two months later, Democratic presidential candidate Robert F. Kennedy was assassinated in Los Angeles.

In the presidential election on November 6, Richard Nixon narrowly defeated Hubert Humphrey. Rowan and Martin rocked America weekly with their "Laugh-In" TV show. Hippies and "flower-power" protested everywhere against The Establishment. Only 3.3% of the 79 million work force were unemployed.

– 1969 –

The bank prime rate was 7% in January 1969 and, between May and August, the stock market plunged $100 billion. Dwight D. Eisenhower died in April at the age of 78 and on July 20 astronaut Neil Armstrong landed on the moon. On national TV he said "That's one small step for man, one giant leap for mankind." 400,000 attended the rock music festival at Woodstock.

Early in January the agency celebrated its 5th anniversary with a dinner dance at the Grosse Pointe Hunt Club. We had grown significantly – quadrupled in size – and there were now many new people helping to propel our growth. Out of the eleven people that were with E.W. Baker, Inc. on January 6, 1964 only two of us remained – Bob Anthony and me. We needed more office space and were discussing the possibility of moving the agency's offices from downtown to somewhere in the suburbs.

From February 5 through February 9, Joan and I attended a SIMSA meeting in New Orleans. Three of our clients also participated in this meeting, including Priscilla and Tom Ricketts (Standard Federal); Esther and Justin Way (Saginaw Savings) and Lynn and Joe Baker (First Federal of Hollywood). New Orleans was a clean, classy and exciting city in 1969 but in the years to come when I returned to New Orleans for other meetings, there was a noticeable decline in the quality of the environment. Over time New Orleans became a seedy city of strip joints and gambling casinos.

On our first visit to New Orleans in 1969 we were fortunate to see Al Hirt and Pete Fountain perform in their own dinner clubs in the French Quarter. Some years later both of them left the French Quarter. Of course we enjoyed traditional jazz at Preservation Hall, breakfast at Brennan's, and lunches or dinners at other famous restaurants: Antoines, Arnoud's, The Court of Two Sisters, Broussard's, Delmonicos, Galataires and Commander's Palace – unfortunately several of these great restaurants no longer exist.

Early in 1969 we were appointed as the public relations counsel for one of the state's largest architect-engineering firms – Harley, Ellington, Cowin & Stirton. In April, Sheller-Globe informed us they were going to launch seven new products through its industrial products division – which it assigned to us. All required market planning, collateral materials, publicity and advertising. Products included tie-down straps, O-Rings for sealing concrete pipes, redi-hot sink hot water heaters, and gauges for various purposes – not so glamorous products, but a great challenge for creative concepts.

In late May, we made our third presentation to the Fred Sanders Company and were optimistic that this time we'd win the account. Again, no decision.

One of the Most Pleasant Days of My Life

Starting in 1967 my sons and I went on an annual fishing trip, usually over the Memorial Day weekend. A neighbor and good friend, Paul Duika, was the instigator and organizer of these fishing trips. Paul and his sons, Dennis and Michael, plus Bob, Mike and me, would leave home after work on the Wednesday prior to the Memorial Day Weekend. We'd then drive all night, taking turns driving in order to reach our destination in northern Ontario sometime in the afternoon on Thursday. Every year we stayed in cabins at the Sunset View Camp near Wawa, Ontario. In 1969 eight of us went on the fishing trip, and another Dad and his son were invited to go with us.

On May 31 we hired an Indian guide named Joe Picody to take us fishing on Five Mile Lake, one of many lakes in that area. We rented three boats with outboard motors, which accommodated the eight of us, plus Joe Picody, by putting three to a boat. We started fishing at daybreak and had lots of strikes. By 9:00 a.m. we had caught 29 good size lake trout and northern pike – the biggest one-day catch we ever had on any of our annual fishing trips to Canada.

Late in the morning we were all famished, so we pulled into one of the many islands that dotted Five Mile Lake. Some of us gathered good size rocks which we used to make three grills. Joe Picody soon had fires blazing in each grill using dry, dead wood for fuel. While the fires in our rock-formed grills were burning down to hot beds of coal, Joe cleaned and cut up nine of the biggest fish into fillet strips. These fillet strips were then rolled in a mixture of flour, cracker crumbs, salt and pepper then dropped into two big skillets half-filled with Wesson Oil. A big pan of baked beans bubbled away on the third grill. Joe carefully turned the fish for seven or eight minutes in the hot oil until they were golden brown and crispy like french fries. I thought to myself, watching Joe do this, "We'll never eat all this fish." Not only did we eat all the fish and the baked beans, but we also polished off a big loaf of soft white bread, two large bags of potato chips and all the pop and beer in our cooler. There wasn't one bite or swallow left of anything.

The island we selected for our shore lunch was about two acres in size and on the high ground in the middle of it was a big patch of soft grass. All of us stretched out in the grass and slept for hours in the warm sunshine. There was never another day to match this particular one on any of our fishing trips. Even though there were other good catches of fish and other great shore meals, none would ever equal or surpass that particular day – Saturday, May 31, 1969 – which I remember as one of the most pleasant days of my life.

George Sperry Joins Our Staff

On July 14, George Sperry, formerly our primary client contact when he was promotion manager for CKLW-TV, became a member of our staff. He was a great addition. He took over the production of all radio and television commercials. George was an expert at this

George Sperry

and there was a marked improvement in the production of our radio and television commercials. Frank Bob, who owned several Howard Johnson's restaurants, also owned, with his partner Budd Schaefer, the Red Barn's fast food restaurant franchise for the entire state of Michigan and the Ponderosa franchise for the eastern half of the state. Frank and Budd operated more than 30 restaurants as we were now handling the Red Barn's and Ponderosa Steak House advertising in addition to Howard Johnson's. Most of Red Barn's and Ponderosa's advertising budgets were spent on television so George had plenty to keep him busy as our savings and loan clients were also advertising extensively on radio and television.

On July 31 we made a presentation to Magnetic Video, and were awarded the account on August 5. Sperry was assigned to handle the account because of his expertise in video tape production. He knew their business and markets.

In the fall, Ken Reeves, who headed our public relations division, resigned and Robert Klepinger was offered that position. Bob accepted and joined the agency on November 3. Bob particularly enjoyed working on new

Robert Klepinger

business and was successful in adding a number of accounts which needed both public relations and advertising to promote their businesses. Carriers Insurance Company, Microdot and the Michigan Trucking Association joined the agency shortly after Bob took over the public relations department. In time, Bob became a principal of the agency, a stockholder and director, and served as president of the agency in later years.

Through the tumultuous 1960s, E.W. Baker, Inc. grew steadily year after year with increased billings and an expanded staff. Downtown Detroit though, was not the same following the riots. Muggings and purse snatchings became common. George Sperry was mugged twice in broad daylight on downtown streets. One secretary had three of her purses snatched. Fortunately no one was hurt but concern about crime and the steady decay of downtown Detroit accelerated our plans to leave the area and move to the suburbs. The move occurred in March 1971.

Chapter 5

We Launch The Decade Of The '70s With Some New Key People On Our Staff And Five New Clients

The harder you work the luckier you get.
– Gary Player, Golfer

Jerry Abbs committed to joining E.W. Baker, Inc. on January 5, 1970. His joining the agency a few months later brought more than a million dollars of additional billings. Jerry had been a principal of Behr, Otto, Abbs & Austin, Inc. When Speed Austin died and Karl Behr retired, he and Rudd Otto decided to dissolve their company and join other agencies. Rudd Otto joined Gray & Kilgore. Jerry and I had met a number of times during the last six months of 1969 to discuss the possibility of his joining the agency. He brought with him the following accounts:

Awrey Bakeries, Inc. (quality baked goods)

Cross & Peters, Inc.
(Better Made Potato Chips)

Fidelity Federal of Kalamazoo
(savings and loan)

Plumbing and Heating Industry Association

Better Investing Magazine
(Published by the National Association
of Investment Clubs)

Jerry began his advertising career as a copywriter with BBDO Chicago. He worked on the Frito Lay account there and was responsible for writing the well-known and still used phrase "Munch...Munch...Munch a bunch of Fritos... Corn Chips." Jerry was an especially competent writer for all media and had few peers, particularly when describing food. On several occasions I heard Bob Awrey, chairman of Awrey Bakeries comment, "No one can write better copy about food than Jerry Abbs."

I welcomed Jerry Abbs to the staff of the E.W. Baker, Inc. advertising agency. Prior to joining the agency in 1970 Jerry had been a principal of another Detroit-based agency for 20 years. Before coming to Detroit he worked for two of the nation's largest advertising agencies in Chicago. Jerry was elected chairman of the board and in addition to writing copy for several of the agency's consumer accounts he also accepted responsibility for supervising our research and media departments.

Awrey's...America's Hometown Bakery

Founded in 1910, Awrey Bakeries is one of the largest privately owned baked goods producers in the country. Its reputation for baking excellence began in the Detroit kitchen of Mrs. Fletcher Awrey, where she became famous for the delicious baked goods from her wood-fired oven. A few years later, Fletcher and Elizabeth Awrey opened a succession of neighborhood baked goods stores, supplied from the first "volume baking" facility with a Ford Model-T truck. The three Awrey boys – Elton, Wilbur and Thomas – became active in their parents' business.

Today, third- and fourth-generation members of the Awrey family continue the tradition of producing the highest quality baked goods in their modern facility in Livonia, Michigan. Over 300 employees produce more than 125 different kinds of high quality, frozen bakery products around the clock, utilizing five state-of-the-art production lines. This broad line of baked products enables Awrey's to meet the diverse needs of its customers – primarily the food service industry – as a true one-stop shop.

The Awrey's product line includes:
- Danish Pastries
- Biscuits
- Coffee Cakes
- Dinner Rolls
- Torte Cakes
- Sheet Cakes
- Muffins
- Donuts
- Croissants
- Sandwich Rolls
- Layer Cakes
- A Variety of Specialties

While Awrey's products are efficiently mass produced, they always start from scratch. Each recipe maintains that homemade taste which earned Awrey's the title of **America's Hometown Bakery**. Even with its effective, state-of-the-art equipment, offering computerized lamination of croissant and danish doughs, its baked goods always have a handmade appearance. And Awrey's offers that homemade quality with pre-baked and frozen convenience.

The addition of the Awrey Bakeries account to our client roster made us feel quite proud as we now represented another company with a great local reputation. They were – and remain – a Detroit institution!

Better Made Potato Chips – "The Naturals"

Jerry Abbs had positioned Better Made Potato Chips as "The Naturals" long before any other company had jumped on the natural foods bandwagon. With per capita consumption of potato chips in Southeastern Michigan the highest in the United States, competition in the 1960s and '70s had been understandably fierce. Out of the 13 local potato chip companies that had existed a few years earlier, only Better Made was still in business in Detroit by 1973.

Better Made chips were first made in the early 1930s by Cross Moceri and Peter Cipriano in their home kitchens and sold for 5¢ a bag on Belle Isle. The company was incorporated as Cross & Peters, Inc. in 1934 when they decided to go into the potato chip business full time. They operated out of a small store front location on Gratiot on the east side of Detroit. Detroiters liked their thin high quality chips and over the years the company grew steadily, adding other snack products and expanding their production facilities.

By the early 1970s their state-of-the-art plant covered a city block and their advertising budget was almost entirely dedicated to television. It is still a family-owned business.

Several Outstanding, Talented People Join the Agency

We got a big bonus when Jerry Abbs came on board as Judy Neuharth, who was the traffic/production manager of Behr, Otto, Abbs & Austin, Inc., also joined E.W. Baker, Inc. Judy was amazing. Energetic and focused, she actually did the work of three people. She became our traffic manager and also assisted Carol Trzos, our production manager.

Norm Shadley

On February 3 Norm Shadley joined the agency as an art director. Norm had been an art director for J. Walter Thompson for many years working primarily on the Ford account. In the last four years of his career with E.W. Baker, Inc. he made a great contribution to our creative output. Norm was also an ordained Episcopal priest and after he retired from the agency in late 1973 he served the Episcopal church full time for a number of years. Norm and I became good friends and we continue to stay in touch.

In June, B. H. Tornow (later B Cunningham) became the head of our financial department. Advertising agencies handle a lot of money – placing millions of dollars of their client's money in media – and accounting for those expenditures is a big responsibility. We were fortunate to hire B as she was not only exceptionally capable but also an extremely hard worker. She set high performance standards for her staff and herself and we had one of the best financial operations of any advertising agency in the midwest.

B (Tornow) Cunningham

In the future years when we computerized our media and production billing and our cost accounting, we had a number of advertising agencies from all over the country come to our offices to study our operation.

Another Invitation From Sanders To Solicit Its Account

Fred Pantillon, Marketing Director of Sanders, called in early March inviting me to visit some of its stores and restaurants. On March 19 we visited a number of its outlets, including a new restaurant concept it was trying which was located in a shopping center in a Toledo suburb. At the end of the day, Fred asked if we would make one more presentation, to which I agreed. We made our "pitch" on April 29 and on May 22 we were officially notified that we were finally going to be Sanders' advertising agency.

Although the Fred Sanders Company and Awrey Bakeries were competitors in baked goods, we were able to get the approval of the heads of the companies – Bob Awrey and Jack Sanders – to handle both accounts. Awrey Bakeries was already moving aggressively in the direction of providing frozen baked goods to the food service industry, with far less emphasis on baked goods at retail, while Sanders' main business was candy, followed by baked goods at retail, ice cream and fountain and restaurant service.

While we were very excited to win the Sanders account, we quickly learned that it had a great **many problems**. Its troubles started in 1951 when it began to market its products (candy, ice cream and baked goods) in local supermarkets in addition to the Sanders stores. While the move created additional sales at reduced profit margins, it also inhibited future retail sales growth at the company stores – the mainstay of Sanders' business. Also, a number of its company stores had been located at or near bus stops on busy main thoroughfares which provided great visibility. Parking, however, was inconvenient or at best difficult. Since fewer people were using public transportation, these stores were being closed, largely in older neighborhoods. The outlying, new stores served areas of less traffic and could not make up the lost sales.

While the older stores were "homey," they were not very eye appealing. They looked behind the times and the impression was that service was slow – even if it wasn't. Fast food restaurants like McDonald's, Burger King, Wendy's and others were now serving many former Sanders food service customers. In addition, most Sanders products were made in small batches to achieve the highest quality possible. By not automating, however, its cost of production was higher than its competitors. In 1941 Sanders sold more than five million pounds of candy. In 1970 its production was less than half that amount. More and more consumers were becoming concerned about diet and health

and this concern was impacting candy sales – which was also a very seasonal business.

We went to work for Sanders with lots of enthusiasm and our efforts were soon apparent or visible everywhere. For years, its newspaper advertising had consisted of copy that was basically an item and the price. We made their advertisements far more eye-catching, compelling and interesting with delicious copy describing its products, written by Jerry Abbs. All point-of-sale posters and danglers became more colorful with bright colors using a new silk screen technique.

New menus and table tents were part of the makeover and much effort was put into a four-color special order tabloid that was inserted in the Detroit daily papers late in November. Special order business set a new record for Sanders in 1970. We added radio to the media mix, running schedules prior to the major holidays.

Sanders' philosophy or strategy had been "Holidays are when we're going to get the business anyway so why do a lot of advertising then?" Our belief was "Sure that's when you do most of your business but it's also the best time to significantly increase your sales." Our strategy really worked!

We Come Up With a Really Big Idea For the Detroit Tigers

In 1966 Hal Middlesworth assigned us the advertising for the Detroit Tigers for the 1967 season and the total advertising expenditure for that year was about $50,000. The budget had grown a little by 1970 but the Tigers didn't do much advertising. The Detroit Baseball Club traditionally ran a small newspaper advertisement in early December suggesting that Tiger tickets for the next season made a good stocking stuffer. Then it ran an advertisement in the spring to announce that the box office was open, followed by small space advertisements all during the season to announce an upcoming series of home games. In addition to this advertising, we produced a two-color folder that described the season ticket packages and another small folder promoting group sales.

If you were a box holder or had season tickets, you were set for tickets for the season. However, for the average fan it was necessary to go to the stadium box office for tickets or if you were planning far enough in advance you could order tickets by mail. I had heard many complaints about how inconvenient it was to get tickets ahead of time but the Detroit Tiger management was truly a traditional operation and if you wanted to go to a baseball game, then you bought your tickets at the stadium box office.

I convinced Hal that they should try running a large space newspaper advertisement that was essentially a mail order coupon. All the Tiger games would be listed for the entire season along with the four season ticket packages that were available. Then the fan could check off the games for which he or she wanted tickets, as well as the number of tickets, then send in the entire advertisement along with his or her name, address and a check or money order. We made it simple and easy to order tickets by making the advertisement an order form. We created a three quarters of a page advertisement with a snappy headline and illustration to get attention.

Hal tried the advertisement. It ran in the Sunday *Detroit News* and *Detroit Free Press* early in the spring. The results were incredible. Orders came in by the thousands – not just from the Detroit area but from all over the state and Canada.

The advertising budget was significantly increased the next year and went up year after year as this highly successful approach was expanded. Other major league teams copied the idea for their own use. Eventually the first of these mail order advertisements ran in mid-December offering tickets for the next season, followed by additional insertions in January and February. In March, the advertising was expanded to include daily newspapers in outstate Michigan, as well as the Windsor (Canada) Star and the Toledo (Ohio) Blade. Radio and television spots on the stations that carried the Tiger games were used to direct listeners or viewers to the mail order newspaper advertisement. This idea not only made it easier to buy tickets and significantly increased sales, but the money was deposited in the bank by the Detroit Baseball Club weeks or months before the tickets were actually used.

Many years later, this advertising strategy changed when the budget was substantially larger and tickets were also available through Ticketmaster and other ticket outlets. Television became the main advertising medium, augmented by outdoor billboards.

Interestingly, in 1996 the Detroit Tigers spent more than a million dollars on advertising in an effort to attract fans. It turned out to be the worst season in the history of the club as it lost a franchise record 109 games. Only 1,168,610 fans showed up during this long season. The Tigers' advertising in 1996 was handled by Young & Rubicam, which created a great campaign in all media. Even great advertising, however, can't sell a bad product. People simply will not spend their money on a loser. Nevertheless, in 1970 the Tigers lost 83 games and won 75 to finish last in their division. They were able to sell 1,501,293 tickets, though, with an advertising expenditure of under $100,000. Our big idea to use a large space newspaper advertisement as an order form sold many thousands of tickets before the losing season even began. The return on their advertising investment in 1970 was many times greater using the mail order approach we pioneered.

Standard Federal Merges With Birmingham Federal

This was the first of many mergers or acquisitions that Standard Federal would make. Little did we know how much this one, on February 10, 1970, would also impact the

E.W. Baker, Inc. agency. For many years Standard Federal's headquarters had been located at the corner of Griswold and Jefferson, which was the site of St. Anne's Church, the first building constructed when Detroit was established. Following the merger with Birmingham Federal, Standard Federal moved its headquarters to Birmingham. Birmingham Federal's headquarters were in a building it owned at the corner of Woodward and Maple in downtown Birmingham. The management staff of Birmingham Federal had been based in offices on the second floor while the banking facilities for customers were on the street level. A jewelry store, Lake Jewelers, also leased a sizable area of the building on the street level. The management and support staff of both Birmingham Federal and Standard Federal were then consolidated after the merger in a new headquarters facility at 1500 North Woodward, which made the vacated second floor of the Woodward and Maple building available for a tenant.

We had been looking at office space in various buildings in different suburbs and Tom Ricketts was aware of this. In the fall of 1970 Tom casually mentioned, one day during one of our frequent meetings, that we might like to take a look at the space available in Birmingham above what was now one of the branch offices. A group of us – Bob Klepinger, Jerry Abbs, George Sperry, Wynne Garlow, B Tornow and several others – went to look at the offices and to our surprise, all of us immediately decided that this was where we wanted to be – in the heart of this vibrant suburban downtown. The space suited our needs better than any other facility that we had seen and we were surrounded by more than 200 different kinds of retailers and specialty stores. Everything we needed was within easy walking distance, including low-cost enclosed parking decks, a great variety of good restaurants plus art galleries and suppliers such as photographers, quickie printers, typesetters and art studios.

In December of 1970 we finalized a lease for our offices to be located at 55 W. Maple in Birmingham and started planning our move, which would occur in the spring of 1971. In the meantime, considerable alterations had to be made in the space we were to occupy to accommodate our staff and allow for some expansion. The entire staff looked forward to the move and we arranged for everyone to see the new offices well in advance of the move so they could share the excitement. It was the start of a new decade and the future looked even brighter for an advertising agency that was only six years old.

The Circus Comes To Town

In the fall of 1970 we also handled the advertising and publicity for Ringling Brothers, Barnum and Bailey Circus for its appearance at Cobo Hall in downtown Detroit. We had been contacted by the circus in the early spring and were offered the account on a local basis and decided to go for it. It was a fun account to handle. A member of our staff, Karen Denton, had always wanted to ride an elephant, so she rode one of the elephants from the circus train to downtown Detroit. We all went to the circus, of course, taking our entire families. The next year the circus did not hire local agencies but used one agency for its entire schedule of appearances – which was a disappointment, as we would have gladly handled it again for Detroit.

My Brother Saves the Hollywood Sign

In 1970, my bother, Joe, was president of the Hollywood, California Kiwanis Club. It was the club's custom to select a project each year to benefit its community. During a discussion by the club's board of directors of various projects to consider, the refurbishment of the decaying "Hollywood" sign in the hills of Hollywood was mentioned as a worthwhile activity. There was not a unanimous consensus to take on this project as some of the board members knew that the Hollywood Chamber of Commerce had sought to refurbish the sign and had received a bid of $50,000 to bring it back to life. This was an amount substantially above what the chamber had available or could raise from its members. Furthermore, the sign had rusted quite badly and a few of the letters had toppled over, so that the sign nearly blended into the vegetation – making it only an eyesore to those who could see it from a fairly short distance away. One of the directors, a long-time Hollywood businessman and major property owner, said the best thing the club could do was to forget about the sign and let nature take it over completely.

My brother, Joe G. Baker, when he was president of the Kiwanis Club of Hollywood, California in 1970.

Joe was intrigued by the possibility of restoring it, so he basically took it upon himself to get the job done. As the sign was located on property owned by the city of Los Angeles and supervised by Los Angeles City Parks Commission, the club needed to receive permission from the city to do the work. He called Los Angeles Mayor Sam Yorty to arrange a meeting with a representative of the mayor's office and the head of the city parks at the Hollywood Brown Derby restaurant. They were enthusiastically in favor of the idea and Yorty sent a letter to Joe giving the club permission to proceed.

Following this step, Joe called a painting contractor, Ted Zobrist of Zoco Painting. Ted had worked for him previously on several projects and Joe asked him to take a look at the job and to give him a bid. The letters of the sign are 40 feet high and the site is located on some rather rugged terrain on the side of a hill. Ted checked out the sign and reported to Joe that he could do the job for $20,000. Ted reported that he would bring in some telephone poles to support the letters that had fallen, corrugated metal for the sign face and lumber to replace some of the wood that had rotted away on frames and supports for the letters.

With this bid in hand, Joe called the presidents of the Hollywood Rotary Club, Hollywood Lions Club and the Hollywood Chamber of Commerce and asked each of them to contribute $5,000 to the project to match the contribution of the Hollywood Kiwanis. The Rotary Club and Chamber agreed, but the Lions were unable to make a contribution. Joe then requested the chamber to raise its contribution to $10,000, which it did. Ted Zobrist was given the go-ahead. Ted and his crew used boatswain's chairs that were attached to the top of the telephone poles to lower themselves to paint the sign. As soon as Ted started painting the H, the local TV stations had their helicopters flying around the sign to shoot film of the work as it progressed. The film appeared on the evening news. The public was very pleased, especially in Hollywood, to see the sign restored and repainted.

After the work was completed, pictures of it began to appear extensively in movies, TV, newspaper and magazine commercials. It also became the target for pranksters, and one group changed the letters from "wood" to "weed." The Chamber of Commerce took over the responsibility for maintaining the sign, and every few years had it repainted. Later, the sign had become such an important landmark for Hollywood and Los Angeles, that the chamber decided to seek contributions to replace the wooden telephone poles and supports with steel structures. An engineering firm provided the design for the new support of the sign and bids were taken for the job. Individual contributors such as Andy Williams (the W) and Hugh Hefner (for the H) and others each made contributions equal to the cost of replacing one letter of the sign. After the new sign was completed, Hugh Hefner held a party at the Playboy mansion in West Los Angeles to celebrate the event.

One enterprising promoter purchased the scrap metal from the face of the sign, cut it into small pieces, and offered it to the public as a souvenir of the old Hollywood sign. Little did they know that Ted Zobrist had picked up most of this corrugated metal from scrap yards a few years earlier and reused it on the sign.

Today, the images of the sign or its representation are seen in numerous forms and many people consider it to be as important to Los Angeles as the Eiffel Tower is to Paris.

The sign had been built originally for a real estate development known as Hollywoodland. Later, the "land" letters were removed and it became a well-known landmark in the Hollywood Hills. Prior to World War II it was lighted by incandescent lights strung around the letters. A caretaker lived in a small nearby building and replaced the bulbs as needed. The lights could be seen by boaters from a considerable distance at sea. With the advent of World War II, the lights were turned off, as it was feared they could become a beacon for a Japanese military attack. During its history, an aspiring, but depressed, actress committed suicide by jumping off one of the letters. But to my brother Joe goes the credit for saving the Hollywood sign.

Other Significant Events That Occurred In 1970

My father – Ernest W. Baker, Sr. – died in his sleep in June shortly before his 65th birthday, which was the fourth of July. He died of heart failure brought on by many years of heavy smoking. Little did we know when we gave him cartons of cigarettes for his birthday or for Christmas years earlier that it was only hastening the end of his life. While he appreciated these gifts, I regret that we gave him so much tobacco. Fortunately, I have never smoked – nor has my brother – but our father more than made up for both of us. Dad set an example that Joe and I didn't want to follow.

During 1970, I became a trustee of Cleary College in Ypsilanti, Michigan, attended the SIMSA meeting in Palm Springs, California and the NAAN meeting in Hawaii. Joan had planned to go to the meeting in Hawaii with me but my father died suddenly two weeks prior to the time we were to depart for Honolulu. She then decided to stay home and help my mother and let our son Mike accompany me – which would also be a high school graduation present for him.

On June 21, Mike and I flew 4,350 miles nonstop from Detroit to Honolulu – a nine-hour flight. The NAAN meeting was at the Makaha Inn, which was on the island of Oahu but miles from Honolulu. As soon as we checked in at the Makaha Inn we went to bed, as we were exhausted from the long plane ride and lack of sleep. Next morning the meeting started and while I was in meetings every day, Mike was having a great time with friends he had made the year before at the NAAN meeting in Maine.

On Thursday evening the meeting ended with a luau and Mike and I went to our room to pack as we were scheduled to leave very early Friday morning to go to the airport to return home. When we finished packing, Mike said he wanted to go say one more good-bye to his friends, particularly Kari Milici, the daughter of Ray Milici. Ray was then the president of our host agency, Milici Advertising, which is located in Honolulu. I said, "Okay but please don't be long" as we need to get to sleep. I waited and waited and waited for Mike's return. Shortly before it was time to depart for the airport, Mike showed up. He and Kari had gone to Honolulu to a disco for a night on the town. Mike explained that he thought I'd gone to bed and would be asleep so he didn't want to wake me. Actually, I had no sleep wondering where he was and worrying that we weren't going to make our early morning flight. We caught our plane but it was a quiet trip home as we didn't talk much.

– 1971 –

We Move Our Offices To Birmingham – An Affluent, Vibrant and Well-Established Suburb of Detroit

During the first three months of 1971, we did a lot of cleaning of files and other materials in the office in the Buhl Building preparing for our move to Birmingham. Everything was ready to go on March 26. We hauled a lot of critical small items to our new offices late in the day. The physical move of all the desks, furniture, files and other heavy items took place on Saturday. The movers arrived at the Buhl Building at 7:30 a.m. and by 10 a.m. their trucks were loaded and ready to go to Birmingham. By noon the movers' ramps were in place at our new offices at 55 W. Maple and all the furniture and equipment was being hauled in and placed in the appropriate offices. In the midst of all this activity John Albert, the sales representative for WWJ-TV and a good friend of the agency,

arrived with a big hamper full of sandwiches, pop and coffee.

The move to Birmingham proved to be the right thing to do at the right time. One of the most significant things that occurred was that people started arriving at work much earlier in the morning and staying later in the evening – particularly those who lived near the office. Productivity increased significantly. Most of our staff were now much closer to the office, so travel time was reduced. They felt safe and the location of the office in the center of a busy small town business district made it a pleasant place indeed.

I had been paying $70 per month to park my car in the garage in front of the Veterans Memorial Building in downtown Detroit. In Birmingham, it cost just $12 a month to park in a parking deck a short block from the office and we no longer had to pay a Detroit city income tax – which put more money in all of our pockets. It took me 35 to 45 minutes to drive to or from work when our offices were in the Buhl Building, however, and it now took from 50 to 70 minutes to go to or from Birmingham from our home in Grosse Pointe on the far east side of the Detroit metropolitan area. (The I-696 expressway did not exist in 1971).

We had considerably more office space in Birmingham, so our individual offices were larger and we had a much bigger conference room, a library – even a screening room – plus lots of storage in the basement. In time, we would outgrow the 7,000 square feet of space and expand into an adjoining building, as well as add offices on the second floor of two other buildings in downtown Birmingham.

In 1971, we were so swamped with business from our clients that we made only five new business presentations during the year. We won three of the five, adding American Central, Stanley-Berry and Detroit Stoker.

We Lose the Bin-Dicator Account

We also lost the Bin-Dicator account, which came as quite a surprise. The Bin-Dicator company had been acquired by a conglomerate and when George Schemm, the president, retired, a new president was transferred from a Colorado division to Michigan to head Bin-Dicator. As soon as he arrived we received a letter from him canceling our services – giving us 90 days notice. Bob Klepinger and I drove to Port Huron to meet with the new president to find out why our services had been terminated. The new president explained that his closest friend was with an advertising agency in Denver and that he also loved to ski. He was now going to use his friend's advertising agency in Denver to handle Bin-Dicator's advertising, which would give him the excuse he needed to return frequently to Denver, particularly during the ski season. And that was that! A strange way to lose an account.

Sanders Tries Some New Things To Improve Its Business

Sanders opened an ice cream parlor in Toledo early in the year which was to serve as a prototype in a franchising effort. We also developed a "Happy Hour" promotion for all their stores to encourage people to enjoy the "soft stuff" as an alternative to going to a bar for the "hard stuff." The franchising never received strong support at that time from Sanders management – which was really needed in order for such a program to succeed – but the "Happy Hour" campaign helped generate considerable traffic and sales late in the afternoon for its soda fountains.

Late in the year Sanders opened two cafeteria dining-style stores in Lansing, in major malls, to try this type of operation. Both stores featured fountain service and were opened with great fanfare. The restaurant and dining area in both units occupied 80 percent of the total floor space with the remainder reserved for candy, ice cream and baked goods displays in the front of the stores. Sanders had high hopes that its investment in these two new concept stores would provide the impetus it needed to ignite the company.

At the end of December 1970, Sanders stores numbered 58, with Sanders products available in 181 supermarkets and 834 candy agencies. They were surviving, but not moving ahead significantly in sales or profits.

All of our clients, though, had lots of projects for us to handle and we were opening new jobs and tackling advertising and public relations assignments at a hectic pace.

The Agency Is Reshaped and Strengthened As a Result of Changes In Personnel

On April 30, George Sperry left the agency to become the promotion manager of Channel 50 in Detroit. Jack Costello was hired to handle the production of radio and television commercials for our clients. Bob Klepinger was elected executive vice president of the agency on July 1 and assumed responsibility for general management of the agency. Bernie Thomas was added in August to manage the PR department. On September 1 Gil Testa joined the agency as an account executive and Keith Schoen became the agency's creative director on September 7. Carole Trzos, our production manager, left at the end of October and was replaced by Nancy Olzem. While it was disappointing to lose George Sperry and Carole Trzos, the agency was reshaped and in many ways greatly strengthened.

Nancy Olzem, Judy Neuharth and B Tornow worked together unbelievably well to provide us with a virtually flawless internal operation. They became the backbone of the agency as work flowed smoothly through the agency under the direction of the traffic department, was expertly produced by the production department and billed by our

Nancy Olzem
Production Manager

Judy Neuharth
Traffic Manager

accounting department with great efficiency with these three highly competent, hard-working professionals in charge. Media, account service, public relations and creative were able to focus on their respective responsibilities without having to be concerned about determining deadlines, being involved in production problems or when and how all the work was being billed.

During the year, I attended the SIMSA meeting in Fort Lauderdale, Florida, and the NAAN annual meeting held in Sea Island, Georgia. In August, I went deep sea fishing with my brother Joe and six other executives of First Federal of Hollywood. We chartered a large fishing boat in San Diego, which we boarded just before midnight. As soon as the boat was underway we got settled on board and in our bunks to get some sleep. We were up before dawn and, using live anchovies for bait, soon caught more than 300 pounds of tuna. It was my first experience deep sea fishing and we hit several large schools of albacore, making it an exciting experience. Late in the morning we had a big breakfast and most of the day we relaxed, snacked, napped and enjoyed being many miles out on the Pacific ocean. Late in the

evening we caught another 100 pounds of tuna, which made our fishing trip very successful. This became an annual event for the next eight years. Sometimes we caught a lot of fish and in other years very few, but these fishing trips were always enjoyed by all the participants.

The fish that we caught were turned in at a receiving station operated by a tuna cannery near where the boat we chartered was docked. They weighed our catch and then paid us in canned tuna – one can for every so many pounds, plus a 25¢ per can canning charge. This was an easy way to deal with all the fish we caught and in 1971 I took home two cases of canned tuna.

In future years, though, I hauled home fresh tuna packed in dry ice, as well as cases of canned tuna. Some great tuna barbecues were enjoyed on several occasions when I returned from California with fresh tuna.

In the fall of 1971 we started working for our three new clients: American-Central, Detroit Stoker and Stanley-Berry. American-Central was a division of a large paper company and needed help selling vacation property in Northern Michigan. We questioned its sales ethics and resigned the business a year later. Detroit Stoker, located in Monroe, Michigan, was an interesting and successful company in the environmental field. Stanley-Berry, which was located in Birmingham, would not only expand to become a large national company but would also become one of three divisions of The Stanley Works in the Detroit area. Ultimately, it became our largest account for several years after the advertising budgets for all three divisions were consolidated from an accounting standpoint.

The Stanley Tool Works, which is a large international company headquartered in New Britain, Connecticut, acquired the Berry Door Company, a manufacturer of garage doors, in 1964. After Berry became part of The Stanley Works, the name was changed to Stanley-Berry. When we became Stanley-Berry's advertising agency in late 1971 it was in the process of expanding the business and adding manufacturing facilities in other states – with the goal of becoming a national company. The expansion also included additional product lines comprised of replacement doors and complete entry systems for homes. In future years the name of the company would become Stanley Door Systems.

In 1972, The Stanley Tool Works purchased the Vemco garage door opener business in Detroit which was then renamed the Stanley Vemco Division of The Stanley Works. This division also became an agency client and in 1987 the name of the company was changed to Stanley Home Automation and the product line further extended to include gate operators and radio controls.

A third division was added in the Detroit area in 1976 when The Stanley Tool Works purchased the electronics production facility of Multi-Elmac, which manufactured remote control units for garage door openers. This division also appointed E.W. Baker, Inc. as its agency in order to coordinate its activities with the other two divisions of The Stanley Works.

During the 1980s these three divisions of The Stanley Works grew tremendously and the agency became totally involved in their communications to the extent of even planning and producing their sales meetings. This was in addition to handling their trade and consumer advertising, package designs and all their collateral materials.

– 1972 –
Another "Grow-Ahead" Year
For the Agency

On January 6 – the eighth anniversary of E.W. Baker, Inc., – we met with Bud Hudson and Bill Speed of the R.P. Scherer Corporation. Speed was vice president in charge of sales and Hudson headed a subsidiary and was a large shareholder in the corporation. Bill and Bud came to our offices in Birmingham, where we made our agency credentials presentation to them and a few weeks later we were notified that they had decided to appoint us as their agency.

R.P. Scherer Corporation

The R.P. Scherer Corporation is an international company that started in Detroit in 1933 when Robert Pauli Scherer invented the rotary die method of encapsulating soft elastic gelatin (SEG) capsules. The first SEG capsules were created by Mothes, a French pharmacist, in 1833 using the "dip" method. Encapsulation is a process by which a powder, liquid or paste is encased in a gelatin capsule. Soft gel is a one-piece, soft elastic gelatin capsule which typically contains water soluble liquids, oil soluble liquids, pastes or solids in solution or suspension. R.P. Scherer became – and still is – the leading international developer and manufacturer of drug delivery systems and is the world's largest producer of softgels for the pharmaceutical and nutritional supplements industries.

We created impressive and elaborate direct mail pieces for R.P. Scherer for customers and prospects. The mailing list was not large because there are not a great number of companies producing drugs and vitamins. In addition to direct mail we created and produced a series of advertisements for trade publications, placed R. P. Scherer's listing in various directories and handled press releases whenever it needed assistance. The company had gone public in 1971 and we were assigned the production and printing of its annual report.

R.P. Scherer remained an active client of the agency until 1979, when the company went through a reorganization. Robert Scherer, Jr., who was president, left the company and Peter Fink, a Scherer director and husband of Karla Scherer, succeeded him as president and chief executive officer. Our primary contacts with the company also left and our relationship with R.P. Scherer ended at this time.

I Receive an Honorary Doctorate Degree

At the Cleary College commencement ceremonies on June 10, 1972, I received an honorary Doctor of Science in Business Administration degree in recognition of the seven years that I served as a trustee of this college in Ypsilanti, Michigan. I was honored, of course, but Joan was particularly thrilled and her reaction meant more to me than the actual degree itself. Founded in 1884, Cleary College provides an outstanding business education for its approximately 900 students with a curriculum that really prepares its graduates for the real world of business.

Joan was especially pleased when I received an honorary Doctor of Science in Business Administration degree from Cleary College in Ypsilanti, Michigan.

Chuck Blore Does Some Great Work For First Federal of Hollywood

Early in July I attended the NAAN annual meeting at the Broadmoor Hotel in Colorado Springs, Colorado and from there went to Hollywood, California to meet with our client, First Federal of Hollywood. While I was in California I also met with Herb Klein and Chuck Blore of Chuck Blore Creative Services. They had a national reputation for producing highly effective radio commercials. Since their offices were on Argyle Avenue in Hollywood, a short distance from First Federal's headquarters at the corner of Hollywood and Highland, they were already very familiar with First Federal and the communities like Hollywood, North Hollywood and Santa Monica where the branch offices were located.

First Federal's offices were located in communities where the population demographic was skewed heavily to men and women 50 years of age and older – ideal prospects for savings accounts, but not for home loans. After considerable discussion it was decided that we would build on the name First Federal of Hollywood – and make it a positive by emphasizing all the positive aspects of the movie industry. As an example, one of the founders of First Federal of Hollywood was C.E. Toberman, who had a real estate business in Hollywood. He donated the land to the city of Los Angeles for the site of the Hollywood Bowl, so First Federal's roots ran deep in the area. We also believed that a great many of these older savings prospects residing in First Federal's marketing areas would either directly or indirectly have some current or past personal or business relationship with the movie industry. It turned out many of them did – which made our marketing strategy even more effective once the advertising campaign got underway. We were involved in what is now defined as relationship marketing.

The first three radio commercials Chuck Blore created and produced utilized George

Raft, Arlene Judge and Richard Arlen as the talent and they were incredibly effective. These three former big name stars had dropped out of sight, so it was a real surprise for radio listeners to hear each of them doing a radio commercial for First Federal of Hollywood. The message in each commercial was simple, honest and sincere. George Raft stated that "he wished he'd saved some of the money he made when he was a star as he wouldn't be doing radio commercials now." The commercials were talked about and written about in the press because they were so different and they refocused attention on a number of personalities or movie stars who had been well known names in the late '30s and early '40s. Some of them lived in the communities where First Federal had offices and several even saved at their offices. Johnnie Carson commented on the radio commercials at some length on several occasions on his television show as he – like many others – wasn't aware that the people doing the radio spots were still alive and living in Los Angeles.

We also arranged for Western International Media to handle the placement of all First Federal of Hollywood's advertising and this too proved to be the right decision, as the buys made enabled our client to achieve the reach and frequency needed to make the advertising a success.

Western International Media is headquartered in Los Angeles and they knew this huge market better than any media planner or buyer in Detroit. As a result of this arrangement, I became well acquainted with Dennis Holt, who started and built Western International Media into the largest media buying business in the country. A few years later as a personal favor, Dennis flew to Detroit on a red eye flight to participate in an agency new business presentation. Friends like this are hard to find and Dennis truly deserves the success he's achieved through hard work and dedication.

The second series of radio commercials for First Federal of Hollywood utilized Patrick Knowles, Faith Domergue and John Agar. The third series featured Jean Parker, Jackie Coogan, Margaret O'Brien and Johnny Mack Brown.

And they were followed by Hoagy Carmichael, Helen O'Connell and Kathryn Grayson. More than half of First Federal of Hollywood's advertising budget was spent for radio advertising but it was backed by advertising in local newspapers, zoned editions of the *Los Angeles Times* and large outdoor billboards in its marketing areas. Our campaign ran for several years. During this time, there were displays or exhibits at the main office of movie memorabilia and a "History of Hollywood" was published and offered as premium for opening or adding to a savings account.

Bill Anderson, who had become the Director of Marketing for First Federal of Hollywood, discovered that Jim Jordan had a savings account at First Federal of Hollywood. Jim Jordan was best known as Fibber McGee. "Fibber McGee and Molly" had been one of the most popular shows on radio for many years. Molly had passed away but Fibber (Jim Jordan) was eager to get back on the air again doing First Federal of Hollywood radio commercials. We did a whole series of radio commercials with Fibber McGee starting early in 1976 and they ran for the next several years. In the first five months of 1976 alone, First Federal had a 31% increase in savings deposits and they ranked well up in the top 10% of all S&Ls in the nation in savings growth. This advertising campaign really worked.

One of the best known signs in the world is the HOLLYWOOD sign, which consists of large individual letters and identifies that area of Los Angeles known as Hollywood. In the late '60s this sign had deteriorated to the point where it was falling apart and several of the letters had actually fallen over. As already reported, my brother Joe raised the funds to rebuild and restore this sign in 1970, when he was president of the Hollywood Kiwanis Club. His efforts saved the sign and this achievement, along with the tie-in and promotional activities relating to the movie industry, really enhanced the advertising campaign and helped make it a fantastic success.

September Is Full of Surprises

September 1972 was full of surprises. Wynne Garlow, who had been with the agency for over seven years, resigned to take another position managing a major shopping mall. My mother decided to move to Sun City, Arizona. She sold her home in Grosse Pointe, packed up and moved there in December and spent the next 20 years enjoying the sunshine and all the amenities of this retirement community.

Also in September, Fred Pantillon resigned from the Fred Sanders Company and shortly after that Dick Herrle, Sanders new vice president and general manager, came to our offices for a meeting that he had requested. He said that one of his goals as the new general manager was to put Awrey's out of business. Therefore, we could not handle both the Awrey's account and Sanders, as far as he was concerned. We then made an economic decision. Sanders' advertising budget was three times larger than Awrey's at that time so we reluctantly resigned the Awrey's account. (In 1977, though, we resigned the Sanders account and got the Awrey's account back; you'll read later about the circumstances that brought all this about).

The Public Relations Department Expands

Jack Muir, who operated a small public relations business, joined the agency in December. We now had a staff of seven highly competent professionals in our PR department. The two major PR accounts that Jack Muir brought to the agency were the Carboloy Systems Division of General Electric and the Prestolite Company, a division of Ultra Corporation – both large accounts in the business-to-business category.

– 1973 –

On January 10, I attended the American Business Women's Association's annual banquet at the Chicago Road House restaurant in Dearborn, where I was recognized as the "Boss of the Year." I was nominated for this honor by Bertha Brooks, a member of our accounting staff, and the trophy I received still resides on a shelf in my den at home.

The following week, major management changes took place at Standard Federal Savings. On January 16, Michael Fury was named as the new head of the marketing department. The next day, the board of directors elected Robert Hutton to be its chairman and Thomas R. Ricketts its president. Mike Fury had been an outstanding branch manager and his new position recognized his past accomplishments. He was a very intense, ambitious young man and he made no secret of the fact that his goal was to follow Tom Ricketts as the next president.

In the months that followed, I spent a considerable amount of time indoctrinating Mike Fury so that he would understand how advertising is produced for newspapers, magazines, radio, television and direct mail and the amount of time needed to do it properly. There was also a special challenge for us to consider – Standard Federal expected to reach and pass a billion dollars in assets sometime during the year and this would be used as the basis of a special advertising and promotion effort. Standard Federal did pass this important milestone and we created and published a special tabloid section that was inserted in several daily newspapers and utilized a 30-second TV commercial that was a great brand builder. The TV commercial started with a little boy handing a teller a $1.00 bill along with his passbook. The teller then asked, "Do you know what this is?" The little boy said "No" and the teller exclaimed "It's a billion dollars, a billion dollars…we've now reached a billion dollars." With that a brass band marched in and a big cake covered with lighted candles was wheeled into the office lobby. The little boy was carried around on the shoulders of employees celebrating this achievement and the commercial concluded with a tight close-up of the little boy saying "They sure do appreciate you here!" It was one of those warm, delightful and entertaining television commercials that leaves you with a happy feeling. The "100 Billion in Assets" campaign was a huge success, as a significant increase in savings deposits was generated by the promotion that was carried out around this special event. During the year Standard Federal moved their headquarters to a much larger building on Big Beaver Road in Troy, as they had outgrown their Birmingham offices.

It's Back To New Orleans In February

The 1973 Savings Institutions Marketing Society of America (SIMSA) meeting was held in New Orleans February 6 through 11 and Joan and I attended along with nine others representing our three S&L clients. The Furys and Ricketts from Standard Federal, Esther and Justin Way from Saginaw Savings, Jane and Ken Lyons and Joe Baker from First Federal of Hollywood. At this meeting I was elected a director of SIMSA for a three-year term.

We Find a Home In the Country

Every weekend starting early in January, Joan and I looked at property in north Oakland County and, on March 4, we found the home we were hoping to find in the country. We closed on the purchase on March 22 and moved to Ortonville, a village just off I-75 north of Pontiac, on June 16.

Our home in the country – Baker's Orchard – located between Clarkston and Ortonville in north Oakland County, Michigan. Moving from an affluent suburban community – Grosse Pointe Farms – to the country was a radical change in lifestyle. It turned out to be a very good and positive change.

We found a comfortable, spacious home that was less than five years old set in the middle of an apple orchard. There was also a 45,000 gallon swimming pool enclosed by an iron fence and a large cabana that contained all the pool equipment, two dressing rooms, and a storage room, as well as two garages for storing power equipment or a boat or snowmobiles.

The Apple Orchard Was Going To Be My Avocation

For 24 years I had been almost totally immersed in the advertising business and long days were the norm rather than the exception. Even before we moved to the country in June we spent weekends at our 13.5 acre "farm" pruning apple trees and doing the necessary spring spraying. Our producing orchard contained more than 200 apple trees and the varieties included Red and Golden Delicious, McIntosh, Jonathan, Winesap, Northern Spy, Rome, Steel Red, Paula Red, Ida Red and Cortland. I immediately read several books on apple production, joined the Michigan Horticulture Society, the Eastern Michigan U-Pick Association and the Lapeer County Co-op.

I was very fortunate to meet Roger Porter who owned and operated a large commercial orchard near Goodrich, the next little village north of Ortonville. Roger became a good friend and my mentor as he showed me how to prune trees, sold me the various kinds of chemicals I needed for spraying, told me when I needed to spray and even bought a lot of our apples, which he used for making cider. Porters Orchards contains many thousands of apple and other fruit trees as well as a big nursery. Roger and his son operate a large farm market and they make the best apple cider in the world. Porters Farm Market is open year 'round but I especially like to go there in the fall to watch the tractors pulling long trailers, each loaded with 20 bushel bins of apples from the orchard for sorting and storage, to smell the donuts being made, and

to experience the pleasure of drinking a cup of cold, freshly made apple cider. All summer long that first year at our little farm we watched our apples grow and finally ripen, starting early in September. We invited friends, relatives and clients to come and pick apples in the fall and many of them did. For them, the apples were free but we also sold apples to pick-your-own customers and this was an interesting experience.

Our apple marketing season lasted about eight weeks, starting right after Labor Day. By the end of October, all the apples were gone. I handled the pick-your-own paying customers on the weekends while Joan took over during the week. We charged the pick-your-own customers $7.50 per bushel and I placed a small advertisement in several newspapers to announce that we had apples for sale. People would call on the phone asking what varieties we had and how much we charged for "windfalls." Joan would run through the list of varieties we kept near the phone and tell the caller, "Sorry, we don't have windfalls." One Saturday when we were out in the orchard a young couple with small children came over to us and asked "How much are your windfalls?" Joan and I looked at each other and said, "We don't have windfall apples." They then pointed at the apples on the ground and asked "What do you call those apples?" We suddenly realized – yes, we do have windfalls. It was all part of our learning experience. We made many new friends in the country and Joan liked to tell them the "windfall" story. The story was repeated all around our new little hometown and Joan became known as *Windfall Annie*.

Our country home near Ortonville was a few miles off I-75 and it was much easier and faster for me to get to our offices in Birmingham than it was from Grosse Pointe Farms. I also usually made several trips a month to Saginaw, as I handled the Saginaw Savings account. I now could drive to or from Saginaw in an hour's time and that made a big difference, particularly if I had to stay in Saginaw in the evening to produce television commercials at a local TV station. Commercials had to be produced in the evening because that's when production people were available. Now I could be home before midnight, whereas I usually didn't get home until 2:00 a.m. or later when we lived in Grosse Pointe.

I was in Saginaw on May 17 for a meeting with Justin Way, at which time he told me he was retiring the end of June. His replacement would be Dick Morford, who worked in the mortgage department. Dick turned out to be an exceptionally pleasant and astute individual with whom to work and one of his closest friends was Dick Weinberg, a first cousin of Joan's. I've discovered over and over again that it's really a small world.

One of the things that I was going to miss were Justin's martinis. Over the years, when one of our meetings ended around 5 p.m., Justin would invite me to his home for a martini. Justin shared a home with two sisters, Esther and Mary, and none of the three of them had ever married. They had many other brothers and sisters who were married, so they were part of a large family. Esther was the society editor for the *Saginaw News*, a daily newspaper, and Mary was the head bookkeeper for a large manufacturing company.

The three of them would arrive home around 5:30 p.m. and then make a ritual out of preparing their martinis. They kept a small silver pitcher in their refrigerator which was ice cold. The gin was also refrigerated but not the vermouth. They would carefully measure the gin and vermouth, stir the ingredients very slowly in their little pitcher, then carefully pour the contents into chilled glasses, in which they had already placed an anchovie-stuffed olive. It was enjoyable to have a cocktail with them and listen to them discuss some of the local gossip, which was the basis of Esther's livelihood. After sharing a drink with them though I then had to either drive home or go to WNEM-TV to produce new TV spots. Thus, I could never drink more than one of their special potent martinis or I would have been in trouble.

In July, I was a real traveling man. First to a meeting at the Broadmoor in Colorado Springs of the officers and directors of SIMSA. Ray Foley, the president of the Colle & McVoy advertising agency in Minneapolis, was also serving as a SIMSA director and we had an opportunity to get much better acquainted at this meeting. We spent an evening at the Golden Bee lounge where Ray suggested that we consider merging our agencies. We talked about this possibility several times over the next few years but the timing never seemed quite right to have this happen.

From July 17 through 22 I was in Hollywood for meetings with Dennis Holt, Chuck Blore and various people at First Federal of Hollywood. We also went deep sea fishing again on the weekend and caught a lot of albacore. It was a very successful trip in every respect. When I returned to Michigan it was back to Saginaw for meetings, now with Dick Morford, and taping of more TV spots. Then, on July 26, Bob Ross and I left Birmingham at 4 a.m. in the morning to attend the annual advertising meeting of Ponderosa Steakhouses in Dayton, Ohio. Bob Ross had joined the agency the year before as our media director and was a very bright young man and an excellent presenter. He elevated the stature of our media department and our clients respected his media expertise. Bob and I drove to Dayton and arrived at the Ponderosa Restaurants national headquarters by 9:15 a.m. in plenty of time for our 9:30 meeting. It was a long day, though, as we didn't get home until late in the evening after stopping for dinner in Toledo – it seemed like every day was a long day back then.

The rest of the summer and early fall were somewhat routine at the office but we were really enjoying our life in the country – especially the weekends. I discovered that a swimming pool is not only a lot of work, but that it was also very interesting how many small critters we fished out of the pool. Living in the country, the swimming pool attracted moles, ground squirrels, mice, 'possums, salamanders and muskrats. Brandy, a neighbor's dog, also liked an early morning swim. I pulled her out of the pool frequently, as the stupid dog couldn't remember where the steps were at the shallow end of the pool. It's a wonder she didn't drown, as Brandy always ended up at the deep end of the pool, where she couldn't possibly climb out of the water. The NAAN annual meeting was held in New York City October 18-24 and Jerry Abbs and I attended it. I was elected a director of NAAN at this meeting to serve a three-year term.

The agency had enjoyed consistent, solid growth year after year but that was about to change due to circumstances over which we had no control.

– 1974 –

Crude oil from 1947 until 1970 cost about $1.79 per barrel. In January 1974, OPEC was virtually holding the world hostage with oil prices soaring to $7.00 a barrel. The U.S. established the Federal Energy Office to set and administer fuel needs to all sectors of the economy. Britain went on a three-day work week to conserve energy. The prime interest rate climbed to 11-3/4% in June.

The impact of the high cost of crude oil was felt by every business and it created a troubled economy, which severely impacted E.W. Baker, Inc. We had been growing steadily

Custom neckties featuring the agency logo were broadly distributed in early 1974 to recognize the agency's tenth anniversary. From left to right: Jerry Abbs, myself and Bob Klepinger display the special anniversary tie. Once, when I was in Chicago on business, I stopped a young man on the street wearing one of these ties. He told me that his father (who was with Microdot) gave it to him. I was particularly pleased whenever I spotted anyone – especially a client – wearing one of these neckties.

for ten years but that suddenly changed in 1974 when our billings dropped by almost $2,000,000. Nearly every client reduced its advertising budget, while Carboloy notified us that there would be **no** budget for public relations in 1974. They were our largest public relations client, providing the agency with an annual income in the $100,000 range.

We were also notified on January 21 that the Red Barn and Ponderosa restaurant accounts were going to move their advertising to the W.B. Doner advertising agency – which they did at the end of April. We then solicited the Sign of the Beefcarver restaurants' advertising and were assigned their account on October 1.

Sign of the Beefcarver Restaurants

The Sign of the Beefcarver restaurants were started by Bob LaJoie and Jack Joliat. The original name was Sign of the Beefeater but the owners were sued by Beefeater Gin and subsequently lost use of the Beefeater name in a court battle. Their first restaurant was on Woodward Avenue in Royal Oak. It was essentially a buffet-style cafeteria with no fried foods, (everything was baked) and it was open for lunch and dinner only. They developed a real winner and a highly profitable operation.

In 1972, Montgomery Ward purchased the eight restaurants in the Detroit area and opened four more in affluent Chicago suburbs. In 1979, when Mobil Oil acquired Montgomery Ward, Jack Joliat formed a management group and repurchased the restaurants, which had grown to 16 in the Metropolitan Detroit area, plus the four in Chicago. Bob LaJoie had retired in 1978 due to health problems. Unfortunately, Jack died of a heart attack in 1988 when he and his wife were vacationing in Ireland.

The Sign of the Beefcarver restaurants were far more successful and profitable than our former restaurant client and I had known both Bob LaJoie and Jack Joliat for a number of years, as they also owned a Howard Johnson's

restaurant. Jack had served as treasurer of the Howard Johnson's Southeast Michigan Advertising Association when it was first organized in 1960.

The Sign of the Beefcarver account was a good replacement for the Red Barn and the Ponderosa accounts that were lost. The Red Barn's restaurants eventually went out of business and Ponderosa went through a difficult period which it barely survived.

Sanders Makes a Disastrous Decision

Early in the year, Sanders decided to go into the frozen dough business. Many of the large food chains were putting a "bake off" operation in their stores where you could purchase freshly baked bread and rolls. The dough for these operations was provided frozen by large commercial bakeries and Sanders wanted to be a major player. It suffered substantial losses and encountered a disaster, arising from the extraordinary cost of distribution and the closing of food chain accounts. There were other major problems it hadn't foreseen as well. Sanders was in trouble and its problems would only get worse.

Meanwhile, Back On the Farm

In the spring, Joan and our sons Bob and Mike decided we should have horses. Over my many objections they purchased two gentle quarter horses – Star and Chester. We had a large pasture available in back of the orchard where they could graze, so we divided this pasture into three separate fenced-in areas. As soon as one area was grazed we could then move them to another area so there would be time for the grass to restore itself. We built a shelter, and a fenced-in riding rink, and bought a large water tank. Star and Chester were a lot of work and a considerable expense – feed, vet bills and new shoes on a regular basis – but they were ridden a lot, particularly when our sons' girlfriends came to visit.

Joan is astride Star, and I'm riding Chester – the quarter horses purchased in 1974 over my objections. I knew that it was going to take a lot of work and expense caring for them – and it was!

Next we decided we needed a barn. We had several hundred apple crates that were stored outside on skids. The cabana was already crowded with a tractor and other equipment so we ordered a barn from Lapeer Co-op. They built a beautiful red steel enameled barn 40' x 80' with a mansard roof and concrete floor. There were three horse stalls in the back of the barn with a huge second floor loft for hay storage as well as an enclosed work room on the first floor. It had two water outlets and we installed an intercom system between the house, cabana and barn. In front of the barn we added an electric gas pump with a 600 gallon in-ground storage tank. It was a beautiful barn of which we were really proud and it was the focal point of our little farm. Construction started early in August and it was finished by the end of November.

The red barn we added to our little farm was where we spent a lot of our time. We filled the loft with hay in the summer, stored our apple crates here, sorted apples and frequently used the workroom for repairing equipment, etc.

On the advice of my apple mentor, Roger Porter of Porters Orchards, I had joined the Lapeer County Co-op. This cost $1.00 and was the best investment I ever made in my life. Farm Co-ops are big operations. They are owned by its members and they're where farmers go for supplies, feed and fertilizer – virtually anything needed for farming. Lapeer County Co-op also had a construction division that built pole barns and that's why we ordered the barn from them. Best of all, I received dividends on my purchases. You have to wait several years for a dividend on the purchases made several years earlier at the Co-op but my first check was for more than $600. Year after year I received sizable dividends based on the amount of my purchases from Lapeer Co-op. Once a year they also held a membership meeting at which you enjoyed a delicious "free" dinner and received a financial report on the operations.

An Improved Apple Crop

We had a much larger and better apple crop in 1974 than we had the year before. Weather has a lot to do with the size and quality of an apple crop. If it's too cool in the spring when the trees are in blossom, then the bees don't leave their hives and pollinate as well as they should and this can substantially reduce the size of your crop. If there's not enough rain, your apples are smaller unless your orchard has irrigation, which we didn't have. I quickly learned to respect and admire commercial fruit growers who raise fruit for a living, as their livelihood depends so much on weather.

In 1974 we again sold apples to pick-your-own customers and gave hundreds of bushels to friends, relatives and clients. I also had half-bushel apple bags imprinted with the Baker's Orchard logo, which I would fill with apples and take to the office. Every Monday morning I would place a dozen or more of these bags of apples on the steps inside the back door of our Birmingham offices, which the account executives would then take to our clients.

I soon discovered that there were seven cider mills in the north Oakland County area – all needing apples. Joan received a 3/4-ton Chevrolet truck for her birthday in 1974 and she really did enjoy driving it – although she also had a station wagon. We could haul 80 bushels of apples in the truck and over the years sold many thousands of bushels of our apples to the cider mills. It was a good way to clean up the crop and, after several years, we stopped selling apples to the pick-your-own customers altogether, as this was becoming too much of a hassle. Our clients, friends and relatives, though, showed up in bunches on the weekends

and enjoyed picking apples. We added a big pumpkin patch behind the barn and in late October, when the pumpkins were ripe, we invited children to select and pick their Halloween pumpkins. It was a special treat for them and we really enjoyed entertaining our clients and friends on the weekends. There were lots of picnics and there are many, many happy memories of the good times we had every fall at Baker's Orchard.

I was also very fortunate that there were a number of really nice boys and girls in our neighborhood that I could hire to pick apples. They liked earning the money for picking apples and I tried to make it fun for them by providing lunch. I would run to Ortonville for pizza or burgers, which they thought was great. There was always plenty for them to eat and drink. Over the years I also had several young men who really liked working at the orchard – pruning trees, cleaning up the brush, cutting grass or doing other chores. It would have been impossible to operate the orchard without them because I only had the weekends and some evenings to work in the orchard. These young men would come and work after school during the week as well as on the weekends. Jim Enerson, Walter Dixon and Ricky Briggs were three of the outstanding teenagers who were a great help to me. They are now adults and doing exceptionally well in their business careers. I'm truly proud of them and hope that I made some contribution to their lives. They became good friends and I still remain in contact with them.

Chapter 6

In The Second Half Of The '70s, The Agency Evolves Into A Different Organization

"We cannot direct the wind...but we can adjust the sails."

– 1975 –

The "good" winds that had been pushing our ship faster and faster every year since 1964 really died in 1974 due to the oil crisis. But there were favorable signs of better times ahead, even though there was rampant inflation worldwide. The U.S. cut taxes by $15 billion per year to stimulate the economy and there was a big oil boom in Alaska. We had trimmed our sails by reducing agency staff – which is always a difficult thing to do. In late January, several new business "pitch" opportunities became available to us: the outstate Michigan McDonald's Association, *The Detroit Free Press*, Boblo (an amusement park) and the Chevrolet Dealers Association. We won the Boblo and the Chevrolet Dealers accounts. I took on the Boblo account and Gil Testa was assigned the Chevrolet Dealers.

Boblo amusement park was located on an island in the Detroit River in the downriver area. It could be reached by a ferry boat from Amherstberg on the Canadian side of the river. Two large cruise ships also carried Boblo visitors from downtown Detroit to the island. These ships also stopped in Wyandotte to pick up or drop off passengers. The business was owned and operated by the three Browning brothers – Red, Bill and Ralph. I worked primarily with Bill, who was general manager. Red was president and Ralph was in charge of ticket sales.

Since 1898, the 272-acre island had been a favorite haunt for Detroit area school kids, church groups and picnickers. Boblo's halcyon days were the 1950s, when at least one million people boated to Boblo each year. The cruises, particularly the midnight cruises, were still very popular but the amusement park had started deteriorating and needed a major investment by 1975 for new attractions and improvements to facilities. Boblo offered 38 rides, including a 2500-foot-long 60-m.p.h. roller coaster, a sawmill log flume ride, an antique car ride, swan boats and a sky-ride. Unfortunately, Cedar Point in Northern Ohio had far surpassed Boblo as an amusement and entertainment venue and now attracted many former Boblo patrons.

Our efforts were directed at making Boblo more "FUN" with a new logo and advertising that expressed this attitude. Boblo's advertising in the past had not been very exciting as they had focused on the destination of the ships, with most of the advertising concerned with departure and arrival time information for the cruise ships. It did not turn out to be a FUN account to handle. Client meetings usually took place late in the afternoon and there were frequent changes in sailing schedules and other problems. I was delighted when the season ended and the advertising ceased.

We resigned the business and went on to better things. Several years later Boblo was sold to AAA Michigan and they invested millions to improve the operation. After several years AAA Michigan sold it to International Broadcasting Corporation but Boblo ultimately ended up in bankruptcy. The two cruise ships are in storage and Boblo island is now being developed into a residential community.

Sanders Celebrates Its 100th Anniversary

June 17, 1975 marked the 100th anniversary for the Fred Sanders confectionery business in Detroit. We executed a celebration that lasted for more than two years. Special promotions of various Sanders products were scheduled for every month starting in July 1975 and the focal point of the celebration was a replica of the horse-drawn candy and ice cream cart used by Grandpa Fred Sanders. The frame and wheels for the candy cart were purchased from an Amish wagon builder in Shipsewana, Indiana. This base for the cart was shipped to a company in the Detroit area that specialized in restoring antique cars. This company then finished building it and installed a large cooler in the rear of the cart to hold ice cream. This cart was a handsome replica of the original. We located an individual with a well-trained pony to pull the cart. Fortunately, he had a pickup truck large enough to hold the cart, as well as a horse trailer to accommodate the pony. This individual received a nice income for two years moving this horse-drawn Sanders cart all over southeastern Michigan to appear in parades, shopping center activities, fairs and grand openings of super-markets that carried Sanders products.

For grand openings of stores or for shopping center promotions the cooler in the back of the cart was filled with ice cream bars which were either sold or given out free, depending on the situation. Pictures of the cart frequently appeared in the press and on television news programs. Sanders gave the cart to the Detroit Historical Museum at the conclusion of the 100th anniversary celebration and it is still in the museum's possession.

Let's Change Our Name

In the fall of 1975, Saginaw Savings decided they wanted to change its name because most of its offices were in Northern Michigan, not in Saginaw. We researched the names of all S&Ls that existed in the United States at the time. Our client wanted a name that no other savings and loan was using and ended up selecting Family Federal from a list of possibilities we presented. This was a challenging and interesting project involving the design of a new logo that could be applied to everything from signs to imprinted pencils, followed by an intense campaign to establish and build the new "brand" name. The advertising budget got a nice boost to accomplish this assignment.

We Start Advertising Squirt and Hires Root Beer

In the fall of the year we added another new account – the Squirt Detroit Bottling Company. This included both the Squirt and Hires Root Beer beverages. The company was owned by Bud Nicolay, a friend of Jerry Abbs. Bud also owned the Kar's Nuts Company, for which we had handled several special projects. Both companies were located in Ferndale.

The agency operated in the red in both 1974 and 1975 but the deficit was not nearly as bad in 1975 as in 1974. These were the only two years in the agency's history in which we failed to make a profit. Thankfully, we had built up resources to help us through a rough period and 1976 would see us back in the black again.

– 1976 –

Two major events occurred in the United States in 1976: the Bicentennial Celebration that began on July 4 to herald the 200th Anniversary of the Founding of the Republic and the Presidential election on November 5, in which Jimmy Carter beat President Gerald Ford with 51% to 48% of the popular vote.

One of the most popular shows on television in 1976 was "The Waltons," which we watched regularly. On a flight from Detroit to Los Angeles early in 1976 I sat next to

Ellen Corby, the actress who played Grandmother Walton in this popular TV series. She had been to Montreal, Canada for a get-away vacation and to add to her collection of tea cups. She had a shopping bag filled with carefully wrapped tea cups cradled between her legs the entire flight to protect the cups.

During the flight, she told me interesting stories about the people in the show and particularly the actor who played her husband, Grandpa Walton, as he was a real "ladies' man."

When we arrived in California, I offered Ms. Corby a ride home courtesy of my brother, who was meeting me, and she readily accepted. My brother Joe and I drove her to her house off Sunset Boulevard. I remember she had a comfortable, small home which she shared with five or six cats.

Several months later on another flight from Detroit to California, I sat next to another well-known business man and personality – John DeLorean. He certainly must have enjoyed talking that particular day because, by the end of the flight, I felt there was very little that I didn't know about him.

A Terrible Ice Storm

On March 3, Michigan experienced a terrible storm that resulted in extensive damage, particularly to trees. A freezing rain built up a thick coating of ice on everything and there were broken limbs everywhere, as trees simply split apart because they couldn't bear the weight of the ice. Our orchard was littered with broken limbs but, worst of all, we lost electrical power for a week. Joan and I "toughed-it-out" while most of our neighbors did not. They left their homes and moved in with family or friends that did have electric power. We kept a fire going in our wood burning fireplace night and day, as this was the only source of heat in the house. A bed was moved directly in front of the fireplace and Joan bunched all her houseplants and flowers around the bed so they would

survive. It was like sleeping in the middle of a garden.

Since we had our own well we had no water in the house, as the pump couldn't function without power. We flushed the toilets using water dipped from the swimming pool, and bottled water for drinking and brushing our teeth. It was a terrible week and we were especially grateful when friends who did have electric power invited us for breakfast or dinner or allowed us to use their facilities for a much needed shower. I suppose we could have left our home and gone somewhere else but, with the horses (Star and Chester), a dog (Monty), two cats (Frick and Frack), and all of Joan's flowers and plants to take care of, we were reluctant to do so.

Michigan Apples Become a Client

On April 6, Bob Klepinger and I went to Grand Rapids to make a presentation to the Michigan Apple Committee. The Michigan Apple Committee is made up of seven apple growers who are appointed by the Governor for three-year terms and the organization functions under a public act. Consequently, every five years it must open bidding on its advertising account. A significant number of agencies had submitted their credentials in 1976 and ten were selected to make formal presentations. Each finalist had one hour to make its "pitch." This was followed by a half-hour question and answer period. Presentations were scheduled for Tuesday through Thursday and on Friday the Michigan Apple Committee would meet to make a decision. On April 9 we were notified that we had been selected!

Michigan apple growers are indebted to the gigantic glaciers of the last ice age, some 10,000 years ago. These glaciers, in their retreat, scooped out the Great Lakes and thousands of smaller lakes to create near idyllic growing conditions for flavorful apples.

Apple trees need a cold winter dormant period and Michigan gets plenty of cold winter weather. But come spring, apple blossoms need protection against late frosts and the lakes help by tempering the cold winds. In the fall, the lakes protect the apple crop by postponing early freezes, permitting late varieties to mature to crisp perfection in the lazy autumn sun.

Michigan usually ranks second behind the state of Washington in apple production. Once in a while, New York sneaks in second. An ideal season occurs when there is virtually no spring frost damage. This requires warm, moist growing conditions through the late spring and summer followed by cool nights early in the fall to add color and high sugar levels. This yields apples that are juicy, pleasing to the eye and especially flavorful. Michigan produces between 25,000,000 and 30,000,000 bushels of apples each year and the advertising budget is based on assessments that the growers pay, depending on whether the apples are sold fresh, or for processing or for juice.

The fact that I was an apple grower, albeit a small one, paying apple assessments each year, and had a firsthand knowledge of apple production was, undoubtedly, a significant factor in our winning this account.

Our creative department was especially excited about our new client. They had the opportunity of doing some unusual and exciting creative work on everything from point-of-sale to trade and consumer advertising in various media. We would win a great many creative awards year after year for the work that we did for Michigan Apples.

The Hectic Summer of '76

In the hectic summer of 1976, the celebration of the 100th Anniversary of Sanders was underway; Standard Federal introduced a new check-a-month savings account; Microdot was involved in a tender offer which generated a great amount of work for the agency; First Federal of Hollywood – through its Hollyfed Subsidiary – was building and selling homes in

several developments with great success; Allentown Cement was merged with Huron Cement and we were handling an ever increasing workload from every client.

On top of all this client activity, we won another new account – the Vocal Interface Division of the Federal Screw Works which was located in Troy, Michigan. This company produced devices to aid the blind. Thus, the marketing of these products was especially challenging. A few years later, the name of the company was changed to Votrax and they pioneered phoneme-based speech synthesis. They packed their expertise into a tiny silicon chip that toy, game, calculator and other manufacturers could incorporate into a variety of talking products.

We were called on to create and place advertisements and to prepare advance publicity materials for this silicon chip. Announcement of the new chip was timed to coincide with the huge four-day CES trade show held at McCormick Place in Chicago, where Votrax demonstrated the unique features of the new chip to potential OEM buyers, as well as to fascinated members of the electronics industry and to the business press.

The recession of the past two years was definitely over.

Our social life was just as busy as the business side of our life. My mother spent the summer with us and a number of her new friends from Arizona came to visit – some for as long as 3 or 4 days. My father-in-law, who was now a widower, spent most weekends with us and he enjoyed riding our tractor to cut the grass in the orchard, an all day job. He was a terrific help, as was my mother – it seemed like the washer and dryer never stopped running with all the bedding that had to be changed after various guests departed. We had a big picnic on the 4th of July to celebrate the 200th birthday of the Nation and on Labor Day we hosted a picnic for the staff of the agency and their families. I joined the Clarkston Rotary Club and, through this affiliation, made many new friends in the area. Tom Rademaker, the Chevrolet Dealer in Clarkston, invited me to join this Rotary Club. Tom was president of the North Oakland Chevrolet Dealers Association, one of our clients. Rotary met every Monday evening for dinner at the Deer Lake Racquet Club in Clarkston and the meals were exceptional. From August 11 through Saturday, August 14 , I was in California for meetings and to participate in the annual deep sea fishing trip, during which I caught eight big albacore tuna.

The summer flew by with every day packed with activity and then we had to shift gears in mid-September to get ready for the fall apple harvest season. We had our best crop yet that fall and lots of friends, clients and relatives came out to pick apples and to raid the pumpkin patch.

Early in October 1976, our creative director, Keith Schoen, resigned from the agency. He was replaced by Alan Marshall. We also hired a new receptionist by the name of Kathryn (Kit) King. She would not remain a receptionist for long. Kit's career in communications began in the area of public relations and event marketing in St. Paul, Minnesota. The clients of her company, Kathryn King Associates, included health care organizations, a state-wide gourmet grocery chain and other regional retail outlets.

Kathryn "Kit" King

Kit's husband Bob had been transferred back to the Detroit area where they had lived prior to moving to Minnesota. With their children in school, Kit wanted to get back into the business world.

Her talents were immediately recognized and she quickly moved into account management. She made herself a very valued member of the staff and later was elected president of the agency and chief operations officer. Kit also became a member of the agency's new business team and her efforts helped the agency acquire such clients as the Michigan Department of Transportation, Michigan Department of Commerce, Hardee's Restaurants, Olga's and Century 21 Great Lakes Region.

We dropped our membership in the National Advertising Agency Network – which had evolved into a network of mostly small agencies (under $5,000,000 in billings) – to join the Advertising Marketing International Network (AMIN) which was comprised of mid-sized agencies with billings of $25,000,000 or more. We also applied for membership in the AAAA's, the American Association of Advertising Agencies, something we should have done much sooner. We were accepted for membership in both AMIN and the AAAA's early in 1977.

On October 20, 1976 I Hit the Big Five-O.

It was hard to believe, but I was now half a century old. The staff used the occasion to play an April Fool's joke on me in October. I left home a little later than usual that particular October morning because I had phone calls from my sons and my mother wishing me a Happy 50th Birthday. I drove to Birmingham and parked in the deck, then walked up Pierce Street to the office. There was a back door to the agency's office on Pierce Street and, when I passed this rear door, I saw a big sign in the window that read "Closed Today For Ernie Baker's 50th Birthday." I found this somewhat amusing but when I arrived at the main entrance on Maple this same sign was in the window and the front door was locked. I unlocked the door, walked up the stairs and into the lobby and there was no one there. I looked around the office and couldn't find anybody. I thought to myself "Well, I'll be damned they must have really closed the office."

I went to my office and sat behind my desk for a while wondering what I should do – stay there or go home? While I was trying to make up my mind I thought I heard something so I again made a round of the office but found no one.

We had expanded our offices, taking over the second floor of the adjoining building, and an entrance had been cut through to that office space which was reached by going through a fire door.

I hadn't checked that area but now decided to go over there to see if there was anybody in those offices? What I found was the entire staff packed into one corner office waiting to yell "Surprise" and "Happy Birthday." After sharing some cake the "closed" signs were removed and it was back to business.

The Michigan Horticultural Society annually holds a three day conference and exposition at the convention center in Grand Rapids. One night is designated as Michigan Apple Night and the Michigan Apple Committee hosts a reception and then presents its marketing program for that crop year. Joan and I attended and I participated in the meeting with a slide presentation showing all the advertising and printed materials that we had prepared for our client.

We stayed at the Pantlind Hotel, which is an exceptional facility. This was the first of many such meetings, as we represented the Michigan Apple Committee for the next 16 years.

1976 was a good year from every standpoint and it was a great relief to become a profit-making business again.

– 1977 –
We Become Baker, Abbs, & Klepinger, Inc.

The year was launched by changing the name of the agency to Baker, Abbs & Klepinger, Inc. to recognize the contributions of Jerry Abbs and Bob Klepinger to the firm.

January 1977 was an unusually cold month with a number of days below 0°. It was terribly cold – 40° to 45° below zero when factoring in the wind chill. I went to California for several days in January for meetings and then attended the SIMSA (Savings Institutions Marketing Society of America) meeting in San Diego from February 20-24. When this meeting ended, I went to Los Angeles for several days of meetings with our client, First Federal of Hollywood and its subsidiary, Hollyfed, which was now a separate account. I also attended a meeting at Squirt's national headquarters. All of this helped me avoid some of the bitter cold Michigan winter.

In the spring, on June 18, son Bob married Jane Kaser and they decided to have the wedding reception in our barn. They cleared and cleaned the barn loft and had plenty of room for the wedding party and guests and even an area for dancing. The caterer didn't exactly enjoy hauling everything needed for a wedding feast up a flight of stairs to the loft but it turned out to be a great party. The only casualty was one guest who fell off one of our horses, which he insisted he knew how to ride. Fortunately he didn't break any bones.

In July my father-in-law Ed Bauman bought 13.8 acres of property near us in the Ortonville area and built a chalet style home on a rise in the land between two lakes – a beautiful setting for a home, among huge oaks. This property had once been part of a large parcel of land owned by the Purple Gang, a notorious prohibition era gang from the 1920s and early 1930s in Detroit. They smuggled choice Canadian whiskey from Canada and controlled many Detroit area speakeasies, and for years the

Purple Gang was the major whiskey supplier for Al Capone and his Chicago criminal empire. Taxes had not been paid on this Ortonville area property for many years and, at the end of World War II, Elaine and Robert Kerley purchased the land at a tax sale.

When the Purple Gang owned the land it was known as "The Wildwood." Located on the property was a big house with many bedrooms. It was used for gambling and prostitution and patrons could hide their cars in one of three large barns in back of the big house. The Kerleys removed two wings of the home, tore down the barns and planted thousands of trees from the late 1940s until they sold off all the property in 1977 and 1978. They divided the acreage into various size parcels. My father-in-law acquired a prize site and our son Bob and his wife Jane bought 25 acres of property adjoining my father-in-law's – Bob's grandfather. Jane and Bob then built a log house in the middle of their property on a hill side surrounded by large white pines and red pines. That is where they've made their home and raised their children, Matt and Emily – my oldest grandson and only granddaughter.

It's Off To Hawaii

In late September, Joan accompanied me to California, where I had several days of meetings. We then flew to Hawaii, where I attended some sessions of the California Savings and Loan League meetings. Following this meeting, Joan and I stayed in Honolulu for a week's vacation, which my wife often said was the most enjoyable one that we ever had. We spent most of our time walking Waikiki beach or just enjoying the sea and watching people. One night we went to The Third Floor Restaurant for dinner and were seated at a table next to a large party of celebrities including Burt Reynolds, Sally Field, Dom Deluise and Jim Nabors.

Meanwhile, Back In Michigan

The Sanders account was causing us great concern because we knew Sanders was in serious financial trouble. We decided to resign the Sanders account and then try to reclaim the Awrey's Bakeries account.

We resigned the Sanders account October 14. On October 25, Abbs and I met with Jerry McClellan and Bob and Tom Awrey. Jerry was then the president of Awrey's and Bob was the chairman of the board. A few days later, we were informed that they had decided to reassign their account to us – a decision which I have always admired and respected considering the circumstances.

A Tragic Death

Mike Fury, the marketing director of Standard Federal Savings, died of a heart attack on December 1. He was 38 years old! I had met with Mike only three days prior to get his approval of all the elements we had prepared for a Preferred Mortgage Program. Standard Federal opened a new branch office in Farmington Hills on December 2 and I attended the ribbon cutting ceremony. There was not the same excitement associated with opening a new office, as everyone with Standard Federal was shocked and saddened at Mike's sudden passing.

On December 9, Bill Yaw was named the new marketing director of Standard Federal. It would be hard to find a better person to work with than him. Standard Federal was to experience tremendous expansion in the years ahead as it converted from a savings and loan to a mutual savings bank, changed its name to Standard Federal Bank and then became publicly owned, with its stock listed on the New York Stock Exchange.

Through all this, there came to be more reliance on us for communications assistance, necessitating a close personal working relationship with the entire marketing department. We became real marketing partners, and that is what makes the agency business truly rewarding.

– 1978 –

We had a double celebration at the office on January 6, to acknowledge the fourteenth year that the agency had been in business as well as the anniversary of the change of the company's name to Baker, Abbs & Klepinger, Inc.

The next week Bob Klepinger and I were in Philadelphia to make a presentation to the Pontiac Dealers of the Delaware Valley, which included the Pontiac dealers in eastern Pennsylvania and all of Delaware. Steve Kulcher, who was the Pontiac zone manager for this dealer group, had invited us to make a presentation. Steve's mother-in-law, Bernice Moore, was a very feisty, elderly widow who lived down the road from our home in Ortonville and was one of the first neighbors we met when we moved to the country in 1973.

Steve and his wife were frequently at Bernice's home either for visits or for Steve to attend meetings at the nearby Pontiac Motors headquarters. Steve had become aware of the advertising we were creating for the Chevrolet Dealers in North Oakland County, which was significantly better than what his dealer group was getting from its agency. The Pontiac Dealers of the Delaware Valley liked our presentation and hired us to handle their advertising.

The dealers called themselves the "Pontiac Giants of the Delaware Valley" and made it immediately clear that they had no intention of changing the name. With this "given," we created a Pontiac Giant. Our giant was a warm, friendly, good giant who stomped out high prices for Pontiac cars, looked out for widows and children and did only good deeds. We created outstanding radio commercials in addition to newspaper and billboard ads. We raised the awareness of the Pontiac Dealers to a much higher level.

The week after Bob Klepinger and I were in Philadelphia, I went to Los Angeles for several days of meetings with our client, First Federal of Hollywood. It was enjoying strong, steady growth adding offices and expanding into other financial services for its customers. We were now servicing clients on both the east and west coast with the addition of the Pontiac Giants of the Delaware Valley advertising account.

In early February Joan and I went to Phoenix for the SIMSA meeting at the Regency Hotel in Scottsdale. Carol and Bill Yaw from Standard Federal; Dick Morford from Family Federal; and Lynn and Joe Baker and Bill Anderson from First Federal were also present for this conference. Joan and I stayed over several days to visit my mother in Sun City, then Joan flew back to Detroit, while I returned to California for more planning meetings with our client and several of its subsidiaries, which were also needing more and more advertising and promotional assistance.

"Your Horses Are In Our Backyard"

In mid-March of 1978 we had an unusually heavy snowfall. One snowy night around 4 a.m. the phone rang. Keith Wandell, a neighbor down our road, called to inform me that our horses were in his backyard. I got up, put on heavy clothes, pulled on my boots and got two lead lines out of the garage for the horses. There was at least six inches of new snow on the ground and I trudged through it, walking down the road to Keith and Dolores Wandell's home to round up our horses. When I reached the back of the Wandell's house I looked at the horses and immediately realized they were not our horses. I returned to our property and walked back to the field where the horses were kept and there – standing in their shelter, heads down, out of the falling snow – were Chester and Star.

I vowed then that, as soon as the weather improved, the horses were going to be sold. The first four years Star and Chester had been ridden a lot but the past three years they had seldom been saddled. Bob was married and no longer interested in the horses and Mike was attending the University of Detroit Dental School.

Just as soon as the snow melted I put an ad in the classified section of the Ortonville Reminder newspaper offering the two horses for sale at $300 each. We had bought the horses for $1,000 each but I figured that horses were like used cars – the older they were the less you could sell them for. WRONG! The first week the ad ran I didn't receive a single call. I repeated the ad and I received one call and it was from a man asking "What's wrong with your horses?" I explained nothing was wrong, they were just getting old and I figured they were worth about $300 each. The caller explained that I'd never sell the horses for $300 each because I could take them to Fenton, a town nearby, where they'd fetch $600 to $800 each based on their weight for processing into dog food. I didn't really want to turn Star and Chester into dog food, so I ran the advertisement again raising the price to $700 each and sold them immediately. The saddles, bridles and all the other equipment we had accumulated were sold separately, so I was delighted with the unexpected way the sale of the horses turned out, but most of all I was just plain relieved not to have to care for horses anymore. I had "mucked out" the horse stalls enough to last me a lifetime. The sale of the horses marked the end of a very interesting chapter in our lives.

In the spring of 1978 both Standard Federal and Family Federal initiated major premium promotions. Premium promotions had become a very effective way for savings and loans to attract large sums of money, both in new accounts as well as for additions to existing savings accounts. The premiums were purchased from companies that specialized in providing brand name merchandise for promotions of this type and there were numerous details involved, not the least of which were the federal regulations relating to the use of premiums.

My last ride on old Chester – as this picture was taken the day he was sold. Our other horse, Star, had already left with his new owners. Owning and caring for horses was quite an experience. In selling them, I learned that the old saying "A horse's value depends on its age" no longer applied.

In May, in the midst of these campaigns, the Federal Home Loan Bank authorized a change in the rate of interest that could be paid on savings accounts. This made it necessary to revise all the materials created for the premium promotion which Standard Federal and Family Federal had underway.

In July, we won the account of the Besser Manufacturing Company, which was located in Alpena, Michigan.

On August 1, Bob Johnson became the agency's creative director. We had committed a lot of time and effort to fill this position. We recruited Bob from Toledo, where he was a partner in the Carr/Johnson Advertising Agency.

One of Johnson's first tasks was to write five 30-second television commercials for Family Federal. The commercials were for various products and Dave Diles was our client's spokesperson. Dave was a well-known sports announcer in Michigan who also had authored several books. We shot TV spots in five different locations including Saginaw, Frankenmuth and Owosso. The commercial produced in Owosso was particularly interesting, as it was shot in front of the Curwood Castle. Owosso was home to James Oliver Curwood, author of many adventure novels. His home was built in the style of a miniature castle. Several of his books were made into movies, the most famous of which was "Back to God's Country," a thrilling story of the far north published in 1920. His unique home, which is where he wrote his novels, is now a museum. We were successful in getting permission to use the Curwood Castle for the background of a home loan commercial which was part of this new series of TV spots. It would have been a very expensive set to build for such a commercial but we were allowed to use the Curwood Castle free of charge.

I returned to California again on August 15 for meetings at First Federal of Hollywood. This was followed by our annual two-day fishing trip. On Friday morning we caught more than 30 large albacore and then relaxed most of the day, enjoying being out on the Pacific Ocean. We encountered several schools of whales and, Friday evening, anchored near some picturesque islands off the coast of Mexico. The weather was perfect and we enjoyed excellent fishing and great meals. The ship was captained by Dick Highfill whose wife, Mary, prepared all the meals. We caught more than 20 different kinds of fish in addition to albacore, including yellowfin tuna, rock bass, barracuda, mackerel and blowfish. I returned home with a styrofoam chest full of albacore fillets packed in dry ice, as well as several cases of canned tuna.

In September, the agency was invited to make a presentation to the Diamond Crystal Salt Company in St. Clair, Michigan but we did not win this account. The latter part of September, I was back in Los Angeles again for meetings and while there, attended some of the sessions of the California Savings and Loan League at the Hotel Del Coronado in San Diego. I was becoming very familiar with Southern California.

A Bumper Apple Crop

The apple growers of Michigan, including Baker's Orchard in Ortonville, had a bumper crop in 1978. My wife Joan experimented with every apple recipe in her cookbooks.

Baker, Abbs & Klepinger, Inc. ended 1978 with a good profit in spite of the fact that there was deepening recession and increasing unemployment. The prime rate hit 10-3/4% in November and regular gas cost over $1.00 a gallon. 1978 was a year of riots, mass demonstrations and political and social unrest throughout the world. Chrysler Corporation was broke and the outlook for 1979 was not very bright. In spite of all this, the agency was prospering.

– 1979 –
Service Is What It's All About

The very heart of the advertising business is SERVICE. Everything that an advertising agency provides its clients centers on this single concept. Account supervisors and account executives are in the front line, meeting frequently with clients to direct all the efforts on their behalf, but behind them are specialists in particular areas of the business. This includes market researchers and planners, traffic and production managers, media planners and buyers, legal and accounting personnel and that truly critical area of the business – the writers and artists who serve in the creative department. When clients change agencies they often state that they are doing so because of dissatisfaction with the creative work – or for philosophical reasons – but when you look below the surface, the real reason most often is due to a lack of service. The level of service must meet the clients' expectations. Research has confirmed this. Two descriptions of service that I have found to be particularly appropriate are:

"Service when present is taken for granted – when absent – breeds hostility!"

Another good description written by Leon Gorman is as follows:

"Service is just a day-in, day-out, ongoing, never-ending, unrelenting, persevering, compassionate type of activity."

The first six months of 1979 we rededicated our efforts to our clients and did not solicit any new business. Actually, all of our clients were quite active and we had a heavy load of assignments, primarily from Standard Federal, Family Federal, First Federal of Hollywood, Michigan Apples, Detroit Tigers, Sheller-Globe, Better Made Potato Chips, The Cement Divisions, Interstate Alarm, Microdot, our three Stanley Divisions and Awrey Bakeries, plus the more than twenty other clients that we served.

I participated in monthly planning meetings in Los Angeles with our client, First Federal of Hollywood, meeting with Dave Freeman, who had replaced Bill Anderson as the marketing director. In February it was back to New Orleans for five days for the SIMSA conference, which our three S&L clients also attended. On May 1, SIMSA held a one-day conference in Chicago just for advertising agencies in which I participated, making a presentation of the work we were doing for our three S&L clients.

In June, Bob Klepinger and I met several times with Bob Cunningham who was the president of the Smith-Winchester advertising agency. Bob had married B Tornow who was the head of our financial department. Prior to joining Baker, Abbs & Klepinger, B was employed by Smith-Winchester and had worked with Cunningham at that agency. Several years later, both had divorced their spouses and eventually started dating, which led to their marriage. It took a lot of serious discussion

but Bob Klepinger and I were able to convince Bob Cunningham that he should join our agency. On June 7, Bob decided to sell his stock in Smith-Winchester back to the agency and join Baker, Abbs & Klepinger, Inc.

Bob Cunningham

After Bob Cunningham joined the agency, we then contacted the accounts he had handled at his former agency. Most of them moved their advertising to Baker, Abbs, Cunningham & Klepinger, Inc. (BAC&K), as the name of the agency was changed when Cunningham came on board. De-Sta-Co, (a division of Dover Corporation), Huron Office Products, Port Huron Paper Company and Palmer-Shile Company were the accounts that followed Bob.

Joan Turns 50

On June 13, Joan turned 50 and the occasion was celebrated with a surprise birthday party at our home that more than a hundred friends and relatives attended. The best surprise of all, though, was that Joan and I would become grandparents – Jane, Bob's wife, announced she was pregnant. Our first grandson, Matthew, was born December 13, 1979.

You Belong In Birmingham

In August, the Birmingham Merchants Association, consisting of more than 250 retailers, hired the agency to create advertising to help bring business into the downtown shopping area. Bob Johnson devised a series of entertaining radio commercials based on bringing parts of your anatomy to Birmingham. For instance, you should bring your head to Birmingham for hair styling, a wig or a hat, etc.; your mouth for lipstick, lunch or dinner at one of a variety of restaurants or to see a dentist; your ears for earrings, recorded music or a theater show; your feet for shoes, a pedicure or dance lessons, and so on for noses, hands and legs. It was a successful campaign, but ran its course after a few years because a few of the non-contributing merchants tried to ride on the coattails of the many stores that did contribute. There was no way to force every merchant to participate and the non-contributors were responsible for the effort's eventual end.

Hal Retires and Dan Replaces Him

Hal Middlesworth, public relations director of the Detroit Tigers, retired in December and Dan Ewald replaced him. Dan had big shoes to fill but did so and in time earned the same kind of respect that the media had for Hal. Dan learned well from Hal. He was just as buttoned up and organized as Hal was when it came to turning over to the agency all the information needed to create and produce the Tigers' advertising.

One of the last projects that I handled for Hal turned out to be quite interesting, primarily because of another individual who also became involved. In the fall of 1978, Hal provided me with all the information and photos needed to prepare and produce the season ticket mailer for the 1979 season. One of the photos was a crowd shot in which everyone was seated except for one individual who was standing holding a large, homemade sign reading "GO TIGERS." Hal wanted to use this particular photo for the cover of the mailer. When I asked if there were photo releases for the people in the photo Hal said, "No, but don't worry about it." I cautioned that he was taking a chance in using this photo but he said if there ever was a problem they'd handle it. The folder was produced and distributed early in 1979 and several months later I got a call from Hal during which he asked, "Do you remember the guy holding the sign in the photo we used for the cover of the season ticket mailer?" I said, "Yes, what about him?" "Well, he's sitting in my office and wants to be paid for the use of his picture. What should I offer?"

I thought for a few seconds and suggested that Hal offer him a season ticket. If he accepted, be sure to get him to sign a photo release. Joe Diroff – the man in the picture – was absolutely delighted to get a free season ticket. Joe then proceeded to make himself the self-proclaimed, resident cheerleader at every Tiger game. He was a real character, usually with Tiger pins and baseball items adorning his hat and clothes. He soon became known as "The Brow" because of his heavy, extra bushy eyebrows. "The Brow" roamed the stands at will imploring the crowd to get behind the home team. "Let's Go Bananas!," he'd scream waving a plastic banana. With the Tigers ahead, he would wave squeeze bottles of ketchup and mustard in the air and shout, "They'll never ketch up – cuz they can't cut the mustard!" When the mood struck him he'd break into a wild rubber-legged jig and his unabashed antics as a cheerleader entertained the crowd. Joe became a fixture at Tiger games and later at Pistons, Red Wings and Lions games, but his involvement with Detroit's sports teams began with the use of his photo on the cover of a Detroit Tigers' season ticket folder. Joe died in January 1997. At the Tigers home opener on April 7, 1997 – 42,749 fans stood for a moment of silence in memory of Joe Diroff.

Joe Diroff – Also Known as "The Brow"

An Exciting End To 1979 and To the '70s

Standard Federal carried out another major premium promotion in December and opened its forty-ninth office in Madison Heights, Michigan.

Fortunately, 1979 was another good year for the agency, with increased billings and an even better profit than the year before

The '70s – What a Decade!!

In the 1972 Presidential election, Richard Nixon defeated George McGovern, but the tactics he used in his political campaign culminated in the Watergate scandal and his resignation from office in August 1974. The Vietnam stalemate, which had cost 50,000 casualties, was brought to a close by our ignominious early withdrawal early in the decade. The national mood was one of bickering and back-biting as confidence in the government and the military reached an all-time low.

Concerted efforts by consumer groups finally forced cigarette makers off television and radio. The cigarette companies took their hundreds of advertising millions and increased advertising in newspapers, magazines, outdoor, special sports events sponsorships, sampling, etc. Their sales increased every year.

Television was supposed to kill radio, but it just didn't work out that way. Advertising volume on radio reached the $2.5 billion level and radio sets in use exceeded 325 million. FM grew prodigiously.

A new wrinkle developed in media buying. It was called media buying services, working both with agencies and with clients directly. In the middle of the decade, their volume exceeded $100 million, their appeal based on cut rates and economies of so-called "bulk buying." But, as the decade drew to a close, many of them went out of business.

The gasoline shortage, which started with OPEC's sharply increased prices in 1973, had an enormous impact on all segments of the economy, especially the automotive industry and its more than 100,000 suppliers. General Motors, Ford, Chrysler and American Motors shifted as quickly as they could to the production of smaller cars. But the German and Japanese manufacturers already had a firm foothold in the U.S. market, which they increased each year until they had a 20% share.

In electronics, especially television and radio sets and TV video cassette recorders, the Japanese practically swept U.S. manufacturers from the marketplace.

Because of concern for the environment, air and water pollution finally became a matter of national and government action. The Environmental Protection Agency, with strong enforcement powers, was established. Here are a few highlights for the decade of the '70s:

- Coca-Cola and General Foods were both spending $200 million annually for advertising.

- "Light" was the magic word in beer; "diet" was the secret of soft drink sales.

- Fast foods, led by McDonald's with 5,000 outlets, grew at a geometric rate, especially in the larger cities.

- With increased use of jumbo jets, such as the 747, DC-10, L-1011, the airlines became very aggressive advertisers and tourism increased.

- Wine consumption in the U.S. became a national drinking habit as the California and New York vineyards stepped up production and promotion.

It was a decade of growth and conglomeration. Total advertising was at the $40 billion level at the end of the decade. The advertising agencies billed about $15 billion, with the top advertisers accounting for almost $9 billion. It was big business and getting bigger every day with agency mergers and acquisitions.

These are the people who would guide the agency through the next decade. We were backed by a staff of more than 30 very talented advertising professionals. Consequently, BAC&K would enjoy exceptional growth and financial success in the 1980s.

With me, left to right: Jerry Abbs, chairman of the board; Bob Cunningham, executive vice president; B Cunningham, treasurer and vice president of finance; and Bob Klepinger, president. I was then chairman of the executive committee.

Chapter 7

The Eventful '80s – 1980 Through 1984

*"Do something. Either lead, follow, or
get out of the way!"*

Merger discussions between our client, First Federal of Hollywood and Santa Fe Federal, initiated during 1979, had become very serious by early 1980. Santa Fe Federal was headquartered in San Bernadino and plans for the merger had progressed to the point where Costa Mesa in Orange County had been selected as the future site for the home office once the merger was finalized. Costa Mesa was agreed upon for the location of the main office for a number of reasons but it also represented a site that was nearly equal distance between Hollywood and San Bernadino. Once the merger was completed, the name of the new financial institution would then become Pacific Savings Bank as the directors had decided to convert from a savings and loan to a savings bank charter as part of the merger process.

Dave Freeman, the new marketing director for First Federal of Hollywood, and I met for two days in mid-January in Hollywood. I returned two weeks later in early February for additional meetings to help plan the 1980 advertising program of First Federal of Hollywood.

The annual SIMSA meeting was at the Fontainebleau Hotel in Miami, Florida from February 18 through February 22 and Dave Freeman attended, along with Mark Letter and Ron Warren from our California client. Carol and Bill Yaw (Standard Federal) and Dick Morford (Family Federal) were present, as well as Kit and Bob King and Joan and I.

During the meeting, Freeman came very close to being killed in a bizarre way when the entire ceiling, along with some of the floor and furniture in the room above his, collapsed into his hotel room. Water had been left running in the bathtub in the room above his and had overflowed the tub. The weight of the water eventually became so great that the floor and its contents fell into the room below. Fortunately Dave was off to the side of his room talking on the phone when the crash occurred. The hotel management apologized and moved Dave to their Presidential suite.

Some personnel changes took place in the spring of the year. Karen Aaberg, the associate creative director, replaced Bob Johnson as our creative director. Cheryl Collins and Andrea Langlais became the two key people in our media department. Bob Ross had left to join an agency in Baltimore, Maryland.

The Metropolitan Detroit Buick Dealers Association held an advertising agency review in which we participated. We did not win the account but a few months later the Michigan Dental Association selected BAC&K to handle its advertising.

The big highlight that spring occurred on Saturday, June 21, when our son Mike, now Michael Baker, D.D.S., married Kathleen Papi. The wedding reception was held in our apple orchard under a huge tent. The big surprise, though, came at midnight when a helicopter suddenly appeared and landed next to our barn. Kathy and Mike jumped into the helicopter and left for their honeymoon in California. They had told no one that they had arranged to depart in such a dramatic way. When the helicopter took off, all of us still present at the wedding reception watched them disappear from sight as they headed for Metropolitan Airport.

NOW Accounts Introduced

During June and July we were quite busy preparing advertising programs for Standard Federal, Family Federal and First Federal of Hollywood to announce the new NOW accounts. This advertising was launched in August.

At Stanley – Vemco (soon to be renamed Stanley Home Automation), Dan Meyvis and Dave Demorotski were flooding us with assignments, including package designs for their various models of do-it-yourself garage door openers and for other products such as home thermostats.

In October, Standard Federal acquired First Federal of Niles and Kit King was elected a vice president of Baker, Abbs, Cunningham & Klepinger, Inc. Kit was now managing the Standard Federal account, working with Bill Yaw and the bank's marketing department.

On November 29, the Adcraft Club of Detroit celebrated its 75th anniversary with a dinner at the Westin Hotel in downtown Detroit, which Joan and I attended. December 4 turned out to be a very hot day in the office as we had a fire in our basement storage area. Two of our employees – Laura Staats and Suzie Houseman – took the elevator to go investigate the source of all the smoke. The elevator stopped halfway to the basement and they was overcome by the smoke and had to be pulled through the top of the elevator by firemen to save their lives. It was a close call. The fire was confined to the basement storage area but the cleanup was a nightmare.

Joan and I attended the Michigan Horticulture Society annual meeting in Grand Rapids from December 7-8 and Fred Hasler, executive secretary of the Michigan Apple Committee, announced his retirement. His replacement, Mark Arney, was introduced to all the Apple Growers attending the annual conference. This was the beginning of a new special relationship, as Mark, his wife Marla and daughters Molly and Mindy, soon became close personal friends.

During 1980 the troubled Carter presidency gave way to the Republican challenger and the beginning of what became known as the "Reagan Revolution" in Washington. John Lennon, one of the Beatles, was killed on a New York street corner. "Who Shot J.R.?," a November episode of the CBS hit show "Dallas," revealed the identity of the attacker of J.R. Ewing (played by Larry Hagman) and broke records by drawing a 53.3 rating and 76 share of the TV audience. Young & Rubicam knocked J. Walter Thompson out of the top spot as the largest advertising agency when they reported a worldwide gross income of $340.8 million for 1980. While BAC&K, Inc. didn't come anywhere close to this record we did have a very good year and made a very respectable profit.

– 1981 –

In mid-January, I spent two days in California for meetings with our client First Federal of Hollywood. I also met with the Cochrane Chase, Livingston & Company Advertising Agency in Costa Mesa, as they were the agency for Santa Fe Federal and also happened to be a member of AMIN – the same network of advertising agencies to which BAC&K belonged. The big question, of course, was "Which agency would end up with the Pacific Savings Bank account when the merger was completed?" I visited and toured Cochrane Chase's offices, met its staff and spent time with Phil Salvati and Pat Anderson, who were assigned to the Santa Fe account. Cochrane Chase, Livingston & Company, I had to admit, was a very impressive shop.

On January 19 Mark Arney and I met for the first time in a business capacity and we reviewed the past advertising, promotion, public relations and research activities conducted for Michigan Flavorbest apples and the plans for the balance of the season to help move apples harvested in the fall of 1980 that were in storage. Apples are available to us year round because of CA (Controlled Atmosphere) storage. In Michigan about half the crop is sold during the fall season and the balance goes into storage to be sold in the late winter, spring and summer months before the next crop is ready for harvesting. In CA storage the apples are put in huge rooms with controlled atmosphere where the apples essentially "sleep" and maintain the same crispness and flavor as when they were first picked and went into storage.

Oakland County Parks & Recreation Commission Appoints BAC&K, Inc. To Promote Family Fun

We bid on and won a FUN account which got us involved in event marketing and a wide variety of promotional activities. Our job was to encourage the use of the various Oakland County Parks offering hiking, picnicking, golfing, water sports, camping and various kinds of recreational activities. Like all governmental contracts, an RFP (Request For Proposal) had been issued by Oakland County in the fall of 1980. We responded to the RFP and, fortunately, our proposal and fee were acceptable. This was the beginning of a long relationship that was pleasant and rewarding because we worked with exceptionally nice people, notably Ralph Richard and Jan Pung. The goal of all our efforts was to enhance the quality and enjoyment of life for families in Southeastern Michigan.

The Year's Biggest News Story

Ronald Reagan assumed office as the President of the United States on January 20 and, simultaneously, Iran released 52 American hostages they had been holding for 14 months. The negotiations had been going on for months with the Carter Administration but the timing was such that most of the credit went to President Reagan. This type of historical event puts advertising and all business activities into proper perspective.

A Terrible Fire In Las Vegas

On February 9, my wife Joan and I went to Las Vegas to attend the SIMSA meeting, which was scheduled to take place February 10-13 at the Las Vegas Hilton Hotel and Convention Center.

The meetings got underway Tuesday morning and that evening a group of us went to dinner. When we finished, we went to the front of the hotel to take taxis back to the Hilton. We were in for a shock – the place was an inferno! Flames billowed out of a large window on the eighth floor, where the fire had been deliberately set, and roared skyward, cracking glass in the upper floors and setting rooms there afire. The noise and confusion was terrifying. Helicopters were taking off from the lawn in front of the hotel to pick up people on the roof and deliver them to the ground. Altogether there were more than 100 people that were saved this way. Others were less fortunate. Some fell to their death trying to escape by climbing down sheets tied together that were lowered from their room windows, or were overcome by the smoke and fumes. Eight people died and more

The Hilton Hotel in Las Vegas when it was on fire.

than 100 others were seriously injured. Damage exceeded $20 million with only 1900 of the 2783 rooms in the hotel escaping damage. Philip Cline, a busboy, admitted starting the fire. He was tried, found guilty of the terrible crime he committed and is serving a life sentence with no chance of parole.

The Red Cross arrived bringing truck loads of cots and blankets, as well as bags containing toilet articles, a tooth brush and paste, soap, disposable razor, etc. At about 3 a.m., Joan and I decided to go to the Sands Hotel rather than stay overnight in the Convention Center.

The next morning we returned to the Hilton and became part of a large mob of people congregating in front of the hotel waiting to learn what was going to happen next? The SIMSA meeting was cancelled, as four of the people who died in the fire were there for our convention. In mid-afternoon, Joan and I were taken to our tenth floor room by a bellboy. Even though the carpeting, walls and ceiling of the hallway on our floor had burned, our room had not caught on fire. It was filled with smoke and all our clothes reeked of it as a result.

We packed our things and checked out. We then went to the Las Vegas Airport and flew to Phoenix to visit my mother for a few days. Since we had planned to be away for the week anyway, we were fortunate that this alternative was available to us. Peaceful, relaxing Sun City, Arizona was just what we needed after what we had experienced in Las Vegas.

Sanders Declares Bankruptcy

Soon after we returned to Michigan, a major news story stirred the community. The Fred Sanders Company had filed for protection under Chapter 11 of the Federal Bankruptcy Law. It had unsecured debts of more than $4 million owed to 734 creditors. Thank goodness our agency was not one of them. Even though our relationship had ended in 1977, it was truly sad to see this landmark company on its knees.

Various investors tried to rescue the company without success and Sanders eventually was acquired by Country Home Bakers, Inc. Fortunately, Sanders candy, ice cream flavors, a small variety of cakes and its famous ice cream toppings are still available in many Detroit area chain stores, in specialty food stores and by mail order.

An Important Meeting In California

It was back to California in mid-March for three days of meetings with Pacific Federal Savings. In early April, the merger with Santa Fe Savings, a San Bernadino-based savings and loan with 23 branch offices and assets of more than $700 million, was approved by the Federal Home Loan Bank. Vern Potter, president of Santa Fe, became president of the combined associations. Joe Baker, my brother, became chairman of the board and CEO. With combined assets of more than $1 billion, the merger made them one of the largest savings and loans in the country. Since they were both highly successful they were strengthened financially and able to offer a variety of new services through their 40 branch offices in San Bernadino, San Diego, Los Angeles and Orange County.

Speas Apple Juice Becomes a Client

In late April, Greg Holub and I went to Bear Lake, Michigan (near Traverse City) to meet with Jarvis Franzblau and Rick Bierndorf to solicit the Speas Apple Juice account. Greg had joined Baker, Abbs, Cunningham & Klepinger, Inc. January 12, 1981 as an account manager to spearhead our new business efforts. Greg, a very upbeat, enthusiastic individual, loved working on new business.

Jarvis Franzblau was the president and Rick Bierndorf the vice president and marketing director of the Speas Company, a division of Sawyer Fruit & Vegetable, the company that had

Greg Holub

acquired the Speas Apple Juice brand from Pillsbury. The main plant for processing Speas Apple Juice was in Fremont, Michigan, while the company headquarters was located in Bear Lake – where Sawyer Fruit and Vegetable owned thousands of acres of fruit trees.

While we were at the Bear Lake plant, as part of a tour, Rick drove Greg and me to the top of a high hill near Lake Michigan from which the company's orchards spread north and south almost endlessly over thousands of acres! On the way back to Detroit, Greg and I went to Fremont to tour the plant where the apple juice was processed. Speas Apple Juice was available in a wide variety of bottles and cans and even in paper cartons, the latter something very new at that time.

Aseptic packaging was an innovation developed in Europe in which apple juice, as well as other beverages including milk, is processed at a high temperature and put in paper boxes that do not need to be refrigerated. Speas was one of the first companies in the United States to introduce aseptic packaging of apple juice, and the small cartons with a straw attached quickly became very popular.

A few weeks later we were notified that Baker, Abbs, Cunningham & Klepinger, Inc.

would be the agency for Speas Apple Juice, effective immediately, and we were very excited to now have the responsibility for an account with national distribution and seeking further market penetration. Speas became a very heavy user of free standing inserts with coupon offers and, in 1986, hit the television airwaves using Soupy Sales, a nationally recognized television personality, very effectively in a series of 30-second commercials. He was a "natural" salesman for a natural product like apple juice.

On May 21 I attended a meeting of the SIMSA advertising agency committee at the U.S. League offices in downtown Chicago. I flew to Chicago that morning in plenty of time for a meeting which lasted from 10 a.m. until 1:30 p.m. I was back at Metro Airport in Detroit by 4 p.m. and in my office in Birmingham before 5 p.m. and did an hour of work before Joan arrived at my office. We then had dinner with several couples representing Stanley-Vemco and took them to see the Adcrafollies Show at the Detroit Institute of Arts Theatre. *There was a lot packed into that particular day.*

A Wonderful Trip To Germany

Joan's Dad, Ed Bauman, had talked to us for years about going to Germany. He didn't want to go there alone and he kept urging us to join him. We decided to make his dream come true and during June, July and early August we made our travel plans, got our passports, tickets and handled other arrangements. Lynn and Joe Baker also planned to be in Germany at the same time, as they were picking up a Mercedes they had ordered and would then drive it around Europe before having it shipped to California.

On August 22, we flew on Northwest Airlines from Detroit to Toronto, then transferred to Lufthansa for a flight to Frankfurt where we had a car reserved. Seated next to us on our flight from Toronto to Frankfurt was a very charming and interesting couple from Sao Paulo, Brazil – Heleana and Peter Kocher. They had been to the Mayo clinic in Minnesota for their annual physical exams and were now going to spend several months at their home in Bavaria near the village of Reit'im Winkle. The Kochers lived most of the year in Sao Paulo, where they had a sizable manufacturing business producing a variety of products made of plastic. They invited us to visit them and we decided to do so as our itinerary the second week would take us very close to where they lived.

Early Sunday morning we landed in Frankfurt and found that one of Joan's suitcases missed the flight. We decided to come back for it later rather than delay our travel plans, as we would be near Frankfurt again in three days. I checked out our reserved car from Avis, loaded our bags in the trunk and drove immediately onto the Autobahn. What an experience! It took me several days to feel comfortable driving on the Autobahn. Consequently, I stayed in the far right, slower lanes at first but, as my confidence improved, I ventured over into the faster lanes. There is no speed limit in Germany and it's exciting driving there.

Our first destination was Cologne, where we would also meet my brother Joe and his wife Lynn. Our travel agent had briefed me before we left and told me that the hotel we would stay in at Cologne was on the far northern outskirts of the city. As we drove through Cologne, Joan and her Dad kept telling me to stop and ask directions but I kept on driving until I was in the area where I believed the hotel would be located. I finally stopped at a service station, where I asked the attendant how to get to the Regent Hotel. He pointed at it across the street. Joan and Dad were amazed. After checking into the Regent Hotel, we rested for awhile and then drove downtown to see the Cologne Cathedral and more of the city.

The next morning, Joe and Lynn arrived and we joined them and some friends of theirs from California who were also visiting Cologne for breakfast. Then it was off to officially start our tour of Germany. We returned to downtown Cologne to spend the time needed to properly tour the magnificent 4000-year-old cathedral that towers over the city. Especially spectacular are the church's two spires that are 515 feet high. We then drove down the Mosel Valley, famous for its wines and ancient castles. Late in the day we arrived in Cochem, where we spent the night. Next day we visited the restored Castle Cochem as well as several wineries and made stops in a number of villages to eat or just look around. Late in the day we reached Wiesbaden and after dinner, Joe and I drove back to Frankfurt to retrieve Joan's suitcase at the airport. Lufthansa assigned a young man to take us to the area where the suitcase was being held and he rode a bike while Joe and I jogged. We went through huge rooms, some as big as a football field, before we finally arrived at the secured area where the bag was held. We signed all kinds of release forms and made our way back – with great difficulty – to the Central Hotel in Wiesbaden.

The next morning we said good-bye to Joe and Lynn as they were taking a different itinerary than ours. Over the next several days Joan, Dad and I went to Stuttgart, toured the Mercedes plant and museum at Sindelfingen, visited a huge farm near Alzey which was owned by friends of Joan's Dad and enjoyed visiting Heidelberg for several days, where there was lots to see and do. Then it was on to Ulm, Augsburg and Munich, with a side trip to the Dachau Concentration Camp – the latter an experience I'll never forget.

On September 1, we arrived at the Kocher's estate in the Alps. The main house – built in 1805 – had more than 20 bedrooms. In the 1800s many of the workers lived in the main house or in an adjoining house with more than 10 bedrooms. They leased out all the farmland as well as a sawmill and several small homes up in the mountains that were on their property.

This provided Peter and Heleana with enough income to pay the taxes and the wages for a young couple who lived on the property year round as the caretakers. All this property once belonged to Peter's mother but had been confiscated by the German government early in World War II. Peter won the property back after a long court battle after the war ended.

They were wonderful hosts and wouldn't let us leave. We stayed for the next three days, during which we visited Mad King Ludwig's Palace at Lake Chiemsee, Reit'im Winkle and a number of charming villages in the area. This was the highlight of our vacation in Germany, as we also had time to walk up into the mountains as well as just relax at the Kocher's and enjoy the fantastic views from their home.

Heleana and Peter Kocher in front of Kocherhof, their home in Austria.

Reluctantly, we said farewell to Heleana and Peter and crossed the border into Austria to reach Salzburg. In the following days we visited St. Johann, Innsbruck and Garmish,

Phartenkirchen and Friederickshaven. We then took a ferry boat across the inland sea to Switzerland and drove across the top of Switzerland, crossing back into Germany near the French border. We drove into and around Strasbourg, France, then back into Germany and to Baden-Baden and Karlsruhle. We decided to return to Heidelburg to purchase some items we had seen there earlier that we hadn't found anyplace else. From Heidelburg we returned to Frankfurt for a day of rest at the Park Hotel before returning home. Except for a few minor problems, we had a wonderful time and, incredibly, did not have a single bad meal during our entire vacation in Germany.

We Part With Two Clients In One Month

A few days after returning from the vacation to Germany, I was back in California the 15th and 16th of September for meetings with Pacific Federal Savings. We were finishing a number of projects and not starting any new ones, as it had become evident that the only way we could effectively handle the Pacific Federal Savings account would be to open a branch office in California. We explored this possibility and I met with an agency in San Diego that was interested in a merger.

We mutually decided that the best course for Pacific Federal Savings to take was to consolidate all their communications needs with the Cochrane Chase, Livingston & Company agency in Costa Mesa, which is where the headquarters of Pacific Federal was now located.

We Run Into An Unfortunate Client Conflict

A conflict also had developed between Standard Federal and Family Federal. Standard Federal had acquired Landmark Savings in Saginaw/Bay City and now there were overlapping offices. We would have to resign the Family Federal account, which we did on October 20, my birthday. Some birthday present! We continued to service the account through the end of the year.

In addition to the merger with Landmark Savings, Standard Federal also merged with the First Savings Association of Dowagiac (Michigan) and, during 1981, introduced checking account services. Standard Federal's advertising budget was increasing as a result of this steady expansion and the addition of new services like checking accounts.

Robert Hutton retired as chairman and Tom Ricketts was named chairman and CEO and continued to serve as president of Standard Federal. Major changes took place in 1981 at Standard Federal and as a result, Kit King, who was serving as the account executive, took on more responsibility managing this growing account.

Just a few years earlier we had four savings and loans for clients. As 1981 came to a close we served only Standard Federal. But this client would become one of the largest and strongest savings banks in the nation in the years ahead. Oddly, Family Federal merged with another association and became part of Heritage Federal, which was eventually acquired by Standard Federal. Many of the Standard Federal branch offices in the northern part of Michigan's lower peninsula were originally Family Federal offices – which we had promoted years earlier when they first opened.

Our relationship with First Federal Savings and Loan of Kalamazoo had ended in 1979, when they decided to move their account to a local advertising agency. However, they too became part of Standard Federal in 1989 as the result of a merger.

We Arrange a Trade-Out With the Machus Restaurants

Within easy walking distance of our Birmingham offices were several Machus restaurants offering outstanding food, service and decor. In the fall of 1981, we decided to approach Machus Enterprises, operators of eight popular restaurants, to determine whether they would consider a "trade-out" with us. Under this kind of arrangement, Machus would pay for all their media expenditures and any out-of-pocket costs for artwork, printing, etc. while our services would be repaid with food and beverage at their restaurants. Such an arrangement requires a fairly close exchange of services – as well as good accounting – to work out well.

After a careful review of their communications and advertising needs, we entered into a mutually rewarding trade-out arrangement which lasted for the next seven years. We used the credit for the hours of service time that we expended handling their advertising to entertain our clients, for staff lunch meetings and employee recognition dinners, as well as the agency's annual Christmas party and for several retirement dinners. It turned out to be a good arrangement for both parties and we created a variety of promotional projects that helped their business. "Meet Me At Machus" was an especially successful campaign.

Harris Machus

The most distinctive Machus restaurant and the flagship of their chain was the Red Fox on Telegraph Road in Bloomfield Hills. It had an elegant hunt club atmosphere and a Certified Master Chef – Leopold Schaeli – but its greatest notoriety came from the fact that the last place Jimmy Hoffa was ever seen alive was in the Red Fox's parking lot. Another large and very distinctive restaurant was the Sly Fox in Birmingham. A number of their restaurants were identified as a Foxy's – Foxy's of Troy, Foxy's of Rochester, Foxy's of Clarkston and Foxy's of Dearborn, etc. – which were more casual but still featured top quality food and service, as well as the famous Machus salad. Several of the restaurants and cafeterias also contained a separate bake shop featuring the highest quality baked goods – primarily cakes, pies, pastries and cookies.

Harris Machus was president of the company during the years we served as its agency. The business was started by Harris' father, Hans, as a bakery and coffee shop in downtown Birmingham, in 1933. When Harris returned from the service after World War II, he came into the business with big dreams. Actually, Harris was fortunate to have survived the war. He had twice been taken prisoner but managed to escape both times and returned to lead his tank battalion into battles with the Germans.

Harris Machus was a cavalry reserve officer, so when the war started he was immediately activated and shipped to North Africa. His wife, Elaine, and his mother had to take over management of the Birmingham bakery, as his father had died a month to the day before Pearl Harbor, leaving his mother alone in the bakery without a baker.

But Harris was having problems of his own. His tank unit was overrun in Africa, and he was one of the few survivors. His wounds were well-treated and he was shipped to Italy with other prisoners. He escaped in Italy and lived in the mountains until he walked over the crest of a hill where he met a German patrol face to face. Other German patrols sweeping the forest for escapees converged from the sides and rear. He made another attempt to escape from a forty and eight box car, but when he had wriggled most of his body out of an upper window, the train suddenly sped up. He hung outside the car as it passed over a bridge and past German guards, who miraculously didn't see the dangling prisoner. That effort failed.

However, Harris did manage to escape a second time and started walking the 300 miles across Poland to Warsaw hoping to get through the retreating German lines and behind the advancing Russian army. He had visions of the Russians escorting him to their headquarters and being flown to his own troops.

His first encounter was with a Russian lieutenant and driver in a one-horse cutter. Machus threw off a large, heavy outer coat given to him by a Polish family so that the Russian soldier would recognize him as an American soldier. The cutter stopped. Machus announced that he was an "Americanski Offizier" which was the Russian terminology for an American officer.

The Russian soldier, about five feet tall and wearing a fur coat and fur hat with the Russian insignia on the hat, stood up and slapped his chest and exclaimed, "Russki Offizier – General Motors, Studebaker, Stalin, Churchill and Roosevelt!" Then he laughed.

Machus felt relieved, even though the rest of the conversation was in sign language and he still had to finish the rest of his journey to Warsaw on his own!

In Warsaw he traded his outer coat for a loaf of bread in a small bakery. Machus thumbed his way on ox carts, sleighs, freight trains, and sometimes on military trucks, to reach Odessa on the Black Sea where he just made it aboard a small tramp steamer as the gang plank was being pulled in.

His next stop was Istanbul, then through the Bosporus, across the Dardanelles, down the Aegean, across the Mediterranean to Port Said, Egypt, and finally, to the American Armed Forces. Harris Machus came home a Major, having been promoted while he was a prisoner.

He then took up the fulfillment of his dream – to build a chain of fine restaurants. The bakery in Birmingham moved into larger quarters in 1948 and was expanded and remodeled several times as the business prospered.

Not only did Harris see his dream of a chain of fine restaurants come true but his peers recognized his success by electing him president of the Michigan Restaurant Association and, later, of the National Restaurant Association, both of which he served with distinction. During his career he received a great many civic, restaurant and food service awards.

Harris is now retired. His son, Robert, now leads the management team. The Machus family has returned to its roots and now emphasizes the bakery business. Most of the restaurants have either been sold or closed.

Farmer Peet Becomes a Client

In 1981, the Peet Packing Company was a major processor of meat products in Michigan, distributing a wide variety of franks, hot dogs, sausages, luncheon meats, bacon and hams. We had met with them several times during the summer months at our offices in Birmingham as well as at their offices and plant in Chesaning. After not hearing from them for several months, we were somewhat surprised when George Peet called to tell us in early November that he wanted BAC&K to handle the advertising for Farmer Peet's People Pleasing Meats.

Bob Wert, who was handling several divisions of our Stanley account, was assigned to the Peet account. I went with Bob to Chesaning for the first meeting. They gave us a major packaging assignment. They wanted all their products, as well as some new products, to have fresh new packaging. Creative people love to tackle projects of this kind. In addition, we were to develop trade, as well as consumer and point-of-sale advertising, to launch the new packaging once it was finished and available in the stores. This was an exciting way to start with a new account.

Over the next 10 months we completed all the packaging assignments and put together a strategic plan to help Farmer Peet schedule and coordinate its promotional activities for its products with the advertising. Unfortunately, the account never developed due to differences of opinion within the Peet family relating to management succession. Two years later we resigned the account and the company self-destructed. Eventually, the company went out of business when Denny McClain (former Detroit Tiger pitcher) got control and cleaned out the pension fund and sold off assets.

We Call In "Mac" McDonald – The Best Consultant In Advertising

From time to time we utilized "Mac" McDonald as a consultant to help us with some sticky client problem, put together an acquisition or merger proposal or resolve some situation as an arbitrator. Mac operates out of his home in Rancho Palos Verdes, California which tells you he's a pretty savvy guy when it comes to picking a site for his consultancy. However, a lot of his life has been spent on planes. He's in constant demand by agencies all over the country as well as by the AAAA's in New York. Mac was born and reared in Kansas City. After service in the Navy in World War II, he went to Tulane and Wharton. After working for several large agencies, he decided to become a management consultant to the advertising agency business and did so very successfully. Mac was an avid Detroit Tiger fan because he and his son both admired Al Kaline so much, and he loved to come to Detroit, particularly if he could include attending a game at Tiger Stadium. He thought BAC&K was really special because we handled the Detroit Tigers' advertising.

In mid-November, Mac spent a day with us to help us plan Jerry Abbs' retirement, which would take place in two years. He was very helpful with this, as well as with several other matters that we asked him to help us resolve.

The viewpoint of someone outside the business who is unbiased, yet highly knowledgeable about the business, is a very valuable resource.

The Conclusion of 1981

Early in December, Joan and I again attended the Michigan Horticulture Society's Annual Convention in Grand Rapids. The decorating of our offices under the direction of Mary Sue Piggott (Piggott Design) was completed in December, so our facilities were bright and fresh. And, on December 11, I became a 30-year member of the Adcraft Club of Detroit. This meant that I no longer had to pay dues and would be a member for life.

I then went back to Costa Mesa for another meeting with Pacific Federal Savings – the last one held as a client of BAC&K, Inc. Late in December, Fred Zimmerman retired. He was an especially capable and talented art director who served the agency for fifteen years. The entire staff, as well as Fred's wife Catherine, attended his retirement dinner at the Machus Red Fox restaurant.

1981 was a very good year for the agency. We had continued to grow even though many things over which we had little or no control had severely impacted our operations.

The agency was evolving and changing because our clients' needs and expectations were changing. The fields of communication and marketing were also changing rapidly and dramatically, and that greatly impacted our operation. Very few of the things that we did in 1981 to produce advertising were done the way they had been done even five years earlier. The agency now had computerized typesetting, a Telmar computer terminal for media analysis, and advanced word processing and telecommunications capabilities, as well as a systematic method for determining the correct strategic direction for our clients' communications efforts.

We fully intended to continue to grow, knowing that many things would continue to change. But we were dedicated to the factors basic to good advertising: *strong creative work*, a *full range of services* and a *commitment to long-term client and employee relationships*. We believed that our dedication to these goals would serve as our basic operating principles, define our purpose as a company and assure our future success in the decade of the '80s.

– 1982 –

The first three weeks of January 1982 were extraordinarily cold. New records were set for the coldest days ever recorded on a number of occasions. On January 17, the temperature stayed at 15 degrees below zero all day. Not only was it frigid, but there was also lots of snow on the ground. In spite of the severe wintry conditions at the start of 1982, our focus at the office was on summer and specifically on the Michigan State Fair, which would be held over a 15-day period in late August through early September.

We had received an RFP (Request For Proposal) from the Michigan Department of Management and Budget for an advertising, promotion and publicity program for the 1982 Michigan State Fair. The fair had been languishing for years under the Michigan Department of Agriculture and the responsibility for the event had recently been transferred to the Department of Natural Resources. Bill Upina, the general manager, and Willis Watkins, the assistant manager, had been selected to head the effort to turn things around, and extra funds had been allocated for a much needed facelift of the facilities. We were excited to have won the account.

Meetings With the Craft, Kennedy & Higgins, Inc. Advertising Agency Prove To Be Very Worthwhile

During February 1982, we had three meetings with Chester "Chet" Craft, Charles Kennedy and Pat Higgins, who were the principals of the Craft, Kennedy & Higgins, Inc. advertising agency. These three individuals had been with Zimmer, Keller & Calvert in 1969, when the agency was in the process of being acquired by Ross Roy, Inc. Not wanting

Chester (Chet) Craft

to become part of Ross Roy, they broke away and started their own advertising agency, which they had operated successfully for more than 10 years. Charlie Kennedy, who was the production manager at ZKC when I was there in 1948 and 1949, was ready to retire, but needed to recover the financial investment he had made in Craft, Kennedy & Higgins, Inc. to do so. Consequently, the three principals had decided to dissolve their agency, after which Pat Higgins and Chet Craft would join other agencies. A well-known federal judge, Cornelia Kennedy, was Charlie's wife and she had been transferred to Cincinnati. Charlie was anxious to move there to join her as soon as he retired.

Chester (Chet) Craft was the president of Craft, Kennedy & Higgins and he decided to join BAC&K. Chet was a specialist in business-to-business advertising and he brought with him three accounts, including the Aeroquip Corporation (a division of Libbey-Owens-Ford), DeVlieg Machine Company and Ross Operating Valve Company.

Pat Higgins joined another agency, while two other members of this agency's staff – Ron Lindroth, an art director, and Carolyn Staats, an account coordinator – officially joined BAC&K with Chet on May 3, 1982. The Aeroquip Corporation had already assigned its account to BAC&K as of April 1 and, at a meeting with our new client in Jackson, Michigan, I was surprised and delighted to discover that, James W. (Jay) Fullerton, my classmate at Smith-Cotton High School in Sedalia, Missouri, was the director of corporate planning.

Jay and I enlisted in the Army Specialized Training Reserve Program in 1943 when we turned 17. One week after we graduated from high school in May 1944, we left for Fort Leavenworth together to be inducted into the U.S. Army. Jay was sent to Colorado State while I drew South Dakota State. After completing two college terms, we met again when we went through 16 weeks of basic training at Camp Hood, Texas.

When we got out of the service, we both attended the University of Missouri and both of us graduated from the School of Journalism. After graduation, Jay joined the U.S. Foreign Service and served in Indonesia and Germany. In 1955, he became a sales engineer for Republic Rubber Company and, in 1966, transferred to Aeroquip's Industrial Division in Los Angeles. He moved to the division's sales and marketing department headquarters in Jackson, Michigan where he advanced to group product manager and worked closely with the Craft, Kennedy & Higgins advertising agency. When we met

again, Jay had recently been promoted to director of corporate planning, but he moved from that position to become vice president, Far East Operations in 1986. Jay retired in 1989 and he and his wife Lanni live in Spring Hill, Florida. We stay in touch and look forward to seeing each other at our high school reunions in Sedalia.

In 1982, we added three new clients: Aeroquip, DeVlieg, and Ross Operating Valve.

Aeroquip's Origin and Development Is An Amazing Story[2]

Peter Hurst

Peter Hurst, the founder of Aeroquip, was born on August 3, 1910 in the village of Bruchsal, near Karlsruhe in Southern Germany. He enrolled at Karlsruhe Institute in 1928, and graduated in 1933 with a degree in mechanical engineering. This led to his employment with a development engineer in England, who was developing a disk brake for Argus Motors, a German aircraft engine and brake assemblies firm. When currency transfer problems (due to the deteriorating political situation in Europe) made it difficult for the British engineer to

---

[2] From "The Flying A" 50th Anniversary Issue written by Mel Borger.

continue the Argus work, Hurst was assigned to take over the project at Argus headquarters in Berlin. Only 24, he organized and managed a successful Argus subsidiary named Rotadisk. Like Aeroquip, Rotadisk was a name he created. Hurst quickly won acceptance of Rotadisk brake products on the leading German military aircraft.

At the same time, the firm developed flexible hose assemblies with detachable, reusable fittings, and self-sealing couplings.

Hurst came to the United States in late 1939 to interest U.S. manufacturers in licensing Rotadisk's products. He was permitted to make this business trip, which was unusual in view of the worsening international situation, largely because Germany needed more U.S. dollars (which licensing could earn).

Working with business contacts supplied by U.S. officials, including the Navy Bureau of Aeronautics, Hurst found that American manufacturers were interested in the Rotadisk products, but were not ready to enter into licensing agreements.

One week after arriving in the U.S., World War II unofficially began with Germany's invasion of Poland. Opposed to the Nazi party and its goals, he worked to extend his official three-month visa rather than return home.

Through the U.S. Navy's Bureau of Aeronautics, he made contact with Charles Hollerith, vice president of engineering for Hayes Industries, Inc., in Jackson, Michigan. This contact eventually led to a licensing agreement under which Hayes Industries would produce disk brakes. Arriving in Jackson by train, Hurst was soon introduced to several leading members of the Jackson business community, including (in addition to Mr. Hollerith) Don T. McKone, Sr. (who later became Aeroquip's chairman of the board); Stuart M. Schram, president of the National Bank of Jackson; Donald M. Teer, president of Teer-Wickwire Company, and others.

Putting his natural charm, enthusiasm and technical knowledge to good use, Hurst's "sales" pitch proved successful, prompting 10

investors (including those previously mentioned) to invest $1,000 each to start his new company, provided that he establish it in Jackson and could secure the patent rights from Argus. The German company agreed to license its patents and Aeroquip, a derivation of the names <u>Aero</u>nautical and <u>equip</u>ment was on its way. The new company was incorporated on April 26, 1940. Though business was slow at first, by early December 1941, Aeroquip had about 100 employees.

When the U.S. entered the war, because Hurst was a German citizen, he was classified as an enemy alien and was not permitted to enter his own plant due to its defense-related activities. But work at Aeroquip continued, and Aeroquip hose assemblies were soon designated as the standard hose and fittings for U.S. military aircraft. In the meantime he kept busy by starting another company which recycled bottle caps for a local bottler.

Now, a different problem arose. Suddenly Aeroquip couldn't produce enough products to meet the demand. Recognizing that his organizational skills were needed, the U.S. government finally gave Hurst permission to return to work, 21 months after he was ordered out. He returned to the company in September 1944 as executive vice president.

Hurst became an American citizen in 1945. When the war ended, demand for Aeroquip products fell dramatically. New markets were needed, and the company began to cultivate the commercial aviation market, as well as the industrial hydraulics market, which was still in its infancy. By 1953, industrial business had reached a point where more production capacity was needed to fulfill orders, prompting the opening of a plant in Van Wert, Ohio.

Expansion to overseas markets followed later in the same decade, and Aeroquip was becoming a worldwide leader in the production of hose assemblies and fittings, self-sealing quick-disconnect couplings and other fluid power and fluid conveying products for aerospace and industrial markets.

Recognizing that Aeroquip needed additional capital to continue its aggressive growth and expansion, Hurst entered into negotiations which resulted in the company's acquisition by Libbey-Owens-Ford Glass (LOF) Company in September 1968.

When the acquisition was completed, Aeroquip's annual sales were almost $125 million. The company had 4500 employees and 14 plants.

Peter Hurst died on April 8, 1969, leaving a legacy which lives on today in a company which has more than 12,000 employees in 90 plants around the globe.

A Great Stock Investment

In July 1950, Aeroquip initiated its first public stock offering of 162,010 shares of common stock at $4 per share and this offering increased the number of Aeroquip shareholders to 805.

On March 2, 1954, Aeroquip stock began public trading at $6.75 per share on the American Stock Exchange under the "ticker tape" symbol "AQP." By 1955 Aeroquip boasted more than 3,000 stockholders. In less than 15 years, an original capital investment of $10,000, which started the company in 1940, had grown to a market value of more than $10 million.

The company's common stock moved up to the "Big Board" when it was accepted for listing on the New York Stock Exchange on July 28, 1955. AQP commenced trading on August 10. The first trade enacted was for 100 shares at 14 7/8 ($14.875 per share).

The familiar AQP symbol went off the board in 1968, following the company's acquisition by Libbey-Owens-Ford Glass Company, which also was listed on the New York Stock Exchange under the symbol "LOF."

Libbey-Owens-Ford stock had been publicly traded since May 29, 1930, shortly after the company was formed as a result of the merger of two glass companies – Libbey-Owens

Sheet Glass Company and the Edward Ford Plate Glass Company which was discussed in Chapter 2. On April 28, 1986 Libbey-Owens Ford sold its glass business to Pilkington Brothers PLC of Merryside, England – the biggest glass manufacturer in Britain. Aeroquip and Vickers had surpassed glass as LOF's largest business segment. LOF then changed its name to TRINOVA Corporation and its New York Stock Exchange listing became "TNV" on August 1 of 1986.

The TRINOVA name was coined by combining "Tri" (meaning three) with "nova" (a bright new star). TRINOVA represented the company's three bright productive stars – Aeroquip and Vickers in fluid power and Sterling in Plastics, and also signified a new beginning for the corporation.

At the close of business on December 31, 1989, TRINOVA had 32,973,726 shares of common stock outstanding, which were held by 15,324 shareholders.

DeVlieg Machine Company

DeVlieg Machine Company, headquartered in Royal Oak, Michigan was a leading manufacturer of machining centers and other machine tools, as well as an international supplier of the Microbore line of standard and special cutting tools.

Ross Operating Valve Company

Ross Operating Valve Company was a leading manufacturer of air control valves, lubricators and regulators for pneumatic control systems. Ross was also an international corporation with operations in Japan and Germany.

An Exceptionally Well-Balanced Agency

The addition of these three new clients in the business-to-business account category combined with the other industrial/commercial accounts that we already served, made us the leader in Detroit in this category. We were equally balanced in volume (revenues), though, with accounts in the consumer category, so we could not be identified as an agency specializing in just business-to-business clients. Agencies that specialize in business-to-business accounts have a very difficult time winning consumer accounts, which usually have bigger advertising budgets than those in business-to-business. In order to recognize and promote our new status as the largest business-to-business agency in the city we celebrated with an open house on May 12 for our clients and media representatives. More than 60 trade publications were represented and the event generated considerable good will and local press coverage.

Grandmother Staples Celebrates Her 100th Birthday

135 relatives of my maternal grandmother, Maude E. Staples, gathered in Sun City, Arizona in early March to participate in the celebration of her 100th birthday. Five generations were present, represented by Grandmother Staples, my mother, me, my oldest son Robert and my grandson Matthew. It was a wonderful, memorable week during which we met and visited with relatives from all over the country – many of whom have since passed away, including Grandmother Staples, who lived to be 104. She was an amazing lady – alert, sharp and fun to talk with – she never ran out of interesting stories to tell.

Five generations represented by, from left to right: my son Robert with his son Matthew on his knee; my mother S. Elizabeth Baker; grandmother Maude Staples (my mother's mother) and me.

A Hotel Chain Registers With BAC&K, Inc.

Servico, Inc., headquartered in Palm Beach, Florida, owned and operated 39 hotels in 14 states in 1982, including three in southeastern Michigan, when we became its agency. Dave Scully, Servico's district manager, hired us to handle the advertising and promotion of the Troy Hilton, Sheraton Southfield and the Michigan Inn, as well as to develop special campaigns that would involve all 39 Servico hotels.

The first chain-wide effort was a "Speedy Breakfast" for less than a "Buck, Buck, Buck" promotion. It was launched August 1 to encourage guests at Servico Hotels to eat breakfast in the hotel coffee shop rather than going elsewhere. The perception was that hotel breakfasts cost more and that service would be slow. The promotion advertised a selection of breakfasts ranging from "Less than one buck" to "Less than four bucks" with a guarantee of seven-minute delivery "or the meal is FREE!" Promotional elements included tent cards, posters, newspaper ad slicks and a brochure to explain the program. A lot of people all over the country were "Buck, Buck, Bucking" at Servico Hotel Coffeeshops.

The speedy breakfast campaign was a resounding success because Servico made it a complete advertising and promotion effort by including an incentive contest for the restaurant and kitchen staff. The prizes for its employees were meaningful and plentiful. The "Buck, Buck, Buck" campaign was advertised throughout the hotels with posters and tent cards. Later, this was expanded to include advertising to consumers on radio, in newspapers and in special publications.

"Buck, Buck, Buck" was followed by a "Gobble Gobble" promotion for Thanksgiving – either eat Thanksgiving dinner in a Servico Hotel or pick up a complete roast turkey dinner with all the trimmings and enjoy it at home. They sold an incredible number of Thanksgiving dinners, so we were off to a great start. The Servico chain grew to more than 50 units, five of them in southeastern Michigan. Several years later, Dave Scully left Servico. With changes in management, less priority was given to advertising and promotion. The account eventually faded away.

Summer of '82 Had Its Bright Spots Along With One Bad Spot

The annual conference of the Advertising Marketing International Network of Advertising Agencies (AMIN) was at the Woodstock Inn in Vermont June 20 through June 24. Joan and I, along with Betty and Bob Klepinger, attended and participated. At the meeting we spent some

time with Cochrane Chase as his agency in California – Cochrane Chase, Livingston and Company – now handled Pacific Savings Bank – our former client.

Saturday night, June 26, was a real bummer! Our home was burglarized. We arrived home around 11 p.m. to find our home torn apart and many things missing. I ran an advertisement in the *Ortonville Reminder* – our local paper – offering a $1,000 reward for information that would result in the arrest and conviction of the robber. Advertising works, because his buddies turned him in for the reward. The thief turned out to be a 16-year-old cocaine addict who lived in the area and was on probation for three other breaking and entering charges. He was tried, convicted and sentenced to one year in prison for robbing our house, but was released in three months. Some justice! I paid his buddies the reward money and had an alarm system installed in our home. The thief who burglarized our home died a few years later in a car crash when he was fleeing from the police.

At the end of July and early August, we took the week-long trip on the Str. Iglehart described in Chapter 2. Our apple crop was looking great and John Feldmann, my next door neighbor, and I managed to spray the apple trees on a regular basis and at all the proper times. Not an easy thing to do when there were so many other distractions, like any regular job.

"More – More Than Ever Before" At the 1982 Michigan State Fair

Compared to previous State Fairs, the 1982 fair featured more top-name entertainers and free entertainment than ever before. With that in mind, we chose the theme "More – More Than Ever Before!" to promote the fair. Attendance was up 27% over the previous year. Our statewide multi-media effort included press releases, advertising in newspapers and on radio and television stations as well as staffing the State Fair press room. Greg Holub was the assigned account executive. He stayed in a trailer on the State Fair grounds for the entire period, putting in long days. The strangest thing Greg handled was delivering $50,000 in cash in a suitcase to Willie Nelson, who was one of the featured entertainers. Nelson insisted on being paid in cash and it fell upon the agency to handle this demand. The State of Michigan reimbursed us, of course, but it was probably one of the most unusual items we ever billed to one of our clients.

Meetings, Meetings and More Meetings

Immediately after the Michigan State Fair, we launched a number of sizable campaigns, the largest of which was a national program to introduce Stan-Guard,™ a combination garage door opener and 24-hour security system designed for do-it-yourself installation in an afternoon.

Introducing a new product is always a challenge. When the product is unlike anything else on the market, the public must be educated as well as motivated to buy it.

For Stanley Automatic Openers, the Stan-Guard™ system represented an important blending of state-of-the-art opener technology with consumer research that indicated home owners wanted added security for their homes.

In addition to functioning as a garage door opener, the Stan-Guard™ system had built-in intrusion, fire and carbon monoxide alarms. And one of its most unusual features was the in-house monitor that let homeowners know at a glance whether the garage door was open or closed, and the nature of the emergency in the event an alarm sounded.

BAC&K began working with Dan Meyvis and Dave Demorotski of Stanley Automatic Openers on an extensive public relations and merchandising program while the system was in the final design and testing stages. By the time the product was ready for shipping, we had succeeded in getting great press coverage and had completed packaging, point-of-purchase materials and both a consumer and a trade advertising campaign.

The product sold well in stores and the agency won several Drummer Awards for the advertising and promotion.

Building Supply News, a highly respected publication in the building products field, established the Drummer Awards competition to recognize excellence in advertising and merchandising materials developed to promote building products.

The judging committee for these awards is made up of a panel of independent and chain store retailers who have been recognized as a Retailer-of-the-Year.

Judges looked for creativity and aesthetics. More importantly, they are interested in determining how well a piece can be used to help move a product at the retail level.

BAC&K had developed substantial expertise in the building products field and in just a few years time had won a total of 40 Drummer Awards in virtually every category, including best audio/visual program, best packaging and best overall merchandising aids program. We had won more Drummer Awards than any other agency in the entire U.S.A.

All Savers Certificate Introduced
By Standard Federal

October was an important month for Standard Federal Savings. The record deposits that the 1981 All Savers Certificate Campaign had generated would reach maturity starting October 1.

Maturing certificates always present a challenge with regard to retaining the funds. And since the amount invested in Standard Federal's maturing All Savers Certificates was one of the highest in the country, there was a lot at stake.

Following a number of meetings and a lot of discussion, an "All Savers Certificate Campaign" was initiated October 1 with a variety of gifts available for certificate renewals and for new deposits of $1,000 or more. Account executive Kit King and her group at the agency put a comprehensive campaign together, working with Bill Yaw and his marketing department staff at Standard Federal. One of the things that we had learned to do well was the use of premiums to retain or attract savings and this campaign was another huge success. On November 9, we held a special anniversary luncheon and presented a plaque to recognize the agency's 30-year relationship with Standard Federal.

In addition to all the meetings with Standard Federal and Stanley Automatic Openers, there were many other meetings with other clients for other programs and projects, including Stanley Door Systems, Detroit Tigers, Better Made Potato Chips, Awrey's, Servico, Speas and Michigan Apples. Greg Holub and I made several trips to Speas headquarters at Bear Lake and I also attended the Produce Marketing Association meeting in Scottsdale, Arizona, as Michigan Apples had an exhibit every year in this big trade show.

A 30-year agency/client relationship was recognized at a special luncheon when the agency presented a plaque to Standard Federal Savings in appreciation and for the recognition of a 30-year relationship. Participants included, left to right: Robert J. Hutton, chairman of Standard Federal's executive committee; Kit King, BAC&K vice president/account executive; Bill Yaw, senior vice president of Standard Federal; Ernie Baker, BAC&K chairman; and Tom Ricketts, president of Standard Federal.

In the last two months of 1982 some good things happened that benefited the agency. In mid-November the Michigan Department of Natural Resources extended our contract on the same terms and conditions for the 1983 State Fair. We were contacted by Dow Corning in Midland, Michigan and asked to submit a proposal to handle a very big project for them. A number of clients informed us that their advertising budgets for 1983 would be increased, while Stanley Door Systems and Stanley Automatic Openers nearly doubled their budgets for the next year.

– 1983 –

One of our clients, First of Michigan Corporation, celebrated its 50th anniversary in 1983 and the agency was requested to prepare a public relations plan, including finding a special, unusual memento to recognize the occasion. On January 7, I met with artist Marshall Fredericks at his Birmingham studio to discuss the possibility of his sculpting a 50th anniversary object for First of Michigan – such as an unusual paperweight – to recognize the anniversary. The sculpture would then be replicated in bronze in quantity and presented in a gift box to employees and clients. It was an interesting meeting, but Mr. Fredericks declined the commission, as he was too busy doing other projects. We did, however, work together on another project a few years later, so it was time well invested.

Agency Restructuring Formalized At Annual Meeting

February 8, 1983 was an important date in the agency's history. With help from consultant Mac McDonald, a long-range plan had been developed for BAC&K, Inc. First the stockholders met to elect the directors and the directors then met to elect the company officers and confirm the direction of the agency as detailed in our plan. In the directors meeting Jerry Abbs retired as chairman of the board and I was elected to that position. I was formerly chairman of the executive committee and CEO. Bob Klepinger continued as president and all other officers were re-elected to their positions. In addition, three new officers were elected: Karen Aaberg and John Logan as vice presidents and Dolores Weatherford as corporate controller.

Karen Aaberg had joined BAC&K in 1979 as associate creative director and became the creative director a year later. John Logan was in charge of marketing services and the media department. His assistant in marketing services was Karen Lewis, director of marketing. Both John and Karen were formerly with the W.B. Doner advertising agency.

Karen Aaberg

Dolores Weatherford had held several positions in our financial department prior to being named our corporate controller. A number of new people had joined the agency in the past several years as the agency had doubled in size in the last three years. Mike Hedge, vice president/public relations, now headed the public relations division and Craig Lesinski and Lorraine McGregor were new PR account executives. Mike Morgan, an outstanding

designer and art director, was now a member of the creative department and we had also added Brad Lang to the creative staff as a copywriter. The strength of any advertising agency is its people because their thinking is an agency's only product. Fortunately we were steadily growing bigger and stronger and it was people who were making BAC&K successful.

SIMSA Meets In San Francisco

On February 27 Joan and I left early in the morning for San Francisco for the Savings Institutions Marketing Society of America meeting at the Hilton. Carol and Bill Yaw were there representing Standard Federal and Kit and Bob King, plus Joan and I, were attending from BAC&K. The three-day meeting featured several outstanding speakers and there were many good sessions. We also managed to find some time to enjoy ourselves. We had dinner at the Cornellian Room on the top floor of the Bank of America Building on Sunday night, the Todish Grill on Monday night and at a Chinese restaurant on Tuesday night, as well as visits to Top of the Mark, the St. Francis lounge and Girardelli Square in between meetings. Following the meeting on Thursday, March 3 Joan and I left San Francisco by car, as we planned to drive to Los Angeles down the Coast Highway. When we reached Carmel we learned that the Coast Highway was closed due to landslides. After a detour through Castroville, the nation's artichoke capital, we drove down Highway 401 and then cut back to the Coast Highway at Morrow Bay. Our primary goal was to tour Hearst Castle at San Simeon. We managed to take all but one of the five tours over a two-day period and found "The Enchanted Hill" absolutely fascinating.

Early in this century, William Randolph Hearst began to fulfill a dream. He had inherited property from his mother and father that included fifty miles of shoreline on a remote stretch of the Pacific Ocean, halfway between San Francisco and Los Angeles. The total area of his property included 250,000 acres of land, and on a spot that he called "The Enchanted Hill" he built his castle. Construction began in 1919 on his 165 room, 90,000-square-foot castle and continued for 17 years in order to build all the buildings needed to house the enormous collection of art and artifacts that he had collected with the help of his mother, Phoebe. So lavish was the estate that it became the basis for Orson Welles' Xanadu in the 1945 film, Citizen Kane.

George Hearst, the father of William Randolph Hearst, was born in Franklin County, Missouri in 1820. I found this most interesting because my mother and father moved to Franklin County when I was six months old and we lived there at St. Albans Farms until I was fourteen years old. In the spring of 1850, George Hearst left his home in Franklin County and headed west across the continent on horseback to seek his fortune. He struck it rich after 10 lean years with a 25% share of a silver mine near Virginia City, Nevada. With the profits from this mine he bought shares in other mines which proved to be even richer than his original claim.

In 1860, George Hearst learned that his mother was ill and returned to Missouri. After his mother died, he turned his attention to Phoebe Apperson, the daughter of a Missouri neighbor, who was twenty-two years younger than he was. George and Pheobe were married a year later, over the objections of her parents. Their only child, William Randolph, was born in Stevenson House atop a San Francisco hill in April 1863.

George Hearst died in 1891 while serving in the United States Senate and he left his entire estate to Phoebe. She died in 1919, at the age of 76, and she left the bulk of her huge estate, including all the land at San Simeon, to her only son, William Randolph, who then proceeded to enthusiastically build his castle and the many other structures that make this such an impressive place to visit and where I would return again in the years ahead.

From San Simeon we drove to South Laguna, where we spent two days with my brother Joe. Then we flew to Phoenix to visit my mother. We arrived home March 9. We had covered a lot of country in two weeks' time and had seen some remarkable things.

Stanley Found the Key To Success With BAC&K Behind Their Doors

Early in 1983, most people knew that Stanley made tools and garage door openers. But not many knew that Stanley also had a full line of entry doors, patio doors and garage doors. So, in 1983, Stanley Door Systems turned to BAC&K for a new comprehensive campaign to inform the trade and consumers.

Our solution was to launch "The Total Door Company" campaign, positioning Stanley Door Systems as one of the most comprehensive and capable companies in the market.

It was a total campaign, with four-color spread advertisements in all the major builder, contractor, architect and remodeler magazines.

129

The results opened doors to totally new vistas. Stanley's share of the market rose to 7.6% in 1984, and 9.3% in 1985. More impressively, Stanley's share of the steel door market rose to an incredible 16.5% and then to 21.5% during the same periods.

This campaign, launched in 1983 and expanded in subsequent years, helped make Stanley Door Systems a leader in the industry.

Our Alaskan Vacation

Joan's father, Ed Bauman, had two big wishes when he retired. One was to visit Germany. The other was to tour Alaska. We had visited Germany two years before and, on August 13, the three of us – Joan, Dad and I – left for Alaska to help Dad fulfill his second wish. We flew to Vancouver and boarded the Sun Princess late in the day to sail to Skagway, where we would leave the ship for our tour of Alaska. We sailed the Inside Passage and saw whales, porpoises, eagles and sea lions, as well as an interesting shoreline dotted with little settlements, lighthouses and logging operations.

In Juneau we met Gino and Madeline Guido from San Antonio, who were in our tour group. We then teamed up with them and, from there on, the five of us enjoyed our meals and field trips together. From Skagway we traveled by bus for three days through the Yukon Territory, staying at rustic inns at Whitehorse and Beaver Creek, arriving in Fairbanks late Saturday afternoon. For the next three days we toured Fairbanks and took a river boat excursion on the Tanana River to visit an Athabascan Indian village. We were learning a lot about

Alaska, its history and how life is lived there. From Fairbanks we went by train to Denali, where we stayed at the McKinley Park Chalet. We spent a day touring this huge park and saw lots of animals but, to our disappointment, no bears. The next day we boarded a train that took us to Anchorage, where we had beautiful rooms at the Captain Cook Hotel.

Joan's Dad had a cousin, Harold, who had moved to Alaska in the late 1930s. They hadn't seen each other in many years. Dad had talked often about his cousin before and during the trip and we could tell that he held Harold in a kind of special esteem because he was a big man – about 6-1/2 feet tall – who loved to hunt and fish. A real man's man! Harold was a retired peace officer and he and his wife were going to join us for lunch at the Captain Cook Hotel. On August 24, Harold met us in the dining room alone, as his wife was not feeling well that day. Joan's Dad was delighted to see Harold again, and being a very outgoing, gregarious individual, Dad kept firing questions or remembrances at Harold. His every reply was either a "yep" or a "nope." Joan and I glanced at each other several times during lunch and we both had the same reaction – why had Dad been so anxious to see his non-conversationalist cousin again? When lunch was finished and we stood up to say our goodbyes, Harold suddenly stated: "A moose fell through my greenhouse last winter." He actually could talk! It was too bad he didn't bring this up earlier, as it would have been interesting to know more of the details.

We left Anchorage by bus the next day, heading for Valdez, but on the way were able to see the Columbia glacier. Some miles out of Anchorage our bus was driven up onto a flat bed railway car and, for the next several hours, we traveled sitting in a bus riding on a train – a strange but interesting experience. An awesome sight was salmon fighting their way up the streams, spawning and then dying – their life cycle ended, but the species would continue. On the way home from Alaska we stopped for a day in Seattle to visit Eunice and George Kurz. George had served as the pastor of St. James Lutheran Church in Grosse Pointe for many years and he was the minister that married Joan and me in 1948.

A Bigger and Better State Fair

Earlier in the year O.J. "Orrie" Scherschligt had been assigned to manage the Michigan State Fair with Willis Watkins continuing as the assistant manager. Orrie had headed a division of the Michigan Department of Natural Resources and his arrival brought a whole new dimension and enthusiasm to rejuvenating the Michigan State Fair. Orrie was bright, energetic, articulate and a natural leader. He got everyone in any way connected or related to the State Fair on his rebuilding team and even started an organization of volunteers called "Friends of the Michigan State Fair" to help bolster his efforts. He challenged the agency to seek corporate funds and sponsors for events and we were successful in raising more than $2,000,000 in corporate funds to underwrite events which the Fair could then offer free to the public. In addition, we developed cross-promotional campaigns with local radio stations in conjunction with big-name talent appearing at the Fair.

Attendance at the 1983 Michigan State Fair was up significantly over the previous year. Because of the results we helped achieve in promoting the State Fair and for raising significant corporate funds, we were awarded a five-year contract extension. Over the next five years, attendance increased 75% and the Michigan State Fair rebounded from a dull, poorly-attended annual activity into an exciting event where winning an award for an exhibit or product really meant something. Prior to 1982 the agricultural exhibits were somewhat meaningless but, by the end of the 1980s, winning a prize for a livestock or other product entered into competition at the State Fair was both prestigious and financially rewarding. All the prize-winning steers, sheep, pigs, cheeses, honeys, wines, etc. were auctioned off at the Fair and Orrie was successful in getting lots of bidders to participate. I usually bought at least one steer, which we would then have butchered and processed. The meat would then be given to our staff or to a charitable institution.

Sadly, all of our efforts were somewhat in vain, as Orrie Scherschligt was promoted to a higher position in the Michigan Department of Natural Resources and there was not the same level of leadership or management when he departed. When we bid on the contract in 1989, another advertising agency submitted a ridiculously low bid and, while they won the contract, it helped put them in bankruptcy. The Michigan State Fair then went into a serious decline, from which it is still trying to recover.

In the fall of 1983 we made several new business presentations but were unsuccessful in winning any of the accounts. There was, however, a virtual flood of activity and projects for existing clients.

– 1984 –

We launched the new year at the agency by adding a "star player" to our team. John Ballantyne joined the agency on January 3 as director of client services. His responsibilities included overseeing the agency's marketing, marketing research and media departments. John had to hit the ground running as we had major research projects underway for Awrey Bakeries, Michigan Apples, Roney & Company and Stanley Door Systems. In addition, he had to help put together a two hundred-plus page analysis, and marketing plan for the three major product lines offered by Stanley Door Systems. This marketing plan included an extensive review of the economy, the housing market, the competition, distribution methods and a seven-year sales analysis, along with the agency's

recommendations for trade promotion programs, creative and sales force strategies and other pertinent marketing data, including five-year volume projections. <u>This was no easy task</u>! Yet John handled everything exceptionally well and helped convince our clients that all the marketing work that we were doing on their behalf had one simple goal – to provide cost-efficient ways to help our clients to communicate better and thereby help them sell their products or services more profitably.

John Ballantyne

We Celebrate Our 20th Anniversary

Six days after our official anniversary – which was January 6 – we had an elaborate open house. Our offices were packed wall-to-wall with friends, clients, media representatives and suppliers. *The Oakland Press* and *The Birmingham Eccentric* ran articles about the event and our anniversary. We published a special "20th Anniversary Issue" of our newsletter "BACK TALK" and this is an excerpt of the comments I made in the publication:

"This agency is obviously not the same agency it was 20 years ago or even two years ago. We have evolved and changed as our clients' needs have changed. The fields of communication and marketing have also changed rapidly and dramatically, and that has greatly impacted our operation. Very few of the things that we do today in producing advertising are done the way we did them even 10 years ago. We now have computerized typesetting, a Telmar computer terminal for media analysis, advanced copying equipment, and word processing and telecommunications capabilities. It's unreal how fast the past 20 years have gone by! And it's hard to believe that so many things could have occurred in that time. Yet, we've survived the past 20 years; we've been buffeted and we've benefited – laughed and cried – enjoyed many successes and also had our disappointments. To everyone who has helped us or contributed to our success, I say a sincere 'Thank You.' There are so many who deserve to be thanked. We are indeed fortunate to serve excellent clients and work with people who are great to be associated with. That makes this business fun, and that's the best reward of all."

Something New For Kmart Shoppers

Early in the year, Standard Federal and Kmart joined together to launch a pilot savings program through Kmart stores. Introduced in three Florida locations, the program included a Money Market Account and a Certificate of Deposit. These accounts were available to Kmart shoppers through special Kmart insurance counters located right in the stores. This program met with great initial success and a few months later was expanded to 25 additional Kmart stores in Florida and then to more Kmarts in Texas. A year later, Standard Federal launched a new marketing program in Indiana that involved opening full-service branches in four Kmart stores.

These new Standard Federal Bank branches in South Bend, Mishawaka and Elkhart, Indiana Kmart stores offered most of the services found at more traditional branch locations.

In all three instances, our agency was instrumental in ensuring the success of the new ventures. Newspaper advertising, direct mail, hand-out pieces, point-of-purchase displays and signboards for the Standard Federal offices and products were produced by the agency. And, to mark the opening of the new branches in Indiana, a grand opening ceremony was staged that generated extensive media coverage from area television, radio and newspaper news editors.

It's Back To New Orleans Again

On February 28, Joan and I left for New Orleans to attend the annual FIMA meeting held at the Hyatt Regency. In June of 1983, SIMSA (Savings Institutions Marketing Society of America) changed its name to FIMA (Financial Institutions Marketing Association). Kit and Bob King and Carol and Bill Yaw completed our group representing Standard Federal. I had dropped a note to Gino and Madeline Guido in San Antonio (the friends we made on our Alaska trip) to let them know that we were going to be in New Orleans. On Sunday, they flew over to spend the day and evening with us. We had a great visit and a delicious dinner together at Begues. While in New Orleans we also enjoyed dinner at Old Noo Orleans and at the Hilton Hotel Lounge, where Pete Fountain performed. On Thursday it was back to work in Detroit, but it was great to have a few days in the warm south in the middle of a Michigan winter.

Our Public Relations Division Handles Some Unusual and Interesting Assignments

The Kresge Foundation preserved a slice of history in Troy and BAC&K's public relations department made sure the news media knew about it.

An open house for the press celebrated the relocation of the Kresge Foundation's headquarters to a renovated nineteenth century farmstead on Big Beaver Road amid Troy's "Golden Corridor" of modern office buildings.

A press kit was prepared consisting of several news releases, fact sheets, and a walking tour of the facilities in print. Also included were reproductions of a lithograph of the farmhouse, modern site plan and aerial photographs of the completed headquarters.

An open house for the news media resulted in numerous national and local news articles, as well as extensive stories in Detroit area magazines, including a multi-page, four-color spread in *Metropolitan Detroit* magazine.

The Kresge Foundation was created in 1924 solely through the personal gifts of Sebastian S. Kresge. Since its founding it has made grants totaling more than 1.458 billion dollars to charitable organizations.

Other accounts using only our public relations division included Federal Mogul and Diversified Technologies, Inc. (Diversitec), a subsidiary of Blue Cross and Blue Shield of Michigan. First of Michigan (stockbrokers) had been inactive for a year and, when Roney & Company, another stockbroker, asked us to handle several public relations projects for them, we decided to do so. Roney & Co. was so pleased that it asked us to be their full-service marketing, advertising and public relations agency. Roney & Co. is the longest-established of all Michigan-based investment securities firms – a full-service investment firm which also deals in insurance, real estate and oil and gas syndications, in addition to various investment services.

Roney had 25 offices in 1984, covering Michigan, Ohio and Indiana, and was a member of the New York, Philadelphia and American Stock Exchanges, as well as other major stock exchanges.

This was the only instance where we resigned an account in the same field to take on a larger competitor. Had First of Michigan been an active account we would, of course, have continued to serve them.

Ah, Spring! What a Beautiful Spring!

Spring of 1984 was delightful. The weather was unusually pleasant and a number of good things happened. For the agency, one of the most significant was winning the Michigan Apple business for another five years.

We Add Two More New Accounts

The London's Farm Dairy, headquartered in Port Huron, invited BAC&K to make a credentials presentation and we were selected its agency of record. Doug Mowat, the president, and Fred Krohn, the vice president in charge of sales and marketing, were on the selection committee and turned out to be great people with whom to work. Our initial assignment was to assist in the development of all-new packaging, along with formulating advertising, public relations and marketing strategies for 1984 and 1985.

Founded in 1936, London's was one of the largest dairies in the state and distributed through supermarkets, independent food stores, drive-in convenience stores, and independent and company-owned dairy stores. The London's Farm Dairy account grew yearly as it added new products and expanded distribution.

Sprague Devices, Inc. of Michigan City, Indiana also named BAC&K its full-service agency in the spring of 1984. Sprague furnished all windshield wiping and cleaning systems for

North American railroad locomotives and is a major supplier to the heavy-duty and off-highway truck market, as well as to the special purpose vehicle industries, including manufacturers of fire trucks, buses, airport crash vehicles, crane carriers and recreational vehicles. This account was added to our roster of "business to business" clients and was managed by Bob Cunningham.

The most important event that spring of '84 took place on April 25, when my granddaughter, Emily Elizabeth, was born. My neighbor, John Feldmann, and I were spraying our orchards when Joan came running out of the house to tell us the exciting news.

On April 28, I attended the final banquet of the Michigan Dental Associations' Annual Meeting at the Westin Hotel. While eating a cup of navy bean soup, I bit down on a small stone and cracked off the side of a tooth. What a thing to happen at a meeting of dentists. When I got home I called my son Michael – a dentist – to tell him about my tooth. He asked me to meet him at his office early Sunday morning to repair the tooth.

The next morning, I went to Michael's office, and his wife Kathy was there to assist him. I climbed into the chair and he immediately started the procedure, as I could hear the hum of the drill. I said, "Wait – aren't you going to give me a shot to deaden the pain?" Michael replied, "No Dad – you're family." "Forget that nonsense," I said, "and give me the shot."

I Take On Several Volunteer Jobs

On May 24, I was elected to a one-year term as president of the Birmingham-Bloomfield Chamber of Commerce. I was also elected a governor-at-large of the Michigan Council of the American Association of Advertising Agencies (AAAA), the national trade association of advertising agencies. I eventually served two terms as a governor of the Michigan Council.

In addition, I was asked to serve as a member of the Advisory Council for the University of Missouri School of Journalism Department of Advertising, which I also did for a number of years.

Better Made Celebrates Its 50th Year With a New Advertising Campaign

In June, a major modernization effort was completed that more than doubled the size of the Better Made production facility, coinciding with the snack food company's 50th anniversary.

To commemorate the milestone, a new advertising campaign was developed by BAC&K, consisting of a full-page, two-color newspaper

135

advertisement that highlighted a special 50th anniversary potato chip package.

A new slogan (Nothin's Better Than Better Made) was developed and used in a TV commercial and incorporated into other company promotions, including new signage on the firm's delivery trucks.

The television commercial ran on all major stations in the Detroit area and my grandson, Matt, was in the spot.

The Detroit Tigers Roar In 1984!

For the fifteenth year in a row, the agency was responsible for the campaign to sell Detroit Tiger tickets. The theme of the campaign was "Hear the Detroit Tigers roar in 1984!" And roar they did! Everybody wanted to get on the winning bandwagon including one of our clients, the Michigan Apple Committee. The agency arranged a Michigan Apple Day at Tiger Stadium on Sunday, September 16.

Growers, shippers and processors – and their families – came by the busload from all parts of the state to watch the Tigers beat the Toronto Blue Jays.

The 1984 Michigan Apple Queen (Kathy Rasch), along with Johnny Appleseed, gave apples to both teams and to the press corps. The Michigan apple growers were also recognized in pre-game ceremonies and got a lot of press for their special day at Tiger stadium.

The Detroit Baseball Club had its best year since 1968 – winning the World Series – and the agency celebrated the Tigers' success with two parties.

Agency staff gathered first during the American League playoffs and again during the World Series to watch the game together on television in the office and cheer the team on to victory.

We practiced "The Wave" around the big conference room table for WXYZ-TV (Channel 7) reporter Bill Proctor, who covered the party as part of a story on Tiger mania in the city.

BAC&Kers watched themselves on a live report on the 11 p.m. news.

But more was at stake than just the outcome of the Series. A friendly bet made a free meal part of the bargain.

Henry DeVries, vice president of Stoorza Advertising in San Diego – the advertising agency for the opposing Padres team – challenged BAC&K to a wager involving the team owners' favorite products: Tom Monaghan's Domino's Pizza and Joan Kroc's McDonald's Big Macs.

Pizza won hands down. Stoorza Advertising, whose Padres fell victim to the Tigers, sent BAC&K gift certificates good for one hundred dollars worth of McDonald's hamburgers and a bushel of avocados.

Speas Farm Apple Juice Account Very Active With New Packaging and Special Promotions

Early in the year, Speas Farm rolled out new aseptic juice packages in 40 markets. The novel packaging of single units in a three-pack side-by-side configuration produced a continuous image of the product on the store shelf thus creating a stronger visual impact on the consumer than the packaging of competitive aseptic products.

The new packages came complete with a straw to be simply punched into the box. Unlike much of the competition, the Speas Farm aseptic packages contained 100% natural fruit juice with no sugar, additives or preservatives and were available in apple, apple and grape, and apple and cherry flavors. We initially advertised heavily in free-standing inserts (FSIs) and in 1985 produced three TV spots, with Soupy Sales as the talent, to sell the juice packs.

In late August and September of 1984, Speas introduced the Napplesack, a backpack for children, designed with a special side pocket to hold one of their aseptic packages of fruit juices. The self liquidating offer was advertised in FSIs in 55 markets with great success.

When we got the Speas account, it was in eighth place as a producer of apple juice. By 1984, it had moved up to number five and was the number-one apple juice producer in the midwest.

Our Creative Department Is Restructured

Our very capable, hard working creative director, Karen Aaberg, left to join her husband on the west coast, where he had been transferred. As a result of this, we began a restructuring of the creative department. We designated Diane Chencharick and Chuck Scholti associate creative directors as part of the plan.

Diane had been the agency's executive art director the past four years. Her responsibilities included the visual end of the creative product, including the production of television commercials and overall design of advertising layouts and collateral projects.

Chuck Scholti

Chuck was new with the agency but his portfolio included award winning work for a variety of clients from consumer, medical, retail and financial spheres. He was made primarily responsible for all the written material for the agency's creative efforts. Interestingly, Chuck held a B.S. degree in aerospace engineering from the University of Michigan. His aerospace knowledge came in very handy when we had to prepare a four-color, two-page spread to run in *Aviation Week* and *Space Technology* magazine for the Aerospace and Vickers Aerospace Divisions of Libbey-Owens-Ford. The two divisions participated in Aerospace Expo 84, a major international exposition of civilian and military aircraft parts, components and new technology.

An Intense Search For a New Creative Director

Throughout the fall we met with a number of potential creative directors to head our creative department. Work was flowing smoothly and well under the supervision of Chuck Scholti and Diane Chencharick but we still needed to fill the creative director position.

Diane Chencharick

We finally settled on Mike Saari, who had extensive experience as a creative director on both consumer and business-to-business advertising. He had served as CD at McCann Erickson's office in Frankfurt, Germany and had worked at Campbell-Ewald, BBDO, Young & Rubicam and D'Arcy MacManus Masius. His credentials included more than 30 significant awards for his creative work. Mike officially joined the agency on January 11, 1985 but his involvement with our clients actually began in December 1984.

We Become the Subcontractor Advertising Agency To Handle the Motorists Insurance Division of General Motors

The Motorists Insurance Division (MIC) of General Motors moved its headquarters from New York to Detroit. Its advertising agency, Gordon & Shortt, Inc. wanted to retain the account, so we worked out an arrangement whereby the strategic planning would be done by G & S in New York but creative, production, media placement, etc., would be handled by Baker, Abbs, Cunningham, & Klepinger, Inc. MIC did business in 15 states, primarily in the Midwest and Texas and was a leader in business volume. The coach of the Dallas Cowboys – Tom Landry – served as its spokesperson, appearing in TV, radio and print advertising. The account billed nearly $5,000,000 annually, so there was a considerable amount of activity that had to be handled.

Bob Klepinger Resigns To Join Another Business He Helped Start

On November 30, Bob Klepinger officially resigned to join Retail Detail, Inc., a company he had started with George Brown, Doug Wright and Zoe Pearson to serve retailers in the hardware/home centers field. Essentially, their business provided a detail service for manufacturers and the business had grown quickly once they secured Kmart's business. Bob's last day with the agency was December 31.

Our Most Successful Year

1984 was by far our most successful in profitability. We were able to pay higher bonuses, to add the maximum allowed to our profit sharing plan and to pay significant taxes to Uncle Sam and the State of Michigan.

In early November, Ronald Reagan won re-election in a sweep, and there was tremendous confidence about the future of the country and the outlook for business from Washington, DC right down to our offices in Birmingham, Michigan.

Standard Federal Savings, carried out two big campaigns starting in the late fall, in addition to continued promotion of its Kmart affiliations. It was now the fourteenth largest savings and loan in the nation and its aggressive promotions for savings accounts, home loans and VISA® credit cards continued right into 1985 in all the markets it now served, including Detroit, mid-Michigan and southwest Michigan, as well as Fort Wayne and South Bend, Indiana.

Our future looked bright indeed as we entered the second half of the 1980s.

Chapter 8

The Transition Years – 1985 Through 1989

"It's not just what you say that stirs people. It's the way you say it."

– Bill Bernbach

On January 4, 1985, the annual meetings of the agency's stockholders and directors were held and Kathryn "Kit" King was elected president, replacing Bob Klepinger. She had been named president and chief operations officer of the agency late in 1984, when Klepinger resigned to join Retail Detail. Kit continued in her role as management supervisor on the Standard Federal account and as a member of the bank's Product Development Committee, in addition to her new management responsibilities.

I continued as chairman and CEO of the agency. New committees to supervise operations and new business were established. Mike Saari was now working full time as our creative director. The agency, though, was in the process of going through a major transition with new management and a new focus, as well as having some new people in key positions.

The Agency Is HOT, HOT, HOT

Agencies that win a lot of creative awards are usually considered "hot." On January 25 the winners of the Michigan Addy Awards were announced and BAC&K received a total of eleven. Four top awards were won for the "Nothin's Better Than Better Made" television campaign for Better Made Potato Chips; another for "Wake Up, George," a radio commercial for Stanley Automatic Openers; a third for our "Win, Place, Show" direct mail program for Stanley Door Systems; and the fourth for a newspaper advertisement for Group Health Plan.

BAC&K also received three Addy Awards for Excellence. One for a television commercial produced for Standard Federal; and another for a print advertisement for Stanley Door Systems. Also awarded to the agency were four Certificates of Merit for a package design for a thermostat marketed by Stanley Automatic Openers Division, for print campaigns for the Michigan Apple Committee, and Standard Federal, and for our own newsletter, *BAC&K Talk*.

A panel of out-of-state judges with top advertising/marketing credentials based its decisions on a clearly defined point system. A total of 474 entries were submitted in 15 categories by 88 entrants.

BAC&K won more awards in the competition than any other competitor except one, winning out over such agencies as W. B. Doner, D'Arcy-MacManus and Masius, and Campbell-Ewald.

The Creative Advertising Club of Detroit also awarded BAC&K two "Caddy Awards" for the Better Made 50th Anniversary newspaper advertisement and the Michigan Apple campaign. The latter also was selected by the Art Directors Club in New York to be shown in its touring exhibit to be displayed throughout the United States, Europe and Asia. The campaign was chosen from over 17,000 entries.

BAC&K also received eight more Drummer Awards from *Building Supply Home Center Magazine* for excellence in the production of promotional material used by retailers in the building supply and home center industries. Six awards were for materials prepared for Stanley Automatic Openers and two for Stanley Door Systems.

Our "Hot" Reputation Attracts New Business

In February, March and April we met with a number of prospective accounts that had contacted us because of the publicity surrounding the numerous creative awards that we were winning. The product manager for Clear Eyes, which is produced by Abbott Labs, came to visit us and we handled several projects for this product.

St. Joseph Mercy Hospital Becomes a Client

On March 25, BAC&K was appointed the advertising agency for St. Joseph Mercy Hospital in Pontiac, a division of Sisters of Mercy Hospital Corporation (SMHC), which operates health care facilities in Michigan, Iowa and Indiana.

The agency developed the theme statement "We treat you in a special way" for the hospital, based on the SMHC commitment to personalized patient care and it was used in all internal as well as external communications. We also created a print campaign stressing the hospital's philosophy of care, which ran in area daily newspapers and in magazines.

AKZO Chooses BAC&K For Public Relations Services

In early April, AKZO Coatings America Inc., headquartered in Troy (MI), chose BAC&K as its public relations agency.

AKZO Coatings America Inc. is a leading manufacturer and marketer of industrial and commercial coatings for the automotive and related industries, as well as for consumer wood finishing products. The firm is a major part of one of seven divisions comprising the AKZO Group, a Netherlands-based international group of industrial companies with 220 operations in 50 countries.

We became responsible for coordinating all public relations with the trade and consumer press, as well as for the preparation of press releases on product information, new products, application, and new personnel and promotions.

Change Is Ongoing

On May 16, I conducted my last meeting as president of the Birmingham/Bloomfield Chamber of Commerce. It had been an interesting year and I met a lot of people that I would never have known had I not taken on this role. In May, I was also called to serve on a federal grand jury but, fortunately, was dismissed. David Harries resigned to join the Abitibi Corporation. We were sorry to lose David, but wished him well in his new position. Michael Murray was promoted to take over as the account manager for our Stanley accounts and Kevin Doyle was added to our staff to assist him.

To Maine and Back the Same Day

LOF Plastics, a division of Trinova (formerly Libbey-Owens-Ford), invited the agency to solicit the advertising of its Laminated Products Group. Our client, Aeroquip, was also a division of Trinova. The Laminated Products Group included Pioneer Plastics, a leading manufacturer of decorative laminated plastics and resins and resin-impregnated products. Pioneer Plastics is headquartered in Auburn, Maine but also had plants in Atlanta, Georgia; Crown Point, New York; and Compton, California, as well as six regional warehouse facilities. Also included in the Laminated Products Group was Consoweld, Inc., based in Wisconsin Rapids, Wisconsin. Sales exceeded $100 million and the advertising budget for the two brands, Pionite and DuraBeauty, was well in excess of a million dollars.

On August 9, John Ballantyne, Bob Cunningham and I – plus Howard Selland and Dan Vosburg of LOF – took off from Pontiac Airport in the LOF Executive Jet early in the morning. Just under two hours later, we were in Auburn, Maine. We toured the plant, learned how decorative laminates are made and became very enthusiastic about the prospect of handling the advertising and promotion of these products.

We quickly planned our presentation to win the business. We made our presentation in November and won.

We Get the John Henry Account Again

Back in 1963, Tony Franco and I made a presentation to the John Henry Company, which is located in Lansing, Michigan, when we were with Denman & Baker, Inc. and we won the business. The account then moved its public relations and advertising to Anthony M. Franco Public Relations when Tony left to start his PR firm.

Now, twenty-two years later, we were again assigned the advertising part of the account. The company had grown significantly, the employees now owned the business, and new management was in charge. For the next ten years we served as its advertising agency and Cathy Delgado was assigned to handle the account. She joined the agency as an account coordinator, and was named assistant account executive in 1984 and an account executive in 1987, working on the Standard Federal account. Cathy also served as office manager with additional personnel responsibilities in the support systems group. *A John Henry Company trade advertisement appears on page 142.*

Standard Federal Converts To a Savings Bank

Standard Federal Bank obtained its Federal savings bank charter early in 1985, but opted to defer the celebration until its new logo, signage and other corporate identification were in place.

Cathy (Delgado) Wing

With that major task accomplished, the Bank celebrated its new status with gala events for employees. To illustrate its expanding role as a full-service financial institution, Standard Federal hosted its own financial expositions for more than 1,500 employees at Somerset Mall in Troy, the Hilton in Fort Wayne and Morris Park Country Club in South Bend. Twenty-five exhibits were prepared by various departments of the Bank in cooperation with BAC&K.

Included were lively demonstrations of the many banking products now available, such as commercial loans, discount brokerage services, insurance, commercial real estate loans, VISA® cards and auto loans.

To get the word out to existing and future customers, Standard Federal and BAC&K produced two newspaper advertisements, two television commercials, a magazine advertisement, a direct mail campaign and an employee information kit that included a lapel pin depicting the bank's new logo.

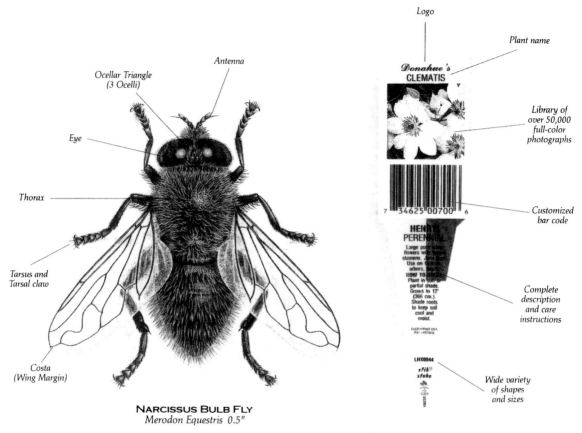

Antenna

Ocellar Triangle
(3 Ocelli)

Eye

Thorax

Tarsus and
Tarsal claw

Costa
(Wing Margin)

NARCISSUS BULB FLY
Merodon Equestris 0.5"

Logo

Plant name

Donahue's
CLEMATIS

Library of
over 50,000
full-color
photographs

Customized
bar code

7 34625 00700 6

HENRY
PERENNIAL

Large pure blue
flowers with yellow
stamens. June-Sept.
Use on trellis,
arbors, fences.
HOW TO GROW:
Plant in sun or
partial shade.
Grows to 12'
(366 cm.).
Shade roots
to keep soil
cool and
moist.

Complete
description
and care
instructions

LHX0044

sFik
sFake

Wide variety
of shapes
and sizes

CLEMATIS PLANT TAG
Tagus John Henryus 4.5"

HOW TO RECOGNIZE A CLEMATIS WITHOUT BEING A NARCISSUS BULB FLY.

Unless your customer happens to be an insect that relies on instinct to identify plants, a John Henry tag is the next best thing.
As you can see, our tags carry all kinds of information to make identification easy. The custom bar code is a great way to provide marketing information, inventory control data and accurate pricing at the checkout. And each tag can be customized with your logo. The
For more information on the industry's best quality tags John Henry
and service to match, give us a buzz at 1-800-748-0517. Company

5800 W. Grand River Ave., Lansing, MI 48906, (800) 748-0517, FAX 800-968-2598

Standard Federal Bank, now with assets of over $5 billion, would experience tremendous growth in the years ahead.

Fred Savage – Future Star Performer – Is the Spokesperson In a Series of London's Farm Dairy Television Commercials

When Fred Savage was only eight years old he touted the taste of London's ice cream, milk and cottage cheese products in a series of television commercials produced by BAC&K and aired in the Detroit area and other eastern Michigan markets. His smiling face was also seen in the dairy's consumer and trade print advertising tying the entire campaign together.

Three television commercials were produced starring a very young Fred Savage, who then went on to Hollywood to star in motion pictures and on television. The commercials for the dairy's milk, ice cream and complete product line marked the first time that London's had ever advertised on television.

In addition to accomplishing its marketing objective, the campaign reaped an unexpected benefit. Management staff at London's Farm Dairy said the excitement generated among the dairy's employees by the television campaign did wonders for employee morale. That alone, they said, made it worthwhile.

The commercials were lauded by the Milk Industry Foundation/International Association of Ice Cream Manufacturers. The entire advertising campaign, of which the commercials were a part, received the Best Dairy Products Campaign award for 1985 from the Association.

Soupy Sales Selected For Speas TV Commercials

With Speas now the fifth largest producer of apple juice in the country, the company, owned by the Sawyer Fruit & Vegetable Cooperative in Bear Lake, Michigan, decided it was ready to take its aseptically packaged juice products to the television airwaves in a significant manner.

After careful study, BAC&K recommended that Speas communicate in its advertising to the primary consumers of juice – school-age children – and the principal purchasers of juice – their parents. To do that, BAC&K needed to secure a spokesperson who would appeal to both groups. We looked for a TV personality who was popular when these boomers-turned-parents were young, a person who would bring back a lot of memories for mom and dad and appeal to today's young juice drinkers.

No one but the incomparable Soupy Sales, we thought, would be better for the job. We contacted him in New York, where he had just signed a three-year contract to host a popular radio talk/comedy show with WNBC. Soupy agreed to star for Speas, and a series of three very entertaining television commercials were written and produced by BAC&K. The spots first ran in selected test markets in the Midwest in the fourth quarter of 1985 followed by a heavy TV schedule in a number of markets in the first quarter of 1986.

A Lot of New Business Activity In the Last Two Months of 1985

In addition to the invitation to make a presentation to LOF Plastics, we were also offered the opportunity to solicit the advertising accounts of Detroit's Renaissance Center, the Metropolitan Detroit Cadillac Dealer Association, Arnold Manufacturing (located in Windsor, Canada) and Ladbroke DRC Race Track (in Livonia, Michigan). I also had a breakfast meeting early in November with Chuck Muer, at his invitation, to discuss the possibility of handling the advertising for his restaurants. Nothing came of the meeting. Chuck Muer and his wife, along with another couple, were lost at sea some years later off the coast of Florida when their sailboat sank during a terrible storm.

On December 13, I was named to the Board of Visitors for the School of Nursing of Oakland University and I still serve on that board.

1985 turned out to be a very good year – in fact, one of our better years in terms of profitability. We again added the maximum allowable to our profit sharing fund, paid bonuses and added to our working capital. Uncle Sam and the State of Michigan also received their share of our success.

Major Events That Occurred During 1985

During 1985 President Reagan and Mikhail Gorbachev met face-to-face for the first time to try to find answers to the arms race riddle. Reagan refused to back off from his Strategic Defense Initiative (SDI), known as "Star Wars," and Gorbachev refused to back away from his insistence that the arms race be barred from outer space. The summit did serve to give diplomacy between the two powers some much needed impetus. As Reagan candidly conceded at the end, "The real report card on Geneva will not come in for months or years."

Bernhard Goetz was tried for New York subway shootings, terrorists seized the cruise ship Achille Lauro and a killer earthquake reduced much of Mexico City to rubble – all big news stories.

The advertising business was affected when Capital Cities Communications bought ABC for $3.5 billion, proving that network TV was no longer an untouchable institution. Advertising agencies also made news. D'Arcy, MacManus, Masius and Benton & Bowles merged, and a TV production company, Lorimar, bought the Bozell & Jacobs agency, merging it with Kenyon & Eckhardt, which it had purchased in 1984. Hal Riney & Partners spun off from Ogilvy, and Scali bought a majority interest in Fallon-McElligott in Minneapolis.

Monday, January 6, 1964 was the first day of business for Baker, Abbs, Cunningham & Klepinger and it so happened that on the 22nd anniversary the January 6 again fell on a Monday. There was no celebration on that date, however, as we had decided to delay the recognition of our anniversary until Tuesday, January 28. This was the date for the annual meeting of the stockholders and the directors. That evening, all the stockholders, officers and directors and their spouses had cocktails and dinner together at the Charlie's Crab restaurant in Troy.

We had a number of things to celebrate besides our anniversary. 1985 turned out to be a very good year, plus we had added significant new business. On January 22, we made our presentation to Ladbroke DRC and five days later we were informed that we had been awarded its advertising account. It was time to celebrate. And celebrate we did!

We Created Thunder For Ladbroke DRC and Brought a Boom In Attendance

As soon as we were selected as the advertising agency for Ladbroke Detroit Race Course (DRC), there was a flurry of activity to prepare for Opening Day of the thoroughbred racing season on April 4.

A strong marketing and advertising campaign, with heavy use of television advertising and innovative ideas for effective use of other media, helped to produce record attendance and wagering on opening day at the Detroit area's only thoroughbred track. A record 10,329 fans packed the grandstands, up nearly 50 percent from the previous year's opening day.

Our strategy was to increase attendance by attracting first-time visitors who may have never experienced the excitement and fun that a day at the races can provide. To create this feeling of excitement, BAC&K developed a theme-line for Ladbroke DRC – "GO FOR THE THUNDER!"

This theme was then used in all print advertising and set to music for all radio and television broadcast advertising.

Because of weather conditions in Michigan, "Go For The Thunder!" television commercials were shot at a racetrack in New Orleans. BAC&K's creative team produced two 30-second commercials during four days of intensive shooting in March.

To announce the opening of the season, Ladbroke DRC and BAC&K coordinated a direct mail campaign aimed at over one million households. Also, free thoroughbred racing seminars were advertised and held at four locations throughout the metro Detroit area. More than 500 people attended these entertaining and informative seminars that explained the fundamentals of racing and wagering.

Throughout the season, newspaper and broadcast advertising ran to promote 12 different premium items during the 24-week racing season. The results were most impressive: the best Opening Day turnout for Ladbroke DRC since 1977; overall season attendance up more than 4% and the handle (amount of money bet at the track) up more than 14% over the previous year. This was a track record we were extremely proud of.

BAC&K Does Well Again In the 1986 Michigan Addy Awards

BAC&K once again made an excellent showing at the 1986 Michigan Addy Awards, sponsored by the Lansing Advertising Club and the American Advertising Federation.

The agency received two Addys – one for a 30-second animated television commercial for Better Made entitled "Marching Chips," and a second for an anti-theft print advertisement for Motors Insurance Corporation, a division of General Motors.

Also awarded to BAC&K were Awards of Excellence for the Sales Aid/Master Dealer Kit for Stanley Automatic Openers and for the agency's quarterly newsletter, *BAC&K Talk.*

Certificates of Merits were received for Stanley Door Systems' direct mail campaign entitled "The Unbreakables" and for Speas point-of-purchase dangler, "We Want Real Juice."

Standard Federal Bank also was honored with a direct mail campaign award by the Financial Institutions Marketing Association at its annual conference in Anaheim, California.

The award was given to Standard Federal for its Equity Line direct mail campaign that we created aimed at long-time homeowners. The campaign was designed to reach an upscale audience to inform them of the Bank's program allowing qualified mortgage holders to write themselves an instant loan of $7,500 to $100,000 based on the equity in their home.

More New Business Comes Our Way

Early in February we were appointed the advertising agency for Michigan Dental Plan and also assigned additional business by The Stanley Works – Stanley Door Systems of Columbus, Ohio. At the end of March we completed a major corporate project for LOF Plastics and on March 26, we were named its advertising agency.

LOF Plastics Decides To Change Its Name

Not long after we became the agency for LOF Plastics, it decided to change its name to Sterling Engineered Products, Inc. When a major corporation decides to change its name, it is usually a symbol for a change in the way that company conducts its business. Sterling Engineered Products, Inc. was certainly no exception.

For Sterling, the change was dramatic, if not a little confusing. Sterling Engineered Products, formerly LOF Plastics, had been a division of Libbey-Owens-Ford (no relation to Owens-Corning or Ford Motor Company). Libbey-Owens-Ford was now called Trinova, which included three companies in its fold: Aeroquip, Vickers and now Sterling.

Sterling marketed plastics through three different product groups: Automotive, Diversified and the Laminated Products Group.

Soon after BAC&K was assigned the advertising for the Laminated Products Group, the agency participated in the name change effort, with a three-page announcement advertisement which appeared in trade magazines targeted toward architects, designers and builders.

Specific brand advertising for Pionite and DuraBeauty, the two brands which were now marketed under the Sterling name, followed the announcement campaign.

Along with Sterling's new name came a change of venue. Sterling moved its headquarters from Troy, Michigan to Maumee, Ohio, right next door to Trinova's headquarters.

The Detroit Coca Cola Bottling Company Makes Us An Offer

During April we had several meetings with the Detroit Coca Cola Bottling Company about handling its advertising account. It turned out it was more interested in acquiring our agency then hiring us to handle its advertising. The Detroit Coca Cola Bottling Company, however, was sold later in the year and the principals then bought the Stroh's Ice Cream business – which was a competitor to our client, London's Farm Dairy.

The "Big Bang"

The "Big Bang" occurred on Monday, April 28, 1986, when three large, well-known and historically successful advertising agencies came together to form a group with worldwide annual billings in excess of $5 billion. This was the merger that ultimately became Omnicom Group, consisting of BBDO, Doyle Dane Bernbach and Needham Harper. Little did I realize when this was announced that a few years later BAC&K would be acquired by the Omnicom Group.

Other April Events

Monday, April 7, was opening day at Tiger Stadium for the Detroit Tigers and I – along with several clients who were my guests – attended. I had not missed an opening day in more than 20 years.

Joan and I were members of a Lutheran Church in Pontiac but decided to join the nearby Ortonville United Methodist Church, where our son Robert and his family were active members. We already knew a number of the people who attended this small, friendly church and, soon after joining, Joan and I started singing in the choir. We enjoyed going to church with Jane, Bob, Matt and Emily and, on most Sundays, we had brunch together following the service.

We held a seminar for our staff at Meadowbrook Hall in Rochester on April 26 and the next week Heleana and Peter Kocher and their daughter Christina came for a visit. They had been to the Mayo Clinic in Minnesota for Heleana's and Peter's annual physical exams and were on their way to their home in Germany. We first met Peter and Heleana in 1981 when we sat next to them on a flight from Toronto to Frankfurt and had become good friends. We enjoyed their annual visits and planned to visit them again in Germany, which we did several years later.

The AAAA's Dominate My Activities

As vice chairman of the Michigan District of the American Association of Advertising Agencies (AAAA's) it was my responsibility to plan a creative seminar for our district – which included all of the advertising agencies in Michigan and Toledo, Ohio. I wanted to make it a truly outstanding event so, with the help of Sean Kevin Fitzpatrick, we were able to get Hal Riney, a nationally recognized advertising executive, to commit to conducting the half-day seminar. Sean was a well-known creative director with McCann Erickson and a friend of Hal Riney.

During May, I arranged for the seminar to be held at the St. Regis Hotel and promoted it with mailings, an advertisement in *The Adcrafter* magazine and a news release.

More than 100 people – a record number – signed up to attend the seminar primarily to see and hear Riney. He was the big attraction. One week before the seminar Riney canceled. Frantically, I called Fitzpatrick who managed to convince Riney not to cancel. Fortunately, he did appear thanks to Sean and the seminar was a huge success. Was it worth Riney's time to do the seminar? In the months to follow, he acquired the advertising accounts of the Stroh's Brewing Company and the Saturn Division of General Motors. Did his appearance at the seminar help bring this about? I think so!

Joan and I attended the annual AAAA's meeting at the Greenbrier, deep in the Allegheny Mountains of West Virginia, from May 13 through May 17. It was a great experience. The Greenbrier, with a heritage of over two hundred years of outstanding service, is an incredible place to stay but the meetings were also outstanding. Lee Iaccoca and Charles Kuralt were featured speakers, along with a number of high profile individuals in the advertising business. One afternoon – which was an open period – Joan

Marilyn (Palliaer) Staargaard

and I wandered around the grounds at the Greenbrier with Phyllis and John O'Toole. He was the former president of Foote, Cone & Belding and was the AAAA's chairman in 1984-1985. John later spent two years as head of the Association's Washington office and then served as Four A's president from 1989 until 1994 when he retired. John was inducted into the Advertising Hall of Fame prior to dying of leukemia in 1995, when he was 66.

At the end of May, we said farewell to Lorraine McGregor, who moved to Dallas to join her husband, as he had become the public relations director of American Airlines. Lorraine had headed our PR operation and she was replaced by Marilyn Palliaer. Jay Pepper also joined our staff as an account executive.

We Help London's Farm Dairy Make Their 50th Anniversary a Major Event

When London's Farm Dairy asked us to develop unique ways to promote their company's 50th anniversary, we responded with some creative ideas. First, we helped create a brand new ice cream flavor that had a great deal of name recognition throughout the state – Ryba's Mackinac Island Fudge.

We responded with a public relations blitz that tied the company's 50th anniversary into key state events. During the opening day celebration of the Michigan sesquicentennial, the world's largest chocolate sundae was created on the steps of the Michigan state capitol. Our public relations division, now led by Marilyn Palliaer, arranged for London's to construct a huge Ryba's Mackinac Island Fudge Ice Cream sundae within a sailboat. From the sailboat, which was later donated to the Bluewater Council of the Boy Scouts, over 12,000 free sundaes were distributed to Lansing festival-goers. This "Sailboat Sundae" turned out to be the most talked-about event at the sesquicentennial kick-off celebration and dominated the publicity coverage received.

From this point forward, promotional activities for London's Farm Dairy's 50th anniversary included a number of exciting advertising and PR events, such as:

- Major sponsorship and participation in the Port Huron to Mackinac Island Sailboat Race festivities, resulting in widespread media exposure.

- Official proclamation by the Governor designating Port Huron as "Ice Cream Capitol of the State of Michigan" and a special tribute to London's Farm Dairy to commemorate the company's 50th anniversary and its past contributions to the state. BAC&K worked with the Governor's office to obtain these two honors.

- Giant cold air balloons with London's logo located at the Bluewater Festival site.

- Public relations activities with the Bluewater Council of the Boy Scouts and the Port Huron General Hospital. Extensive news coverage resulted from each project.

- Popular Detroit media personalities such as Chuck Gaidica, WDIV-TV weatherman, radio station WJR's J.P. McCarthy, and WCZY's radio personality, Dick Purtan, all helped to promote London's Farm Dairy, its 50th anniversary and Ryba's Mackinac Island Fudge Ice Cream.

- A continuous and strong program including both advertising and public relations was scheduled through 1986 and into 1987, including additional new product launches.

A Tragic Drowning Accident

Late Sunday afternoon on June 22, I drove to Grand Rapids to spend the night at the Amway Grand, as I had been invited to speak at a meeting early Monday morning at this hotel. It was a meeting on Michigan Foods, sponsored by the Michigan Department of Agriculture. I stayed at the meeting until noon and then drove back to my office in Birmingham, where I learned that Mark Richmond – the young man in charge of our mailroom – had drowned Sunday afternoon. Mark was an especially fine young man who was attending Wayne University with the goal of entering the advertising business. Mark brightened our days with his smile. He was always kind, patient and eager to succeed and please. His death was a shock and the entire staff was devastated. It was a very, very difficult week.

A Busy Summer Flows Into Fall

Summer flew by with all the activities taking place for various clients. I was in the office nearly every morning before 8 a.m. and seldom was home before 6:30 p.m. The State Fair was another big success and we planned and carried out another Michigan Apple Day at Tiger Stadium. Busloads of apple growers came to Detroit from all over the state for this special day.

On September 3 our first meeting was held with Standard Federal to start making plans for it to make a public offering in 1987. The planning for its new corporate headquarters on Big Beaver Road in Troy was underway, with ground-breaking scheduled for early November. We put together an extensive ongoing campaign for the new headquarters. Following the initial press release, which announced the project and the site approval, we planned an exciting ground-breaking to attract full-scale media and community attention. Elements of this public relations program included:

- A unique invitation consisting of a toy construction vehicle – a bulldozer, cement mixer or earthmover, etc. – which was hand-delivered to key media and civic affiliates with the ground-breaking announcement attached.
- A special press kit including releases and photos on Standard Federal Bank's history and current status.
- News releases and photos on the new corporate building, the architecture and construction firms, and the Bank's commitment to the community.
- Photos and renderings of the new building. In addition, flags, pennants and signs decorated the landscape, while bulldozers and earthmovers provided an authentic backdrop for the ground-breaking ceremonies. Following the ground-breaking we created a series of special events to keep the media aware of the progress of Standard Federal's new financial complex.

Lady Luck Smiles On Me

On October 29, Greg Holub, John Ballantyne and I met with Don Drew, president of Ladbroke DRC. It was a particularly good meeting because Ladbroke was having a very successful race season. Our meeting ended around 3:30 p.m. and we decided to watch the last three races scheduled for that day. I was very lucky and won $1,500. I then gave John and Greg each $100 because they didn't win any money and when I got home I put $1,300 on the kitchen table. Joan asked, "What's this?" I explained it was hers to do with as she pleased, as I had won it at the horse races. Joan scooped it up and I never asked what she did with the money. I'm sure, however, that most of it was spent on our grandchildren.

I Join the Distinguished Clown Corps

When it started in 1925, Detroit's Thanksgiving Day Parade was barely a blip on the radar screen – a mere parenthetical reference buried in a *Detroit Free Press* story about Thanksgiving Day church services. By 1928, not much had changed. What started in relative obscurity, though, grew to become one of the nation's largest Thanksgiving Day parades.

When Hudson's Department Stores announced early in 1985 that it would no longer sponsor this parade, a task force was formed to save this annual event. Tom Adams, the retired former chairman and CEO of the Campbell-Ewald advertising agency, was a member of the task force. He came up with the idea of starting a distinguished clown corps made up of men and women, each of whom would pay $1000 annually for the privilege of being a clown and participating in the parade on Thanksgiving morning. Tom invited me to join the corps and I have been a member since 1986.

The clowns and their families gather at Cobo Hall in downtown Detroit before 8 a.m. on Thanksgiving morning. Breakfast is served and we get our clown makeup applied. After joining in a champagne toast to the parade, the distinguished clowns have a "class picture" taken, after which we board buses and go to where the parade begins on Woodward Avenue. The parade starts at 10 a.m. and lasts until noon, covering a 2.2 mile route with floats, inflatables, bands, equestrian units, drill teams and fantasy – and, of course – lots of clowns. It's really great fun! The Parade Company, which plans and produces the annual parade, is the operating arm of The Thanksgiving Parade Foundation and the 100 members of the Distinguished Clown Corps provide major financial support. In 1996, more than a million people watched curbside at what had become Michigan's largest public event, while millions more watched the parade coast-to-coast on the CBS television network. The Detroit parade had now become "America's" Thanksgiving Day parade.

Fall Quickly Turns Into Winter

Not only did Michigan apple growers have a good season in 1986 but so did Baker's Orchard. Cider mills took all the apples that we didn't give to friends, relatives and clients. Mark Arney, the manager of the Michigan Apple Committee, invited me to attend the Produce Marketing Association Convention in San Antonio. On October 19, we flew to San Antonio and the next morning the convention was underway. This was a big show with many exhibits, including one for the Michigan Apple Committee. October 20 also happened to be my 60th birthday but I didn't mention it to anyone. Mark and I walked through the large exhibit hall to check out the exhibits and also attended a number of sessions that were of particular interest. On Tuesday evening I had dinner with Gino and Madeline Guido – the couple Joan and I met in 1983 on our trip to Alaska. We enjoyed a nice visit and a great dinner at the La Scala restaurant. I returned to my office on October 23.

Much of What We Did Followed a Pattern

Much of what Joan and I did during 1986 followed a regular pattern or routine. Thursday evenings there was choir practice. Most Friday nights we went out for dinner and to see a movie. Saturdays we were usually busy around the orchard or involved with some special social activity. Sunday mornings we sang in the choir at the United Methodist Church of Ortonville and afterwards we had brunch with our son Bob and his family. And, special annual activities – like the Michigan Horticultural Society meeting in Grand Rapids the first week of December – we attended year after year. In 1987, though, our life would not be nearly as routine.

Major Events of 1986

Americans watched in horror as the space shuttle Challenger exploded on take-off. The Duvalier reign of terror in Haiti ended, while tensions increased in the Philippines with the rise of Corozon Aquino. Wall Street was rocked by scandals, with financier Ivan Boesky arrested and jailed for insider trading.

In the advertising business there were a number of mergers and acquisitions, with Saatchi gobbling up Bates, Backer & Spielvogel and Dancer Fitzgerald Sample (DFS). Saatchi and Saatchi upended Interpublic as the top agency group.

The anonymous "Herb" became the object of a national, $40 million manhunt by Burger King in what became the most elaborate advertising flop of the decade. The effort was dropped after four months.

Rupert Murdoch's News Corp. launched the Fox Network with Barry Diller, and General Electric acquired the NBC Network.

– 1987 –

Joan woke up on New Year's Day, with a bad cold that was even worse the next day. On Saturday her cold evolved into a severe case of the flu that lasted the next three days. Also on Saturday, our neighbor Keith Wandell, who was a retired master cabinetmaker, died of a heart attack. Keith was a special person, a good neighbor, and his death was quite a shock. Joan and I had gotten to know Keith and his wife, Dolores, well and Keith had made several things for our home. He had built a beautiful floor-to-ceiling bookcase for our family room to fill an opening next to the fireplace. He constructed it in his home workshop and when he and his sons brought the bookcase to our house to install it, the unit fit the space like a glove. Keith could do anything with wood. He frequently brought us produce from his huge garden. Every spring, he enjoyed making maple syrup from sap he collected from trees on his property, which he also generously shared with us. His funeral was January 6 and, although Joan still wasn't feeling back to normal, she insisted on attending the service with me. This was definitely not the best way to start a new year.

During January there were several heavy snowfalls and the orchard resembled a white fairyland. Our two snowmobiles got a lot of use in the evenings and on the weekends, as a number of our friends came out to ride them. At the office, things were humming, as we were very busy executing advertising plans that had been recently approved by Stanley Door Systems, Stanley Home Automation, Michigan Apples, Speas, Roney & Co., Ladbroke DRC and Sterling Engineered Products (Pionite). We were especially busy with activities for Standard Federal Bank, as it was planning on going public with a stock offering on January 21, 1987.

We Assist Standard Federal Bank In Going Public

In January 1987, Standard Federal Bank was an $8 billion federal savings bank, with 83 offices in Michigan and Indiana. Converting the bank from a mutual to a capital stock organization was one of the most important undertakings in its 94-year history. The decision to convert to a public company was implemented in order to operate the bank in the most efficient manner

for future growth. BAC&K was asked to provide communications counsel for this effort and we developed the following elements:

- A theme line, "SHARE IN OUR FUTURE," appeared in all communications. We believed there was power in the word "SHARE" – inviting the public to participate in a good thing, and considering them partners rather than merely buyers or beneficiaries…sharing in Standard Federal's FUTURE. No promise. Nothing misleading…but based on Standard Federal's long history of growth and success.
- These preliminary materials were developed and prepared by the agency:
  1. Pocket folder and envelope for prospectus and other materials.
  2. Q & A Brochures with both customer and employee versions.
  3. A comprehensive marketing piece presenting Standard Federal's management personnel.
  4. Banners, signs and buttons for use at investor meetings and at branch office locations.
- An announcement advertisement targeted at an investing-oriented public which was accustomed to, and familiar with, new offerings was also developed. The advertisement appeared exclusively in the financial pages of the major publications in each of the bank's service areas.
- We assisted in producing a dynamic audio-visual presentation which presented the bank in the most favorable light as a progressive, growth-oriented organization and poised to assume an even greater leadership role in the future. All of the bank's top management personnel appeared in this film.
- A media relations program was launched through our Public Relations Division. Major financial writers were issued personal invitations to interview top management personnel. An ongoing series of press releases were prepared and disseminated on a regular basis to appropriate media.

- A large-scale introduction event was planned for all 1,700 Standard Federal employees featuring the premier showing of the "Standard Federal Story" film and an exhibition of the bank's products and services. A similar meeting was held for the stockbrokers in the bank's market area, where brokers had an opportunity to meet the bank's management team.
- The agency also produced an internal newsletter called the "Stock Report" which kept employees updated on a regular basis about progress during the conversion period and answered questions which they or their customers might have.

The resulting total number of shares offered was over 30 million and gross proceeds received by the Bank exceeded $250 million. This level of proceeds was the largest amount ever received in an initial public offering by an FSLIC-insured thrift institution, except for three FSLIC-insured California thrifts in 1983. The amount of proceeds received in the subscription and community offering was also one of the largest ever achieved. It was also one of the best stock investments that I ever made. The stock I purchased at $8.25 per share was eventually sold for $59.00 a share in 1997. Plus, I also received quarterly dividends over that 10-year period.

Ernie Baker   **Dick O'Reily**   **Walter Dunne**

"Drug Free America" Program Introduced

On January 15, Walter Dunne and I met to discuss the launching of the "Drug Free America" program. Walter was then a vice president of Saatchi & Saatchi Advertising and we were both serving as governors of the Michigan District for the AAAAs. It would be primarily our responsibility to organize and launch this program in the Michigan 4A District, which also included Toledo, Ohio. On January 16, John O'Toole, who was now with the 4As, spoke at the Adcraft Club of Detroit. He introduced and described the "Drug Free America" program and its goals at this luncheon.

Follow-Up Meetings With Dick O'Reilly

On February 12, Dick O'Reilly, who was now the national director of the "Drug Free America" program, visited Detroit to meet with the governors of the Michigan Four As District. He outlined the program, described what was needed to introduce this huge effort to "unsell" drugs and presented samples of the advertising for all media which we were to distribute in our district.

My Role As Coordinator For the "Drug Free America" Program

The "Drug-Free America" program would be the largest and most ambitious private sector, voluntary advertising effort ever undertaken. This massive media program against drug abuse had been planned to equal $500 million of advertising time and space annually for its first three years. The goal was to produce a fundamental reshaping of social attitudes toward the use of illegal drugs.

The program included more than 50 different television and radio commercials, which would be broadcast thousands of times each year by the nation's networks and stations, as well as hundreds of different advertisements in thousands of magazines and newspapers nationwide.

Coordination and local placement of the campaign would be handled by the 28 regional councils of the AAAA, and this would be primarily my responsibility as head of the Michigan 4A. District. Fortunately, I had a very capable, dedicated administrative assistant in Phyllis Attwater, who did the bulk of the detail work. Our council was recognized a year later as one of the best in the country in getting this program launched. The credit for our success belonged primarily to Phyllis.

Dick O'Reilly Drowns On a White-Water Rafting Trip

I had gotten to know Dick O'Reilly quite well as a result of frequent contact with him regarding the "Drug Free America" program. I was saddened a few months later when he drowned on the Chilko River in British Columbia while on a get-away weekend in early August with eleven friends and business acquaintances. Tragically, five of the eleven drowned. The others included Robert Goldstein, VP-advertising for Procter & Gamble Co.; retired DDB Needham senior VP, James Fasules; and two DDB Needham senior VPs, Stuart Sharpe and Gene Yovetich. The HBO movie called "White Mile" is loosely based on court transcripts and accident reports of this Chilko trip and premiered May 21, 1994.

A Whole Bunch of Us Go To California On Vacation

Joan and I had told our family how much we enjoyed our vacations at Laguna Beach the past several years and now everyone wanted to go with us – and they did! On February 14, thirteen of us flew to California with 24 pieces of luggage – Jane, Robert, Matthew and Emily; Kathy, Mike, Blaine and Bradley (Reid hadn't been born yet); my father-in-law Edward Bauman, along with Jane's parents Marian and Jay Kaser. We all stayed at the Laguna Riviera

right on the ocean and my mother came over from Sun City, Arizona to join us. It amounted to a family reunion on the West Coast and we had a wonderful, memorable week relaxing, soaking up sun and playing on the beach, as well as a day at Disneyland plus a few other fun excursions mixed in! All good times have to end, though, so we returned home to cold, snowy Michigan on February 25.

Our Creative Staff Maintains a Winning Tradition

The BAC&K Creative staff continued an impressive tradition of excellence by once again making an outstanding showing at the Michigan Addy Competition. We received a total of seven awards in various categories.

When the Creative Advertising Club of Detroit held its annual award ceremony at Ford Auditorium, BAC&K won four caddies.

In the 1987 Telly Awards, a national competition honoring outstanding local and regional television commercials, BAC&K was awarded two bronze statuettes for excellence in commercial creativity.

We also held our lead in the Drummer Awards and since 1979 had won a total of 75 awards – more than any other advertising agency in the United States. The 1987 Drummer Awards were officially announced at a luncheon at the Ritz-Carlton in Chicago, where we received the following awards for our clients:

Best Overall Sales Aid Program
Stanley Entry Door Systems	GOLD
Stanley Garage Door Systems	GOLD
Stanley Thermostats	GOLD
Stanley Automatic Openers	SILVER

Best Individual Selling Aid – Sales Literature
Stanley Garage Door Systems	SILVER

Best Individual Selling Aid – Merchandiser Display
Stanley Thermostats	GOLD
Stanley Entry Door Systems	SILVER
Stanley Garage Door Systems	SILVER

Best Individual Selling Aid – Packaging

Stanley Thermostats   SILVER

Best Audio/Visual Program

Stanley Entry Door Systems   GOLD
Stanley Full Product Line   SILVER

"Drug Free America" Program a Demanding Project

The Drug Free America project took a lot of my time in March, as the campaign was scheduled to start in April. While Phyllis Attwater was busy distributing advertising materials to other agencies – which they in turn redistributed to media – I met with service clubs and various organizations that either wanted to know more about the program or wanted to tiein with it. I was interviewed by a number of radio stations and three TV stations and was asked to serve on the Michigan Coalition for Drug Free Youth to help it determine how best to use grants it had received from several foundations. Suddenly, I had become an expert on drug abuse because of my involvement in the Drug Free America program.

The AAAA annual meeting was held at the Boca Raton Hotel and Club and Joan and I left for Florida on March 22. We were there for a week attending meetings. The meetings concluded on March 28 with a presentation of all the advertising developed free of charge by more than 50 advertising agencies for the Drug Free America program. I was back in the office on March 30, and went right to work helping to prepare a presentation for Hardees Restaurants, as we were a finalist for its advertising account for its midwest region.

The Drug Free America program got another big boost in Detroit on April 3, when Allen Rosenshine of the Omnicom Group spoke at The Adcraft Club, providing more insight into this new project. I had an opportunity to visit with Allen before the luncheon, as I was invited to sit at the speakers' table.

The White Gun Controversy

April 1987 saw the kick-off of the campaign against drug abuse. The campaign, officially called "The Media-Advertising Partnership for a Drug-Free America," sought to re-shape fundamental attitudes about using illegal drugs. Public communication companies – advertising agencies, the media, production companies, etc. – volunteered time and money to try to make the program a success.

A variety of television commercials were produced. One, entitled "The White Gun," had been held back. This commercial showed a businessman alone in his office loading a white gun with white bullets to symbolize cocaine. As he put the gun to his head the voice-over said, "Cocaine. It can cost you your brain."

Because many who had seen private screenings felt the commercial could be incorrectly perceived as dealing with suicide as a "solution" to a personal drug problem rather than as an analogy to the damage someone does to himself by using cocaine, the commercial was kept off the air.

Channel 7-WXYZ television in Detroit, agreed to help the Drug-Free America campaign effort by airing the spot and assessing public reaction. I made personal appearances on Channel 7 news programs, as well as on "Kelly & Company" and Dayna Eubanks' "Second Look" program, to introduce the commercial when it was aired.

During the "Second Look" program, debate was encouraged between panelists and me, as well as with members of the audience. While all agreed there was a need for strong action against drug abuse, not everyone thought "The White Gun" television commercial was appropriate.

After the television shows, WXYZ-TV received 211 letters and 41 telephone calls. Most (67%) of those who called or wrote felt that the commercial was appropriate to air nationally. In general, though, people *did* feel that it may evoke thoughts of suicide and, consequently, the commercial was never aired nationally.

Hardees Awards Us With Its
$2 Million Midwest Region Account

In 1987 Hardee's was the third largest fast service restaurant in the United States, based on restaurant sales and customer traffic. It selected BAC&K as its advertising agency for the Midwest Region, which included Michigan, Illinois, Indiana and Ohio. Our first effort was a campaign that included print, radio, direct mail, outdoor advertising and event marketing, all in support of the "We're Out To Win You Over" national advertising program.

A Weekend Get-Away
At the Grand Hotel

Our sons and their families, had given Joan and me a weekend at the Grand Hotel on Mackinac Island as a Christmas present. We left early the morning of May 23 for the Grand Hotel to enjoy our Christmas present and checked in after lunch. Following dinner Saturday night, we went to the theater in the hotel to watch the movie "Somewhere In Time," which was filmed on Mackinac Island and at the Grand Hotel. Christopher Reeves and Jane Seymour starred in this film and, though we had seen it before, it was a special experience to view it where it was actually produced. On Monday morning, we checked out and headed home, as I had meetings scheduled at the office on Tuesday.

Joan's Checkup Reveals
She Has a Tumor

Later in the week after we returned from Mackinac Island, Joan had an appointment with her gynecologist and, during the checkup, Dr. Stanley Dorfman detected something and suggested Joan have additional tests at St. Joseph Mercy Hospital. She spent June 5 at the hospital, taking additional tests, and on June 8 we met with Dr. Dorfman to get the test results. He told us that there was a tumor but that we shouldn't worry, as he didn't believe it was malignant. Surgery was scheduled for early Wednesday morning at St. Joseph Hospital for a hysterectomy and to have the tumor removed. During the surgery it was discovered that, not only was the tumor larger than tests indicated, but it was also malignant. Dr. John Malone, an oncologist/gynecologist at Hutzel Hospital, was called in to assist with the surgery. Late in the afternoon, the surgery was completed and Joan was out of recovery at 9 p.m. She was in a lot of pain but relieved that the tumor had been removed.

When I went to visit Joan the next afternoon, Priscilla and Tom Ricketts were already there to see her. Saturday, June 13, was Joan's birthday and spending the day in the hospital was not the best way to celebrate it.

Joan left the hospital on Monday and she was delighted to be back home again. I took the week off to be with her and to help her but she was running the washing machine on Tuesday and it was difficult to keep her from trying to do too much. Her first chemotherapy was Thursday at Hutzel Hospital. We had decided to have Dr. John Malone supervise her care, as she was scheduled to have chemotherapy every month for the next six months. Each "chemo" treatment lasted five hours and Joan was nauseated for the next two or three days following each treatment. Remarkably, she never complained about the discomfort but I knew she felt terrible. She did everything she could to make our lives as normal as possible.

International Apple Institute Holds Its
Annual Convention In Grand Rapids

At the end of June, the International Apple Institute held its annual meeting in Grand Rapids. Marilyn Palliaer and I attended, representing the agency. We also wanted to see a large special display the agency had designed and installed at the Grand Rapids airport that welcomed the delegates to this meeting.

155

DDB Needham Wants To
Acquire the Agency

Brian Bowler, president of DDB Needham's Detroit office, called to invite me for lunch on July 15. Brian explained at our lunch that the Detroit office, which handled the VW and Audi accounts, needed to have a larger base of accounts in order to attract and hold creative people. This office had experienced a big turnover in its creative staff, as there was great pressure on the agency to create advertising to help these two auto marques regain their share of market. They had both slipped badly in sales in recent years. Along with this, there had been a constant turnover of people on the client side and each change also resulted in a change in strategy for the advertising for VW and Audi.

Additional meetings followed with Brian and we provided information on the agency that would help it put together its proposal for acquiring BAC&K, Inc. It was agreed that two accounts, Hardees and Better Made Potato Chips, would have to be resigned if the acquisition went through, as DDB Needham handled the McDonald's and Frito Lay accounts.

By early September, we had essentially agreed to all the terms and conditions of being acquired and there was one last hurdle to get over. There was the possibility of a potential conflict with our client, Standard Federal Bank, because DDB Needham's San Francisco office handled the First Nationwide Bank account. On September 11, I met with Tom Ricketts, president and CEO of Standard Federal, to review the merger proposal and to discuss the First Nationwide Bank situation. Tom gave us his approval to proceed. He believed there was no conflict as long as the San Francisco office handled First Nationwide's account in that office and the two banks served different marketing areas. I was really relieved to get over this potential obstacle.

On September 14, in the business section of the *Detroit Free Press*, it was announced that First Nationwide Bank, a subsidiary of the Ford Motor Company, had acquired two small savings and loans in Dearborn, Michigan. I couldn't believe it! The next day we canceled our plans to be acquired by DDB Needham because First Nationwide Bank was now doing business on Standard Federal Bank's turf.

Our Client, Stanley Home Automation, Hosts an Appreciation Luncheon For the Agency

Dan Meyvis, Vice President of Sales and Marketing for the Stanley Home Automation Division of The Stanley Works, invited our entire staff to a luncheon on August 21 at the Machus Sly Fox to acknowledge the successful launch of the new LIGHTMAKER™ home control unit. We had already helped our client introduce the LIGHTMAKER™ garage door opener, a unique garage door opener that not only opened and closed the garage door, but also turned on lights inside and outside the home from the safety and security of the car. The LIGHTMAKER™ garage door opener had been very well received by consumers seeking additional security and convenience.

To extend this successful concept, Stanley had developed LIGHTMAKER™ Home Controls. These controls worked the same as the LIGHTMAKER™ opener, sending signals through existing house wiring to control lights and appliances throughout the home – from one convenient location.

The products consisted of four control units, all with different features, and three modules to control any type of incandescent lighting, plus an appliance module for turning TVs, stereos and other appliances on and off.

The Stanley LIGHTMAKER™ Home Controls were introduced to the trade at the 1987 National Hardware Show. To support the introduction of the LIGHTMAKER™ Home Controls, the agency had developed packaging, P.O.P. materials, a trade brochure, a consumer stuffer, trade advertising, direct mail, and promotional material.

Judging by the response at the trade show, as well as by research we conducted to determine consumer attitudes toward the product, it appeared as though Stanley was well on its way to being the leader in the "Home Automation" market.

Our creative staff especially appreciated the recognition that our client gave them at this luncheon. A "Thank You" now and then goes a long way in inspiring enthusiasm for a particular client.

John Deere Appoints BAC&K As Their Midwest Region Advertising Agency

We had met several times in July and early August with Marvin Moeckley and John Steffin, who were with John Deere's Regional Office in Lansing, Michigan. On August 25, they informed us that we were going to handle advertising for their midwest region. This involved co-op programs with all the midwest dealer associations. We immediately went to work planning a big promotion for snow removal equipment.

We were delighted to win this account but it turned out to be a short relationship. Less than a year later, John Steffin was transferred to John Deere's Chicago headquarters and his replacement reassigned the account to John Deere's national advertising agency, even though the dealers were praising the campaign we produced for them.

September – An Interesting But Hectic Month

On September 1, I bid on and bought a 1,335-lb. prize steer at the Michigan State Fair Youth Livestock Association. We had a record attendance at the Michigan Apple Day at Tiger Stadium because the Tigers were leading the Eastern Division, which they clinched on Sunday, October 4. Unfortunately, the Tigers lost to the Minnesota Twins in the playoffs

and didn't make the World Series. I attended a lot of meetings in September, including a 4A Regional meeting in Chicago and several meetings to review the progress of the Drug Free America campaign. Joan had her fifth chemotherapy treatment and each one seemed a little worse than the one before.

The Stock Market Plunges 510 Points

On October 19, the Stock Market plunged 510 points. We happened to be conducting a taste test of 14 varieties of Michigan apples that day. Someone joked that maybe we should have saved the apples, rather than use them for a taste test, in case we needed to earn money selling them on the street corner. Shades of the depression! In time, however, the market more than recovered, but the huge drop was a real shocker.

Our New Campaign For Pionite® Decorative Laminates "Jazzes Up" the Design World

After an initial effort establishing the brand identity of Pionite® decorative laminates and its affiliation with two new corporate names, Sterling Engineered Products and Trinova Corporation, the agency was charged with developing a comprehensive new product campaign.

This was a product category dominated by two names – Formica and Wilsonart. They were so firmly established in the minds of architects, interior designers and remodelers, that they pretty much ran the same kind of advertising – new colors, new patterns, and an application photo.

It would have been simple to have followed this "accepted" pattern. But the need was apparent for something different to break through this monotony and shake up the design world.

"We looked closely at the mind set of our target audiences," John Ballantyne, our director of client services, explained when the campaign was presented to our client. "They are intensely proud creative people – sometimes professionally conservative, sometimes personally eccentric. We wanted a campaign that would show that we understood how creative they are. The feeling was that, if we could do this in a unique way, they would like our advertising and, in turn, like our product," according to John.

Chuck Scholti, our creative director, added, "Our mission then, was to capture the creative moment when the architect's and designer's imagination was running free. And to parlay this dynamism into a 'personality' for the product, as well as the company itself. Everybody has high quality. Everybody has good selection. But no one else can be Pionite!"

The new campaign showed musicians in moments of intense concentration when they create their best music. Artwork was used rather than photography to allow the readers to interpret the mood and feeling in their own way. The overall effect was to tie an intensely creative moment to what it is architects and designers feel when they solve a difficult problem in an elegant way.

The campaign met with great success. Inquiries flooded in for samples of the product and for reprints of the artwork in poster form.

We Add the Biz-Com "Best of Show" and a Gold Regional Addy To Our List of Awards

Having already won three Michigan Addy's and two Creative Advertising Club of Detroit Caddy's early in the year, the Great Doors Campaign created for Stanley Door Systems continued its winning ways.

At the Detroit Biz-Com Best of Michigan Awards; sponsored by the Detroit Chapter of Business/Professional Advertising Association (B/PAA), BAC&K won the "Best of Show" Award. The individual ads – "White House,"

"Pisa," and "Chateau" each won Gold Awards. In all, out of 50 total awards, we won five!

The Great Doors Campaign also won a Gold Award in the American Federation Sixth District Addy Competition. The individual advertisements all won Merit Awards.

Winning a district Addy is especially prestigious because it pits the best of Michigan against the best of Indiana and Illinois, which includes a great many big agencies in Chicago.

The Conclusion of 1987

Early in December, I spent two days at the Michigan Horticultural Society Meeting in Grand Rapids and made a presentation to the Michigan Apple Growers describing how we were doing a good job of competing with Washington Apples despite being outspent three to one in the Midwest – Michigan Apples' primary marketing area. Michigan had a huge apple crop in 1987 of 27,300,000 bushels.

We had recommended that most of the budget should be spent on a heavy print advertising campaign to the trade. At the same time, consumer advertising on radio would be used in a limited way. Because distribution gains were critical, only 50,000-watt radio stations, with their stronger signals that covered large geographic areas, were used early on in the program. These stations were also willing to support our media campaign by writing letters to chain store produce buyers, telling the Michigan Apple story and describing specific promotions.

The goal was to develop and expand the distribution base, i.e., the trade, to set the stage for greater consumer sales. This meant heavier spending on the trade through a "push" strategy rather than through the consumers (as Washington state was doing) with a "pull" strategy.

In the trade advertising we told the produce buyers that the Michigan Apple Committee was sending out impactful advertising to consumers and they should, therefore, be fully stocked year 'round with Michigan apples, since consumers would be looking to buy them because of that advertising.

Consumer research commissioned by the Michigan Apple Committee showed that even though Washington state, the primary competitor, out-spent Michigan three to one, advertising awareness of Michigan apples among consumers went up significantly to 11% versus Washington's 19%. Further, (unaided) brand awareness for Michigan was 46% and 68% for Washington. The strategy worked well. The trade embraced Michigan apples, and the consumers became aware of the Michigan apple story.

More Surgery For Joan

The agency's annual Christmas party was held on December 11, which Joan and I attended. On December 14, Joan underwent "second look" surgery at Hutzel Hospital, as she had received her last chemotherapy treatment in November. We were elated when Doctor John Malone informed us there was no sign of cancer. She left the hospital on December 22 and the family enjoyed a wonderful Christmas together at Jane and Bob's home – a log home situated in the middle of a forest near Ortonville. We had much to be thankful for and there was great joy in celebrating together.

– 1988 –

The hectic pace of the past fall continued right into and through the first quarter of 1988 at the office, as there was an extremely busy work load. Early in February, the annual meeting of the stockholders and directors took place and John Ballantyne was elected a director of the agency. In the first quarter of 1988, we also continued our winning ways by receiving a number of awards for our creative efforts.

A major change took place with the Detroit Tigers, as they established a new position of vice president of marketing, promotion and sales and hired Jeff Odenwald to fill this post. Jeff joined the Detroit baseball club from the Chicago Cubs, where he had been director of merchandising and broadcasting. My first meeting with Jeff was on March 3 and this would be the first of many meetings. Dan Ewald continued to be responsible for the advertising, as Jeff's efforts were initially directed at developing corporate sponsorship programs. He is now the director of marketing and business affairs for USA Baseball and is responsible for managing the marketing, sales and business operations of the organization and its three national teams.

George Pisani

On March 14, I met with George Pisani to discuss his joining the agency. George had been a successful, award-winning designer and had retired. Retirement was not challenging enough and George wanted to become active again. He was 76 years young in 1988. Many of the package designs George created when he was operating his own design company, Trombley,

Pisani & Trombly, are still in use today at Borden's, Dow Chemical, Faygo Beverages, Johnson and Johnson, Dow Chemical Packaging (Saran Wrap), Arrow Liquors and Hiram Walker Distillery. He worked until July 1999 when he underwent surgery. George was 87 when he died October 6, 1999.

At the end of March, Central Michigan University engaged our services to advertise and promote the graduate and undergraduate programs it offered at fifty locations in the U.S. and Canada. Standard Federal's new headquarters was now well underway and, on May 2, several of us from the agency had a tour of the building. On May 6, I met with Bruce Wagner, executive vice president of the Ross Roy, Inc. advertising agency. It was now interested in acquiring the agency.

At the 1988 AAAA annual meeting at the Greenbrier in West Virginia, Tom Hedricks gave a report on the Drug Free America program, which he now headed. John Pepper, president of Procter and Gamble, was a featured speaker. But the most interesting part of the meeting for me occurred on May 20, when Glen Fortinberry and I met. He was the chairman, president and CEO of Ross Roy, Inc. He was following up on my earlier meeting with Bruce Wagner. It was an interesting place to discuss the possible acquisition of the agency – standing in the pool in our swim suits. We agreed to meet for more discussions as soon as we were back in Michigan.

When I returned to Michigan I had several meetings with Glen Fortinberry and Chris Lawson, the financial head of the Ross Roy agency. Talks ended, though, when National Bank of Detroit awarded its advertising account to Ross Roy without a review. That created a definite conflict with our client, Standard Federal Bank.

In July, John Sanders, chairman and CEO of Young & Rubicam, contacted me. Now Y&R was interested in acquiring the agency. Unfortunately, it would mean moving back to downtown Detroit if we joined Young &

Rubicam. We had already committed to moving into Standard Federal's new headquarters. That made the merger impossible and the meetings ended.

Sunday, September 4, Joan and I celebrated our 40th wedding anniversary. Our sons and their wives, Bob and Jane and Mike and Kathy, threw a grand party with a big buffet dinner in a huge tent in front of Kathy and Mike's home on Lake Voorheis. It was a wonderful, memorable party.

40 Years In the Advertising Business

Fall marked forty years in the advertising business and it rolled in with plenty of new challenges – a number of meetings negotiating our space requirements and the lease for our new offices in Standard Federal Bank's headquarters. I was asked to serve on the Detroit Advertising Review Panel, which was a joint effort between The Adcraft Club of Detroit and Detroit's Better Business Bureau. The objective of the Review Panel was to stop misleading advertising. My name was drawn to serve on the first panel, which involved retailers of drapes and window blinds who were using illusory discount pricing by inflating manufacturers' list prices to calculate advertised discounts. Our panel – consisting of Adcrafters Val Carradi, Bill Volz, Saul Waldman and me – didn't achieve what we set out to do, as these retailers still advertise unreal discounts.

During the fall, I regularly met with Dan Ewald of the Detroit Tigers to plan the advertising campaign for the 1989 season and, by December, most of the advertising was approved and in production for release early in the new year. Again in early December, Joan and I attended the Michigan Horticulture Society Meeting in Grand Rapids and, once again, I made a presentation to the state's apple growers at the traditional Monday night meeting sponsored by the Michigan Apple Committee. We decided to have the family come to our home for Christmas, thinking it might be our last one on the farm, as a number of prospective buyers had recently surfaced. It was a warm, wonderful Christmas and, as it turned out, it was the last Christmas we would celebrate in the country at Baker's Orchard.

Major Events of 1988

During 1988, George Bush swept to victory beating Massachusetts Governor Michael Dukakis to ascend to the White House. Soviet troops finally abandoned Afghanistan after being involved for nine years. Broadway was under the "spell" of the "Phantom," which is still going strong in theaters.

In the advertising business, the top 25 agencies recorded higher gross income from foreign operations than they did from domestic operations for the first time. Television viewing was significantly impacted by widespread use of video cassette recorders. Only 4% of U.S. households had a VCR in 1982 but by 1988 more than 60% of TV households boasted one.

– 1989 –

January 6, 1989 was the agency's 25th anniversary and we celebrated the milestone with a champagne and pizza lunch in our conference room for our staff and any clients who wished to join. A few actually did show up. The agency started January 6, 1964 with a staff of eleven people. Now 25 years later, I was the only one remaining of the original eleven. Bob Anthony, Joe Gallagher, Don Brown and Evelyn McSorley were deceased, while the other six were employed elsewhere or, in two cases, full-time homemakers.

MDOT Becomes a Client

Friday, January 13, turned out to be a lucky day for us, as we were awarded a contract by the Michigan Department of Transportation (MDOT) to promote bus travel in the state of Michigan. Greyhound, Indian Trails and other bus companies operated the vehicles, but the state of Michigan actually owned all the buses and the bus stations. Thus, the state had a proprietary interest in encouraging more people to travel by bus. It was an interesting assignment and we put most of our efforts (advertising dollars) into encouraging college students and seniors to use the buses – which turned out to be quite successful.

Two different television commercials were developed to target each distinct audience. These bright, clever spots featured a running dialog geared to our senior citizens and college student audiences. A theme line, "We drive so you don't have to," was developed for the campaign. We also secured a memorable "vanity" telephone number, 1-800-SEE-MICH, that interested customers could call to receive immediate and up-to-date information about bus schedules and fares.

We Part With the Hardees Account

During January we held several meetings with Hardees trying to get it to consider a new financial arrangement. We had a team of people assigned to its account and our income from its business barely covered our overhead. Hardees was unwilling to budge, so we resigned the account on February 7. It then hired several people from our staff to work directly for Hardees.

We Take the A-Train

In preparation for their retirement B and Bob Cunningham had purchased a big RV. They invited Joan and me, Joan's dad, Ed Bauman, plus Janet and Doug Graham, to travel in their RV to Sault Ste. Marie, Canada, where we would take the snow train operated by Algonac Central – which is why we called it the A-Train. We left Friday morning, March 17 and it took all day to travel to the top of Michigan and cross over into Ontario. That evening we had dinner at the Pagoda Chinese restaurant, where we had been told to order the 12-course dinner. The dinner was delicious but we weren't sure what some of the courses were. When we asked our waiter, who spoke very little English, what it was we were eating, his reply each time was – "Chinese food!" After a while, we stopped asking!

Having spent a day on the snow train, I now realized where much of the water in the Great Lakes comes from, as I never saw so much snow in my life. When it melts in the spring, the lakes fill up. It was an interesting, enjoyable weekend with good friends. Fortunately, we arrived back safe at home Sunday night after enduring thirty below zero cold in Canada and slippery driving conditions on our return from the north country.

Plans For Our New Offices Move Ahead

By the end of March, plans for our new offices in the Standard Federal headquarters building were finalized. Then came the task of selecting a company to do the "build-out" of the space. This meant more negotiations, but by mid-June, contracts were signed and the work begun. Our goal was to move to our new offices at the end of August, when our three leases for our offices in Birmingham ended.

Speas Is Acquired By P & G

Baker, Abbs, Cunningham & Klepinger started handling the advertising for Speas in 1981, and the initial advertising campaign consisted of only newspaper advertising. Since that time, Speas had grown tremendously and Speas Farm Juice Blends had become the best selling aseptic brand in America. Using a wide range of advertising media – from black and white newspaper and four-color magazine advertisements to full-page, free-standing inserts and television advertising – BAC&K's account service and creative team had been instrumental in expanding Speas Farm's market share. According to the spring 1989 SAMI Report (this report measures the volume of package goods merchandise withdrawn from warehouses and shipped to food stores), Speas Farm Apple-Cherry, Apple-Grape, Apple-Raspberry and 100% Fruit Punch had become America's leading brands of blended aseptic fruit juice. Dollar volume had gone up 59%, while pint volume had gone up 64% over the same time a year before.

This outstanding growth attracted the attention of the Proctor & Gamble Company and its Suntory Brands Division acquired our client. We tried – without success – to retain the Speas advertising account. Knouse Foods of Peach Glen, Pennsylvania now owns the Speas label along with Musselman's and several other lines of apple products.

A Beautiful Spring

The weather in April and May was ideal – just what spring should be – and my neighbor, John Feldmann, and I got all the spraying of our apple trees done on schedule – quite unusual. Opening day for the Tigers, Friday, April 7, was unusually warm and a capacity crowd watched the Tigers beat Milwaukee.

Joan and I left for the AAAA meeting at the Greenbrier in West Virginia on May 16 and spent that night in Marietta, Ohio, the first town settled in Ohio. We took time to drive around Marietta the next morning and were quite impressed with the number of antebellum homes that were still lived in and well maintained in that city. We then took the turnpike and headed for White Sulfur Springs, where the Greenbrier facility is located. On the way we got very hungry and I took an exit off Highway I-64 into Green Sulfur Springs, where we enjoyed lunch at a small country general store. Not only did we have a delicious lunch, but we had a wonderful experience. Our lunch consisted of sandwiches of stacked ham and cheese on soft white bread with mayonnaise, lettuce and sliced tomatoes. The lettuce, bread and tomatoes couldn't have been fresher, while the ham and cheese were sliced especially for our sandwiches. We shared a big bag of Lay's potato chips. Joan had a Diet Pepsi with her sandwich, while I had a chocolate soda. Then we topped off our lunch with an Eskimo Pie ice cream bar. It was chilly, so we ate our lunch sitting around a warm pot bellied stove, talking with three men and the postmistress (she owned the store). We had a good visit.

As usual, the speakers at the AAAA meeting were outstanding and I participated in several good workshops. Following the meeting, Joan and I took several days to relax in Gatlinburg, Tennessee and again spent time in the Great Smoky Mountains. On Thursday, I was back in my office.

Joan Undergoes Surgery Again

During her regular monthly checkup in early June Dr. Malone discovered another tumor. Joan's CA-125 test had been elevated for several months but CAT scans and X-rays hadn't revealed any tumors. Now there was one. On Tuesday, June 13 our entire family came together to celebrate Joan's 60th birthday. The next day, she checked into Hutzel Hospital in Detroit. Surgery the next morning lasted six hours and I was able to see her briefly in ICU late in the afternoon. Joan finally left ICU late Friday afternoon and I was able to spend Saturday and Sunday and every evening the next week with her, as she didn't leave the hospital until Saturday, June 24. By the fourth of July weekend, she felt much stronger and her monthly chemotherapy regime started again in early August, with different but stronger chemicals than the last time.

We Get the Coffee Beanery Account

On July 10, several of us from the agency met with JoAnne Shaw, president of the Coffee Beanery, Ltd., headquartered in Flushing, Michigan. This rapidly growing company was becoming a popular franchise for shopping centers, with 29 outlets in six states. It was holding an advertising agency review and we were invited to make our presentation on August 4. On August 22, we were notified that we had been selected to handle its advertising and we immediately went to work for it, creating advertising and promotional materials to help sell gourmet coffees, coffee beans, gift packages and novelties. The Coffee Beanery, Ltd. now operates more than 200 upscale retail stores, streetfront cafes, free-standing coffee bars and kiosks in 31 states, and system-wide sales exceed $50 million. It was a client for four years until the account moved to Ross Roy, Inc.

We Make An Offer On a New Home – and Get It

Even though we hadn't sold our country home near Ortonville, we had been looking at other houses in order to be ready to move when ours sold. In mid-July, we looked at a house on Cedar Key Drive in Orion Township on Lake Voorheis. This was the perfect house for us, so we made an offer and it was accepted. Fortunately, we wouldn't have to close until late November, so we prayed someone would come along and buy the farm.

Get Ready – Get Set – Move

All during August we had prepared for our move from our offices in Birmingham to our new offices in the Standard Federal headquarters building in Troy by cleaning files, throwing out outdated materials and packing what we could. On August 31, the staff gathered for a farewell party…which we did as an Irish wake! We had enjoyed our years in Birmingham but now looked forward to going on to a "better place" and for the entire staff being together in one location in a brand new building. On September 5, we excitedly arrived at our offices and everyone's furniture was in place. The move was made flawlessly, with Phyllis Attwater in charge of all the details. There was no disruption of service to our clients.

We Change the Agency's Name – Again

Most clients, suppliers and the media referred to the agency as "Baker" or "Baker-Abbs" rather than using the full name – Baker, Abbs, Cunningham & Klepinger. Consequently, when we moved – since we had to reprint all the stationery and all our forms anyway – the name of the agency was shortened to Baker Advertising, Inc.

Merger Talks With DDB Needham Resumed

Earlier in the year, Ford Motor Company decided that it did not want the advertising for its subsidiary, First Nationwide Bank, handled by DDB Needham because this agency also handled advertising for Audi and Volkswagen in many countries around the world. First Nationwide was forced to change advertising agencies and, when that happened, the potential conflict with Standard Federal Bank no longer existed. Peter Farago, who had participated in the earlier negotiations, then contacted me to initiate new discussions about Baker Advertising becoming part of DDB Needham's Detroit office. Brian Bowler, who was responsible for starting the merger discussions when he was president of DDB Needham Detroit, had left that position and was now president and CEO of Porsche Cars North America, Inc.

The merger talks with DDB Needham resumed. The odds were good that we would be acquired by them unless some unforeseen "glitch" should pop up, as it had the year before. Soon after we moved and were settled in the Standard Federal Financial Center, a number of people from the Detroit office of DDB Needham visited us. Steve Burton, from DDB's New York office, spent a day with us at the end of September to review and discuss all aspects of the merger.

A Brief History of DDB Needham

DDB Needham came into being when Needham Harper Worldwide and Doyle Dane Bernbach merged as part of Omnicom in August 1986 (The Big Bang). Both agencies had great creative reputations. Needham Harper, which was headquartered in Chicago, created, many memorable campaigns for McDonald's, State Farm, Anheuser Busch and other major advertisers. Doyle Dane Bernbach was considered the creative capital of Madison Avenue. From the day DDB opened in 1949 it shook up the advertising business, leading a creative revolution. DDB first caused a stir when it filled New York subways with posters for Levy's bread reading, "You don't have to be Jewish to love Levy's." Sales for the bread skyrocketed! The Alka-Selzer phrase they created, "Mama, Mia, dattsa one spicy meatball" sold unbelievable quantities of that product. The "Lemon" and "Think Small" advertisements for Volkswagen are considered classics. Even today, decades later, the "We Try Harder" campaign for Avis is what most people think about when you mention Avis Rent-A-Car.

Advertising agencies make a great effort to find fresh, memorable and effective ways of selling products and services. DDB succeeded time after time because it regularly turned its back on the safe way of doing things and often poked fun at products it advertised. It used humor in advertising very effectively. The goal of the advertising created by Doyle Dane Bernbach, according to Bill Bernbach, was "to state the products' advantages in a way never

Think small.

Our little car isn't so much of a novelty any more.

A couple of dozen college kids don't try to squeeze inside it.

The guy at the gas station doesn't ask where the gas goes.

Nobody even stares at our shape.

In fact, some people who drive our little flivver don't even think 32 miles to the gallon is going any great guns.

Or using five pints of oil instead of five quarts.

Or never needing anti-freeze.

Or racking up 40,000 miles on a set of tires.

That's because once you get used to some of our economies, you don't even think about them any more.

Except when you squeeze into a small parking spot. Or renew your small insurance. Or pay a small repair bill. Or trade in your old VW for a new one.

Think it over.

The Chivas Regal of Scotches.

Give dad an expensive belt.

Lemon.

This Volkswagen missed the boat.

The chrome strip on the glove compartment is blemished and must be replaced. Chances are you wouldn't have noticed it; Inspector Kurt Kroner did.

There are 3,389 men at our Wolfsburg factory with only one job: to inspect Volkswagens at each stage of production. (3000 Volkswagens are produced daily; there are more inspectors than cars.)

Every shock absorber is tested (spot checking won't do), every windshield is scanned. VWs have been rejected for surface scratches barely visible to the eye.

Final inspection is really something! VW inspectors run each car off the line onto the Funktionsprüfstand (car test stand), tote up 189 check points, gun ahead to the automatic brake stand, and say "no" to one VW out of fifty.

This preoccupation with detail means the VW lasts longer and requires less maintenance, by and large, than other cars. (It also means a used VW depreciates less than any other car.)

We pluck the lemons; you get the plums.

Or buy a Volkswagen.

Avis is only No.2 in rent a cars. So why go with us?

We try harder.

(When you're not the biggest, you have to.)

We just can't afford dirty ashtrays. Or half-empty gas tanks. Or worn wipers. Or unwashed cars. Or low tires. Or anything less than seat-adjusters that adjust. Heaters that heat. Defrosters that defrost.

Obviously, the thing we try hardest for is just to be nice. To start you out right with a new car, like a lively, super-torque Ford, and a pleasant smile. To know, say, where you get a good pastrami sandwich in Duluth.

Why?

Because we can't afford to take you for granted.

Go with us next time.

The line at our counter is shorter.

© 1963 AVIS, INC.

Avis can't afford dirty ashtrays.

Or to start you out without a full gas tank, a new car like a lively, super-torque Ford, a smile.

Why?

When you're not the biggest in rent a cars, you have to try harder.

We do.

We're only No. 2.

It's in, but maybe you shouldn't be in it.

Some girls look sensational in hot pants. Front, back and sideways. So for those gorgeous girls Ohrbach's has an assortment of stylish hot pants and warm pants. All at Ohrbach's fabulously low prices.

But no one style is right for everybody. And a girl who looks absolutely divine in one outfit can look positively dreadful in another.

That's why Ohrbach's has so many thousands of fashions to choose from. We know there's a right look for everyone, and when you come into our store we want to be sure that it isn't right if it isn't right for you.

you'll find the one that's right for you.

And at a price you can afford. At Ohrbach's, we believe

OHRBACH'S Where you always find the right fashion and the price that's right for *you*.

I found out about Joan

The way she talks, you'd think she was in Who's Who. Well! I found out what's what with *her*. Her husband own a bank? Sweetie, not even a bank *account*. Why that palace of theirs has wall-to-wall *mortgages*! And that car? Darling, that's *horse*power, not *earning* power. They won it in a fifty-cent raffle! Can you imagine? And those clothes! Of course she *does* dress divinely. But really...a mink stole, and Paris suits, and all those dresses...on *his* income? Well darling, I found out about that too. I just happened to be going her way and I *saw Joan come out of Ohrbach's!*

Ohrbach's

34ᵀᴴ ST. OPP. EMPIRE STATE BLDG. · NEWARK MARKET & HALSEY · "A BUSINESS IN MILLIONS, A PROFIT IN PENNIES" stated before." He led the agency for three decades. When he died on October 2, 1982, the agency was doing $1.2 billion in annual business in offices around the world.

October Has Highs and Lows

October 4 was an "up" day, as we were awarded the Olga's Kitchen account. We took the account on even though we would have to resign the business after our acquisition because there was a conflict with DDB Needham's McDonald's account. Troy-based Olga's Kitchen, Inc. had 56 restaurants in 12 states, with aggressive plans for growth when we became its agency. Olga's Kitchen is best known for its exclusive menu item, the "Original Olga," which consists of a secret bread recipe, seasoned beef and lamb, onions, tomatoes and special recipe Olgasauce.™

A few days later, though, Joan and I and our family were feeling very "low" because Rocky, our poodle which had been part of the family for 14 years, had to be put to sleep by a veterinarian. For my birthday on Friday, October 20, the agency staff enjoyed eating apple pie rather than a cake, and on Sunday, October 22 I delivered the year's last load of apples to a cider mill. We still hadn't had an offer to buy our farm – but as it turned out it would be the last load of apples I would ever deliver to a cider mill.

The next weekend Joan and I flew to Kansas City, rented a car and drove to Sedalia, Missouri to attend the 45th reunion of my high school graduation class. It was the first reunion I'd ever attended since graduating in 1944. On Friday night a mixer at the Holiday Inn, where the reunion was being held, enabled everyone to renew old acquaintances. Name tags helped a lot.

Saturday morning there was a tour of Smith-Cotton, the high school I had attended, while the afternoon was spent visiting the old "haunts" that still existed – several drive-in restaurants we patronized were still in business. On Saturday evening, a dinner and dance provided an opportunity to visit with many

old high school friends. After a brunch Sunday morning, everyone departed for home. Former classmates from all over the country attended and I was particularly pleased to learn how successful many of them had been in their careers – there were accountants, architects, doctors, nurses, teachers, business owners and corporate executives present at the reunion. The 200 students in my high school graduating class grew up during a very serious period in our nation's history. We all had experienced the depression and World War II. Not one student had a car, no one used drugs and very few ever drank alcoholic beverages when we went to high school. Vastly different from today.

A Two-Home Family

On November 16 we were not just a two-car family, we also became a two-home family, because we closed on that date on our new home on Cedar Key in Orion Township. I got a bridge loan from Standard Federal and started praying even harder that our home in the country would sell, not relishing the expenses of owning two homes. There were lots of families looking at our country home but we still had not received an offer.

Joan, though, was very enthusiastic about moving to our new home in early December, when Bonnie and Ken Bouwman, the former owners, would move out. She took her third chemo treatment in early November and Joan was not only feeling stronger, but Doctor Malone's reports following her exams were also very encouraging. For Joan the prospect of redecorating a new home just down the street from where our son Michael and his family lived was both invigorating and exciting.

On Thanksgiving Day I again participated as a clown in the big parade in downtown Detroit. In the late afternoon we had a wonderful feast at Kathy and Mike's home. It was a fine, crisp Thanksgiving day with a clear sky and no wind.

We Sell Our Farm – Finally

The day after Thanksgiving Joan and I did some shopping. When we returned home there was an urgent message on our phone to call Ron Rodda, the sales representative with our Realtor, Max Broock. Someone had made an offer to buy our country home. The offer was made by Lillian and Jim Bouder and was good for 24 hours. We called Ron and he drove out Friday evening so that Joan and I could sign the purchase agreement. Lillian Bouder was president of the Cranbrook Educational Community in Bloomfield Hills. They had a home on the grounds at Cranbrook but they wanted a retreat in the country and a place where Jim could spend time keeping busy during his retirement. They had looked at the property several times and theirs was the first offer we had received since the property was put on the market early in 1987.

We had, however, reduced the selling price because we didn't want to move in December and have one home sitting vacant. The week after Thanksgiving we had three more offers to purchase – all many thousands of dollars more than the offer we had accepted. Unfortunately, the deed was done and the others were too late. One prospective buyer who called me to confirm that the farm was sold told me he and his family were not only terribly disappointed but extremely angry at their Realtor. They had notified their real estate agent that they had decided to make a bid for our property but she left to go out of town over the Thanksgiving holiday confident our property wouldn't sell because it had been on the market for almost two years. To her surprise, when she got back to her office Monday morning she learned we had sold it the Saturday after Thanksgiving and her client had lost out. Not only did she lose a sale but we would have received $20,000 more than we sold it for to the Bauders. Our listing with Max Broock was scheduled to end in early December and the other two prospective buyers were planning on making a direct offer to try to avoid paying the Realtor's commission.

The End of the '80s

Sunday, December 3, I went to Grand Rapids for the Michigan "Hort" Show and sat in meetings all day Monday. That evening there was the traditional meeting with the state apple growers and a presentation of the advertising, promotion, public relations and research we were carrying out on their behalf.

The move to our new home on Cedar Key in Orion Township took place on Wednesday, December 6, and the moving company we selected did a fine job. By the end of the day we were well settled with the wonderful help of our friends Brigette and Ricky Briggs.

On Friday of that week we closed on the sale of our little farm in Ortonville and we were back to owning just one home. The years that we lived in the country were, for the most part, happy years because we shared our home and the orchard not only with our family but also with our friends. *There were lots of good memories because you never really leave a place you love. Part of it you take with you, leaving part of you behind.*

Soon after we were comfortably established in our new home, we met our neighbors. Fortunately, they not only turned out to be amicable and caring people but also good

Joan and I enjoyed the agency's Christmas Party as we celebrated a very successful year in 1989.

friends – Chris and Doug Peterson on one side, Gina and Frank Gambino on the other side, and Sue and Walter Engh directly across the street.

The agency Christmas party was December 5 at the Somerset Inn and Joan and I felt like celebrating because everything was going so well. We were in a new home, Joan was handling the chemo treatments well and the agency had enjoyed a great year.

DDB Needham Makes Formal Offer To Buy the Agency

We got a very special Christmas message when DDB Needham's formal offer to purchase Baker Advertising, Inc. was received on December 21. Hours of discussions and countless memos, letters and special reports had finally resulted in a firm offer that confirmed its intent to acquire the agency.

There were still a lot of details to work out but now both companies were committed to each other. We could not talk with, or consider an offer from, another agency now that we had reached this stage of the negotiations.

Significant Events of the Past Year

U.S. troops invaded Panama to arrest Noriega, and Chinese students braved army tanks to demonstrate for democracy in Tianammen Square. The Berlin Wall, which had stood for 28 years, crumbled at the stroke of midnight on November 9 and a stunned world pondered the consequences.

In 1989 – for the first time – *Advertising Age* magazine included non-U.S.-based advertising agencies in its annual ranking and the Japanese agency Dentsu took top position with $1.3 billion in worldwide gross income. Pay-Per-View became a popular part of cable TV, reaching about one-fifth of all wired households, while Time, Inc. and Warner Communications merged in a $14 million deal.

Chapter 9

What It's Like To Be Acquired –
1990 Through 1994

"The greatest thing in this world is not so much where we are, but in what direction we are moving."
– O. W. Holmes

In January 1990, we entered into a critical area in the process of merging with DDB Needham, with the receipt of its letter late in December of 1989 confirming its intent to acquire us. Our talks had now reached an even more urgent level and there was one or more calls every day regarding some issue that needed clarification. On January 3, John Bernbach, president of DDB Needham Worldwide, Bob Freeman, president of DDB Needham Detroit and Peter Farago, senior vice president of DDB Needham Detroit, spent most of the day in our offices discussing various issues, the integration of personnel and a variety of details. It was agreed at this meeting that I would go to New York and spend January 24 in meetings with DDB Needham's top management. The head-quarters of DDB Needham Worldwide is at 437 Madison Avenue, where it occupies a number of floors in an office tower.

I met with the president, John Bernbach, and the chairman and CEO, Keith Reinhard. Following lunch, there were meetings with the chief financial officer, Gerald Germain, senior vice president, Steve Burton, and vice president of public affairs, Lou Tripodi. It appeared that everyone was feeling comfortable and enthusiastic about the acquisition of Baker Advertising. Bob Freeman and Peter Farago were also present for the meetings and we flew back to Detroit together late in the afternoon.

The accountants and the attorneys were now ready to take over the negotiations and nothing more happened until February 27, when I received DDB Needham's interim purchase offer. The next day Steve Burton, Bob Freeman, Peter Farago, Kit King and I met to review the purchase offer, which Kit and I signed on March 2. It would then take until August to have all the documents prepared for the final purchase of the agency.

In the meantime, we were busy handling our accounts, preparing a three-year plan, managing the operation and working on new business.

We Win the Michigan Department of Commerce "Say Yes To Michigan" Account In Late January

On January 26, there was great excitement in the office when we learned that Baker Advertising, Inc. was the successful bidder for the Michigan Department of Commerce's "Say Yes To Michigan" account, which had an annual budget of $3,000,000. Unfortunately, the full budget never materialized, as the agency that lost the business to us filed a protest and held up the awarding of the contract for six months. We eventually won the contract but there was only several hundred thousand dollars left in the budget when we finally took over the account.

In November 1990, when John Engler was elected governor, the "Say Yes" campaign was eliminated.

Another Exciting Event Occurred In January

The Gannett Outdoor Advertising Company sponsored a creative contest for billboard designs and a concept that we entered for the Detroit baseball club (Detroit Tigers) won the grand prize. And a *grand* prize it was – a No. 100 showing for the Detroit Metropolitan Market, worth $110,000.00 per month. Doug Wood, the art director who created the design, won a personal prize of $500.00. The Detroit Tigers actually got 160 billboards (a No. 100 showing) for more than one month because many of the boards didn't change copy for two or three months because there was not a strong demand for outdoor boards at that time of the year. Gannett simply let the Detroit Tigers message remain on display until they had another advertiser's copy to replace it.

On January 9, I met with Jeff Odenwald, Dan Ewald, Doc Fenkell and Scott Nickel at the baseball club's executive offices, in downtown Detroit, to tell them the good news about all the "free" outdoor billboard advertising they were going to receive. A presentation ceremony was arranged at the agency's office and we had a very delighted client when the contract for the free advertising was presented. The agency received considerable good PR coverage in the local press and in trade publications for winning this contest. In addition, the agency also won four more Addy's in January in this statewide creative competition.

In early February, Joan had her seventh chemotherapy treatment and, following that, got a very good report from Dr. Malone. A few days later, Joan and I went to the Detroit Boat Show, just to look at boats, since we now lived on a lake. However, we ended up falling in love with a show model – a 26' Sanpan Royale

pontoon cruiser – which we couldn't resist. Over the years we've had a lot of enjoyment from this boat, which we named "The Lollipop," and kept it docked right in front of our house.

AAAA Meeting Held At Desert Hot Springs, California

On March 14, Joan and I arrived at the Marriott Desert Hot Springs Hotel for the start of the annual meeting of the American Association of Advertising Agencies. We really enjoyed attending these meetings and a lot was packed into each session so the meetings were very worthwhile. I was particularly pleased to attend the opening session at which Keith Reinhard, chairman and CEO of DDB Needham Worldwide, was elected chairman of the 4As for the coming year. The meeting ended on March 17 and Joan and I then went to Laguna Niguel, California to visit my brother Joe for three days. We then went to Phoenix to visit my mother in Sun City for three days. We covered a lot of territory in the two weeks we were away.

We Lose the Michigan Apple Account

On April 10, we made a presentation to the Michigan Apple Committee to try to retain an account we had served for 15 years. Every five years the account had undergone a review and the timing this year was not good for us. We informed the committee that we were in the process of being acquired by DDB Needham and that weighed heavily in their decision – they were quite concerned about dealing with an office of a large New York agency rather than with a Michigan-based business. We lost the account, which was particularly disappointing to me, because I had developed a great many personal relationships with growers and shippers across the state during the fifteen years that I had handled the account. We ended our relationship June 30, 1990, when the Grand Rapids agency,

Maxwell Advertising, took over handling the advertising for Michigan Apples.

Late in April though, the Consumers Power Company gave us a sizable trial assignment to develop a campaign to promote the use of gas air conditioning in commercial buildings. Consumers Power had worked with one advertising agency for many years but changes in agency personnel and other factors led them to seek other creative ideas. We were selected to develop the gas advertising campaign which they were very pleased with and which helped precipitate an agency review. Unfortunately, when Consumers Power held the review some months later we were not the agency that won the entire account.

Ursula Crenshaw

The Start of Another Close Relationship

In November 1989, Standard Federal Bank merged with Peoples Savings Bank of Monroe –

a $350 million financial institution with offices in three counties. Ursula Crenshaw, who was in charge of marketing for this bank, then joined the marketing department of Standard Federal Bank as vice president of marketing. She was assigned to develop and implement marketing strategies for the bank's retail deposit products, alternative investment products, insurance products and delivery systems, and to manage the national marketing, brand and image development for InterFirst, the national wholesale marketing division of Standard Federal Bank. Ursula was a great addition to Standard Federal's marketing department. She was not only a highly competent, enthusiastic individual but also very pleasant to work with. With Ursula's key assignments, the agency had frequent contact with her on a myriad of projects. During April and early May, there were numerous meetings with Ursula. This was the beginning of another family-like bond, which occurs when you're working closely together day after day trying to find the solution to a problem or developing a business-building idea for your client.

A Surprising Offer

On May 25, John Bernbach, president of DDB Needham Worldwide, invited me to breakfast with him on May 30 at the Townsend Hotel in Birmingham. Baker Advertising had, for all intents, been acquired by DDB Needham although the final documents and agreements had not been signed. The signing of all the documents would take place in August.

To my great surprise, when I met with him he asked me to be the CEO of the Detroit office of DDB Needham. He explained that the president and CEO of the Detroit office, Bob Freeman, was interested in pursuing something else and that the position was being offered to me. I would not only be the chairman but also CEO of the Detroit office. I explained to John my concern about accepting this responsibility as my wife was finishing chemotherapy treatments and I was very unsure of what the future might hold for us. Furthermore, I had no experience on national car accounts. John pointed out that my involvement in the Audi and Volkswagen accounts would be minimal because these accounts were supervised by Phillipe Defechereux who reported directly to him. DDB Needham Worldwide served as the advertising agency for Volkswagen and Audi in many countries, making these marques multi-national accounts. Accordingly, Phillipe reported to John because he wanted to stay as close to the accounts as possible.

After much discussion, I agreed to become the chief executive officer of DDB Needham's Detroit office for a year, which would provide sufficient time for the agency to find someone to become president and CEO. My immediate responsibility and challenge, though, in becoming the CEO was to find an executive creative director for the Detroit office – a key position that had been open for some time.

On June 1, I spent the day and early evening in Chicago attending a DDB Needham management meeting and dinner. During the day, I also managed to meet with two prospective candidates for the ECD position. Over the next five months, I spent a considerable amount of time interviewing a number of candidates. Bruce Duffey, who was with DDB Needham in Chicago, was offered the post and after long and careful consideration, agreed to become the executive creative director of DDB Needham's Detroit office. He joined the agency at the end of the year.

In the meantime, an executive management committee was established consisting of Phillipe Defechereux, Kit King, Peter Farago and myself. A management advisory board was also initiated, consisting of eight department managers. This board was charged with looking for ways to improve performance and morale by identifying problems, investigating alternative solutions, and making recommendations that would help create an environment in the agency that would make the office a better place in which to work.

Following the acquisition of Baker Advertising Inc., the new management team named to head up the DDB Needham Detroit office included (left to right): Philippe Defechereux, director of client services/automotive; Peter Farago, director of administration and finance; Kathryn King, director of client services/non-automotive; and Ernest Baker, chairman and CEO.

The Acquisition of Baker Advertising Formally Announced By DDB Needham In a Memo From John Bernbach

A memo was distributed to all DDB Needham employees on July 2 and a news release was sent to all the advertising and marketing trade publications to announce the acquisition of Baker Advertising. The memo, reprinted with John's permission, read as follows:

July 2, 1990

To: The People of DDB Needham

From: John Bernbach

Subject: A Stronger Detroit Agency

I am pleased to tell you of a number of important moves we have made to grow and strengthen the Detroit agency of DDB Needham Worldwide.

Our biggest news is that we have reached an agreement to acquire Baker Advertising, Inc., one of the city's most successful agencies, and merge it with DDB Needham Detroit. Ernest W. Baker, founder and chairman of the 26-year-old agency, will become chairman and CEO of the merged agency, which will continue with the name DDB Needham Detroit. Ernie Baker is one of Detroit's best known and most influential advertising professionals, and his appointment as head of the agency will have a significant and favorable impact on our image in the market.

The Baker Advertising agency has billings of over $20,000,000 and includes on its roster clients such as The Detroit Tigers, Standard Federal Bank, Michigan Department of Commerce, Michigan State Fair, Stanley Door Systems, Lafarge Corporation, John Henry Company, Stanley Home Automation, the London's Farm Dairy and others.

All agency personnel will be consolidated at the office presently occupied by Baker Advertising in the Standard Federal Financial Center.

Robert Freeman, who has done an excellent job since his appointment as president of Detroit in January 1989, will now move on to a new opportunity, having successfully completed his assignment. Bob played a key role in finding an appropriate partner for us and in the negotiations that brought this fine agency into the DDB Needham family. We extend our deep appreciation to him.

Philippe Defechereux has been promoted to director of client services/automotive in Detroit and will now be responsible for both Volkswagen and Audi.

Kathryn (Kit) King has been appointed director of client services/non-automotive, and Peter Farago will become executive vice president director of administration and finance for the agency.

The steps we have taken in Detroit represent our commitment to future growth and success in this market that is so vital to our interests. We are confident that this new strength in our roster and our management will make DDB Needham Detroit the agency of the '90s in this market.

# # #

For a couple of weeks early in July, DDB Needham was the "talk of the town" and received considerable attention in the Detroit market but that soon faded away as other new events occurred. The agency did get invited to make presentations to six companies as a result of all the publicity we received, four of which we had to turn down due either to a conflict or to some other problem. On August 9, however, we made a presentation to Murphy Software and the next day we made a presentation to Kelly Services for its recruitment advertising business. We did not win either of these two accounts.

A One-Day "Shoot" On Mackinac Island

Our client, London's Farm Dairy, introduced Ryba's Mackinac Island Fudge Ice Cream in 1986 and the demand for this product had far exceeded everyone's expectations. In addition to the original Mackinac Island Fudge ice cream, the flavors had been extended to include Peanut Butter Fudge, Cherry Amaretto Fudge, Walnut Fudge, Double Fudge and even further extended into a line of novelty ice cream bars. Other dairies had jumped on the Mackinac Fudge ice cream bandwagon and were producing it under a licensing agreement with London's Farm Dairy. To its credit, London's Farm Dairy donated all the license fee income it received to the Blue Water Council of the Boy Scouts of America and to St. Mary's Hospital in Port Huron – where they were headquartered.

Arrangements had been made to shoot audio and video footage on Mackinac Island on

August 25 of Harry Ryba – in various situations or involved in certain activities – which would be used in a television commercial and for a sales presentation video. The film crew and all their equipment were transported to Mackinac Island in a twin engine Beechcraft Baron airplane. Fred Krohn, vice president and general sales manager of London's Dairy, and our primary client contact, thought that he and I should also be present to observe and monitor the eight-hour shoot. Since there was no room for us in the Beechcraft Baron I asked my son Bob if he would fly us to Mackinac Island in his Cessna 182. He readily agreed, as his wife Jane and his son Matt and daughter Emily were going to be in northern Michigan visiting Marian and Jay Kaser (Jane's folks) at Indian River that weekend.

Very early Saturday morning Bob and I went to the Linden airport where he kept his four-seat Cessna and we took off for Port Huron to pick up Fred and his 16-year-old son, John. By 7:30 a.m. we were over Port Huron but a heavy fog had rolled in off Lake Huron so we couldn't land. We contacted Fred by radio and arranged to meet him at the Almont airport. Bob and I then flew there to await their arrival. As soon as they arrived, the four of us then flew to Mackinac Island. It was a clear, bright, beautiful summer day – a perfect day to fly and to shoot footage outdoors. We arrived on the island in plenty of time to watch the taping of all the various sequences and it was a successful, productive day.

Harry Ryba, a very energetic and colorful individual, helped build Mackinac Island into a tourist attraction. In addition to his fudge shops, Harry also operated an ice cream business. He owned the Star Line of boats that transported people to and from the island and the Lakeview Hotel, as well as hundreds of bicycles that tourists could rent. Harry was an entrepreneur who believed in gimmicks. He vented his fudge shops and installed blowers to blow the sweet fudge odor outside his shops to attract customers. He added $60,000 diesel engines to his boats so they would shoot a rooster tail in the air to make the trips back and forth to the island more exciting. The competition followed his lead but he was the leader. Harry and his wife Ethel couldn't have been more gracious or helpful the day we spent with them on Mackinac Island shooting footage. Harry died in 1996.

The Closing of the Merger of Baker Advertising, Inc. With and Into DDB Needham Worldwide, Inc.

The day had finally arrived when all the documents were ready to be signed to finalize the sale of Baker Advertising, Inc. to DDB Needham. Early August 29th I picked up Kit King at our offices in Troy and we drove to the First National Building in downtown Detroit where the offices of our law firm – Butzel, Kidon, Simon, Myers & Graham – were located. When we were ushered into the conference room, the large conference table was completely covered with stacks of documents that had to be reviewed and signed. In addition to Kit and me, Doug Graham and Elliot Spoon of Butzel, Kidon were there representing Baker Advertising. Steve Burton, senior vice president of DDB Needham Worldwide and Janet Wertman of the New York law firm of Davis & Gilbert were there to represent the acquirer. By noon all the documents had been explained, signed and witnessed. It was a done deal.

At noon we all went to the Renaissance Club for a luncheon to celebrate the merger. After 26 years and eight months of operation, Baker Advertising, Inc. no longer existed. Late that afternoon the champagne corks popped at the agency's Troy office so that the staff could share in the celebration and in the start of our new future as part of DDB Needham Worldwide – then the fifth largest domestic advertising agency and the tenth largest worldwide. That evening, I took my entire family, along with friends Carl and Brigette Briggs, to the Clarkston Cafe in Clarkston to celebrate our merger.

The Baker family in October 1990. From the left (seated): Kathy, Blaine, Reid, Bradley, Joan (holding Gitte) and me. Standing (from left to right): Michael, Matthew, Jane, Robert and Emily.

We Win the Century 21 Account

Early in September 1990, marketing representatives of the Great Lakes Region Century 21 office approached the recently merged Baker Advertising/DDB Needham Detroit office to discuss its advertising account. McCann-Erickson's Los Angeles office had recently lost the national and regional Century 21 business, and while the national business was going to CME in Minneapolis, the regional accounts were authorized to hire their own local advertising agencies.

Century 21 Great Lakes Region was especially impressed with our long-standing relationship with Standard Federal Bank.

Because of the bank's well-known mortgage/ real estate expertise, Century 21 felt they had indeed found an excellent marketing partner in the DDB Needham Detroit office – one that truly understood the real estate industry and the specialized marketing needs of the Realtor professional. On September 12, we were notified that Century 21 Great Lakes Region was assigning its advertising to DDB Needham.

For the remainder of 1990 and throughout 1991, DDB Needham planned and placed over a million dollars in television and radio advertising for over 500 Century 21 brokers in six states: Michigan, Ohio, Indiana, Kentucky, Western Pennsylvania and West Virginia. Kaye Helms was assigned to manage the account on a day-to-day basis and, through Kaye, the agency provided extensive field service. Kit King and I participated in sales rallies and broker council meetings, at which we unveiled advertising programs and consulted on local marketing and advertising issues.

Late in 1991, pressured by the need to allocate broker contributions to local newspaper advertising, regional Century 21 offices across the country canceled local broadcast budgets, leaving insufficient agency revenue to justify continued field service. The agency and the client jointly agreed to part ways at that time.

More Good News

The following Wednesday after winning the Century 21 business, Joan had another complete check up at Hutzel Hospital, including CAT scans and X-rays. Late in the day Dr. Malone informed us that no masses or cancer had been detected. Everything was O.K. Wonderful news!

DDB Needham Holds a Series of Open Houses

On September 24, we had an Open House at our offices for our clients and a number of DDB Needham executives came from New York to participate, including Keith Rinehard, John Bernbach, Gerald Germain, Steve Burton and Lou Tripodi. There were representatives from all our clients, including Hans Hungerland, president of VW of America, and Tom Ricketts, chairman and president of Standard Federal Bank, which helped make the client open house a big success. Another well-attended open house was held the next day for media representatives, suppliers and our employee families. The first nine months of 1990 were indeed eventful and a lot had been accomplished.

We Celebrate the 100th Anniversary of the Beta Theta Pi Fraternity

On Friday, October 5, I flew to Columbia, Missouri to attend the celebration of the 100th Anniversary of the Beta Theta Pi Fraternity at the University of Missouri. My brother Joe and his wife Sue came from California and more than 500 Zeta Phi Betas returned to participate in this special event. My wife Joan and I met in Columbia when she was attending Christian College but she decided not to attend this event as she knew it would be very tiring – and it was – but certainly worth it for me.

My pledge class got together for dinner on Friday night and it was great to see fraternity brothers that I hadn't seen in more than 40 years. Saturday morning I had a tour of the Journalism School, followed by a buffet lunch at the fraternity house at 520 College Avenue. Then we went to the Missouri vs. Colorado football game. This was the incredible game where Missouri lost in the

During the centennial celebration of our college fraternity my brother Joe and I toured the University of Missouri campus. The 150-year-old columns – landmarks of the University – are visible behind us as well as Jesse Hall. We are at the north end of the Francis quadrangle and the School of Journalism, which was the first school of journalism, is in the northeast corner of this quadrangle.

final seconds only because Colorado was able to score when it got five downs instead of four – due to an error by the referees.

Saturday night more than 1,000 people attended the Beta Theta Pi 100th Anniversary dinner – the biggest "sit-down" dinner ever held in Columbia, Missouri. Sam Walton, founder of WalMart and a Beta at Missouri, was scheduled to be the speaker at the dinner but canceled at the last minute due to illness. Cancer took his life a few months later. Harold Hook, the CEO of American General, a $4.5 billion insurance company headquartered in Houston, filled in for Sam Walton and made an inspiring talk.

An Aggressive New Business Campaign Launched

Rod Burton and David Horner were added to the staff of DDB Needham's Detroit office to spearhead an aggressive new business effort. Starting in late October and throughout November and December, the agency made a number of new business presentations to accounts that had a prior relationship with Rod Burton and Dave Horner. These accounts included Delta Dental Plan, Health Alliance Plan, the McDonald's Operators of Southeast Michigan, plus several others.

A mild recession was underway, which would become much worse in 1991. There were many reasons for the downturn in the economy but it was starting to hurt the advertising business for the first time in many years. The advertising business had experienced its share of recessions but this downturn was sending shivers through the industry. Total ad spending grew only 3.8% in 1990 – well below the 5% of 1989 – and agencies were reacting by reducing staff as advertising expenditures began to drop. The recession would become more of a depression in 1991 as the situation got much worse. Advertising agency employment peaked in 1989 at 173,000. Thousands of jobs were lost in 1990 and by

the end of 1991, there would be a 6% decline in employment as more than 10,000 jobs disappeared. What was happening in the advertising agency business had already happened on Wall Street and to conglomerates. Now it was happening in advertising, which in turn affected media and marketing services companies.

December Is a "Go-Go" Month

December is usually the most hectic month of the year with all the gift buying, parties and other activities leading up to Christmas and the holiday season. We decided to take a "get-away" weekend and go to Frankenmuth and invited our family to join us. We reserved four rooms at the Bavarian Inn Lodge Friday, December 14 through Sunday, December 16, and took our family there to "kick back" and have fun. This Inn is particularly suited for families, with two indoor swimming pools as well as a huge hot tub where parents and grandparents can relax and still watch their kids. Game rooms, family fun centers, miniature golf and even sleigh rides make it all seem like you are worlds away from the daily grind. Our five grandchildren loved it and we particularly enjoyed these special moments when we could spend "quality time" together enjoying their company and watching them enjoying themselves.

The following week, on December 19, Joan had another complete checkup at Hutzel Hospital including a CAT scan and X-rays. Dr. Malone reported that no masses or areas that needed to be removed were detected, so this was very encouraging, wonderful news even though Joan would continue receiving chemotherapy treatments every month.

Major Events of 1990

During 1990 Germany was reunited for the first time since 1945, after the Berlin Wall came tumbling down in 1989. The most powerful and dreaded firm on Wall Street during the '80s also came tumbling down in 1990 when the Drexel Burnham Lambert Group filed for bankruptcy – adding thousands more workers to the 37,000 already dismissed the past two years by Wall Street firms. Nelson Mandela was released from prison in South Africa from his 27-year imprisonment and Margaret Thatcher lost her position as head of Britain's Conservative Party and was replaced by John Major. Many Americans felt that the "Greed Decade" was over and there was a lot of anger and disgust with the behavior of Wall Street due to the fact that many bankers got rich quick through paper-shuffling deals that manipulated companies at the expense of workers and communities. As the year came to an end the U.S. was on the brink of a war in the Middle East because Iraq had invaded Kuwait.

– 1991 –

Tuesday, January 1, Joan and I enjoyed a really special treat as we were able to sleep late – something we were seldom ever able to do. We had enjoyed dinner New Year's eve at the Haymaker restaurant at Canterbury Village with Joan's dad and our friends Brigette and Carl Briggs and then had returned to our house for a quiet evening watching television, including the traditional program from New York's Time Square. Our son, Mike, and his family spent the afternoon of New Year's Day with us and we played pool, watched football games on TV and enjoyed snacking on a variety of good things to eat – a great way to start 1991!

But it was back to work the next day in a big way, though, as John Bernbach, Gerald Germain and Steve Burton were in the office all day for meetings with Peter Farago, Phillipe Defechereux, Kit King and me on a wide range of topics, including the business plan for 1991, long range planning, client service assignments,

and new business status, etc. There was also a big concern about the economy, as U.S. unemployment was at its highest in three years and we were facing the possibility of more cutbacks in advertising spending by some of our clients, particularly VW and Audi. We fully intended to make up for any reductions in our business volume with new business and by seeking additional assignments on special projects from all our existing clients. With the addition of Bruce Duffey as the agency's executive creative director the national creative work for Volkswagen had been transferred to Detroit from the New York office. So there were many issues to be concerned with and we wanted to make sure that we had all the "i's" dotted and the "t's" crossed as we moved ahead into 1991.

New Business a Top Priority

We had developed a comprehensive new business development plan for 1991 and all the members of the new business team were familiar with it and the objectives. This plan covered the current situation in the Detroit market, including a review of all our competitors and the accounts they serviced. Another section of the plan was dedicated to strategy, including the size and type of accounts we were going to pursue. The third section covered tactics and how we would proceed, techniques we would apply, monitoring our efforts, follow-up procedures and the advertising and public relations the agency would do as a part of our new business effort. A major offer that we intended to make to prospective accounts as a part of our tactics was a Guarantee Program – something no advertising agency had ever offered before. This Guarantee Program concept had been put together at our New York office. It was new, exciting, controversial and provocative but it gave us a unique selling point. The Guarantee Program would make it possible for DDB Needham to "guarantee specific business or marketplace results achieved by the agency's communications program at the consumer, and tie the agency's compensation to the achievement of the these results."

The DDB Needham Guarantee Program could be custom tailored to an account and there were a variety of things that could be guaranteed, such as:

Business Results – volume, share of market, revenue – or,

Consumer Behavior – trial, phone calls, showroom traffic – or,

Consumer Attitudes – awareness, image, intent to purchase.

Also, a number of things had to be taken into consideration as part of the Guarantee Program – such as how long the guarantee would last, establishing the objectives of the guarantee, and defining the conditions, particularly as to what would be expected of the client and the agency to make the guarantee program successful. It was a powerful idea and it would be interesting to see how many prospects would embrace such a concept.

The organization of our new business unit consisted of Peter Farago, executive vice president, who headed the team; Rod Burton and Dave Horner, both vice presidents; three account executives – Jim Coraci, Nan Gerard and Ed Hogikyan; plus Bonnie Hewitt, who was assigned to be the team coordinator, and me. We were excited, enthusiastic and eager to see what we could achieve in 1991 with Rod Burton as the point man for our efforts.

B and Bob Cunningham Retire

Two of the happiest retirees that I know retired on January 4. Their retirement had been planned for a long time but finally the day had arrived. The entire staff gathered for cocktails and farewells late Friday afternoon and a dinner followed at The Whitney restaurant in Detroit. I'm lucky if I am able to catch up with them once or twice a year now as they are constantly on the go, but I don't know anyone who is enjoying their retirement more than my close, good friends B and Bob Cunningham.

It's a Busy, Hectic January

I took Joan to Hutzel Hospital for another checkup on January 9, and Dr. Malone informed us that he believed that the monthly chemotherapy treatments should be continued. Joan had hoped that she had finished the schedule of treatments in December. The next one was scheduled for the following week on Thursday and I stayed home to be with her and canceled a meeting that I was supposed to attend in New York. For the past year the chemotherapy treatments were given to Joan by a nurse who came to our house, which was far more convenient than spending a long day at Hutzel Hospital near downtown Detroit.

In addition to all the other activity, we also had to start making plans to consolidate the DDB Needham offices with our offices in the Standard Federal Financial Center. The main DDB Needham offices were several blocks away in the Top of Troy Tower and all the people at that location would be moved to the Standard Federal building later in the year.

Three design firms had been invited to submit proposals for planning and designing our expanded office space for the integration of our staff but this, too, required meeting time to discuss our needs and to determine the time line to accomplish the consolidation.

We received sad news on January 12 when we learned that Joan's cousin, Bob Mossner, had been killed in a snowmobile accident. His funeral was January 16 – the same day that the allies attacked Iraq to start the Persian Gulf war. There was extensive coverage of this conflict on TV by the television networks and CNN and we watched the events unfold daily on television. Many advertisers, including Proctor & Gamble, Sears, Pizza Hut and all the major airlines, refused to air spots during the news coverage of the war. NBC reported a $45 million loss as a result of canceled advertising during the newscasts of the Persian Gulf war coverage.

Keith Reinhard spoke at the Adcraft Club of Detroit luncheon on February 1. Representatives of our clients were on the dais with him and it was a good opportunity for them to meet and hear the chairman and CEO of DDB Needham Worldwide when he spoke at this important local venue. The next week, on February 5, we had a long meeting with Catallo & Associates – the design firm we decided to use to plan our expanded office space for the consolidation of our staff in the Standard Federal Financial Center. The following day we received very encouraging news, when Joan had her monthly checkup at Hutzel Hospital – as the CA125 test results were favorable, as well as the CAT scan and the other exams she underwent. We had been planning a Florida vacation and wanted to have our family join us. Now we could go!

A Wonderful Vacation In Florida

Joan and I and our sons' families (11 total) left Friday, February 8, for Orlando, Florida. We had a wonderful vacation with a day at the Kennedy Space Station, two days at Disney World, one day at Universal Studios, and two days at Epcot Center, with days off in between to rest, relax and enjoy the outdoor pool at the hotel. The time flew by and Joan and I particularly appreciated all the time we could spend with our five grandchildren and watch them enjoy themselves. We returned home on February 23, the same day Kuwait was invaded by the Allied forces – BIG news!

HAP Appoints DDB Needham As Their Agency

While I was in Florida on vacation the agency won the Health Alliance Plan (HAP) account. This was a significant and exciting new business win, as HAP was and is the largest HMO serving the metro Detroit market. It carried an outstanding reputation. HAP's annual advertising budget exceeded $5,000,000 so our staff was really excited and enthusiastic about this achievement. Our year was off to a great start and we had a number of other new business presentations scheduled in the months ahead – to Siemens, Consumers Power, Kelly Services and others.

We Welcome Spring

While it was not a severe winter, the arrival of spring was most welcome. I participated in the Golden Mile Walk at the end of March – a March of Dimes fundraiser that involves a one-mile walk by business executives followed by lunch. Easter weekend, March 29-31, we invited our family to join us for another get-away to the Frankenmuth Bavarian Inn because we'd had such a nice experience doing this the past December. So we did it again! The following week Joan had her monthly chemotherapy treatment and each one seemed a little worse than the one before.

The Detroit Tigers opened their 1991 season on Monday, April 8, and Bruce Duffey, Peter Farago and I attended as guests of our client and sat in the new Cloud 9 box, high above the field. It was a beautiful spring day and fortunately the Tigers beat the Yankees 6 to 4. That evening, though, I attended a Rosary service for Nancy Olzem, who had died of cancer. Nancy was a very valued member of the staff of Baker Advertising for 13 years. Her funeral was the next morning and a number of us from the agency attended.

Phillipe Defechereux resigned from the agency on April 17 and announced that he was going to Germany to join our client, VW, as its international marketing director. Peter Saad, who had been hired to manage the VW account, was then promoted to Phillipe's position to supervise both the VW and the Audi accounts.

At the end of April we had several meetings with Tom Catallo, the head of the design firm, to review the drawings his staff had prepared for our office layout. Of course, there were some revisions, as we were now proceeding to the final plans for our offices. Friday, May 3 was a sad evening, as my favorite television show "Dallas" came to an end after 13 years. The following Wednesday, I was again rather disappointed when I stayed at the Waldorf-Astoria in New York. I had planned to leave Detroit after lunch on Wednesday so that I could have dinner at the Waldorf and see this famous hotel. As it turned out, I wasn't able to leave Detroit until late afternoon and I got to the Waldorf at midnight – went right to bed and got up the next morning at 6 a.m. to check out in order to attend an 8 a.m. meeting at DDB Needham. I had heard a lot about this hotel from my father-in-law, Ed Bauman, who had stayed there a number of times when he was in New York on business, and I was looking forward to staying there myself. My stay lasted under six hours and I saw virtually nothing of the Waldorf-Astoria.

On May 16, the staff was informed that Bruce Duffey and Peter Saad would become co-presidents of the DDB Needham Detroit office. The CEO responsibilities were divided between them. Now the agency had two captains running the ship. I was asked to spearhead a new project for the agency called "Project Water Rescue" which was a pro bono effort to be carried out in every DDB Needham office around the world to try and help improve the quality of our water. This took a lot of time and I arranged for us to participate in the National Wildlife Association's Great Lakes Natural Resource Center program to assist its efforts to improve the quality of the water in the Great Lakes – a huge challenge.

Mark Van Putten was the director of the Great Lakes Resource Center, headquartered in Ann Arbor, Michigan, and I met regularly with him but also participated in meetings held in Lansing and Chicago. The agency created a variety of support materials, including newspaper and magazine advertisements and a television commercial, while carrying out this project.

A Delightful Mini-Vacation

Joan wanted to get away for a few days between chemotherapy treatments so we invited our friends Brigette and Carl Briggs to join us for a mini-vacation. We left our home on May 23 and by early afternoon we were in Clinton, Michigan in the Irish Hills. We spent the afternoon "antiquing," as there are lots of stores selling antiques in the Irish Hills. Thursday night we stayed in Sturgis and the next morning we drove to Shipshewana, Indiana the heart of that state's Amish country. We drove around the beautiful countryside and admired the big, well-kept farms and had lunch at the Essenhaus in Middlebury, where I enjoyed the best dressing I'd ever tasted. From there we headed north through South Bend and spent the night in Niles, Michigan. The next morning after breakfast, we visited Drier's Meat Market in Three Oaks, famous for its sausage. My favorite actor, Larry Hagman, is one of its regular customers and he likes its sausage so much that he has had Mr. and Mrs. Drier, the proprietors, as guests at his home in Malibu, California.

Drier's opened for business in 1875 and features boneless "ready to eat" smoked hams. Its big volume is in smoked German ring bologna and a liver sausage pate which comes in a ring. We stocked up on sausage and then headed for Holland, where we had lunch at a restaurant on Lake Michigan across the street from where L. Frank Baum and his sister

Dorothy had summer homes. L. Frank Baum wrote all the "OZ" books. After some shopping at Holland's Wooden Shoe Factory, we drove up the coast of Lake Michigan past Grand Haven, Muskegan, Pentwater and Ludington. Late in the afternoon, we arrived in Manistee. For dinner, we enjoyed sampling the various meats, cheeses and wine we had acquired along the way.

On Sunday morning, we headed north on Highway 22 along the lake shore, so we could see the beautiful inland lakes, including Portage and Crystal Lake – the latter being one of Michigan's prettiest. Following lunch in Traverse City, we headed for Houghton Lake, where Joan spent many summers as a young girl at her grandparents' cottage. It was her first visit there in many years. We were home late in the evening but we had enjoyed a delightful mini get-away vacation which we talked about for weeks afterwards.

Spring Quickly Flows Into Summer

Time simply flies by when every day is filled with meetings or commitments. During June and July, if there weren't meetings with clients – London's Farm Dairy, Standard Federal Bank, Lafarge, Oakland County Parks, or others – then there were meetings regarding our office space, the "Water Rescue Project," personnel issues or the new business program. Our client, Stanley Door Systems, had a new president – Steve Anderson – and I spent time with him, and Joan and I entertained Steve and his wife Mary at our home. Joan had her fourth chemotherapy treatment on June 28 and I stayed home to help her and to give her support.

In early July, I had to go to California for meetings. On July 12 I spent the day and that night with my mother – who had recently moved from Sun City, Arizona to Laguna Hills, California so that my brother Joe could help her manage her affairs. Our mother had lost nearly all her sight due to adult-onset diabetes.

Saturday night – July 13 – Joe, Sue, Mom and I went to the Hollywood Bowl to enjoy a concert featuring George Gershwin music. I returned to Detroit Tuesday, July 16, and was back in the office early the next day. The following week I spent a day in Chicago for a meeting at which a number of DDB Needham offices reported on what they were doing as part of the agency's worldwide pro bono effort "Project Water Rescue."

Keith Reinhard

A Special Detroit Tiger Baseball Party

The chairman and CEO of DDB Needham Worldwide, Keith Reinhard, was in our offices for meetings on August 5. Late in the afternoon he addressed the entire staff to update everybody on the agency and its future direction. I introduced Keith but, in the interest of time, had prepared a memo for the staff to help them get to know our CEO. This memo was distributed on August 2, and the information was taken from an article that had recently appeared in a magazine. Keith's background is most unusual and here's what my memo said about him:

To: The Staff

From: Ernie Baker

Re: Getting to Know Keith Reinhard

As you know, Keith Reinhard will be meeting with us Monday afternoon, and we'll all be going to a Detroit Tiger game in the evening. There will not be time for a lengthy introduction so the following information will help you get to know Keith better; and hopefully, give you a greater appreciation and understanding of the man who leads this Company.

The Wall Street Journal, in profiling Keith Reinhard as part of its series on the creative giants of our industry, said "he was the man responsible for creating a new creative legend from the point where two separate traditions merged."

That was, of course, a reference to the merger of Doyle Dane Bernbach with Needham Harper. But those words seem to be just as appropriate today. His ability to create an environment where people and ideas flourish is one mark of his great talents as an agency leader.

But where did Keith come from and how did he get to where he is at today?

Keith Reinhard was born and raised in the small midwestern town of Berne, Indiana, population 2000.

"As soon as I was old enough, I wanted to get out of it," Keith says.

The problem was not family. He had a loving family. The problem was that there were so many things he wasn't allowed to do. His was a family of Mennonites. Berne was a town filled with Mennonites and the farm region surrounding them was Amish. Everything and everybody had to conform to rules.

"We had no television, no advertising, you couldn't go to the movies, you couldn't even go dancing. Against the rules of the church. It wasn't as strict as Amish. We did have cars, we did have electricity, and we didn't have to wear the Amish clothes. But it was a close second," according to Keith.

"Well, I am today a very lousy dancer. But I'll tell you, I am an excellent roller blader. In high school, if you went to an ice skating party which was one of the few kinds of parties we were allowed, then you could touch girls. You'd go with them on the bus to the rink and when you got there, you could hold hands. You could do that."

People in Berne either worked the farms or worked for one of the seven furniture factories in town. The Mennonites were largely from Switzerland, and the Swiss were known as craftsmen. Keith's father worked as an upholsterer, but when he died when Keith was just 3, his mother had to go to work. They were always poor. Fortunately, his grandfather lived in town and, in many ways, became Keith's surrogate father.

Still, it was Keith's plan, somehow, to get out of Berne and the plotting began early. It began, Keith thinks, with the truck that delivered V8 Juice to the grocery store where his mother worked. He sometimes helped in the stockroom, and when he unloaded the boxes there would be the cardboard box full of color promotional posters for V8 Juice. He would take the posters home and put them in his room under his bed. There was lots going on in the outside world that he wanted to know about.

"We'd listen to the radio," Keith says. "That was tolerated. I figured there were two ways out, either I'd be a commercial artist or I'd be a radio announcer. But I didn't know anybody in radio. Then one day, a kid who recently had moved to town from Detroit, told me he had an uncle back in Detroit who was a commercial artist. I went with him to visit this uncle; and sat in his studio (McNamara Art Studio, which was in the Fisher Building) and watched him airbrush the fenders of an automobile for a Ford advertisement. All I could think about is how could it be possible they could pay you to do something that was this much fun. I was hooked."

Keith spoke to his grandfather about art. His grandfather said it was frowned upon by their religion since it could be construed to be a form of creation, certainly presumptuous at best.

Eventually, his grandfather agreed to lend Keith $600 so at night he could take a correspondence course to become an artist.

"And that's how I learned to draw," Keith says. "A two-year correspondence course I took while in high school as a result of answering an advertisement on the back cover of a Popular Mechanics magazine."

The day after he graduated from high school, Keith was out the door and headed toward New York City. The father of a friend of his, Jerry Sprunger, owned the Ford dealership in town. Since they were graduating from high school, Jerry's father was willing to give them a 25-year-old Ford pickup truck to use to drive east to see the sights in New York. Jerry Sprunger and Keith, along with a third graduate, Max Lehman, painted this old truck robin's egg blue and constructed a wooden enclosure on the back with three plank beds in it. They'd go to New York City, see the sights, and they'd come back. Keith, of course, planned to go to New York, see the sights, and stay. But he didn't tell anybody that.

"We were one of the few vehicles ever thrown off the New Jersey turnpike," according to Keith.

"All we could do was thirty miles an hour. It was below minimum. They threw us off."

Eventually, they got through the Holland Tunnel and to the West Side, where they found a parking lot with a chain link fence around it. Here is where they slept every night for four days.

"I tried everything," Keith explains. "From a pay phone, I called every commercial art studio in the yellow pages. I couldn't even get an appointment." On the fourth day, they returned to Berne. "New York wasn't ready for me," Keith says.

It had been a taste, however.

This happened in 1953. Later that year, Keith got his first job in a commercial art studio as an apprentice in Fort Wayne, Indiana, making a dollar an hour. He cleaned brushes. He delivered packages. After saving up some money, he went to Chicago looking for work. He stayed at the YMCA and got a job at Kling Studios, one of the largest commercial art studios in the country. Virtually all the work was for advertising agencies.

It took the next 10 years for Keith to finally break into an advertising agency with his art portfolio. He tried and tried. He went back to Fort Wayne and worked at a studio there. He also worked for a company in Bloomington, Illinois. But nothing he did seemed to get him out of just doing studio work.

In 1963, Keith made an application to work for the Needham, Harper and Steers agency in Chicago. He carried with him a forty-page portfolio of his artwork.

"It absolutely didn't come out the way I had planned," Keith claims. "I presented all this art work, and they looked at me and said, 'Did you ever think of being a writer?' They hired me as a writer."

Ten years it had taken. But now, at long last, he was in the advertising agency business. He was 29-years-old.

"My very first job at the agency was to write 26 humorous radio commercials for State Farm Insurance. I had no idea what to do. I went to my supervisor. He told me just sit and type. When you laugh, show it to me, and if I laugh, we have something. If not, go back and write some more."

As it turned out, inside this commercial artist there lurked one of the greatest advertising writers of all time. Keith won't tell you that. But his credits will. Keith wrote commercials for McDonald's. He wrote, "You Deserve A Break Today," and "Twoallbeefpattiesspecialsauce…"

He wrote "Like a Good Neighbor, State Farm Is There," which is still used by that insurance company, and within five years, at the age of 34, he was creative director at Needham, Harper and Steers.

Keith was one of the chief architects of the unique three-way merger which took place in 1986, bringing together three agencies with rich creative traditions – Doyle Dane Bernbach, Needham Harper, and BBDO – into one agency group called Omnicom.

As head of DDB Needham Worldwide, he is one of the few multi-national agency chiefs who regularly participates in the creative process and directly influences the quality of the agency's creative output. The agency's highly successful campaigns for Amtrak, Michelob, Bud Light, Dial, Wheaties, Michelin Tires and Volkswagen have all benefited from his creative leadership.

He is a results-oriented advertising man who believes that narrow strategies are essential to great creative and introduced the "Planning for R.O.I." disciplines designed to bring more

Relevance, Originality and Impact to the creative product. Keith is also a firm believer in the importance of research to fuel the creative process, and his belief in the strategic use of media is emphasized by his reference to the agency's media professionals as "our other creative department."

Yet beyond his duties as DDB Needham's chief executive officer, Keith is generous in his participation in industry programs and community affairs. We can all be very proud of Keith and his achievements.

# # #

Following the staff meeting we boarded chartered buses and went to a Detroit Tiger baseball game, with a stop on the way at a McDonald's restaurant for dinner. It was an interesting and memorable day.

Another Family Outing

We enjoyed taking our family (Bob and Jane, Kathy and Mike and our five grandchildren) on outings and in mid-August (18-21), we went to Put-In-Bay – which is on South Bass Island in Lake Erie. From there we went to the Cedar Point Amusement Park. We stayed at the Greentree Motel in Sandusky, Ohio, which is a fun place to stay with good rooms, a bowling alley and miniature golf. When we returned home, Joan had her monthly "chemo" treatment and she was nauseated for the next five days.

Joan and I celebrated our 43rd wedding anniversary September 4 with a dinner in the Tack Room at Haymaker's Restaurant. Fourteen family members and friends joined us, sharing a large, specially decorated cake for dessert.

Standard Federal Acquires United Home Savings Bank

The first week of September was particularly hectic, as Standard Federal acquired the United Home Savings Bank in Toledo. This bank had 11 offices, all of which were converted to Standard Federal Bank offices, and the agency was very involved in preparing all the advertising and news releases relating to this important acquisition – its first in Ohio. That same week, we completed our RFP for the State of Michigan Tourism account and submitted it by the deadline. We did not win this account.

Joan's Test Results Are Alarming

On Monday morning, September 23, we were up at 5:30 a.m. to get to Hutzel Hospital for Joan's regular checkup with Dr. Malone. She had X-rays, a CAT scan, and the CA-125 blood test and we were home in the mid-afternoon. Several days later we were notified that Joan should have more tests, and these were done on September 27. This time it was not good news. Two new masses had formed in her abdomen. This would require surgery, which was scheduled for October 17. We went home emotionally drained and both of us took long naps. Later we informed our family that more surgery was necessary for Joan.

For the next several weeks prior to Joan's surgery I went to the office every day and we kept our lives as normal as possible. We met our friends Carl and Brigette several times for dinner and usually went to see a movie together after dinner. We also had dinner regularly with Joan's dad or with our sons and their families. Through it all Joan's courage and resolute determination to survive and beat the cancer was truly inspiring and impressive.

Joan Undergoes Extensive Surgery

On Wednesday, October 16, we went to Hutzel Hospital, where Joan was admitted for the surgery scheduled early the next morning. I was able to stay with her and slept on a cot brought into her room. Late Thursday evening, after the surgery, I was able to see her in the intensive care unit. She didn't return to her room until after midnight and was in considerable pain. I was able to stay overnight again and there was a lot of activity with doctors and nurses coming and going checking her all night. Dr. Malone explained the next day that the surgery was extensive, as the masses were attached in several places. Sections of her bowels had to be removed and reattached and considerable scar tissue from previous surgeries also had to be removed. Worst of all, the masses were malignant and not all of them could be removed. Wednesday, October 30, Joan left the hospital and we were advised that she should try to get into the experimental Taxol chemotherapy program at the University of Michigan Medical Center. Dr. Malone did not believe that further chemotherapy following a standard regimen would be effective. Joan had already gone through three aggressive chemotherapy regimens but this had not stopped new masses from forming.

I took a leave of absence from DDB Needham, as Joan was now having difficulty eating and was not recovering as quickly as she had from the previous surgeries. A visiting nurse came every day to change the dressing that had been placed in her chest, but I had to learn how to attach the various medications and dispense them through this port. I contacted Dr. James Roberts at the University of Michigan Medical Center and, on November 11, Joan and I spent a long day at the hospital where she underwent a number of tests and several examinations by different doctors. We had all her records from Hutzel Hospital with us as well as all the "path" slides from past surgeries. We returned to the U of M Medical Center a week later for more tests and, on November 25, we met with a team of doctors. They informed us that Joan had been accepted for the Taxol program and her first treatment would be on December 16. Our hopes were up again as we had heard of some incredible results from Taxol chemotherapy but also knew that it did not work for everyone.

In spite of everything, we had a pleasant Thanksgiving. Joan and I, along with our sons and our grandchildren, went to the Thanksgiving Day Parade. The weather was mild – in the 40s – and there was a big crowd in downtown Detroit. We had breakfast together, then I participated in the parade. Later in the day we all had dinner at Pree and George Holcomb's home (Kathy Baker's mother and stepfather) and what a feast it was! It was a relaxed and really enjoyable Thanksgiving.

Joan wanted to spend time with our grandchildren, so we arranged another weekend at the Bavarian Inn. On December 13, we went to Frankenmuth and "Grandma Joanie" had a delightful weekend being close to her grandchildren. We arrived back home again late Sunday afternoon and prepared to go to Ann Arbor early Monday morning, when Joan would start Taxol chemotherapy.

Joan Enters the Taxol Chemotherapy Program

We were up very early Monday morning, December 16, to go to Ann Arbor so that Joan could start the Taxol chemotherapy treatments. After a lot of tests, the treatment started in her room and the chemical was administered over a 24-hour period. They put a cot in her room so that I could stay with her, as she would have to remain at the hospital for three days for observation after the Taxol had been administered. We were home again late in the evening on Friday, December 20.

In spite of her weakened condition, Joan insisted on wrapping all the presents – which the family received on Christmas, when we all gathered at Jane and Bob's log home in the woods for dinner and to exchange gifts. In addition to our sons, their wives and our five grandchildren, Joan's father, Ed, was also present. Joan thoroughly enjoyed being with her immediate family but it was tiring and we went home early. She was in bed before 9 p.m. The next day she had a temperature and was nauseated and each day the nausea was a little worse.

The following Saturday morning her temperature was above 100° and the nausea made it very difficult to eat anything but a little Sustacal. Dr. Roberts insisted we return to the University of Michigan Medical Center, which we did Saturday morning, December 28. That's where we stayed until Tuesday, December 31, the last day of 1991 – when Joan decided she was going to leave the hospital to spend New Year's Eve at home. The doctors were opposed to Joan's leaving the hospital but relented and we were home at 7:30 p.m., where we had a quiet evening. And that's how 1991 ended.

– 1992 –

It was nice to be home again and out of the hospital for the start of the new year, even though Joan didn't feel well, with almost constant nausea, which made it very difficult for her to eat anything. We had a quiet New Year's day but did watch the Rose Bowl game as Michigan played Washington, losing 34 to 14. Brigette Briggs spent most of the next day with Joan, and I went to the office for a few hours. Mail and memos were dropped off regularly at the house by David Hudson, who lived nearby and was on staff of DDB Needham, but this was the first time I had been in the office since early the past November.

On Sunday, January 5, we returned to the U of M Medical Center so that Joan could take the second Taxol treatment. Following the treatment, she had a high temperature – making it necessary for us to remain at the hospital. We stayed eleven days and left the hospital on Wednesday, January 15, in a record-setting snow storm. It took us almost five hours to get home from Ann Arbor and it was exhausting for Joan.

A visiting nurse came every day to check on Joan's condition and to make various tests. I had to learn how to attach and administer the IV every night and really came to appreciate what nurses are able to do for their patients. It was necessary to do this with great care and I was very concerned that I might do something wrong. Just getting through a night without having to clear an air bubble in a line was a great relief. On January 27, we returned to the U of M Medical Center for the third Taxol treatment and the CA125 test showed that Joan's white blood cell count had dropped from 1440 to 960. This was encouraging and we were able to go home the next evening.

The next several weeks it became increasingly difficult for Joan to eat, as the nausea became worse and worse. She switched from taking Compazene to Thorozine and this did relieve the nausea slightly. It was obvious that Joan was getting weaker and she slept more – particularly during the day.

When it was time for Joan to take her fourth Taxol treatment, she was so weak that she had to be transported to the U of M Medical Center by ambulance on February 17. The Taxol wasn't administered until two days later and then we had to stay for several additional days for observation and tests. Early on Friday morning, I looked up at Joan in her hospital bed from where I was laying on my cot. I could see a steady flow of tears streaming down her face and I got up to try and comfort her. Joan looked up at me and for the first time said, "Ernie, I'm going to die." Up until that moment Joan had been resolute in her determination to beat the cancer and I really believed that she would do so. I put my arms around her and we sobbed together for a long time. I tried to reassure her and to encourage her to keep on fighting – not to give up hope. She wanted so much to see her five grandchildren grow to become adults and I tried to get Joan to focus on that goal so that she would keep on trying to beat the cancer. A wife, mother and grandmother, she had everything to live for, but five years of struggling with this horrid disease was finally robbing her of her vitality.

We returned home by ambulance again on Friday evening. The next morning, home care started, with nurses caring for Joan 24 hours a day – each nurse working an eight hour shift. A hospital bed and other equipment was set up in the living room. On Saturday afternoon, our two sons came and stayed overnight with us. That evening we looked at slides and had a happy and amusing time looking at family photos that we hadn't seen in years. It was a delightful trip back down memory lane for the four of us.

The next day Joan managed to eat some broth and a little Jello. Her dad and sister came to visit. Barbara decided to stay and help and to be with her sister. Late in the afternoon, Father Richard Herbel of St. Augustine's House came and gave us communion. St. Augustine's House is near Oxford, Michigan and is the only Lutheran monastery in the United States. Joan and I occasionally attended their Sunday services.

Joan's Life Ends

The Home Care nurses were doing everything possible to make Joan comfortable and she slept well Sunday night. The next morning she had a good breakfast and, in the afternoon, she sat in a wheelchair and visited several hours with Brigette, Barbara, Jane (our son Bob's wife) and the nurse. That evening, though, she was very tired and unable to eat. As the evening wore on she became restless and her breathing became more and more labored. Bob, Mike, Barbara and I sat next to her bed talking to her, rubbing her arms, holding her hands and telling her how much we loved her. A few minutes after midnight, she passed away. It just didn't seem possible – or real – that she was gone.

The next morning, Bill Wint and one of his associates from the Lewis E. Wint & Son Funeral Home in Clarkston, came to take Joan to their facility, as that was where her funeral service would be held. That afternoon my family and I went to the funeral home to make all the necessary arrangements. Visitation started that evening and my brother Joe arrived from California. This was a terribly sad and difficult day for my family and me.

On Thursday, my uncles, Jim and Tom Staples, and Tom's wife Dorothy arrived from St. Louis. In the late afternoon, the family gathered at Jane and Bob's home for dinner. Then we all went to the funeral home, which was filled with people who had come to pay their respects.

The funeral service on Friday morning was conducted by Father Richard Herbel. Gary Imms, our pastor at the Ortonville United Methodist Church, was unavailable because he was recuperating from heart bypass surgery. He wrote a special message, however, which was read by Ann Munger, a friend of Joan's and a member of the church. Following the service and her internment at White Chapel Cemetery, a luncheon was served in the fellowship hall at the Ortonville United Methodist Church. During the five years that Joan battled cancer, she had received hundreds of letters and cards of encouragement from the members of this little church. This support was greatly appreciated.

Joan and I had been married 43 years, 5 months and 21 days when she passed away. We met October 3, 1947 when she was a freshman at Christian College in Columbia,

Missouri and I was a senior at the University of Missouri. We had a wonderful year together in college, going to dances, football games, on picnics and to all kinds of activities involved in college life.

Sunday, March 1, my brother Joe returned to California and now I was living alone. This was a strange experience and hard to describe when you've shared your life with a companion for so many years. My days were busy with lots of things to take care of – thank you notes to write to acknowledge more than 80 funeral arrangements, the awful task of disposing of clothing, and so on. Brigette and Carl Briggs invited me to dinner Saturday, March 7, and after dinner we went to see the movie "Fried Green Tomatoes." It seemed unreal to go to dinner and to see a movie without Joan being with us. On Sunday, March 15, St. Anne's Catholic Church in Ortonville held a special mass for Joan, as many of the parishioners at this church knew Joan because of her involvement in Crop Walk.

An Incredible Mystery

I had not returned to the office as of March 11. There was so much to be done in settling things after Joan had passed away. I really wasn't emotionally ready to return to work. On this particular morning, something extremely unusual happened. My three grandsons, who lived down the street from me, had cereal for breakfast and left their plastic dishes and glasses on the kitchen table. Their mother, Kathy, had already left for work and Mike had gone with them to watch them walk to the corner where they caught a school bus. When Mike returned home and went back inside the house, the dishes that had been left on the table had now been rinsed and stacked in the rack on the kitchen sink. Mike knew that neither he nor his sons had rinsed and stacked the dishes and there was no one else in the house. Mike called Kathy's mother,

Pree, to see if by any chance she had stopped by the house while he was at the bus stop. Pree said she had not been there. Mike was – and still is – convinced that somehow his mother was able to do this as she had frequently gone to their house to get the boys off to school when both Mike and Kathy had to leave early for work.

The next morning I heard a strange sound coming from the den down the hall from my bedroom. I got out of bed to find the source of this ringing sound and discovered that the alarm clock on the desk had started to ring at 3 a.m. The alarm on this particular clock had never been set or used before. I had never heard the sound that it made. No one had been in the house for several days except me and I had not touched this clock. It was an odd feeling. I finally turned it off and stood there wondering what could have caused it to start ringing at 3 a.m.?

Later that same day, I had a call from my son Bob who reported that a strange thing had also happened at their house early that morning. When Bob got up to get ready to go to work, he heard an unusual sound coming from their basement. He went to the basement and discovered that a motorized Lego toy that was stored in a box had been turned on. Bob was flabbergasted, as this toy, which Joan had given to her grandson Matthew, had not been touched or played with in months. I then told Bob about the alarm going off at 3 a.m. and the mystery of the rinsed and stacked dishes at Mike's house. All of us believe that Joan's spirit was somehow responsible for these three unusual incidents which all occurred within a 48-hour period. How else could these mysterious events be explained?

It's Back To Work Again

On March 18, I went back to work full time at the office. It was a welcome change and I really appreciated being able to keep busy doing something that I really enjoyed. The days were full of meetings, memos or letters to write and many phone calls.

Easter vacation – the end of April – I took my family to Laguna Beach, California again for eight days. We celebrated Emily's eighth birthday on Friday night while we were in California and returned to Michigan the next day, Saturday, April 25.

Increasing Concern About the Economy

America's stunning victory over Iraq in the Gulf War in 1991 had led to a momentary respite in the ongoing recession. But, by the fall of 1991, the wheels had fallen off the economy and white-collar layoffs exceeded 2,700 a day. There was a significant increase in bankruptcies early in 1992, including such high profile businesses as R.H. Macy & Company and TransWorld Airlines. The big three automakers had announced 1991 losses totaling more than $7.5 billion. Our two automobile clients – Volkswagen and Audi – were struggling. The "Fahrvergnugen" advertising campaign we had created for Volkswagen was getting a lot of attention but sales results were disappointing. A "60 Minutes" program had carried a disastrous report on Audi, as well as a follow-up report some months later that was nearly as bad as the first one. Audi did nothing, believing a reported "sudden acceleration" problem (which was never proven) would blow over. It didn't, and sales plummeted. Dick Mugg, who was the head of Audi, decided to move the Audi advertising account to DDB Needham's Chicago office. A few of our people were transferred to Chicago when this occurred, but it also resulted in some downsizing in our office.

While I was in California for the Easter vacation with my family, Rod Burton, Dave Horner and Nan Gerard all resigned from DDB Needham to join the Bozell Advertising agency. This, following the Audi account moving to Chicago, created considerable turmoil in our office with all kinds of rumors erupting – some started by our competitors. In June, the nationwide jobless rate had hit 7.8 percent but it was even higher than that in Michigan. Times were tough but there were also some signs of the economy recovering, as interest rates had plummeted, creating a boom for the sale of cars and residential housing. Standard Federal financed the Victoria Park development in Detroit and this subdivision, the first in more than 30 years within the city of Detroit, has been credited as the catalyst that started the city's recovery. The concept was developed by Garry Carley, vice chairman of Standard Federal Bank. Tom Ricketts supported the project and became very involved and John Behr was assigned the day-to-day management.

A Room For Women At a Monastery

A number of women had shown interest in going to St. Augustine's House – the monastery near Oxford, Michigan – for a retreat and meditation. There was not a suitable place for a woman to stay there, so I agreed to furnish a spare room as a memorial to Joan. The room was painted and new light fixtures installed. I ordered the furniture, carpeting, bedding and pictures to make it a very comfortable, pleasant place for a woman to stay. This was initiated early in June and the room was finished and dedicated in late September. St. Augustine's House, which sits atop one of the highest hills in Oakland County, is kind of a Christian crossroads, as people are always coming and going from all over the United States, Canada, and other countries. It is a busy place and you meet some really interesting people there. A book has been written about the monastery called, "The Place Where Love Abides" and that title really says it all.

All Dinner Invitations Gladly Accepted

Several weeks after Joan had passed away, and continuing through the spring and summer months, I was invited out for dinner several times a week. These invitations were truly welcomed and appreciated and I had dinner a number of times with Kathy and Mike Baker, Jane and Bob Baker, Ed Bauman, Priscilla and Tom Ricketts, Brigette and Carl Briggs, Beth and Bob Hutton and several of my neighbors, as well as others. When I did eat at home alone, the first thing I did on entering the house was to turn on the kitchen radio for some noise. After changing from a suit to casual clothes, I'd usually try to use the exercise bike and this was followed by a couple of drinks while watching the news on TV – after which I would then open a can of something. *When you eat alone, you just eat – when you eat with somebody, you dine.*

I also attended several support group meetings for widows and widowers, which Bill Wint arranged, but stopped going, as I felt more depressed after the meetings than I did before I attended. I'm sure these are helpful to some people, but they weren't for me. Listening to other people's woes just didn't get me "pumped up."

When the Going Gets Tough the Tough Get Going

We had high expectations when we merged with DDB Needham but had encountered a number of unexpected bumps in the road after the merger. Every time we moved ahead three steps, it seemed like we'd soon slide back one or two. Our enthusiasm was flagging and a new long-range plan was necessary. On June 19, the entire management staff of DDB Needham Detroit met all day at Meadowbrook Hall on the campus of Oakland University for a long range planning meeting. Mark Nichols, a motivational speaker, was the lead presenter. This meeting, which took considerable planning, helped to recharge everyone's batteries. On the positive side, Craig Dunaway had been added to the staff to supervise and manage the Health Alliance Plan account. We also were looking forward to moving to our new offices in Standard Federal Bank's corporate headquarters, as they were nearing completion. The entire staff would soon be consolidated in new offices in this beautiful facility. Our staff was working hard and looking forward to a much improved future.

I agreed to take on another volunteer position on July 1, when I became chairman of the marketing committee of the Greater Detroit Chamber of Commerce. Over the years I had participated in various activities of the Chamber and had been invited to serve on the marketing committee. As it turned out I served as its chairman for two years and met a lot of business people whom I would never have known had I not been involved. This organization later changed its name to the Detroit Regional Chamber and grew to be the second largest in the United States, with more than 11,000 members.

Some Time Out

My brother Joe and his wife Sue came to visit at the end of June. We picnicked, played golf and went to Mackinac Island over a weekend – also spending time at Indian River with Marian and Jay Kaser. A few weeks later, I met Sue and Joe in Wyoming, where we stayed at the Rusty Parrott Inn in Jackson Hole. My grandson Matthew went with me and the four of us enjoyed an exciting week, including a float trip on the Snake River and tours of Yellowstone Park and the Grand Tetons.

The adventure and excitement continued, though, when we got home, as Matthew's Boy Scout Troop went to West Virginia in August for a white water raft trip on the New River. I was invited to go along and that float trip

in a big rubber raft was one of the most thrilling things I have ever done in my life. I'm glad I did it once but I don't intend to ever do it again. This river adventure was arranged through Class VI River Runners, Inc. in Lansing, West Virginia and they also made a video of our day-long trip down the 1,000-foot-deep New River Gorge. Much of the time you drift along past "boom and bust" coal towns and rusty relics of the early 1900s, but every so often you pass through white-knuckle rapids or over ledge-drops. The rapids have interesting names like Upper and Lower Railroad, the Keeneys, Miller's Folly and Double Z. Whenever I look at the video of our float trip, I do so in amazement.

Mike Ilitch Buys the Detroit Tigers

On August 26, I attended the press conference at Tiger Stadium at which Mike Ilitch announced that he had purchased the Detroit Tigers from Tom Monaghan, the owner and CEO of the Domino's Pizza, Inc. chain. Monaghan was elated some years earlier when he became the owner of the Detroit Tigers, but Domino's had incurred a huge debt, forcing him to sell the team – which actually occurred on August 21. By comparison, Little Caesars Pizza, owned by Ilitch, was earning record profits. I was sorry to see this sale happen, though, as I believed our days were now numbered as the advertising agency for the Detroit Tigers, and this turned out to be true.

Homecoming At the University of Missouri

On Monday morning, September 14, we started unpacking boxes and putting everything away to get settled in our new offices. Over the weekend, movers had hauled all the furniture, equipment and files from the Top of Troy Tower to our new consolidated offices in the

Standard Federal Financial Center. Our long awaited move had finally occurred and by late Tuesday afternoon we were functioning as if we had been in this location for years. At the end of the day I started driving to Missouri, as I had already packed before I left for work in the morning. I stayed overnight at a motel in Indianapolis and arrived at Dorothy and Tom Staples' home in St. Louis after lunch on Wednesday. We drove to St. Albans, which was once a 5,400 acre estate owned by Oscar Johnson, the founder of International Shoe Co. I lived at St. Albans from the time I was a few months old until I was 14. When I lived there the estate raised championship Golden Guernseys and provided most of the milk for Peveley Dairy in St. Louis. It took 60 workers to operate and maintain the estate, and they, along with the farmers surrounding the estate, shopped at Pfeiffer's Store, which still exists today. John Pfeiffer owned the store when I lived at St. Albans and it's still in the family, as Mae Pfeiffer Head owns the store and operates it today as Head's Store. Visiting the store, as I did in September 1992, brought back a lot of memories.

I remember Mae's father, John Pfeiffer, helped me – and other kids – learn arithmetic. He used to have us count our candy and tell him how much we owed. The candy counter is still there filled with butterscotch drops, candy kisses, peppermint sticks, horehound drops, rock candy, cigars molded in chocolate, lemon drops, jawbreakers, cinnamon red hots, licorice shoe strings, and bellyburners, along with all kinds of chewing gum. Just name the brand you want to chew. It's there!

The store is now popular with cyclists of all sorts, and they descend on the store in the spring, summer and fall for sandwiches that are made in a special way. On the wall is a plaque from the St. Louis Bicycle Touring Society "for the many years of kindness."

The store is so irresistibly picturesque that, in the summer of 1983, a photographer from *Playboy* magazine used the store as a backdrop for part of the centerfold layout featuring a St. Louis woman, Playmate of the Year, Ruth Guerri. The tasteful photos that resulted from the photography session at Head's store – Mae would permit no nudity – now hang from a support beam in the store along with tear sheets from a *Seventeen* magazine fashion feature that also used the store as a background prop.

Mae Head paid a price for that exposure, however. The two vintage Coke signs that were affixed to the walls of each side of the front door (they were featured in the photograph) were stolen soon after the magazine hit the newsstands.

We always like to go back to our roots and, fortunately, St. Albans has become an impressive upscale community of expensive homes, golf courses and clubs and the like. The home we lived in no longer exists.

My uncle Tom and I played golf on Thursday and that evening I enjoyed a dinner with the Staples family members that live in the St. Louis area – my uncle Jim, cousins Tommy and Mary (Staples) and her husband Dean Vazis, their daughter Colleen and, of course, Dorothy and Tom. Then it was on to Columbia, where I arrived at the Country Club of Columbia before noon. There weren't many participants in the scramble from my college days, except Floyd Eberhard, so we paired up and shared a cart. The golf outing was a benefit for the scholarship fund of the Zeta Phi Chapter. It was a fun day and a cocktail party and buffet dinner followed. When the prizes were distributed, I received one for being the "oldest" alumnus who played in the scramble. Hmmm!

The next morning, I met an old friend, John (Jack) Bloess, at the fraternity house and we went to the homecoming football game after lunch. This was followed by several parties, dinner, and another party. Jack and I were friends in high school in Sedalia, and it was Jack who convinced me that I should join the Beta Theta Pi fraternity. After college,

Jack remained in Sedalia, where he owns and operates a lumber business. He, too, lost his wife to ovarian cancer. On Sunday morning I headed back to Michigan, driving all day and part of the next through a steady rain.

The Condo At Boyne Mountain

My son Mike had recently talked with a friend who knew of a condo coming up for sale in one of the Boynestadt units at Boyne Mountain. These condos seldom were for sale, as most had been held by families from the time they were first built. Bud Shea, who was an original owner, had purchased a home on nearby Lake Charlevoix and had decided to sell his condo. On September 30 Mike and I went to Boyne Mountain to inspect the unit and also played golf at the Monument Course. After much discussion on the way home that evening, it was decided that I'd make Bud an offer. I did so and we quickly came to terms, closing on the deal on October 14. The purchase of this condo was one of the best things I've ever done for my family. They've gotten a lot of use out of it, particularly throughout the skiing season, and my five grandchildren are all exceptionally good skiers. Blaine Baker is on the Park City, Utah Ski Team while Brad Baker is a member of the Rocky Mountain Biathlon Team (in 1999). I've enjoyed the condo during the spring, summer and fall months for get-away weekends to play golf, go morel mushroom hunting, or just to relax and read a good book.

Michigan Lottery Account Up For Bids

Throughout October and into November we put a lot of time and money into a proposal for the Michigan Lottery. We had received their RFP and decided to make an "all out" effort to win this account. David Hudson, vice president and strategic planner, headed the DDB Needham team to put our proposal and bid together. Since DDB Needham already handled the New York and Canada lotteries as well as part of the California Lottery account, we had a lot of expertise upon which to draw. On November 23, the proposal and price bid were delivered to Michigan's Department of Management and Budget in Lansing. We had to wait for the outcome of our efforts.

A Number of Interesting Meetings

I was invited to serve on a committee to plan the celebration of Standard Federal's 100th Anniversary, which would occur in 1993. The first meeting of this committee was November 11 and regular meetings of the committee followed to develop a significant recognition of this important milestone.

In October, we were both delighted and relieved when Volkswagen approved the 1993 creative and media plan we had proposed. Consequently, we were shocked to learn on November 11, that the national creative work was moving back to New York from Detroit at the insistence of a new executive at Volkswagen. This would mean a further reduction of our staff and put into question the future of DDB Needham's Detroit office.

During October and November, I had met with Fred Krohn and Doug Mowat of London's Farm Dairy to get approvals on a number of advertisements that we had prepared for the dairy. They were interested in having the agency assist them in preparing a five-year plan that would move their sales to $100,000,000 annually, at which time they would have a public offering of their stock. In December, Doug Mowat, the president of London's Farm Dairy, gave us the assignment of preparing a strategic marketing plan for the dairy and we started the planning process for executing this important assignment.

A Church Elevator Dedicated To Joan

The Ortonville United Methodist Church needed to add an elevator to meet the new building code for handicapped persons. On Sunday, November 22, this elevator was dedicated to Joan E. Baker. The church had received some memorial contributions in her name and these funds were utilized for this purpose. However, I made the commitment to pay the major cost of this elevator and it is now paid in full.

What Will the Future Be?

During December, I participated in a number of meetings concerning the future of the office. Armond Salerno and Hal Stutt from our New York office came to Detroit frequently and unfortunately a number of people had to be "career adjusted." I tried to help some of them find new positions and, fortunately, most did so, as the job market for people in communications in the Detroit area had improved considerably. In spite of the problems created first by the Audi account moving to Chicago and more recently by the Volkswagen account move to New York, we still had a lot of activity to handle for Standard Federal Bank, Lafarge Corporation, Health Alliance Plan, John Henry Company, London's Farm Dairy and other clients.

Bill Clinton had been elected president November 3 and would take the oath of office in January but he would benefit from various indicators that were detecting a pick-up in economic activity. 1992 was the nation's transition year from recession to growth – the year the recovery really began.

Right after Christmas, I went to California to visit my brother Joe and to help him celebrate his 60th birthday on December 30. The following day Joe, Sue and I went to Pasadena to attend a pep rally at the Civic Center for the University of Michigan football

I enjoyed visiting with Bo Schembechler at the U of M pep rally held in Pasadena, California on December 31, 1992.

team. Bo Schembechler, former U of M football coach and more recently the president of the Detroit Baseball Club, was present and we had a very interesting half-hour conversation together.

Later we went to Leslie and Jack Owen's home in Sierra Madre, where we spent the night. Leslie is my niece and we had a pleasant evening with her and Jack and their three children, Hayley, Justin and Olivia. But, we went to bed early so that we could be up and on our way at dawn on New Year's day to go to the Rose Bowl parade and later to the Rose Bowl football game.

– 1993 –

When you watch a Rose Bowl Parade at home on TV one thing you're not at all aware of are smells. Even though we had reserved seats in stands close to the actual parade, we wanted to arrive early to find a place close by to park the car. When we arrived, there were still many people in sleeping bags or on cots on the sidewalks who had been there all night to secure a good place to watch the parade. Lots of these "overnighters," though, were up and fixing their breakfasts and the aroma of bacon and coffee permeated the air. Later, when the parade went by, we enjoyed the scent of the flowers used to decorate the floats. That afternoon, we watched an exciting football game at the Rose Bowl and this year the University of Michigan came out victorious beating Washington 38 to 31.

The next several days, I stayed with my mother at her apartment in The Wellington, a senior citizen facility in Laguna Hills. We talked a lot, I read to her, and we reminisced about the many happy times the family had experienced over the years. I'm very grateful we had that time together.

Early Monday morning, January 4, Phyllis Attwater called to tell me that Doug Mowat, president of London's Farm Dairy, had died in a plane crash Sunday evening. He was flying his private plane back to Port Huron from Phoenix, where he and his wife had spent the Christmas holidays with their daughter and her family. Doug's wife Nancy had decided to stay in Arizona a week or two longer. In addition to her husband, she lost their son Douglas Andrew and her father John Church, as all three died in the plane crash. Doug was 59 and a very capable, experienced pilot, but when he tried to abort the landing in order to make another circle to land the Cessna T337, it flipped and crashed.

Phyllis Attwater, Kit King and I attended the funeral service on January 8 in Port Huron. It was a combined service, with all three caskets at the front of the church. Each was eulogized by a different minister and the service ended with "Amazing Grace" played on a bagpipe by a Scotsman in kilts standing at the altar. It was a very moving service, resulting from a terrible tragedy.

The following Monday, we were informed that we did not win the Michigan Lottery account. This was a great disappointment, as David Hudson, our vice president manager of strategic planning and his team that helped prepare the RFP had worked extremely hard on our presentation and proposal. Not long after, David Hudson resigned from DDB Needham to join Campbell-Ewald, where he has had a very successful career. He is presently executive vice president and executive director of planning and development for that advertising agency.

The rest of January and February were fairly routine, the only exception being a special project in early February for the Michigan Department of Transportation (MDOT). We were asked to put together a comprehensive advertising and promotion plan to encourage people to use railway transportation between Pontiac and downtown Detroit. This service had existed for many years but, as usage steadily declined year after year, it was discontinued. Now Amtrak, which was a client of DDB Needham in New York, wanted to renew this local passenger service. This client relationship was the reason we became involved. It was just an exercise, however, as this passenger service never came about.

On February 18, I was back in New York for meetings with Armond Salerno, Linda Clark and Hal Stutt. I also met with John Bernbach, as well as Andy Berlin, who had recently been named president of DDB Needham New York. At this meeting, I was informed that I would now report to Andy Berlin. Andy had helped develop a highly successful advertising agency in San Francisco – Goodby, Berlin and Silverstein, Inc. This agency had been acquired by Omnicom and Berlin then moved to New York to join DDB Needham. The following week, Andy, Armond and Hal were in Detroit for meetings with our staff.

Thursday, February 25, marked one year since Joan had passed away. It seemed incredible that a whole year had already gone by but time steals quietly and swiftly by on its ceaseless course and, as we advance in life, we acquire a keener sense of the value of time.

Spring Returns

In late March I took part again in the Golden Mile Walk to benefit the March of Dimes and served as the advertising industry chairperson. I was the guest of Denise Ford at a play at St. Dunstan's Theater at Cranbrook on Saturday, March 27. Denise was then vice president of the Screenvision Cinema Network and, several years later, she married Robert Lutz – the president of Chrysler Corporation. I was still quite involved in the pro-bono "Project Water Rescue," which had recently received considerable media coverage due to new disturbing revelations concerning the poor water quality of certain parts of Lake Superior.

Thursday, April 8, it was back to California again as we kept our "family Easter vacation together" tradition going. My mother especially enjoyed our visit and the time she was able to spend with her grandsons and great grandchildren. She arranged for all of us to have dinner at The Wellington, the senior facility where she now lived, on Easter Sunday. We said goodbye to our relatives in California on Saturday, April 17 and returned to Detroit.

Hello Mary Lou

Mary Lou Vlasov and I met at a dinner arranged by a mutual friend of ours. After being married for more than 43 years, it was a strange experience for me to be invited to a dinner to "meet" someone. Mary Lou was a widow with two grown daughters. The oldest daughter, Nina, was married to Anthony Pacitto and they had a baby daughter, Alexandria. Lisa, her younger daughter, was a senior at Walsh College, majoring in accounting and living at home with Mary Lou in Sterling Heights. We enjoyed doing things together and I particularly looked forward to the weekends and Mary Lou's company.

Early Thursday morning, April 22, I went to New York for a two-day management meeting.

Mary Louise Vlasov and her daughters. Nina Pacitto on the left and Elizabeth (Liza) Duronio on the right.

I invited Mary Lou to accompany me. We stayed at the Omni Berkshire and on Thursday night we attended a DDB Needham-sponsored dinner at the Seashell Restaurant at Rockefeller Center, at which Keith Reinhard gave a very interesting talk.

While I was in meetings during the day, Mary Lou visited art museums but, on Saturday, we did "a day on the town." Following an early morning carriage ride through Central Park, we took an Apple Tour of Manhattan with side trips to the Statue of Liberty and Ellis Island. Apple Tours allow you to get off its bus at various places then catch another one of its buses when you're ready to move on – a great way to see the Big Apple. We had lunch at Fulton Street Market and ended our tour at the Waldorf-Astoria Hotel. This time, I had ample opportunity to see this hotel and some of its unique shops, and we unwound in a comfortable lounge off the lobby with a Beefeater martini. Following dinner, we saw the musical "Ain't Broadway Grand," to top off a full, fun day. Sunday morning we relaxed in the coffee shop at the Omni Berkshire, enjoying a big breakfast and drinking strong coffee while reading several New York newspapers. In the early afternoon we returned home in time to attend a

90th birthday party that evening for my father-in-law, Ed Bauman.

What Will Our Future Be?

From the end of April through June there were a number of meetings regarding the future plans for DDB Needham's Detroit office. We had down-sized the office considerably over the past year and a half as a result of the Audi and VW accounts moving to our Chicago and New York offices. There were still VW Dealer Associations' advertising to handle and a volume of special projects for VW, but the lack of a definite commitment as to the future of the office caused considerable uneasiness for the entire staff.

Bruce Duffey, the executive creative director, resigned to take another position and we held a farewell party for him on May 14. In late May, Health Alliance Plan (HAP) notified the agency that they were going to hold an agency review and this only helped fuel the anxiety of our staff. On June 10, while in New York for meetings, I was informed that BBDO Detroit, another division of Omincom, had been approached about taking over the general accounts. This was exciting news!

The plan that had evolved was to move the DDB Needham Detroit staff members assigned to the VW account to a new location. The space this group occupied in the Standard Federal headquarters building would then be occupied by PentaCom, a free-standing media planning and buying operation developed by BBDO Detroit to service all divisions of Chrysler Corporation. PentaCom was a new concept in media planning and buying, in that it would interact with the client (Chrysler) and its agencies (BBDO and Bozell) to develop media strategies and plans. The planning groups would then work directly with Chrysler brand management and the account and creative groups at the respective agency to produce strategic plans. The buying groups then would

take over and deliver the desired media vehicles. PentaCom was unique, in that all media planning, buying, trafficking and invoice reconciliation and paying would be done in one place. This would provide continuous coordination of all elements of the media planning/buying/paying cycle and as it turned out, this concept worked with great success under the leadership of David Martin, the president and CEO.

In late June the strategic plan that we had prepared for London's Farm Dairy was presented to Sharon Spradling, the new president of the dairy, and Fred Krohn, vice president. It was well received and detailed the strategy and steps needed to reach the goal of $100 million in annual sales in five years. Carl Hendrickson, who prepared the plan, made the presentation and led the discussion, which took most of the day.

A Wonderful Invitation From BBDO Detroit

Bill Oswald, the president and chief executive officer of BBDO Detroit, and I met for lunch on June 30. At this luncheon meeting, Bill extended an invitation for the General Accounts Group of DDB Needham to join BBDO Detroit. I had somewhat expected – and sincerely hoped – that Bill would inform me at this meeting that the management of Omnicom Group Inc. had decided that this should occur because of the questionable future status of the Detroit office of DDB Needham. I was quite surprised, then, when the offer to join BBDO Detroit was presented in the form of an invitation. I was tremendously impressed, enthused and thrilled by this offer, as I had the highest respect for the Batten, Barton, Durstine & Osborn Advertising Agency – now known as BBDO. The image and reputation of BBDO has consistently been one of an exceptionally solid, growing, innovative, professionally managed and profitable advertising agency.

George Batten

Bruce Barton

Roy Durstine

Alex Osborn

George Batten founded the agency, then known as the George Batten Company, in New York City in 1891.

In 1928, the George Batten Company merged with Barton, Durstine and Osborn, founded by Bruce Barton, Roy Durstine, and Alex Osborn, to form Batten, Barton, Durstine & Osborn (which eventually became known as "BBDO"). By 1971 BBDO, Inc. had grown into a network of agencies and was renamed BBDO International, Inc. Growth and evolution continued as BBDO International became BBDO Worldwide, Inc. in 1986. From the beginning, BBDO has been at the forefront of industry developments. In the early Batten Company years, it was the first "full-service" agency, providing clients with the writing and design as well as the placement of ads. In the '20s, when Batten merged with Barton, Durstine & Osborn, it became the hottest – and very likely the first – agency on Madison Avenue. In the '30s and '40s

it led the industry into radio, and in the '50s, BBDO was the first agency to propel clients into television, producing shows as well as creating advertising. During the '60s, BBDO was a leader in the "Creative Revolution," producing landmark campaigns for Schaefer Beer, Chrysler, Dodge, and GE. And in the '70s, BBDO developed into a leader in the global marketplace.

During the '80s, BBDO distinguished itself as a premier agency network with exceptional creative strengths. Among the hundreds of awards won by BBDO in recent years is the 1985 Grand Prix from the Cannes advertising film festival for the Pepsi "Archaeology" commercial. In 1990, BBDO's Diet Pepsi "Apartment 10G" was named the best commercial of the past 30 years by the Hollywood Radio and Television Society. In 1992, BBDO's "Foreman" spot for HBO was awarded an Emmy – the only TV commercial ever to be so honored.

In 1983 and 1985, respectively, BBDO was named Agency of the Year by *ADWEEK* and *Advertising Age*. In 1993, BBDO Worldwide was one of the world's largest advertising agencies, with billings of more than $6 billion and it was the largest operating unit of the Omnicom Group, spanning 117 cities and 66 countries.

Following the lunch meeting with Bill Oswald, I met with Kit King to tell her about the invitation from Bill Oswald to join BBDO Detroit and we started making plans to inform our clients about this in order to get their support and approval. I also called all the people at DDB Needham in New York that I had been discussing the future of the office with – Arnold Salerno, Hal Stutt and Andy Berlin – to tell them that we wanted to become part of BBDO Detroit. They were all in favor of this move.

I spent most of the next day on the phone talking with clients to tell them about this anticipated change in our status and to answer any questions they might have about BBDO Detroit. That evening I was a dinner guest at Wendy and Robert Freeman's home in Metamora and Bob, who had preceded me as CEO of the Detroit office of DDB Needham, was delighted to learn about our good fortune.

On July 6, I went to my office for a meeting to help plan a presentation to BBDO management scheduled for the next day. At this meeting, Kit King, Matt Duff and I presented samples of the print and broadcast advertising we had created for our clients to Bill Oswald, Ray Schneider, Pete Swiecicki, Joe Caponigro and Kathy Tebbe. Kit, Matt and I were also given a complete tour of the Southfield offices of BBDO and introduced to a great number of people. The next week we were back and forth between the two offices nearly every day for meetings with various people in different departments, as there were many details to be handled in the transition. Key meetings were with Dave Harrelson to become familiar with the traffic and production systems and with Carol Maynard, head of human resources, to complete all forms required of new employees as well as to become familiar with the company's policies and benefits.

Bill Yaw, Vince Carducci, Kathleen Clancy and Ursula Crenshaw – our primary contacts in Standard Federal Bank's Marketing department – visited BBDO's Detroit headquarters in Southfield on Wednesday, July 14 for a tour and presentation on the credentials and background of the agency. This meeting went especially well and we were over another hurdle in our transition from DDB Needham to BBDO Detroit.

Later in July, Standard Federal Bank merged with Heritage Federal Bank, which had a number of offices in the northern part of Michigan's lower peninsula. At one time, these offices were Family Federal offices – we had handled the grand opening advertising for most of them. When Standard Federal acquired Landmark Savings, which had overlapping offices with Family Federal, we had to resign the Family Federal account. Now the Family Federal offices were back in the fold as part of Standard Federal Bank.

It's All Systems GO!

On July 28, Bill Oswald informed me that everything was in order for the General Accounts to become part of BBDO Detroit effective Monday, August 2. What a great relief it was to hear those words! The next day, Thursday, July 29, Phyllis Attwater, Matt Duff, Dan Busto and I had a lengthy meeting with London's Farm Dairy in Port Huron. Matt Duff, our creative director, and Dan Busto, copywriter, presented a new consumer and trade advertising campaign which the client enthusiastically approved along with the media plan for the advertising. Things were actually going well!

Matt Duff joined BBDO Detroit in August 1993 as vice president, associate creative director, responsible for overseeing and directing all creative work prepared for the General Accounts clients of BBDO Detroit. At DDB Needham Worldwide, Matt had served as group creative director.

The Start of a New Career

There are particular days in one's life that are extra, extra special and Tuesday, August 2, ranks in that category for me – for that's the day I became a member of the staff of BBDO. I felt very proud when I joined BBDO because of the agency's reputation for building brands, and because of its great heritage. Men who are legends in the advertising agency business, like Ben Duffy, Charlie Brower and Tom Dillon, spent their careers at BBDO and I was familiar with them from reading *Ad Age* magazine. In 1891, more than one hundred years ago, a minister's son named George Batten put the word "Company" after his name and opened the first agency to actually write ads.

Three months later he signed his first client – The Macbeth Lamp Chimney Company – and, in the years that followed, saw business boom.

Since then, BBDO, the agency born out of the 1928 merger between Batten and Barton, Durstine & Osborn, has led the industry in all manner of innovations, producing some of the most memorable, effective and distinctive campaigns in history.

Who can forget *"Better Things for Better Living...Through Chemistry,"* *"Which Twin has the Toni?,"* Chiquita Banana, and the *"Pepsi Generation?"* And more recently, *"GE Brings Good Things to Life", "Visa Is Everywhere You Want To Be,"* and *"Apple Offers You The Power To Be Your Best."*

It was Bruce Barton, for example, the second "B" in BBDO, who named General Motors and General Electric; and some say it was a good thing he stopped there before BBDO wound up with a roster of clients all bearing the same name. Roy Durstine, the founding "D," was "the father of commercial broadcasting." And Alex Osborn, the "O," invented the concept of "brainstorming."

On August 4, I had lunch with Bill Oswald at Morton's Chicago Steak House in Southfield. Bill told me at this luncheon that the board of directors of BBDO Detroit had elected me executive vice president, manager of general accounts; Kit King, senior vice president, management supervisor of general accounts; and Matt Duff, vice president, associate creative director of BBDO Detroit.

I now reported to Bill Oswald, the president and chief executive officer of BBDO Detroit. Bill joined BBDO Detroit in 1982 as a senior vice president and account management supervisor for the Chrysler Corporation Dodge Division account. In 1988, he was named executive vice president and senior management representative. While on the Dodge account, Bill was part of the marketing team responsible for the Chrysler Corporation's turnaround, assisting with the development of the highly successful "Ram Tough" concept for Dodge Truck.

Prior to joining BBDO Detroit, Bill worked for several agencies in New York City, including Kenyon & Eckhardt and Lennen & Newell. He gained extensive account experience working for clients such as Colgate, National Distillers and Beecham products. In addition, he had owned his own car dealership, a Ford franchise, one of the largest in northern New York.

Happy Days Are Here Again

With the resolution of our employment status and a vastly improved outlook for the future, the world seemed a better and brighter place. There no longer was a cloud of doubt hanging over us. Even though it was a busy summer there was also time to have fun! Nearly every weekend I managed to get in several rounds of golf at different courses and even squeezed in a few nine hole outings late in the day during the week. On August 15, Mary Lou and I watched the final round of the 1993 PGA Tournament at Inverness Golf Club in Toledo. Mary Lou's daughter Liza and her fiancee, Robert Duronio, joined us. It was an exciting event as Greg Norman and

Paul Anzinger ended up in a tie, forcing a sudden death overtime. Paul Anzinger won by a stroke on the second playoff hole.

At the end of August, my two uncles in St. Louis, Jim and Tom Staples, and Tom's wife Dorothy came to visit. Tom and I played the beautiful and challenging Pine Knob golf course in Clarkston before we all headed north for a few days to the Boyne Mountain condo, where we played more golf. Tom is a very good golfer with a six handicap and I appreciated the suggestions he made to try to help me improve my game. After spending a day touring Mackinac Island, we headed north to Sault Ste. Marie, Canada to take a one-day trip on the Algoma Central (the A-Train again) to see the fall color change already underway in Canada. Nearly every evening, the five of us played dominoes (Mexican train) or *SkipBo* and had a most enjoyable week together over an extended Labor Day weekend.

In mid-September, I returned again to Mackinac Island as the guest of London's Farm Dairy to attend the annual meeting of the Michigan Grocer's Association at the Grand Hotel. Mary Lou accompanied me and we shared some fun activities and great meals with Sharon and Fred Krohn in between business meetings.

A Return Trip to Germany and Austria

A week later, on September 22, we flew to Munich, Germany where Mary Lou, my sister-in-law Barbara Watts, Barb's father Edward Bauman, and I enjoyed a memorable vacation. Munich has a great airport – easy to find your way around and with free carts everywhere to haul your luggage. We picked up our reserved rental car and headed for Oberwassen, as Peter Kocher had invited us to visit Kocherhof – where we first stayed in 1982. Late in the afternoon, we arrived at his home in the Alps and received a warm welcome. Peter's daughter Cristina prepared a wonderful dinner for us and the next morning

her husband, Claudio Pareto, cooked breakfast for everybody. Peter's wife Heleana had died since our last visit and was buried in a cemetery next to a small church in the valley below their home. On Sunday afternoon, we all walked to the village, stopping at the cemetery, and later had dinner at a restaurant built in 1701.

Standing in front of Kocherhof, from left to right: Peter Kocher, Cristina Pareto, Barbara Watts, Ed Bauman and Mary Lou Vlasov.

Enjoying lunch in Reit 'im Winkle, a village in the Alps. From left to right: Ed Bauman, Ernie Baker, Barbara Watts, Cristina Pareto and Mary Lou Vlasov.

On Monday we went to see King Ludwig's Palace, which is on an island in Lake Chimsee and is an incredible facility. That evening, after

204

dinner, we took a long walk together, taking in the spectacular scenery and watching the shadows fall across the valley as the sun set. We said our farewells to Peter, Cristina and Claudio after breakfast on Tuesday morning and then drove to Vienna, Austria, where we stayed for several days at the Böck Brunn Hotel on the outskirts of the city. Rail transportation into downtown Vienna was available near our hotel, so we left our car at the hotel and took the train, which first ran above the ground but soon ran underground as it entered the city, becoming a subway. When we arrived in downtown Vienna, we had to go up several levels by escalator to reach the streets.

There are many museums in Vienna and we visited a number of them. We and also took a Grey Line Tour – always a good way to see any large city. On Thursday evening, Mary Lou and Barbara wanted to see the Frank Lloyd Webber musical "Elizabeth," but Dad and I opted to return to the hotel to have a good dinner and get to bed early. Dad and I returned to the subway and boarded the train and then Dad discovered his wallet was gone from his back pocket – a pick-pocket had taken it. Dad was devastated that such a thing could happen to him as he was very trusting of people – especially Germans. When we returned to our hotel we called the police. They came to take a preliminary report but they told Dad that he should go to the police station in the morning to file a complete report.

The next morning, after checking out of our hotel, we went to the police station. It took more than an hour to complete the huge form to report the stolen wallet. Later, when we were on our way to Salzburg, Dad said, "I'm going to get my wallet back, I'm sure of it." And I said, "Dad, you'll never see that wallet again." I was wrong! After we returned home, Dad's wallet did come back in the mail – someone had found it and turned it in to the U.S. Consulate office in Vienna. The money was gone but the photos, credit cards and other documents were all intact.

We spent the weekend in Salzburg, staying at the Hotel Taunhof, where we had a huge bathroom that, strangely, was bigger than our bedroom. We had some great meals at the Glockenspiel and K&K restaurants in Salzburg (which means Salt City), as well as delicious sausage treats and other snacks we purchased at food stands while walking and exploring the streets and alleyways of this old city. Again, we took a Grey Lines Tour to see more of the city and the outlying areas. From Salzburg, we returned to Munich, where we enjoyed a great dinner at the famous Hofbrau House. We arrived home midnight Tuesday and I was back in the office Wednesday morning trying to catch up on everything that had happened while I was away. There was plenty to catch up on!

A Special Wedding

Saturday, October 9, Mary Lou and I attended the marriage of Priscilla and Tom Ricketts' daughter Karen to Robert (Bert) Struck at Christ Cranbrook Church. Their reception was at The Townsend hotel in Birmingham. We sat with Beth and Bob Hutton for dinner and enjoyed the company of many long time Standard Federal Bank officers and their wives whom I had gotten to know quite well over the years: Mary and Jack Ray; Carol and Bill Yaw; Nancy and Garry Carley; Carol and Ron Palmer; Cheryl and Joe Krul; Leslie and Durwood Allen; and Beth and Jack Beauchamp, plus others. It was a beautiful wedding and we had an exceptionally good time in the company of especially nice people.

The next weekend, I was in Columbia, Missouri for the Beta golf scramble, which took place on Friday afternoon at the Columbia Country Club. Floyd Eberhard and I paired up again and our foursome included Floyd's son Mark and Bob See. The outing raised more than $5,000 for the Zeta Phi scholarship program. At the fraternity house on Saturday, I had lunch with Jack Bloess and Ray O'Brien.

205

Ray and I were in the same pledge class and he has been recognized by a number of business publications as one of the top chief executive officers in the country. In 1993, he was chairman and CEO of Consolidated Freightways, a $4.2 billion company, headquartered in Menlo Park, California. Ray's company employs over 40,000 people and handles more than 25 billion pounds of freight annually, making it the largest in the world.

1993 Winds Down

From mid-November through Christmas, it seems that everything accelerates – especially time – because you're so busy shopping for gifts, addressing cards, participating in all kinds of activities and, in the advertising agency business, there's always more business activity. Clients want projects that have been underway for months finished before year-end, and assisting in the preparation of business or marketing plans for the coming year takes considerable time. Keeping it all in perspective and under control is a real challenge, but you must do so if you're going to enjoy this special part of the year.

On November 14 I was the guest of Dave Martin, president of PentaCom, at the Huntsman Club in Dryden, where we spent a beautiful fall day pheasant hunting. Dave and I had a lot of shots and bagged a number of pheasants, primarily because we had a well-trained hunting dog working the fields for us. Later in the week, we had a delicious pheasant dinner prepared by Mary Lou and we invited my sister-in-law, Barbara Watts, and my father-in-law, Edward Bauman, to join us.

On Thanksgiving morning, my sons and their families and I were all up at 5:30 a.m. in order to be at Cobo Hall in downtown Detroit for the 7:30 a.m. breakfast that precedes the annual Thanksgiving Day parade. It was a crisp, clear day and a huge crowd lined Woodward Avenue. I participated again as a

Dave Martin   **Tom Gribble**   **Ernie Baker**
                       (Dog Handler)

member of the clown corps and used up a dozen cans of silly string spraying children along the parade route.

From Thanksgiving to Christmas I was invited to a series of holiday parties starting with the annual *Business Week* brunch at Pine Lake Country Club on Saturday, December 4. This was always a special, well-attended event because it was also an opportunity to visit with many people who were either old friends or long-time business acquaintances that you didn't see very often. The annual Christmas breakfast for the agency's staff took place on December 9 at Forest Lake Country Club. Tom Clark, chairman of BBDO North America, welcomed everybody and gave us an update on the company's 1993 progress and achievements, as well as the outlook for the coming year.

Over and above all the year-end work we were doing for our regular clients, we were also asked to handle the advertising and promotion for a major event scheduled for New Year's Eve at the Dearborn Hyatt Regency Hotel. The Hyatt chain was a client of BBDO New York and the local Hyatt Hotel had requested our assistance. We put a campaign together for them that sold out the event.

On Christmas eve, Mary Lou and I were invited to Brigette and Carl Briggs' home for the traditional fondue dinner which Brigette worked hours to prepare. Chunks of beef, pork, venison and veal, along with shrimp and fish, were cooked in electric fondue pots at the dining room table (a-cook-it-yourself dinner), which generated a lot of lively conversation while we satisfied our appetites.

A few days after Christmas, we gathered at our condo at Boyne Mountain. It was a wonderful way to end the year with the family together. My sons, their wives and my grandchildren went skiing every day and built up hearty appetites. Mary Lou and I did a little cross-country skiing but, mostly, we saw to it that there was lots of food for everyone to eat. On New Year's eve, we decided to go out for Chinese food and we got a big variety of take-out items which we also shared with friends and neighbors who stopped by the condo. Everybody had plenty to eat and with all that day's fresh air and exercise, no one stayed up very late. A good way to end 1993.

Interesting Statistics and Events of 1993

93% of U.S. households owned at least one TV set in 1993 and 65% had two or more sets. The final episode of "Cheers" aired, a sitcom carried by NBC for 11 years. David Letterman jumped to CBS, and NBC issued a humiliating retraction and apology to General Motors on "Dateline NBC" for a staged on-camera explosion during a report on alleged safety problems with GM trucks. The Midwest had the worst floods ever recorded – fifty people died and the lives of thousands of others were disrupted. In Detroit Coleman Young was out – too ill to run again – and Dennis Archer became the new mayor with big plans for the city.

– 1994 –

The automobile manufacturers and their suppliers shut down from the day before Christmas through New Year's, and consequently, Detroit advertising agencies that serve automotive clients close their offices for the same time period. There are always some people in ad agencies, though, that have to report to handle emergencies or "hot" assignments but most employees (except for the accounting and financial staff) have this extra time off, which adds considerably to the enjoyment of the holiday season. Very few advertising agencies outside the Detroit area, however, get this special "perk."

One of the first assignments I received when I returned to work on January 3, came from the New York office. They needed a comprehensive report on the automotive after-market in a big hurry. I turned for help to Reid M. MacGuidwin, who had just retired at the end of 1993 as the director of marketing for *Automotive News* magazine. Reid provided all the information and materials I needed to prepare this report. When you know whom or where to turn for assistance the job is half done!

Tom Clark, chairman of BBDO Detroit and chairman of BBDO North America, addressed the Adcraft Club of Detroit on January 7. There was a big turnout to hear his talk on a company's most valuable asset – its brands. He dramatically showed why a brand requires constant focus, constant nurturing and constant nourishment by using the car business as an example. Out of 1,500 American companies that produced automobiles since the beginning of the century only three have survived – Chrysler, Ford and General Motors. It was a terrific talk because Tom provided a lot of information about the history of the car business and about branding, and did it in a very entertaining way.

Tom Clark is an Ad Man's Ad Man – someone I've been very proud to be associated with at BBDO Detroit. He joined BBDO in the agency's San Francisco office in 1968 as an account supervisor, and was later elected a vice president. He was transferred to BBDO's Cleveland office in a similar capacity three years later. In January 1973, Tom moved to New York to serve as a management supervisor. He was promoted to the position of general manager of BBDO's Detroit office in November 1974, at which time he was elected to the Board of directors of BBDO. For a period of five

Tom Clark

years in Detroit, Tom managed this full-service office as well as a 40-man field force responsible for the Dodge dealer business in 22 satellite offices. He returned to New York in 1979 and assumed executive management and administrative responsibilities. In 1984, he became chairman of the agency's account management committee and in June of 1986 assumed the titles of president and chief executive officer of BBDO. In 1987, Tom returned to Detroit as chairman of BBDO North America, a newly-established

region of the BBDO Worldwide network. All of BBDO's offices in the United States (except for the New York office) and Canada reported to Tom. BBDO was, and still is, the largest advertising agency in Canada by a wide margin.

Every Day is Busy – And Different

During January, our creative director, Matt Duff, copywriter John Brogan, and I put together a comprehensive capabilities brochure for BBDO Detroit for use in soliciting new business. We had a variety of projects to handle for our clients – Lafarge, London's Farm Dairy, and others – and a great many assignments for Standard Federal Bank. The bank was enjoying outstanding growth and great success under the leadership of the chairman and president, Thomas R. Ricketts. The following memo, prepared by Kit King, describes this progress:

Memo to: Ernie Baker
From: Kit King
Subject: Overview of Client Activity
Client: Standard Federal Bank

Standard Federal had its most profitable year in 1993 with ROA and ROE ratios which continue to place them among the top performers in the financial services industry.

The unprecedented volume in mortgage lending ($4.3 billion in residential home loans) contributed significantly to this; more than 90% of revenue is generated from this source. In addition, Standard Federal expanded its franchise during 1993 with several acquisitions, the most notable being Heritage Federal Savings Bank which added 45 branch offices to their retail operations. And the InterFirst Federal Savings Bank, which gave the Bank a national presence in the wholesale mortgage lending arena.

Two key components of Standard Federal's performance in the future will continue to be the strength of its retail mortgage lending operations and the servicing of loans generated through its InterFirst wholesale division. Since mortgage volume has slowed considerably, the Bank will concentrate heavily in both of these areas throughout 1994.

For instance, during the last several months, the agency has designed and produced numerous advertising and collateral materials for InterFirst; starting with a complete corporate identification system through trade advertising, sales materials and displays. (BBDO recently received the "Best of Show" at the National Convention of Wholesale Mortgage Bankers for all of this work on behalf of InterFirst.) Our efforts throughout the remainder of the year will focus on strengthening their brand identity and solidifying their emerging position as a major national player in wholesale lending as they expand into new markets.

On the retail lending side, the agency recently presented a comprehensive campaign designed to facilitate a surge in mortgage lending for Standard Federal during the second half and help them maintain their leadership position.

However, the need to continue building a strong full service retail presence will demand that marketing efforts be expanded toward the deposit side of the business as well; particularly in expanding the checking account portfolio and garnering low-cost savings dollars.

To assist in both these efforts, we will debut some of the new television advertising which was produced recently by BBDO. It is product-driven while highly image oriented because of the superior production quality. The client is very pleased with the final result of the commercials.

Last but not least, our media group just completed and presented a media analysis that included several innovative strategies for the Bank's consideration; which should significantly increase brand awareness and make the most of a current budget which needs to be increased; given their recent growth spurt and the aggressive acquisition strategy they continue to pursue. This analysis should also make a strong case for a larger budget.

Overall, our relationship with Standard Federal remains strong, both personally and professionally. They take a great deal of pride in being represented by an agency with the reputation ours enjoys around the world. And we all do our best every day to deserve the loyalty and respect that they accord us every day. They are a terrific client!

Standard Federal Bank's Annual Report Is a Major Assignment

For years we had prepared an annual report for Standard Federal Bank in the form of a small folder that was mailed to its savings and mortgage customers. After it went public in 1987, the annual report then turned into a major assignment as it became an important communications vehicle with stock holders. The 1993 annual report consisted of 80 pages, plus cover, and included a card insert. It was printed on high-quality paper with full-color photos and graphs to illustrate the bank's highly successful and profitable operation. In the marketing department, Vince Carducci, vice president in charge of corporate communications, was responsible for this important project. Planning started in September of the prior year and the report had to be presented and available for the bank's annual stockholders' meeting which took place on April 26, 1994.

At the Bank, a number of top officers were also involved in the approval process for the annual report, including Tom Ricketts, president and CEO; Joe Krul, senior VP, chief financial officer; Michael Maher, senior VP and controller; and Ron Palmer, senior VP and general counsel.

Headquarters of Standard Federal Bank on Big Beaver Road in Troy, Michigan.

On the agency side, Kit King was very much a part of the process, working with the General Accounts Group creative, production, traffic and studio staff. Art director Diane Schroeder designed the annual report with supervision by Matt Duff. Laura Pizzo, production director, was intensely involved from start to finish, including attending the inevitable final all-night press check at the printer. And Kathy (Grobbel) Canapini of the BBDO Art Studio got her first opportunity to typeset an annual report.

Never a Dull Moment

Many changes occurred in the first half of 1994, as well as many new developments – all requiring attention or some involvement. This is typical, though, in the advertising agency business. Kaye Helms' husband Steve, who was with the Taubman Company, was transferred to Denver, so we said farewell to Kaye.

A few weeks later, Kristi Slack came on board as an account executive, assigned to Standard Federal Bank and the Oakland County Parks and Recreation Commission. Kristi joined us from Ross Roy but she was quite familiar to us, as she had worked at Baker Advertising and later at DDB Needham.

On February 14, "The Fridge" – Michigan's first and only refrigerated toboggan run – opened at Waterford Oaks. It was an immediate success.

Facing page: This full page advertisement for Standard Federal was one of the first ads for the Bank produced at BBDO Detroit.

HOW TO FEEL AT HOME WITH YOUR MORTGAGE.

 There's a lot to understand about a mortgage. At Standard Federal, we'll take the time to answer all your questions, and do everything we can to make you feel comfortable with the entire home loan process. Call us at 1-800/643-9600 for more information. We'll make you feel right at home.

PROUD SPONSOR OF
PARADE OF HOMES

100 Years Of Helping You Along The Way.™

Standard Federal Bank
Savings/Financial Services

1-800/643-9600

 Member FDIC — EQUAL HOUSING LENDER

©1993 Standard Federal Bank

Standard Federal

I attended the press preview and was fortunate to be one of the first riders. After a 55-foot drop, the toboggan races at more than 30 miles per hour down 1,000 feet of dips and straight-aways in a flume – exciting! My ride was videotaped by Channel 50, and that evening I saw myself on the local news. A few people who saw this on TV thought I was crazy.

The Motor City Exhibit

The Detroit Historical Society decided to recognize the 100th anniversary of the car business in Detroit with a special exhibit at the Detroit Historical Museum, to open in December 1995. The actual anniversary would be in 1996, as Charles Brady King's car and Henry Ford's quadricycle launched Detroit on the path to leadership in automobile manufacturing in 1896.

Bill Oswald was invited to be on the planning committee, but asked me to represent the agency as he did not have the time to participate. The first meeting of the committee was on February 21. The committee, in addition to me, included:

Peter Brown
Automotive News

William Chapin
Chapin and Company

John Emmert
Global News Bureau

Ida Hendrix
Motor City Exhibition

Maud Lyon
Detroit Historical Museum

Oscar B. Marx, III
Ford Motor Company

Blaise Newman
J. Walter Thompson

Dave Tarrant
ASG

Mike Smith
Motor City Exhibition,
Detroit Historical Museum

John Sonego
Detroit Historical
Society

Oscar Marx and Bill Chapin were selected to serve as co-chairmen of this committee, which was charged with planning a permanent $2 million interactive exhibit that would dramatize the immense contributions of the automotive industry to Detroit, as well as with examining the nature of the industry, the people who built the cars and the future of the industry. The exhibit would occupy 8,000-square-feet of space on two levels in the Museum's Dodge Hall and was scheduled to open in December 1995. It was necessary to meet regularly to check progress in order to meet the deadline for completion.

I soon learned that BBDO had handled the advertising of more car accounts than any other advertising agency and that we had a great amount of reference material in our library. Thus, I was able to provide old advertisements for a number of automotive accounts, many of which ended up in the exhibit.

The automotive accounts that BBDO has served since 1903, showing that BBDO has had ties to the auto industry since shortly after 1896, are listed on the following page.

Lots of Good News About the Agency

BBDO Detroit won many awards for the advertising it created in 1993 at the various award shows held early in 1994, including two Gold Effies for the Dodge division. Both *Advertising Age* and *Ad Week* magazines selected BBDO as the "Agency of the Year" and the American Marketing Association named the agency "New Products Agency of the Year."

On St. Patrick's Day, Kit King and I attended the special service held annually at Holy Trinity Church in Detroit's Corktown. Ursula Crenshaw, vice president of Standard Federal Bank, was involved in the service and arranged for us to be seated near the front of the church, which was packed with parishioners, dignitaries and politicians, including Michigan Governor John Engler and Detroit Mayor Dennis Archer. Following the service, we enjoyed a corned beef and cabbage luncheon at the Porter Street Station restaurant with Ursula and a large group of her friends.

A few days later, I participated again in the annual Golden Mile Walk, the benefit for the March of Dimes.

BBDO Automotive Accounts

Account	Years Handled	Client Location
Cadillac Automobile Co.	1903-1907	Detroit, Michigan
Peerless Motor Car Co.	1905-1911	Cleveland, Ohio
Dragon Automobile Co.	1907	Philadelphia, Pennsylvania
A.L. Kull Automobile Co.	1908	New York, New York
Oldsmobile	1908-1911	Lansing, Michigan
Stevens-Duryea	1910-1912	Chicopee Falls, Massachussetts
Baker Electric	1912-1916	Cleveland, Ohio
Standard Steel Co.		
Standard Eight Automobile	1914-1921	Pittsburgh, Pennsylvania
Mercer Motors Co.		
Mercer Automobiles	1922-1923	Trenton, New Jersey
General Motors Corp.		
GMAC Auto Purchasing/Financing	1928-1933	New York, New York
Oldsmobile	1933-1934	Lansing, Michigan
GM Institutional Advertising	1923-1938	New York, New York
Pierce Arrow Car Co.		
Cars and Trucks	1933-1935	Buffalo, New York
Chrysler Corp.		
DeSoto Division	1944-1960	Detroit, Michigan
Plymouth Valiant Division	1959-1960	Detroit, Michigan
Dodge Division	1960-1979	Detroit, Michigan
Dodge Division	1982*-Present	Detroit, Michigan
Dodge Automobiles		
Dodge California Marketing		
Dodge Dealer Advertising/Factory Co-op Across U.S.		
Dodge Northeast Marketing		
Dodge Truck and Car		
Dodge Neon		
Dodge Intrepid		
Dodge Stratus		
Dodge Viper		
Dodge Avenger		
Dodge Caravan		
Dodge Ram Pickup		
Dodge Dakota		
Dodge Ram Vans and Wagons		

*When Lee Iaccoca became head of Chrysler in 1979, he fired all Chrysler agencies and consolidated the entire advertising account with Kenyon & Eckhardt (now Bozell). In 1982, BBDO was re-appointed as Dodge Division's advertising agency.

Advertisements created by BBDO Detroit for Dodge Intrepid and Dodge Neon appear on the following pages.

WHAT'S AUTOMOBILE MAGAZINE'S OPINION OF THE DODGE NEON ?

HIGH.

Dodge would like to thank *Automobile Magazine* for giving the roomy, zoomy Neon Sport Coupe a 1995 All-Star award. Apparently, what with the multi-valve DOHC engine, the 4-wheel independent performance suspension and such, they had as much fun testing it as we had building it. We promise to put the award in a place of honor. Right next to Neon Sedan's *Automobile Magazine* 1994 "Automobile of the Year" and European magazine *Motor* "World Car" awards.

NEON SEDAN & COUPE

THE NEW DODGE
1-800-4-A-DODGE

I Lose My Mother

My brother Joe called on March 28 to tell me that our mother had suffered a massive heart attack. We had planned to go to California the next week for our family vacation at Laguna Beach, but Mary Lou and I left the very next morning instead, and the rest of the family followed on the weekend. We were able to spend Tuesday evening with Mom at Saddleback Hospital and most of the next six days. She seemed to rally to the point that we were hopeful she would be able to leave the hospital. That was not to be. Early on Tuesday morning, April 5, she passed away. Fortunately, I was able to spend the week with her before she died and her grandchildren also got to spend some time with her as well.

Her funeral service was held on April 9 in Sedalia, Missouri, where she was laid to rest in Crown Hill Cemetery next to dad and a son, Billy.

When my mother was a senior in high school, she was driving the family car when it turned over on a sharp curve. There were three other young people in the car with her and, while no one was killed, they were all severely injured. As a result of that accident, my mother vowed that she would never drive a car again, and she didn't! She managed to go the rest of her life without ever driving an automobile. The curve where that accident occurred is less than 500 yards from where she is buried.

An Interesting Trip To the East Coast

After being back in the office for just 2-1/2 weeks, Mary Lou and I left for the east coast on April 29. First stop was the Russian Monastery and Religious Center at Jordanville, New York. This is where Mary Lou's husband is buried. We attended the Russian Orthodox Easter services while we were there, which were truly impressive. Our next destination was Annapolis, where we stayed at the Kent Motor Inn just off the Atlantic

Ocean shore on Kent Island. This inn was opened in 1820 and is a delightful place to stay. While we were in Annapolis, we had lunch at the Middleton Tavern, built in 1740, and enjoyed its famous crab soup. We then traveled on to Washington D.C. In the six days we stayed there, we were able to visit Arlington Cemetery, the Lincoln Memorial, the Vietnam Memorial, the Nurses Memorial and the Washington Monument. We also toured the Smithsonian Museum, the National Gallery of Art, the Museum of Natural History, the Arts and Industries Museum, the Holocaust Museum, the Freer Gallery and the Hirsh Museum, the Air and Space Museum, and the National Postal Museum. We walked our tails off! Michigan Congressman Joe Knollenberg met with us in his office and arranged a personal tour of the White House, conducted by a secret service agent. Following that tour, we had lunch in the Senate dining room. Of course we had Michigan navy bean soup – which, by law, must be served every day in the Senate dining room – one of our better laws because I love navy bean soup. On our way out of Washington D.C., we visited the National Cathedral.

On To Gettysburg

Arriving in Gettysburg late in the day on May 5, our first priority was to find a place to stay. We were lucky that a bed and breakfast, "The Tannery," had a vacancy. That evening, we skipped dinner and enjoyed sitting on the inn's big front porch while sipping complimentary wine and eating cheese and crackers along with several other guests.

The next morning, we had a relaxing breakfast in The Tannery's dining room. It was a comfortable and appropriate place to stay in Gettysburg, as this bed and breakfast started as a tannery in 1868. After breakfast we went to the Gettysburg visitor center, where we saw a reenactment of the Battle of Gettysburg on a large topographical map, with various colored lights representing the military units. A narrator described the three days of carnage in which more than 50,000 men died – the worst battle ever fought in the United States.

When you tour the battle grounds, you can either go on a bus with a narration describing what you are seeing presented by either the bus driver or a guide, or you can purchase an audio cassette to play in your car and do-it-yourself – or you can also hire a guide to drive your car and describe what happened in each area of the battlefield. We opted for the latter and our expert guide, Russ Cunningham, was our source of information for the three hours that it took to cover the large area where the battle took place, including Roundtop, Little Roundtop, Cemetery Hill and Seminary Ridge, as well as many sites in between. More than 1,300 monuments, some very elaborate, are sprinkled all over the Gettysburg battlefield. I found it very impressive. We also visited the Eisenhower farm on the outskirts of Gettysburg, after which we headed for home in Michigan.

The Kmart Account

When I returned to the office on May 9, I learned that Tom Clark had scheduled a meeting the next morning to consider the Kmart account. There were indications that they were going to hold an advertising agency review. Bill Oswald, Tom Neman and I met with Tom to discuss the account and whether or not BBDO should prepare to get into the hunt. The Kmart Corporation was a large advertiser but was in trouble financially. Its stock had dropped significantly in value. Its reputation for service and the availability of merchandise in its stores was not good. A major turnaround was absolutely needed to restore Kmart to a healthy financial condition and the status it once enjoyed as a leading retailer.

It was decided that we would watch what developed. In the meantime, Tom Neman, senior vice president and research director, would gather information about this prospect, while I would assemble copies of Kmart's advertising in all media for reference.

The Nightingale Awards

In 1985, when Bob Hutton was the chairman of Standard Federal Bank, he suggested that I join him as a member of the Board of Visitors of the Oakland University School of Nursing and, following that, I was appointed to the board by Sandra Packard, then the president of Oakland University. In 1988, I served as the chairperson of the Board of Visitors and, in 1989, helped to initiate the Nightingale Awards. These awards are sponsored by the Board of Visitors to recognize professional nurses throughout the state of Michigan for excellence in nursing practice, administration, research, education, long-term care and home care. The winner in each category receives a bronze statuette of Florence Nightingale and $1,000.

In 1994, I was the chairman of the committee to plan the annual Nightingale Awards dinner, which was held on May 11, the start of National Nurses Week. I had written M. Joycelyn Elders, M.D., Surgeon General of the United States, inviting her to be the keynote speaker at the dinner, and she accepted. Although she later became quite controversial, she gave a non-controversial talk at the Nightingale Awards dinner, that was well received. Her appearance generated a lot of interest in our annual awards dinner and there were more than 740 people in attendance. It also resulted in extensive press coverage in both the print and the electronic media. Best of all, the dinner made a profit of more than $40,000. These funds enabled the School of Nursing to purchase equipment and materials that otherwise would not have been available.

Beautiful Spring Weather

Spring came early, and we had a number of warm, pleasant days early in May. I was

A reception and dinner followed the marriage of Cindy O'Linger to Robert Ricketts at the impressive Hotel St. Germain in Dallas. Couples attending from Detroit included, from left to right: Joe and Cheryl Krul, Garry and Nancy Carley, Carol and Ron Palmer, Mary Lou and me. In 1994, Joe Krul was senior vice president and chief financial officer of Standard Federal Bank; Garry Carley was executive vice president and a director; and Ron Palmer was senior vice president and general counsel. Hotel St. Germain is rated as one of America's top hotels and its elegant grand dining room overlooks an ivy-covered New Orleans-style garden courtyard.

busy with a variety of things, including preparing proposals to submit to various Michigan foundations to solicit funds for Orion Oaks Parks. This 927-acre undeveloped park, which is part of the Oakland County Parks system, had not been developed because voters of Oakland County turned down a special millage proposal. A number of volunteers had emerged – led by Margie Pollick of the Telephone Pioneers of America – who were willing to donate their time and energy to develop the park. Funds were needed for materials to build bridges across wetlands in order to extend the trail systems, as well as for a wheelchair-accessible fishing pier at a large lake inside Orion Oaks Park.

The agency also received a questionnaire from the La-Z-Boy Chair Company in Monroe, Michigan, requesting information. It was holding an agency review. The information was provided, but it was BBDO's Chicago office that was invited to make a presentation to solicit the business, as Steve LaGattuta, president of BBDO's Chicago office, had worked on the account when he was with the W. B. Doner agency in Detroit. Doner handled the advertising for the La-Z-Boy Furniture Galleries account but, in the review, Doner won the entire account, including the national brand advertising.

At the end of May, I was off to northern Michigan for a few days at Boyne Mountain and then on to Mackinac Island to attend the Greater Detroit Chamber of Commerce meeting at the Grand Hotel. This meeting features outstanding speakers and an interesting, challenging program which results in a capacity crowd. I chaired the chamber's communications advisory committee and most of the members of this committee were in attendance at this conference.

During June, we had some of the hottest days on record in southeast Michigan, as the temperature hit 99 degrees on June 18 and 100 degrees the next day. My brother Joe and his wife Sue arrived on June 30. We then went to northern Michigan for several days where it was much cooler. Then we went to Toronto for a week to see shows and to visit the Royal Ontario Museum and the Bata Shoe Museum.

During July and August, I was invited to play in several golf outings and attended a dinner at the Grosse Pointe Yacht Club to celebrate the 50th wedding anniversary of dear friends Beth and Bob Hutton. We also made several new business presentations – including one to Detroit Edison – but we were not the winning agency.

In late August and early September, Mary Lou and I had dinner with Priscilla and Tom Ricketts several times, and we went to various concerts. On September 10, we flew to Dallas to attend the marriage of Priscilla and Tom's son Robert to Cindy O'Linger, returning home the next day.

The Lewis E. Wint Memorial Golf Outing

On September 19, the first annual Lewis E. Wint Golf Outing was held at Springfield Oaks Golf Club, one of the Oakland County Parks golf courses. I was on the planning committee. Lewis E. Wint, who passed away in 1992, was a founding member and trustee of the Oakland Parks Foundation, and chairman of the Oakland County Parks and Recreation Commission for 15 years. Under his leadership, the parks system grew and expanded, serving more than 1.5 million visitors every year. I first came to know Lew when I was a member of the Clarkston Rotary Club. The goal of the foundation was to raise $50,000 for the expansion of a nature center. This was accomplished in three years, using golf outings as fundraisers.

"Make A Difference Day"

October 22 was national "Make A Difference Day," so a volunteer work-day was scheduled for Orion Oaks County Park. The solicitation letters and proposals that I had put together the past spring resulted in more than $5,000 in contributions. These funds were used to purchase the lumber necessary to construct a six-foot-wide by 120-foot-long bridge across a wetlands area to link the park's east side with its west side trail system. The bridge took $2,500 worth of lumber and the balance was used to buy seedlings and saplings and other materials to help develop the park.

BBDO Detroit Invited To Solicit the Yellow Pages Publishers Association Account

In addition to BBDO Detroit, agencies in Boston, Cleveland, Chicago, Minneapolis and Detroit were invited to solicit the advertising of the Yellow Pages Publishers Association for its "Marketing the Medium" effort, which had a ten million dollar budget. We were one of three finalists out of eight contenders, but an agency in Chicago won the account.

Early in November the Kmart account went into review and the invitation to pursue the business went to BBDO's New York office. The woes of Kmart were getting lots of attention in the press, as institutional shareholders were demanding that this giant retailer spin off its specialty stores, restructure its operation, and close all poorly performing stores. In response to the pressure, Kmart announced it would close 110 stores in 1995, fire 6,000 employees and 2,300 managers, and cut millions in operating costs. Just before Christmas, it laid off 900 employees at the Troy headquarters, which is located on Big Beaver Road just one block east of Standard Federal Bank's headquarters. It was not a pretty picture and any downturn in the economy would have been devastating for Kmart.

1994 Winds Down

On November 12, Priscilla and Tom Ricketts and Mary Lou and I were guests of Karen and Tom Clark at a fundraiser for the Detroit Institute of Arts that was held there. The DCT Companies assigned a corporate design program to us, and Bill Sidenstecker, one of our art directors, handled this project. The Dearborn Hyatt Regency also gave us several assignments. The annual Thanksgiving Day parade downtown was well-attended by a crowd estimated at over 1,400,000 and I participated again as a clown. The Mike Baker family joined me for breakfast and to watch the parade. The weather was ideal.

The annual BBDO/PentaCom Christmas breakfast was held on December 9 at Forest Lake Country Club. Bill Oswald, Dick Johnson, Dave Martin and Tom Clark each addressed the staff and shared a lot of information with us.

In the United States, the advertising industry had improved growth in 1994, and BBDO benefited with record gains in revenues and net income. Shareholders of Omnicom, of which BBDO is a part, enjoyed increased earnings per share and the outlook for 1995 was very good. In terms of new business, BBDO Worldwide added Russell Athletic, Sterling Health, Campbell's Condensed Soups, three major brands from Best Foods, and Ortho in the United States, as well as all media responsibilities for General Electric.

During December, I attended several meetings of the committee planning the 100th anniversary of the car business exhibit at the Detroit Historical Museum. There were now just twelve months left before it was scheduled to open. There was lots of work to handle for our clients but, in spite of all the activity, Christmas was full of joy with the exchange of gifts and good things to eat. There was so much for which to be thankful! The family gathered at Boyne Mountain, where we enjoyed being together sharing the fun of outdoor activities and eating hearty meals. After dark on New Year's eve, we watched about 50 skiers with torches slowly ski down the mountain, criss-crossing back and forth like two long snakes sliding down the mountain. This was followed by a big fireworks display. Then we returned to the condo, where we enjoyed the hilarious movie, "The Blues Brothers." A happy, fun way to end the year.

Major Things That Happened In 1994

"The Lion King" became Disney's most successful film, while "Beauty and the Beast," Disney's first stage musical, opened on Broadway, The Winter Olympics set ratings records, with 83% of the country watching at least some of CBS' coverage. A Major League Baseball strike derailed the Baseball Network, a joint venture between NBC, ABC and the league. The venture lost $95 million in advertising and $500 million in national and local spending. The world TV premiere of "Gettysburg" on TNT attracted the largest viewership ever for a movie on basic cable, as 23 million people watched all or portions of this outstanding two-part special. O.J. Simpson was arrested as the primary suspect in the brutal murders of his former wife, Nicole Brown Simpson, and her friend, Ronald Goldman. Former President Nixon and Jacqueline Kennedy Onassis died during the year.

Chapter 10

Heading Towards The Millennium – 1995 Through 1999

Sometimes work is more fun than fun!
– Noel Coward

In anticipation of the turn of the millennium on January 1, 2001, articles on the subject began appearing during 1995 in newspapers and magazines. There were also special reports on radio and television concerning a big computer problem and how it would affect mankind, entering in the year 2000. This concern received more and more attention and press coverage with each passing year, as we moved closer to this important milestone. Computer programmers had decided at a 1960s programming convention, to save a few bytes of precious space by specifying years as two digits instead of four – "98" rather than "1998," for example. The programmers believed that this software would be replaced long before the year 2000 – but they were wrong. Some of the forecasts for the economy, the airlines and the government were horrific, but we can only wait and see, hoping that the computer glitches will not be as bad as forecasted by the press during the years leading up to the critical date of January 1, 2000.

More New Business Opportunities Come Our Way

In the first quarter of 1995, a number of new business opportunities "popped up," which required considerable time and attention. Three companies that invited us to make presentations to solicit their accounts were politely thanked for considering BBDO Detroit but, for various reasons, were not pursued.

While we did not win the Yellow Pages Publishers account, Harvey Winn, director of communications for the Association, offered us a major project involving the publishing of its monthly magazine. Again, after careful review and consideration, we decided not to tackle it. The Kmart saga was ongoing and I participated in meetings held to review the progress of the upcoming presentation that would be made to Kmart, by BBDO New York. In the meantime, Kmart was "biting the bullet" and restructuring, disposing of many non-core assets. It sold its investments in the Borders Group, Office Max, The Sports Authority and Coles Meyer and also closed 214 under-performing stores.

At BBDO New York, though, a number of new business opportunities came their way. In the first quarter of 1995, the agency won the biggest account in its history – billing approximately $250 million annually – when it became one of Mars, Incorporated's three core international agencies. But this record-breaking victory was exceeded later in the year, when Bayer A.G. consolidated its $275 million global consumer care account at BBDO. Other important new business wins in 1995 included an AT&T Olympics assignment, an agency of record designation from LensCrafters and getting advertising responsibility for the U.S. Department of Housing and Urban Development account.

The SPRING Newspaper Network Becomes a Client

Late in January, the SPRING Newspaper Network invited BBDO Detroit to solicit its advertising account. SPRING (Detroit Suburban Press Ring) consisted of a network of 50 Detroit suburban newspapers published by the Adams, Associated, Heritage, HomeTown and Observer & Eccentric publishing groups. SPRING was founded as a pre-print vehicle and then broadened to include ROP ("run of press") advertising, delivering advertisers 50 suburban newspapers with one set of materials and one invoice – a big convenience for advertisers. We put our presentation together during February and early March and made our "pitch" on March 31 to a large committee comprised of representatives of all the publishers.

Kit King, Matt Duff, John Brogan, Diane Schroeder, Pat Pearson and I participated, using a PowerPoint presentation projected on a large screen.

Our second presentation to the SPRING Newspaper Network occurred on April 3. This one was made to top management and the publishers. Late in the day, we were notified that BBDO Detroit had won the account. The objective of the advertising and promotion for this account was to significantly increase awareness about the SPRING network and its primary benefits among a target audience representing a vast potential for increased revenue. Our strategy for achieving this objective consisted of positioning SPRING as a network that delivers more prime prospects to advertisers than other advertising vehicles, at a lower cost. This strategy was supported by facts, which made this position believable. We immediately created advertising materials for SPRING with the new umbrella theme, "Reach People Where They Live."

The Detroit News and *Detroit Free Press* unions struck on July 13 and our new client SPRING reaped big benefits from this strike, which was to last for several years. The strike drastically changed the media market in Detroit.

Taking a Break From Winter

I also managed to squeeze in a short vacation to California in late February and early March. Sue, Joe Baker and I drove from their home in Laguna Niguel, up the coast to Carmel, with stops along the way. On February 25, we toured the Hearst Castle at San Simeon – this day marked three years since Joan's passing. Joan and I had really enjoyed our visits to Hearst Castle and a lot of memories came flooding back. Sue, Joe and I spent three days in Carmel, visiting galleries and various attractions such as the aquarium in Monterey and just wandering around the area. Sue is a big fan of Doris Day and we were hoping that we would run into her in Carmel, as that is where she lives – no such luck! Sue has met her a number of times, however, and has a large collection of Doris Day memorabilia – movies, records, posters, photographs, coloring books and other items.

It's a Cold But Interesting Spring

April Fools Day – Saturday, April 1 – turned out to be a day full of fun, as Mary Lou and I attended a "Bop Till You Drop" party at Bloomfield Hills Country Club as guests of Karen and Tom Clark. Mary Lou wore a poodle skirt – popular in the 1950s – and I dressed as a Blues Brother in a black suit, fedora and dark glasses. We were among the last to leave the party – we bopped all night but didn't drop. The weather in early April was unusually chilly and a 100-year-old record was broken on April 5. I had put my winter coat away but I got it out again, as we had snow and sleet all the next week, unbelievable for early April.

Walking With Dr. Jonas Salk

On April 12, it was a clear but very crisp day when my secretary, Linette Neumeyer and I went to Ann Arbor to participate in the annual March of Dimes Golden Mile Walk. This year, Dr. Jonas Salk led the walk around the University of Michigan campus and along the way, he pointed out the building where he and Dr. Thomas Francis, Jr., a former professor, developed commercial vaccines against influenza, which were used by American troops during World War II. After the war, Salk headed the viral research program at the University of Pittsburgh, where he eventually devoted his studies to the eradication of polio.

The year 1952 was one of the worst years of the polio epidemic – nearly 58,000 cases were reported in the U.S. and more than 3,000 people died. On April 12, 1955, a Salk colleague announced that a vaccine, developed by Salk, had been tested on more than one million schoolchildren and had proven to be "safe, effective and potent." A nationwide mass inoculation followed and by 1962, new cases of polio in the U.S. dropped to fewer than 1,000. Dr. Jonas Salk became one of the most celebrated men of the 1950s, ranking in opinion polls with Gandhi and Churchill as heroes.

One of my uncles, James Staples, contracted polio when he was a young boy in the 1930s and it severely impaired one of his legs. Parents were especially fearful of this horrid disease and my mother and father were no exception – especially since it had affected someone in our family. To this day, I avoid using handrails or other things commonly touched in public buildings, as I can still hear my mother's cautious words – "Don't touch – you'll pick up germs." We also washed our hands before every meal, all of which probably is the reason I've had so few colds in my life.

Following our walk around the University of Michigan campus, Dr. Salk gave a brief talk. He reminisced about the years spent in Ann Arbor in the 1930s and then described the AIDS research that was being done at the Salk Institute for Biological Studies in La Jolla, California. I was particularly glad that I took the time to drive to Ann Arbor to participate in the Golden Mile Walk again, because it

provided the opportunity to meet Dr. Jonas Salk and to hear him speak. He passed away on June 23, 1995 – just 72 days after the Walk – when he failed to recover from heart surgery. He was 80 years old and truly a hero of modern history, but most of us have already forgotten how much we owe this man.

Something New and Different Every Day During the Months of April and May

Our first monthly meeting with the full marketing committee of our new SPRING account occurred on April 13. It took the better part of the day and was held at the Heritage Newspapers headquarters in the downriver Detroit area. The next day – Good Friday – I was off to the Boyne Condo for the Easter weekend. Mary Lou joined me and we played golf three days at three different courses. Weather was ideal, making it a delightful long weekend in Northern Michigan. Back in the office on Tuesday, we learned that Kmart had appointed Campbell-Mithun-Esty, headquartered in Minneapolis, as its new advertising agency.

There was horrible news on April 19, when it was reported that a terrorist car bomb had exploded at 8:05 a.m. outside the Alfred P. Murrah Federal Building in Oklahoma City – in the heartland of America. Rescue workers eventually recovered the bodies of 168 people, including 19 children, from the ruins, while hundreds more were injured by the blast.

It was a much happier time the next evening, though, when I attended a surprise 70th birthday party for Chuck Clark, a friend of many years. Chuck started a printing company in 1966 – Clark Graphics – which over the years grew to be one of the largest printing businesses in the midwest. I was his first customer. At the party, I presented him with a large framed mural consisting of a montage of a variety of pieces Chuck's company had printed for our clients, along with personal messages from many of the people at BBDO who worked with and knew Chuck. I tried to express to Chuck how much the efforts he had made on behalf of our clients were appreciated, because over the years he had "saved our butts" many times by delivering jobs with virtually impossible deadlines. He was a great friend to have!

For a little diversion, we went on a weekend bus tour, leaving early Saturday morning, April 22. First stop was in Toledo for breakfast. We then went to Dayton to visit the Air Force Museum. We ended up in Cincinnati, where we toured the Meier's Wine Cellars late in the day. Mary Lou, Barbara Watts, and her dad Ed Bauman, and I signed up for this get-away weekend. On Saturday evening, we went to a dinner theater, where we saw an excellent performance of "Gypsy," and then stayed overnight at a Country Inn. Following breakfast at this inn on Sunday morning, we reboarded the bus and went to a huge flea market. This was followed by lunch aboard the "Star of Cincinnati" and a cruise on the Ohio River. We arrived back home late in the evening after enjoying a most unusual weekend, vowing to do things like this more often.

Tuesday morning, April 25, I went to a breakfast meeting at ITT headquarters in Rochester Hills to participate in a fundraiser to benefit the Clinton Valley branch of the Boy Scouts of America. That same day, I attended Standard Federal Bank's annual stockholders meeting at the headquarters facility. In early May, my father-in-law, Ed Bauman, and I went on another get-away weekend, this time to Holland, Michigan for the tulip festival. We left on Thursday morning, May 11, and stayed at the Rosemont Bed and Breakfast Inn on Lake Michigan. For the next two days we explored the area, enjoying the spectacle of huge fields of vivid, blooming tulips, watching wooden shoes being made at Veldheers Tulip Farms and having some wonderful meals. On May 22, I played in a golf scramble benefit at Wabeek Country Club for the Oakland County Secret Witness program. Luckily, I won a clock radio.

Back To Boyne For the Memorial Day Weekend Then On To Mackinac Island

Mary Lou joined me for the Memorial Day weekend and we left on Saturday, May 27 for five days of golf at Boyne Mountain and to search for morels. Hunting for these "wild things" is like being in an Easter egg hunt when you're six-years-old. Thousands of people flock to the northern Michigan woods every spring to go mushroom hunting and I wouldn't miss it. We enjoyed the morels we found for breakfast in our scrambled eggs. On June 1, we moved on to Mackinac Island to attend the Greater Detroit Chamber of Commerce Conference. We joined Priscilla and Tom Ricketts for dinner that evening and heard a speech by Jack Kemp. Other speakers at the meeting included Malcom S. Forbes, Jr., Governor John Engler and Hillary Clinton.

Starting Monday, June 5, there were meetings every day with clients, organizations in which I was involved, and with several new business prospects. Diversey Corporation and Kelly Services were both having an advertising agency review. We met with both of them in response to their request for information about BBDO Detroit. The Diversey opportunity fizzled out and Kelly Services assigned its account to a Cleveland advertising agency.

There were several nice events that I enjoyed in June. I went to the Grand Prix race on Belle Isle as a guest of Crain Communications. I played golf at the TPC in Dearborn as a guest of the Wall Street Journal and my golf partner was Jim Berline. Jim has his own advertising agency, The Berline Group, and some years earlier, had served as general manager of BBDO Detroit.

So much happened in the first six months of 1995 that the time simply flew by! BBDO was named "Agency of the Year" by both *Adweek* and *Advertising Age*, and "New Products Agency of the Year" by the <u>American Marketing Association</u> for the second year in a row. The agency also won the most television

In 1995, some of the members of BBDO's Detroit management group included: Bill Oswald (seated behind desk), president and CEO; Bill Hackett (far right), executive vice president and director of strategic planning. Other members are (left to right): Dave Harrelson, executive vice president and director of operations; John Hammond, executive vice president and senior management representative; Ernie Baker, executive vice president; and Pete Swiecicki, executive vice president and chief financial officer. Cocoa, the office mascot, is sitting at far left.

Lions at the Cannes Film Festival, so BBDO received a lot of attention in the trade press.

The Second Half of '95

In early July, I met with Dwight Cunningham, editor of *The Detroiter* magazine, to discuss an article about BBDO's 93-year history handling advertising for various automobile manufacturers. I had met Dwight at the Greater Detroit Chamber of Commerce meeting on Mackinac Island in early June and had suggested the possibility of his magazine doing this feature story. The story appeared in the December 1995 issue. In addition to the

cover, the feature covered 11 pages and there were eight pages of congratulatory tie-in advertisements. It resulted in a very special issue and a great promotion for BBDO. For the Chamber, it was the biggest single issue it had ever published and it won several awards – "a win-win" situation.

A BBDO Management Training Seminar In Toronto

I was off for Toronto on July 9, to attend a management training meeting held at the Royal York Hotel. Meetings began promptly at 8:30 a.m. and ended at 6:30 p.m. and we had homework assignments every evening. Bruce Liebowitz and Nancy Weeks from the BBDO New York office conducted the sessions, assisted by Paul Burke, a consultant from Boston. The meetings lasted five full days, ending late Friday afternoon. For completing the session, we celebrated with beer and champagne and a big dinner at the Asia restaurant.

Lots of Fun In the Good Old Summertime

During July, August and September I participated in a number of golf outings sponsored either by a publisher or to benefit some charity. BBDO Detroit is generous in supporting a number of worthwhile causes and I was fortunate to be invited to participate in several outings, representing the agency. The agency hosted a cruise on Lake St. Clair for the marketing department of Standard Federal Bank on August 20. It was a perfect summer day and, after a pleasant four hour cruise, everyone enjoyed dinner at Rachel's restaurant in St. Clair, Michigan.

Off For Boston and a Drive Up the Maine Coastline

Both Mary Lou and I wanted to visit Boston and then drive up the coast to Bar Harbor, Maine. We made our plans to do so and left August 30 for what turned out to be a great vacation. By noon we had already checked into our hotel in downtown Boston. We then immediately took a Grey Line Tour of the city. I find that this not only helps you to learn a lot about the city but that it also helps orient you to the area. During the five days we spent in Boston we enjoyed lunch or dinner at several well known restaurants that had been recommended to us. Carol and Paul Burke joined us one evening for dinner at the Legal Seafood restaurant and later we took a harbor

cruise. Paul was the consultant from Boston that helped conduct the management meeting I attended in Toronto in early July.

A most enjoyable afternoon was spent with my old friend Steve Cosmopolous at the Hill, Holliday, Connors, and Cosmopulous advertising agency in the Prudential building. Steve introduced us to a Greek restaurant, Omonia, where the food and service were truly outstanding.

Steve Cosmopulous and Ernie Baker

While in Boston, we managed to do just about everything tourists are expected to do, but it required a lot of walking. We hiked a good portion of the Freedom Trail, starting at Boston Commons, with stops along the way to see the State House, old burial grounds, Park Street church, Faneuil Hall and other historic sites. We visited the "Cheers" bar on Boston Hill, saw the Kennedy Museum and took the subway to Cambridge, where we walked around the campuses of Harvard and Radcliffe. I made a special pilgrimage to the Omni Parker House hotel where Parker House rolls originated, as my mother and her mother were both especially proud of the Parker House rolls they made.

On Sunday, September 3, we attended the 11 a.m. service at Old North Church and following the service, joined the congregation in the courtyard for lemonade and cookies. We then walked to Paul Revere's home nearby and stopped for lunch at an Italian restaurant, which had a very attractive display of food in the front window. It turned out to be a good choice. In mid-afternoon, we left Boston, driving around Cape Ann through Essex, Ipswich, Rowley and Newburyport. We stayed overnight at a bed and breakfast in Portsmouth, New Hampshire. The Abercrombe and Fitch restaurant in Portsmouth was recommended to us for dinner and we were not disappointed. The next day we went exploring, visiting antique shops and having lunch in Kennebunkport. We then drove to Freeport to shop at L.L. Bean. We then went on to Brunswick and to Bath, where we stayed overnight at Sebasco Estates. In 1967, I had attended a National Advertising Agency Network annual meeting at this resort. We took the time to visit the Marine Museum in Bath – a very worthwhile institution to see. By late afternoon we arrived at Boothbay Harbor and found a place to stay right on the wharf. We discovered a restaurant that served two large lobsters, fresh from the bay, for just $13.95 – delicious! We then drove up the coast to Camden, where we were held up because the movie "Thinner" was being shot there. The entire downtown area, including the highway through town, was involved in the movie. We joined the crowd watching the movie being produced. We decided to stay overnight in Camden at the High Tide Inn and found another excellent restaurant, Chez Michel, where we had dinner.

Following a breakfast of hot popovers the next morning at the High Tide Inn, we decided to end our trip up the Maine coast and return to Boothbay Harbor for several days to go whale watching and to spend more time in that beautiful area. We took two whale watching trips without success, but the view of the coastline from the ocean was really impressive.

On Friday afternoon, we headed back to Boston, stopping in Brunswick at the Stowe House – which I had first visited in 1959 when

I spent several days at the Warren Paper Company plant in Sebasco, Maine learning about paper production. We arrived at Boston's Logan airport at noon on Saturday, turned in our rented car, and flew back to Detroit with a lot of good memories and a determination to do this all over again sometime in the future.

The Beta Reunion In Columbia, Missouri

After two busy weeks in the office, we went to Columbia, Missouri on September 20, to participate in the 125th anniversary celebration of the Zeta Phi Chapter of Beta Theta Pi at the University of Missouri. We arrived in Columbia on Thursday afternoon and stayed with Mary Lou's niece and nephew, Kathy and Jerry Ogelsby. Jerry manages the Sam's store in Columbia. On Friday Jack Bloess, Floyd Eberhard, Floyd's son Mark, and I teamed up as a foursome to play in the Beta scramble to benefit the scholarship fund. On Saturday night, at the reunion dinner, I had an opportunity to meet with good friends from my college days – Joe Hurley, Ray O'Brien, Jack VanDyne, Ben and Viga Hall, John Huston, Max Simpson and Ben Morris, among others, most of whom I hadn't seen since I graduated in 1948. My brother Joe and his wife Sue came from California for the reunion and we were able to spend time together as well.

A Number of Special Activities

The Nightingale dinner, sponsored by the Oakland University School of Nursing, took place on September 20, coinciding with the 20th anniversary of the School of Nursing. On Saturday, September 30, "Make a Difference Day," I joined more than 200 other volunteers helping to build trails in Orion Oaks Park – which borders our subdivision. The first – and so far the only – reunion ever held for former staffers of the Zimmer, Keller & Calvert advertising agency took place Saturday,

October 21 at the Main Event restaurant in the Pontiac Silverdome.

On November 13, Mary Lou and I attended a formal dinner in the ballroom of the Westin Hotel. The dinner was sponsored by B'nai B'rith International and honored Tom Ricketts of Standard Federal Bank with the Great American Traditions Award – in recognition of his many accomplishments and service to the community. Marvin Hamlish provided the entertainment and it was truly an impressive evening.

On Thanksgiving, I attended the traditional early morning breakfast at Cobo Hall in downtown Detroit and participated again as a Distinguished Clown in America's Thanksgiving Day Parade.

Selling Condos In Chicago

On November 30, Frank Henderson and Tom Clark introduced Kit and me to Bart Berman, who was the head of The Barton Group. His company was involved in the building of many commercial enterprises and he wanted to hire BBDO Detroit particularly to help promote his property, The ParkShore Condominiums, which were located in downtown Chicago. The twenty-four floor building housed one, two and three bedroom condos, ranging in price from $139,500 to $270,000. Amenities included a gourmet grocery, a health club, underground parking, a rooftop pool, and tennis courts – PLUS a spectacular view of Chicago's lakefront. He appointed BBDO Detroit to help sell these condo units with newspaper and radio advertising and, like all entrepreneurs, he expected immediate gratification in terms of results! We advertised every weekend and sales were tracked on a weekly basis, so our feet were held to the fire every Monday morning. Our client also expected to be able to summon us to Chicago at a moment's notice to fix whatever he believed to be broken that particular week. The project eventually did sell out and we got out of the real estate fast lane for more conventional business – never to forget, however,

our time spent with a dynamic, demanding "man on the move." Our friend Bart Berman was definitely all that and more. It was a good learning experience about a very volatile category of business and, fortunately, we all parted as friends in the end.

A Really Hectic December As the Year Winds Down

Meetings during the day and receptions or parties nearly every evening filled the first three weeks of December. For example, on December 3 we met all afternoon at BBDO's Southfield office with our new client, Bart Berman, to discuss and plan the advertising and promotion for his Chicago Condo project.

In the evening, a press preview was held at the Detroit Historical Museum to announce the opening of the exhibit commemorating the 100th anniversary of the car business in Detroit. It opened with great fanfare and proved to be a very popular exhibit.

Painted billboard designed by BBDO Detroit for the Motor City Exhibition at Detroit Historical Museum.

The Adcraft Club of Detroit celebrated its 90th anniversary with a luncheon in the ballroom of the Westin Hotel, in Detroit's Renaissance Center, and more than 1,000 members attended. That evening, I went to a client's Christmas party and, the next morning, BBDO Detroit held its annual Christmas breakfast for the

While most people seek the key to happiness, ParkShore residents find it right at their door.

Meet Ray. Besides making sure that you have a cab waiting any time of the day or night, and offering you a helping hand after a successful shopping trip, Ray prides himself on knowing who you are...by name. At The ParkShore, happiness is often defined by attention to details.

All the comforts at home.

Once you have experienced the many comforts and amenities of The ParkShore, you may never want to leave. And you won't have to, thanks to our fully equipped health club, rooftop pool, tennis court, party room, gourmet market and on-site dry cleaner. Sometimes happiness is defined by convenience.

Your choice of options right outside your door.

Located at the foot of Randolph Street and Lake Shore Drive, you're never far from where you want to go. The ParkShore is just minutes from the Loop, Michigan Avenue, Grant Park and the

lakefront. Plus you'll enjoy some of the most spectacular residential views in the city...Chicago's magnificent lakefront and harbor, the river with its graceful bridges, the golf course, Buckingham Fountain. Happiness can be simply enjoying your options.

Value. The ultimate amenity.

The ParkShore's most appealing feature is its overall value. No other condominium in downtown Chicago can match The ParkShore's unique combination of friendly service, beautiful surroundings and ideal location. When you add our affordable prices (from just $139,500) and attractive financing programs, The ParkShore clearly becomes Chicago's best condominium value.

Come visit The ParkShore's five beautiful decorator models, tour our fabulous Design Center, meet your own personal design consultant and experience the key to happiness for yourself. And say hello to Ray. He'll be waiting for you.

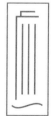

| THE MERIDIAN | THE PLAZA | | THE MAYFAIR | THE PENINSULA |

The ParkShore Condominiums
Where it's good to be home.

195 NORTH HARBOR DRIVE, CHICAGO **312-540-4300** • A DEVELOPMENT OF THE BARTON GROUP, L.L.C. • 1 BEDROOM HOMES FROM **$139,500**
2 BEDROOM HOMES FROM **$182,500** • 2 BEDROOM PLUS DEN HOMES FROM **$233,000** • 3 BEDROOM HOMES FROM **$270,500**
DIRECTIONS: MICHIGAN AVENUE TO RANDOLPH STREET. TURN EAST ONTO RANDOLPH. GET IN THE EXTREME RIGHT LANE AND FOLLOW RANDOLPH TO
ITS END AND BEAR LEFT. FOLLOW SIGNS TO THE PARKSHORE CONDOMINIUMS, 195 NORTH HARBOR DRIVE. WE'RE AT THE END OF THE CUL-DE-SAC.

entire staff at the Forest Lake Country Club. A scrumptious breakfast was followed by comments from our president, Bill Oswald. Tom Clark presented the founders award to Gordon Berg of BBDO and Cindy Nelson of PentaCom. They each received the handsome, solid silver Founders Award Medal along with 100 shares of Omnicom stock – quite a recognition. The next two weeks were more of the same and the end of the year was a repeat of 1994 activities.

Major Things That Happened In 1995

Omnicom acquired the Ross Roy Communications, Inc. agency in Detroit and our client Standard Federal Bank took over Bell Savings in Chicago during 1995. Disney purchased Capital Cities/ABC for $19 billion and released "Pocahontas," its 33rd animated feature. Westinghouse bought CBS for $5.4 billion and O.J. Simpson, who most people believed murdered his former wife, Nicole Brown Simpson, and her friend Ronald Goldman, was declared not guilty by a Los Angeles jury and set free.

– 1996 –

The first business activity for the new year was a status meeting for the General Accounts Group at 9 a.m. on January 2, at BBDO Detroit's Southfield office. Status meetings are held weekly and last about an hour. The traffic coordinator conducts these meetings and reviews the status of every client assignment with the creative, production, and account service staff. There's usually someone also present from media, the art department, and accounting, so there's a large group gathered around one big conference table.

Status meetings are valuable because everyone gets an update on every project (usually between 50 and 100 different assignments),

whether each job is on, ahead of, or behind schedule, and what problems, if any, have been encountered. Following the status meeting, the creative, account service, traffic and production personnel meet to handle specific problems, as well as any revisions or changes necessary in an assignment. The rest of the participants leave as soon as the status meeting ends to go about their business.

Two New Business Prospects Surface

On January 3, Bill Hackett, Michael Graham, Tom Neman, Pete Swiecicki and I met to discuss whether we should pursue the Eaton Corporation account. We had received an invitation to make a presentation to solicit a corporate advertising campaign that Eaton was considering. Again, we turned to Reid MacGuidwin, now retired but formerly director of marketing for *Automotive News*, as well as Barbara Hoffman, Detroit sales manager for *Design News* magazine, to get their insight and background information. They were both quite familiar with this company. After considerable discussion and some "soul searching," the consensus was not to pursue this prospect, as Eaton's recent history in carrying out corporate advertising campaigns was not good. We made the right decision because nothing did happen and the individual who initiated the proposed corporate advertising campaign left the company.

The Air Bag Problem

The following week, John Hammond, Michele White and I met with Ron Zorowitz of Chrysler Corporation to discuss a national advertising campaign under consideration to educate the public concerning accidents and fatalities related to air bag deployment. Air bags were originally developed for those drivers who would not buckle up and, although they were very effective for saving lives in many instances, they were also sometimes inflicting great bodily harm because of the tremendous force with which they deployed. Further, with new federal requirements for dual air bags in new vehicles, the incidence of injuries to riders on the passenger side was expected to increase unless a very effective communications program was carried out to communicate how to significantly reduce injuries – wear seatbelts and do not sit too close to the wheel.

A number of groups had come together to attempt to solve the problem – the auto manufacturers, insurance industry, governmental agencies and special interest groups. All agreed that a concerted effort had to be made to educate the public, particularly those at greatest risk:

- Children under 12 months of age in child seats in the front seat – these children should be placed in child seats in the rear.

- Older children who are not restrained properly – these children should wear seat belts.

- Males in the 20-30 age group who do not wear seat belts and also take other risks while operating a vehicle: speeding, drinking while driving, etc.

- Drivers (mostly women) who sit too close to the steering wheel or who have their hands wrapped around the steering wheel, and those who have objects (pipes, cigarettes, suckers, etc.) in their mouths while driving.

During the meeting, Ron, the manager of Vehicle Safety and Regulatory Affairs for Chrysler Corporation, showed us a video of test dummies being hit by exploding air bags, which graphically and dramatically presented the possible hazard that exists with air bags.

It was appalling to see the test results, but it was also a great learning experience. I have been a consistent seat belt user and do not sit as close as I once did to the steering wheel, ever since viewing those test videos.

Over the next several months, there were additional meetings as the situation changed constantly. The anticipated budget of more than $10,000,000 never materialized and the responsibility for the public education campaign was assigned to the National Safety Council, in coordination with the National Highway Traffic Safety Administration. The total budget for the two-year education program starting July 1, 1996, through June 30, 1998, ended up being just $4 million dollars. A public relations agency was hired to handle the project, as there was not enough money for a national advertising campaign.

The North American International Auto Show

Every year, Detroit's International Auto Show has a preview night before the show opens to the public. This black tie event raises millions of dollars for several charities. A large contingent from BBDO Detroit always attends. Late in the afternoon on January 5, Mary Lou and I joined the other attendees from BBDO Detroit at Daniel's restaurant in Royal Oak for cocktails and hors d'oeuvres. From there we went by bus to Cobo Hall, where we spent several hours looking at all the new cars and trucks in elaborate displays at this huge, impressive show. Then we were back to Daniel's for dinner, entertainment and dancing, making it a full, exciting and fun evening.

The Record-Breaking First Six Months of 1996

For the General Accounts Group of BBDO Detroit, there was an abundance of activity and a tremendous amount of work accomplished in the first six months of 1996. A new billings record was achieved due to the sharply-increased volume of media advertising and collateral production handled for Standard Federal Bank, for its InterFirst Division and for the newly acquired Bell Federal in Chicago. Advertising for the ParkShore Condo project in Chicago was now in full swing and the Spring Newspaper Network program was also underway. A major project every year for Standard Federal Bank was the design and production of its annual report, which we handled, and we also assisted BBDO Dusseldorf with the creation and production of several advertisements for the U.S. division of one of its clients in Germany.

In spite of the record volume of work during the first six months of 1996, Mary Lou and I managed to get away for a week to visit my brother Joe and his wife Sue in California in early March and we also spent several weekends at the Boyne Mountain condo. We were there over Easter weekend, when my granddaughter Emily won the Boyne Mountain Easter bonnet contest for a hat she made. Her prize was a gold ski pass for the 1996-1997 season.

On Memorial day weekend, we went back to The Grand Hotel on Mackinac Island for the annual Detroit Regional Chamber of Commerce Conference. As usual, Mary Lou and I spent some time with Priscilla and Tom Ricketts. Tom was selected to be chairman of the Chamber for 1997 at this meeting. Speakers at the four-day conference included Robert Eaton, chairman and CEO of Chrysler Corporation, Elizabeth Dole, Newt Gingrich and Governor Engler. During the first six months of 1996, there were the usual benefits to attend – dinners and golf outings – nothing much different from previous years and, so, time went by in a flash!

Greece, Turkey and London

Dorothy and Tom Staples, my aunt and uncle who live in St Louis, celebrated their 50th wedding anniversary with a trip to Greece and Turkey. To help them celebrate their anniversary, they took their immediate family with them. This included their son Tommy and daughter Mary, as well as Mary's husband, Dean Vazis, and Mary and Dean's 17-year-old daughter, Colleen. Dorothy and Tom invited Mary Lou and me to join them, so the eight of us met at John F. Kennedy airport in New York on June 17, and flew together to Athens, Greece. This turned out to be the most memorable vacation I've ever experienced and a great learning experience. While in Athens, the birthplace of Western civilization, we visited the Acropolis, walked all around the Parthenon, and visited the major tourist attractions. We left Athens after several days to take a bus tour of the interior, including legendary Thebes and Delphi. We stayed overnight at the Hotel Amiklia near Delphi, where we had a fantastic view of the valley below that was filled with thousands of olive trees. The Bay of Itea was visible in the distance.

The next day, we visited Myceneae and Nauplia. Our professional guide, Nikos, continually pointed out interesting things to see and explained what we were seeing. We crossed over to the Peloponnesus peninsula on a huge ferry and proceeded down the coastline to Corinth. This is where St. Paul lived for a time, writing, preaching and establishing a church. This is also where St. Paul is reported to have written the two epistles to the Corinthians in the Bible. We then went to Epidaurus, built in the 4th century BC. We then went to Mycenae, stopping to see the ancient sites of Tiryns and Argos on our way. From Mycenae, we proceeded to Nauplia, on the gulf of Argos – a beautiful town in an exquisite setting between twin fortresses. We stayed overnight at the Hotel Amilia.

We were awakened the next morning by a rooster crowing. After breakfast we took our tour bus to Naplion, where we boarded the cruise ship Marco Polo for a seven-day cruise to various Greek Islands. After sailing all night June 22, we arrived at tiny Delos Island in the Aegean Sea. Delos was the reported birthplace of Apollo and Artemis and once was the religious and political center of the Aegean Sea. Today, however, it is inhabited only by a wondrous assortment of ruins. We were tendered ashore and took a guided tour. We saw the Avenue of the Lions, three beautiful temples dedicated to Apollo, and houses with splendid mosaic floors.

We went back to the ship for lunch and then on to Mykonos – a ritzy, whitewashed town with nice beaches and boutiques. Mykonos is also interesting for its labrynth of narrow, winding streets that were designed to foil attacking pirates in the 15th and 16th Centuries.

On Sunday, June 23, we went ashore to the town of Mykonos on the island of Mykonos to have lunch and do some shopping. From left to right: Colleen Vazis, Tommy Staples, Dorothy Staples, Dean Vazis, Tom Staples, Mary (Staples) Vazis, Mary Lou and me.

The next stop was Santorini, where we toured the ancient ruins at Akrotiri – which was buried by a volcanic eruption in 1500 B.C. On the way to the ruins we passed many vineyards – there are several wineries on the island. We proceeded to Fira, perched on the rim of the caldera, which offered charming shops and spectacular views of the sea. We rode the funicular back to the beach and took the tender out to the Marco Polo.

We then sailed on to Crete, docking at Iraklion. We wandered all over town and bought some souvenirs, including a mask of Bacchus, the Greek god of wine and fruit. We then sailed for Rhodes at 9 p.m., arriving there at 7 a.m. on

June 25. After breakfast, we went ashore to tour the medieval stronghold of the Crusader Knights of St. John. We also visited the Church of our Lady, which was built upon the foundation of the ancient temple of Athena, and catacombs from early Christian times. Following our walking tour of the Knights of St. John Fortress, we took a bus tour of the city, ending up at a small village by the sea for lunch.

Our ship arrived at Kusadasi, Turkey early Wednesday morning. We went ashore and boarded a tour bus and then drove to Selcuk, successor of the great city of Ephesus – which is now three miles from the sea but was once the major trading port in the Mediterranean.

The ruins which survive at Ephesus, belong almost entirely to the Roman Imperial period. Among these, the Harbor Bath, built during the second century, is one of the largest structures.

Harbor Street is also known as Arcadiana, named after Arcadius, who remodeled it in 395-408 AD. It stretches between the harbor and the theater. Paved with marble and lined with colonnades and stoas, this was one of the few thoroughfares in antiquity to be furnished with street lamps.

After our tour of Ephesus, we returned to Kusadasi, where we had a fascinating experience shopping for a Turkish carpet.

Thursday, June 27, was our first full day of sailing without stops. It was pleasant to have all three daily meals on board the Marco Polo and relax on the deck. We sailed past lots of islands as we cruised along the coast of Halkidiki, and past the Athti Peninsula on our way to Mt. Athos, the holy mountains where no women are allowed to visit.

After breakfast on Friday, we were tendered ashore at Canakkale, Turkey, where we boarded a bus for Troy, a half-hour's drive outside the city.

The first thing we saw on the site was a replica of the famous Trojan horse ("beware of Greeks bearing gifts"). But the most impressive relic of Homer's original Troy are the massive Mycenanean walls of Troy VI. It was the

German archeologist, Heinrich Schliemann, who actually discovered this legendary city, long thought to be merely a figment of Homer's imagination. Schliemann came to the Troad (the region around Troy) in 1868 to locate the legendary city of Priam and Hector. He subsequently found not only its remains, but those of nine other civilizations dating back 5,000 years. Inside, near the chariot ramp, Schliemann also unearthed the controversial "Jewels of Helen."

Schliemann smuggled the "Jewels of Helen" out of the country, and his wife was later seen flaunting them at fashionable social events. They disappeared during World War II, and it wasn't until 1993 that Moscow announced that the State Pushkin Museum of Fine Arts housed the lost "Treasure of Priam."

Early on Saturday morning, June 29, the Marco Polo arrived in Istanbul. We had our bags packed ready to go ashore after breakfast. Most of the day was spent touring Istanbul, the largest city in Turkey.

Our tour included the Chora Church, which boasts the finest collection of Byzantine mosaics and mural paintings in Turkey, as well as the Hippodrome, the spectacular Blue Mosque and the Grand Bazaar.

In the evening, we went to the Hasnad Restaurant on the Bosporus, about eight blocks from the Conrad Hilton. We had a really enjoyable dinner costing 12,500,000 lira.

On Sunday morning, our tour began with a visit to Suleymaniye Mosque, built by the famous Turkish architect, Sinan, and dedicated to Sultan Suleyman, the Magnificent. Next, we went to St. Sophia Museum, formerly the Church of Hagia Sophia (Divine Wisdom). This museum is the most important Byzantine monument in Istanbul, especially famous for its immense dome and the magnificent frescoes and mosaics inside. Our final stop was the world-famous Topkapi Palace, the imperial residence of the Ottoman Sultans for almost 400 years. It occupies 700,000 square meters and is a complex of courts, pavilions, mosques and fountains.

Early on Monday morning, July 1, we said goodbye to Tom, Dorothy, Tommy, Mary, Dean and Colleen and went to Istanbul airport, from which we flew on British Air to Heathrow Airport in London. There we were met by a driver, who drove us to the Hilton Hotel on Park Lane overlooking Hyde Park.

The next morning, bolstered by an excellent breakfast in the Hilton Hotel dining room, we were ready to go sightseeing. We took the Big Bus Company tour, as they offered "Hop On-Hop Off" sightseeing. We started from Marble Arch and got off the bus at Piccadilly Circus. We walked around the area, down Whitehall Street past the House of Parliament, and took a tour of Westminster Abbey. Later, we did more walking and saw the horseguards, Downing Street, Big Ben and Scotland Yard. We also had lunch in a British Pub – awful food. Still later, we saw Covent Garden, London Transport Museum, St. Paul's Cathedral, and the Tower of London. Mary Lou and I covered a lot of London by bus and by foot.

Elizabeth & Paul Wassmandorf of La Jolla, California were with us on the tour we took of Greece and Turkey. We were together again in London and Mary Lou and I enjoyed dinner with them. Paul retired from General Electric, where he was responsible for the advertising of various divisions. He worked with many people at BBDO New York including Tom Dillion when he was with GE and I enjoyed hearing him describe the many interesting experiences he had over the years with the agency.

On Wednesday morning, we walked through Hyde Park to Harrod's Department Store and did a lot of shopping. From Harrod's, we went to the British Museum and saw the Elgin Marbles. In 1801 Lord Elgin, the British Ambassador to the Ottoman Court at Constantinople, had gotten permission from the Turks to plunder the Acropolis – Turkey then ruled Greece. Elgin took large parts of the Parthenon frieze back to London along with a number of large sculptures. They are now all on display in the British Museum. Greece has waged a long campaign to get these treasures returned. In the evening, we had dinner at Luigi's in Covent Garden and then went to the theater to see *Sunset Boulevard* – a great show with an outstanding cast.

On Thursday, July 4, we left London. Our limo driver gave us an interesting tour on the way to Gatwick Airport. My son Mike met us at Detroit's Metro airport that evening and drove us home. It was good to be back in the U.S.A. again after being gone for almost three weeks.

A Super Summer

When I returned to the office in early July, I learned BBDO had recently cleaned up at the 44th Cannes International Advertising Festival, the industry's leading awards competition. BBDO won 26 Lions overall, more than any other agency. With 16 Lions in TV and 10 in print, our network led the world in both categories. As a result, BBDO was named "Agency of the Year" in the United States at the close of the Cannes International Advertising Festival. This marked the first time a U.S. agency had ever captured this coveted honor. This award is given to the agency that receives the most points for Lions won in the press/poster and film competitions. This honor capped the most successful overall award performance by BBDO Worldwide of any year in its history.

A Major Reorganization For the Agency

Tom Clark's 60th birthday was celebrated with a big party at his home, which Mary Lou and I attended. Shortly after that, BBDO Worldwide announced the creation of PentaMark® – a new and unique subsidiary that manages the combined communications assets on behalf of the Chrysler Corporation, the largest worldwide client of BBDO.

Clark became president and CEO of PentaMark. In addition, John Hammond and David Jones were appointed managing directors of PentaMark. Hammond and Jones had previously been executive vice presidents at BBDO Detroit for National and Dealer Association Advertising programs.

Many other individuals were also assigned roles in the evolving PentaMark structure.

The PentaMark organization, dedicated to providing Chrysler Corporation with the most effective and innovative integrated brand marketing programs in the industry, is comprised of: BBDO Detroit, handling all Dodge car and truck advertising and Dodge Dealer Association advertising in the U.S.; Ross Roy Communications, providing below-the-line services for all Chrysler brands, Chrysler/Plymouth, Jeep/Eagle, Dodge as well as their dealers, Mopar and Chrysler Corporate and International programs; and PentaCom, the media planning and buying entity for all Chrysler Corporate and Brand national advertising.

Bill Oswald, the president and CEO of BBDO Detroit, became chairman and CEO of Ross Roy Communications. Ross Roy founded this agency in the 1920s on the premise that better-informed dealers and sales people would sell more cars and trucks. Working with Chrysler, he transformed the raw product data into information salespeople could use to facilitate the sale. Ross Roy Communications still provides that service for Chrysler Corporation, but the service is now identified as "Customer Relationship Management" (CRM).

Dick Johnson

Dick Johnson, BBDO Detroit's chief creative officer since 1991, assumed the position of president of BBDO Detroit. Under the leadership of Johnson, BBDO Detroit's work for Dodge set the automotive industry benchmark for innovative, effective advertising.

In 1996, for the second year in a row, the agency won the Chrysler Gold Pentastar for outstanding performance and marketing achievement. Completing one of the most award-winning years in its history, BBDO Detroit was the recipient of more than 40 major awards for Dodge advertising at the Effie, Clio, New York Festivals, Mobius and Houston International Film Festival competitions.

All the Usual Summer Activities – and Then Some

Not only was there a lot happening at the office, but weekends were also filled with the golf outings and social activities. On Sunday, August 11, the marketing department of Standard Federal Bank was invited to a picnic barbecue at my home on Lake Voorheis. We had a good turnout including Priscilla and Tom Ricketts, and it was a prefect summer day, weather-wise.

For several years, I had been on the Advisory Committee for the "Friends of Orion Oaks," a volunteer organization dedicated to developing Orion Oaks park in Oakland County. Entirely through volunteer efforts, this park had been transformed from a 927-acre tract of land eroded by misuse and full of debris, to a haven for wildlife and a great place to escape to for those seeking peaceful recreation. Volunteers, led by Marjorie Pollick of the Telephone Pioneers of America, have planted more than 10,000 seedlings, hundreds of trees and developed five miles of trails. Our most significant project was the construction of an 8-foot wide by 168-foot long wheelchair-accessible fishing pier in Lake 16, which covers more than 90 acres in Orion Oaks Park. This project took 1,500 hours to build and was dedicated on August 21. This fishing pier was built entirely with funds received from private donors and foundations, most of which I raised by writing letters to businesses soliciting contributions or by submitting proposals to foundations and service clubs requesting funds. I was successful in raising more than $25,000.

The dedication of the pier was a real "high" that day but, little did I know, that bad news would soon follow. Later that same day, I learned that my 93-year-old father-in-law, Edward Bauman, had leukemia. Dad and I were close friends and he was truly "one-of-a-kind." Tall and distinguished with his white hair – a man of strong convictions and a dedicated Christian – he was the patriarch of our family. Dad had enjoyed exceptionally good health and we thought he'd live to be 100 years of age, or more. Just 30 days after he was diagnosed with leukemia, he passed away. His immediate

The wheelchair-accessible fishing pier, which extends 168 feet into Lake 16 at Orion Oaks Park in Oakland County, was built entirely by volunteers led by Margie Pollick of the Ameritech Telephone Pioneers. There is a parking lot adjacent to the dock with a wheelchair-accessible toilet and a special barbecue unit for paraplegics. The lot and walkway are hard surfaced, as the goal was to make this facility an easy-to-use place for wheelchair anglers. I raised the $25,000 from private donors on behalf of BBDO Detroit that it cost. The pier was dedicated on Wednesday, August 21, 1996, when Dan Stencil, chief of park operations, and I participated in the dedication ceremony.

family cared for him, up until the last few days, when nurses from Hospice became necessary.

The following weekend, Mary Lou and I went to Tiverton, Ontario to visit Jeannette and Keith Evans at their summer retirement home on Lake Huron. After dad's funeral, this get-a-way was most welcome and Keith and Jeannette were wonderful hosts.

Son Mike and Family Move
To Park City, Utah

During the summer, my son Michael sold his dental practice in Lake Orion and he, Kathy and their three sons moved to Park City, Utah. They wanted to start a new phase in their lives and, after investigating a number of possibilities, decided on Park City as the place they particularly wanted to live. Mike had

returned to Michigan for his grandfather's funeral and now I decided to go see their new home – we made quite an interesting trip out of it.

First, we drove to St. Louis, staying Friday night, October 21, with Dorothy and Tom Staples. The next morning, we had breakfast with Sally and Jack Higgins and then drove on to Columbia for lunch at the Beta fraternity house with Jack Bloess. It was homecoming weekend and Jack had gotten us tickets to the Missouri vs. Oklahoma State football game that afternoon, at Faurot Stadium. Missouri beat Oklahoma State in overtime. We stayed overnight in Columbia in order to visit relatives and friends on Sunday. Late on Sunday afternoon, we drove to the Kansas City airport, staying at a nearby hotel, so that we could fly to Salt Lake City early Monday morning. My son Michael met us when we arrived at Salt Lake airport, and on the way to Park City, we visited the Mormon Center.

My brother Joe and his wife Sue, were also in Salt Lake visiting Susan and Dorothy Bale, and the four of them joined us for dinner at Kathy and Mike's that evening. It was a busy, interesting week that we spent becoming familiar with Park City and the surrounding area. We made several trips to Salt Lake – once to visit the impressive Genealogy Center operated by the Mormons and another time to attend a Halloween costume party at Susan and Dorothy Bale's home. On Sunday afternoon we had an early Thanksgiving feast – turkey and all the trimmings – at Kathy and Mike Baker's. Sue, Joe, Susan and Dorothy were included. On Tuesday, November 7, I saw Blaine, Brad and Reid off for school and, later in the day, we returned to the Salt Lake City airport and flew back to Kansas City – but this vacation was not over yet!!

We stayed overnight at the same hotel near the Kansas City airport where we'd left our car. Early Wednesday morning, we drove to Madison County, Iowa. There we visited several covered bridges and had lunch in Winterset at the Northside Cafe. All were included in the movie

"*Bridges of Madison County.*" The actor, John Wayne, was born in Winterset and his childhood home is now a museum, which we took time to see. The next day we drove to Dyersville, Iowa, where the movie "*Field of Dreams*" was made. We stopped briefly at the farm where the movie was shot but our real motive for going to this town was to visit the National Farm Toy Museum. We spent several hours at this museum and also did some shopping in the outlet stores operated by the model car, truck and farm equipment toy manufacturers located in Dyersville. Then we went to Chicago and finally arrived home on Sunday, November 10, so that I could go back to work Monday morning (after being away for two-and-a-half weeks).

Standard Federal Bank To Be Acquired

The rest of 1996 followed pretty much the course of the last several years, with one big exception – the acquisition of our client, Standard Federal Bank, by ABN AMRO North America, Inc. On November 22, it was announced in a press release and in a memo to the staff of Standard Federal Bank that ABN AMRO was purchasing the outstanding common stock of Standard Federal Bancorporation, Inc., (the parent of Standard Federal Bank of Michigan and its Bell Federal Bank division in Chicago) in cash for $59 per share. Based on the then-current number of outstanding shares and options, the acquisition was valued at approximately $1.9 billion, making it the largest acquisition in the Netherlands-based bank's history.

Standard Federal Bank, the principal operating subsidiary of Standard Federal Bancorporation, Inc., operated a network of 182 banking centers, over 390 automated teller machines (ATMs) and 11 home lending centers in Michigan, Indiana, Northwest Ohio and Illinois. As of October 31, 1996, it had assets of $15.5 billion, deposits of $10.8 billion and $10.1 billion of loans serviced for others. It

was announced that, upon closing, current Standard Federal Bank branches would continue to operate under the Standard Federal name.

Standard Federal's mortgage operation, including InterFirst, a wholesale mortgage banking unit, was the largest thrift lender in the nation. Together with ABN AMRO's LaSalle Home Mortgage Corp. of Northridge, Illinois, the largest single family lender in Chicago, the combined operations would form the country's eighth largest mortgage originator.

In Chicago, Standard Federal's Bell Federal branches would be integrated into LaSalle Bank FSB's branch network.

We also learned that, upon closing, Scott K. Heitmann, president and CEO of LaSalle Community Bank Group, would assume the additional responsibilities of president and CEO of Standard Federal Bank. The current chairperson and CEO, Thomas R. Ricketts

Scott Heitmann is chairman, president and chief executive officer of Standard Federal Bank, and is also executive vice president of ABN AMRO North America, Inc. He serves on the board of directors of Detroit Renaissance, Inc., the Economic Club of Detroit and the Detroit Regional Chamber Commerce.

would remain chairman of Standard Federal Bank and become a member of the board of directors of LaSalle Bank FSB.

Even though I was aware that a merger was under consideration and the news releases and memos provided a lot of information, there were still questions and concerns which, hopefully, would be resolved in the months ahead.

It was most encouraging, though, when I read in the bank's employee newsletter this statement from Scott Heitmann:

"Long-term goals for the Bank are to build a platform on which ABN AMRO can grow future business not only in this geographic region, but throughout the United States. We will maintain the commitment to excellence of customer service and earnings performance that Tom Ricketts and the management team at Standard Federal have successfully created here."

1996 Comes To a Close

Our company Christmas party was held at Plum Hollow Golf Club on December 5, and an early light snowfall helped put everyone in the spirit of the season. BBDO Detroit enjoyed an outstanding year in 1996, while BBDO Worldwide grew significantly in the volume and scope of its operation. The agency's roster of multinational clients rose to 56 served in five countries or more and the agency's network of offices now covered more than 70 countries.

There were a number of parties in December, including two that I attended to honor Lee Wilson for his 40 years of service to the Adcraft Club of Detroit as its executive secretary.

Overall, 1996 was a good year for the Baker family, for most of my friends and associates at the office, for BBDO and for the nation.

The major news story of the year occurred when Paris-bound TWA Flight 800 exploded shortly after take off, killing 230. In terms of marketing, Beanie Babies and Tickle Me Elmo

dolls were huge sellers and The Procter and Gamble Company introduced Olestra with great fanfare, after approval by the Food and Drug Administration. This "no-fat" food product took 25 years and cost $200 million to develop.

– 1997 –

On New Year's Day, Mary Lou and I drove home from Boyne Mountain, where we had spent the last week of 1996. The roads were slippery, so we took our time, arriving home in time to watch the second half of the Rose Bowl game on TV. It was a thriller, with Ohio State beating Arizona State in the final seconds of the game. The first day at the office – Thursday, January 2 – there was a huge pile of mail and memos to wade through and many calls to be returned.

One important letter was from Dee (Marx) Prosi, director of advertising for Select Care, informing us that BBDO was a finalist for its account. Dee Prosi's letter outlined how and to whom we were to make our presentation on January 16. For the next two weeks, much of my time was dedicated to helping prepare our presentation to this large HMO organization. We made our "pitch" but an advertising agency in San Francisco won the account.

During the first quarter of 1997, there were the usual activities and some special events, such as the annual preview night for the North American International Auto Show at Cobo Hall, in downtown Detroit. This year all the participants from BBDO Detroit gathered at The Detroit Club for hors d' oeuvres and, after spending several hours at the auto show, returned to The Detroit Club for dinner and dancing. On March 7, Tom Ricketts was honored at the formal "Champion of Hope" Tribute Dinner, sponsored by the National Kidney Foundation. Priscilla and Tom were as happy and excited that evening as I'd ever seen them and I felt quite privileged to be among those present to see Tom receive this prestigious recognition.

Priscilla and Tom Ricketts at the Champion of Hope Dinner held in the International Center Ballroom in Greektown, Detroit on Friday, March 7, 1997. This was an evening dedicated to the celebration of their lifetime achievements and generosity.

The Tragic Death of Priscilla Ricketts[*]

Only hours after voluntarily recording a science textbook to be nationally distributed to blind students, Priscilla Ricketts was struck on Monday afternoon, March 24, by a hit-and-run driver as she loaded groceries into her car outside a Kroger store in Troy. A passerby found her unconscious, lying two parking spaces away from her car, and called police. The groceries in her trunk and shopping cart were untouched, but her purse was missing.

I did not learn about this tragedy until the next morning when I was at our weekly status meeting, which is held for the purpose of reviewing every client assignment. That afternoon, I went to the new dream home (which Tom and

Priscilla had just built and recently moved into), in order to try to console and support Tom. Priscilla and Tom's daughter, Karen, and her husband, Bert Struck, as well as their son Robert, his wife Cindy and their baby son Austin, were also present. Everyone was devastated by this incredibly horrible, senseless hit-and-run robbery. Priscilla died Wednesday, March 26 as a result of the injuries she suffered and her funeral service was held March 31 – the day after Easter Sunday – at Cranbrook Church in Bloomfield Hills. Garry Carley, Robert Hutton, John O'Hara, Ron Palmer, Bert Struck and I served as pallbearers, and the church overflowed with mourners. Priscilla and Tom were an exceptionally close, loving couple and they had many, many friends through business and the numerous social and charitable organizations with which they were involved.

In 1999, just prior to the publication of this book, two young men were put on trial for causing the death of Priscilla Ricketts.

It's Discovered That Tom Ricketts Has Terminal Cancer

A few days after Priscilla's funeral, I called Tom to invite him to dinner. Tom said he wasn't feeling well and asked for a rain check, explaining that he planned to see his doctor the next day. Early the next week, I learned that Tom was at Beaumont Hospital undergoing tests. On April 11, I was shocked to learn that he had undergone surgery for removal of a stomach tumor and that he had widespread abdominal sarcoma – a form of cancer that is usually terminal. It was unbelievable that this could be happening to Tom less than a month after he had lost his wife. He died early in the morning on April 22 and his funeral service was held on April 25 at Christ Church Cranbrook. I was a pall bearer and Garry Carley and I eulogized Tom during the service. This is what I said about my friend of many years – Thomas R. Ricketts:

Thomas R. Ricketts

Eulogy For Thomas R. Ricketts

Dr. Martin Luther King, Jr. in one of his sermons said:

"If a man is called to be a street sweeper, he should sweep streets even as Michelangelo painted, or Beethoven composed music, or Shakespeare wrote poetry. He should sweep streets so well that all the hosts of heaven and earth will pause to say, here lived a great street sweeper who did his job well." Tom Ricketts was a <u>great</u> banker who did his job exceedingly well and your presence here this morning attests to that fact.

Tom was well educated. He earned a degree in Business Administration and a Doctor of Law Degree, both from University of Michigan. That, however, was just the beginning of his education. He was an avid reader. He attended many marketing and financial seminars and also graduated from the School of Savings and Loan

at the University of Indiana in 1965. Tom listened to others, absorbing information, and became an exceptionally well-informed and knowledgeable individual. He never stopped learning. In 1962, when Bob Hutton became president of Standard Federal, the marketing and advertising responsibilities were assigned to Tom. As the representative of Standard Federal's advertising agency, I had almost daily contact with Tom – either in person or by phone – for the next 11 years. Consequently, we got to know each other very well and became close friends – a friendship that has grown for these 35 years.

In 1967, we were both charter members of the Savings Institution's Marketing Society of America and Tom's abilities were immediately recognized by this group, as he was elected the president in 1968 – the first actual year of operation – as 1967 was dedicated to establishing the organization.

Working closely as I did with Tom over a number of years, I was frequently amazed and impressed with how quickly he could assimilate information, mentally sort through a lot of facts and make a decision.

He never hesitated making decisions – frequently involving sizable sums of money – and incredible as is seems, I believe he <u>always</u> made the right decision. I am not aware of any decision that Tom ever made that was not the right decision.

Tom – like his wife Priscilla – gave back to their community. Tom served on the boards of a number of organizations, usually ending up as the leader with the title of president or chairman.

When he became president of Standard Federal in 1973, he blossomed in that role and became not only a great manager, but also a highly respected leader. His achievements as a manager and a leader were recognized by many prestigious publications such as *Financial World* magazine and the *Wall Street Journal*.

He and Priscilla had an unusually close relationship. They were best friends. He was especially proud of her and Priscilla, in turn, was very proud of her Tom. They smiled at each other a lot. They especially enjoyed quiet evenings together discussing what each had done that day…plans for a trip somewhere… watching some special show on TV…or going to a movie together.

I was with Tom the night after Priscilla was struck in the parking lot and was on life support so that certain organs could be donated the next morning. Tom frequently said – "What am I going to do without Priscilla?" or "I'd gladly give anything to get my Priscilla back." If there's a bright spot in this tragedy it's that the two of them are now reunited. Tom's got his Priscilla back again.

Volunteering Proves To Be Beneficial

April 26 – the day after Tom's funeral – was the spring work day for volunteers at Orion Oaks Park. The weather was ideal and there was a big turnout of volunteer workers. I joined a group installing benches in various locations in the park and I really appreciated just being out in the woods. It was healing and I thought about the words of Thoreau which I've seen on signs in parks offering inspiration and contemplation for visitors:

"I went to the woods because I wished to live deliberately, to front only the essential facts of life, and see if I could not learn what it had to teach – and not, when I came to die, discover that I had not lived."

In the following weeks, I attended the annual Nightingale Dinner, sponsored by the Board of Visitors for Oakland University School of Nursing and a fundraiser for "Habitat for Humanity" and participated in several golf outings for various benefits.

In mid-May, we went to Boyne to hunt for morel mushrooms and to golf. Mary Lou's brother, Jere Keyes, and his wife Pat, joined us at the condo and we had a very pleasant weekend together. We didn't find many morels but we enjoyed being out in the woods – which were alive with new growth and spring flowers.

We returned to Boyne the end of May for a few days, before going to Mackinac Island for the Annual Regional Chamber of Commerce Conference at the Grand Hotel. This meeting started May 29 and that evening Karen Struck accepted the Van Dusen Award presented posthumously to her parents, Priscilla and Tom Ricketts.

Scott Heitmann, the new president, chairman and CEO of Standard Federal Bank, and Edward "Chip" Miller, executive vice president in charge of Standard Federal's Commercial Banking Division, were at this conference. Scott's wife Kathy and Chip's wife Patty accompanied their husbands and Mary Lou and I enjoyed being with these two couples at various functions. We returned home on Sunday and I was back in the office on Monday. From early June through September, it was virtually a repeat of all the media functions, golf outings and social activities that I have reported attending in prior years. My son Mike and his family came to visit for several weeks in July and, in September, I went to visit them in Park City, Utah. Mary Lou accompanied me and we rented a car during the time we were in Utah to go to Jackson Hole and Yellowstone. Mary and Jack Ray have a home in Jackson Hole and we spent a delightful day with them, driving through Grand Tetons National Park – where we saw lots of wild life. Before retiring, Jack was with Standard Federal Bank and for many years he headed the mortgage department.

The Detroit Newspapers Tournament of Champions Pro-Am

During the summer, I was invited by *The Detroit News* to play in the Tournament of

Champions Pro-Am at Boyne Mountain and it was a great experience. I am just an average golfer and have gone to a number of PGA tournaments, to watch the professionals play golf but it's quite another thing to play golf with a professional golfer. For this two-day tournament, each foursome was really a fivesome with the fifth player being a Michigan PGA professional golfer. David Smith was the professional assigned to our foursome and the other players were Teresa Lucido, senior advertising sales director with The Detroit Newspapers; Dan Hiller with Farmington Hills Chrysler/Plymouth; Gary Morrison with Joe Ricci Automotive Group; and me. We took second place and won a number of nice prizes.

Hard to Believe It's Fall Again

The American Heart Association's annual Heart Walk at the Detroit Zoo took place on Saturday, October 4 and I was involved as a Recruitment Leader. My charge was to get five companies or organizations to participate in this fundraiser. Clark Graphic Services, Oakland County Parks, Oakland University's School of Nursing, Standard Federal Bank and the King family were the participants that I recruited.

BBDO Detroit supports the annual Heart Walk of the American Heart Association. Participants from the agency in the early morning walk at the Detroit Zoo, in 1997, included Carol Maynard, Ernie Baker, Ron Fularczyk, Kathy Nichols and Sue Fularczyk.

Ursula Crenshaw of Standard Federal Bank rewarded all the walkers that she got to participate with an elaborate Italian-style picnic lunch, when they finished the walk, complete with bottles of wine. Her scrumptious feast covered several picnic tables and a good time was had by all, including myself. This one-day walk raised over $403,000 for the American Heart Association – a new record.

Dennis Goschka, Esq. joined BBDO Detroit in 1983 to oversee legal matters and is executive vice president, chief legal officer and secretary of the company. He graduated magna cum laude from the University of Detroit Law School and also obtained a graduate law degree in Corporate & Finance Law at Wayne State University Law School.

A Seminar On "Advertising and the Law"

A seminar on legal issues associated with advertising, was held on October 14 for our clients. PentaMark was the sponsor and

Dennis Goschka, executive vice president, chief legal officer of BBDO, and I organized the seminar. Dennis lined up the speakers and I made all the meeting arrangements while the General Accounts creative and production staff produced a series of mailers to promote attendance at the seminar.

The seminar was held in a large meeting room at the Troy Marriot Hotel and started with a continental breakfast and ended with a luncheon. It was a big success – our clients were delighted – and a capacity crowd of 136 people attended.

Seminar speakers included:

Tom Clark
President/CEO PentaMark – Tom welcomed the attendees and explained the purpose of the seminar.

Dennis Goschka
Executive Vice President, Legal Officer BBDO/Detroit – "Advertising Review: Why Do It and What To Look For"

Judith Shumaker-Holland
Senior Staff Counsel at Chrysler Corporation – "Chrysler's Advertising Review Procedures"

Don Fraser
Partner, MacMillan, Sobanski & Todd, LLC – "Intellectual Property Issues in Advertising (Patents, Copyrights, Trademarks and Intellectual Property Issues)"

Ken Gluckman
Assistant General Counsel at Chrysler Corporation – "Product Liability Issues in Advertising"

Rick Martin
Attorney, MacMillan, Sobanski & Todd, LLC – "The Internet and The Law (Domain Names, Jurisdictional Issues and Their Application)"

Back To My Roots

On the day after the seminar, I left for St. Louis late in the afternoon and drove to Terre Haute, Indiana, where I stayed overnight. The next day, I arrived, shortly after lunch at Dorothy and Tom Staples' home. My brother Joe had already arrived there from California. That afternoon, Joe, my uncles, Jim and Tom Staples, and I went to Grant's Farm (operated by Anheiser Busch) for a tour and to see where the Budweiser's Clydesdale horses are raised and trained.

The next day, the same foursome – Jim, Tom, Joe and I – drove to St. Albans so that Joe and I could "*return to our roots.*" Since my last visit, more houses had been built, the Country Club was being expanded and, to our surprise, the house we lived in for many years no longer existed. It had been bulldozed and a golf cart path now ran right through the area the home once occupied. We recognized the trees that were in the yard even though they were considerably larger than when we had lived there in the late 1930s. A visit to Head's Store and with Mae Head was a must and she was pleased to see us. We then drove to Hermann, Missouri, where we visited several wineries. We then returned to St. Louis for a family get-together dinner.

Ernie Baker   Joe Baker   Mae Head

On Saturday morning, Joe and I met Sally and Jack Higgins for breakfast at Schneithorst's restaurant in Clayton, and then traveled on to Columbia.

We had lunch at the Beta fraternity house with Jack Bloess and Jack VanDyne, and then went to the homecoming football game to watch Missouri beat Texas in a hard-fought game. After the game, Joe and I drove to Sedalia, stopping at Crown Hill Cemetery to visit our family's grave site. That evening we had dinner with Jack Bloess and some of his family and stayed overnight at Jack's, gabbing until after midnight. I took a slight detour returning to Michigan and drove my brother to Dayton, Ohio so that he could visit his daughter Julie, her husband Bill, and their son Jordan. On Sunday night, we stayed at a hotel on the east side of Indianapolis. The next day, Monday, October 20, was my birthday. When I woke up Monday morning, Joe had already been to the hotel lobby and had brought juice, coffee and muffins back to the room. He also had managed to find a candle, which he stuck in my muffin. When I woke up, he lit it and sang "Happy Birthday." I arrived home that evening in time for a birthday dinner with my family and, the next weekend, was invited to B and Bob Cunningham's home in Birmingham for dinner. It turned out to be a surprise birthday party for me, attended by many people that I had worked with over the years. There was a lot of celebrating for my 71st.

The Conclusion of 1997

The last two months of the year were similar to years past. Again, I participated as a clown in the Thanksgiving Parade, attended three different fundraisers, and the usual company and media holiday parties. Bill Yaw retired as marketing director of Standard Federal Bank and there were several retirement parties for him, including one hosted by BBDO. Our creative department redid the movie "It's A Good Life"

Maggie Allesee and me at the Michigan Thanksgiving Day Parade. Both of us have been members of the Distinguished Clown Corps for more than ten years and are the two longest-serving members of the Board of Visitors for the Oakland University School of Nursing.

into a video titling it, "He's A Good Guy." It was hilarious and my part in the video was that of Ernie – the angel in the original movie who saved Jimmy Stewart when he jumped off a bridge.

Since the University of Michigan was going to the Rose Bowl, we decided that this was a good excuse for us to go to California. Mary Lou and I left on December 28 to soak up some sunshine and help my brother celebrate his 65th birthday on December 30.

1997 turned out to be an excellent year for BBDO Worldwide, with strong growth in revenues and profits and broad recognition of its creative excellence. BBDO now operated 285 offices in 72 countries, allowing it to serve 24 of its multinational clients in 10 or more countries.

For the second year in a row, BBDO was named the "Most Creative Agency Network in the World" by *Ad Age International*.

In the U.S., BBDO's TV commercial for HBO won the first Emmy ever awarded in the advertising category, and our commercial for Pepsi was the most-liked Super Bowl spot in the *USA Today* Ad Meter Poll. It was the fifth year in a row that a BBDO commercial had taken the top spot, and BBDO created five of the top 20.

It was major news during the year when 36-year-old Princess Diana of Wales died in Paris in a car crash and 39 Nike-clad members of the Heaven's Gate Cult committed suicide in southern California. A new $50 bill was introduced that looked more like a coupon or play money than real money, and the price of PC's dropped under $1,000.

– 1998 –

On New Year's Day, we rose early to drive to Pasadena for the Rose Bowl Parade. We enjoyed the spectacle and the splendid buffet of flowers decorating the floats in the parade. It was our intention to buy our tickets for the Rose Bowl Game from someone around the stadium. Instead, we decided to go back to Sue and Joe's home in Laguna Niguel and watch the game on their new, large screen TV – all the way to California to watch the game on TV! At least Michigan beat Washington State, 21-16.

On January 12, I was back in the office. There was plenty of catching up to do – mail and memos to read and answer – as well as phone calls to be returned.

The months of January, February and March were unusually mild and, except for a few mornings when the roads were a little slippery and one snowfall of six to seven inches, getting around the Metropolitan Detroit area was much easier than it had been most winters. El Nino, which was the reason for our mild weather, became a household name. Our friends, Carol and Jim Lueders, went to Frankenmuth, Michigan with

Mary Lou and me for the ice festival on February 7, and it was amusing to see the ice sculptures melting almost as fast as they were made.

We participated in several different kinds of fundraisers in late winter and early spring for various causes, but the most enjoyable one was the Tony Bennett concert. This was a benefit for the J.P. McCarthy Foundation held at the Fox Theater, and Sue and Vince Carducci joined Mary Lou and me to attend this very successful and entertaining fundraiser.

In early April, Vince Carducci was named head of the marketing department of Standard Federal Bank – a position that had been open since Bill Yaw's retirement at the end of 1997.

Vincent Carducci is first vice president director of marketing of Standard Federal Bank, responsible for the promotion of all products and services of the Bank, its divisions, subsidiaries and related brands. He is the author of more than 100 articles, essays and reviews on art and design for various publications.

Earlier in the year, Ursula Crenshaw had left the marketing department to join a family business, but InterFirst – the wholesale mortgage division of Standard Federal Bank – wanted her to become its marketing director. It pursued her and eventually convinced Ursula to join it at its Ann Arbor headquarters, where she is now a First Vice President in charge of marketing for ABN AMRO Mortgage Group.

Early on Saturday morning, April 25, I was at Orion Oaks Park along with more than 200 other volunteers for the spring work day to help improve the park. Volunteers planted trees and seedlings, installed benches, improved the trails and cleaned up trash. It was a perfect spring day to be outside. This was also my granddaughter Emily's 14th birthday, and as a special present I sent her and five of her girlfriends in a limousine to the Fox Theater in downtown Detroit to see the play "The Wizard of Oz." She was thrilled. I was delighted that evening to attend the Discovery Ball, sponsored by the Michigan Chapter of the Leukemia Society of America.

Photo by Santa Fabio

Mary Lou and I arrive at the Ross Roy Building in Bloomfield Hills for the Discovery Ball. The highlight of the evening was the presentation of the Glen W. Fortinberry award to Tom Clark.

The highlight of this formal ball is the presentation of the Glen W. Fortinberry Award and the 1998 recipient was Tom Clark, the chairman and chief executive officer of BBDO Detroit, vice chairman of BBDO Worldwide, a member of the Board of BBDO Worldwide and president and chief executive officer of PentaMark. Tom received this award because of his support of numerous community affairs and charitable events and truly deserved this recognition, even though he prefers to stay out of the spotlight on the causes he supports. The 1998 Discovery Ball

netted more than $170,000 for the Leukemia Society's use in its efforts to eradicate leukemia and its related cancers. The Glen W. Fortinberry Award commemorates and celebrates the life of Glen Fortinberry, the former chairman and CEO of the Ross Roy Group, who died of leukemia.

A Special Reunion

In May, a number of employees of the erstwhile Baker, Abbs, Cunningham & Klepinger and the Baker Advertising agencies met for a reunion organized by former staff members. This reunion was held in the evening in a private dining room at a Royal Oak restaurant and I enjoyed visiting with people that I had worked closely with in the past – some of whom I had not seen or talked with in many years.

The Fascinating Story of How Heinz Prechter Served as the Matchmaker In the Merger of Chrysler Corporation and Daimler-Benz

In the third week of May, I was a guest of Heritage Newspapers for a dinner at the St. Regis Hotel. Heritage Newspapers are part of Prechter Holdings, which also includes ASC Incorporated, Heritage Development, Heritage Beef Cattle Company and the Heritage Network. Heinz C. Prechter founded the American Sunroof Company, as it was initially known, in 1965 in a two car garage and turned it into a global automotive supplier enterprise and one of the largest private businesses in Michigan.

What I found most fascinating was his account of how he introduced Robert Eaton, chairman and CEO of Chrysler Corporation, to Jürgen Schrempp, chairman and CEO of Daimler-Benz, during the North American International Auto Show in January 1997. The merger discussions between Chrysler and Daimler-Benz were being reported nearly every day in the business news and, according

Heinz C. Prechter
Chairman and Founder, ASC Incorporated

to Heinz, he was the matchmaker who introduced Robert Eaton and Jürgen Schrempp. Subsequent to Jürgen Schrempp addressing the Detroit Economic Club, Heinz hosted a private dinner at the Detroit Athletic Club for Schrempp with Governor Engler, Mayor Archer, the chairmen of the Big Three automakers, and other business leaders. According to Heinz, Eaton and Schrempp started developing "a very close friendship" that evening.

In a follow-up meeting held a year later in Eaton's office at Chrysler's Auburn Hills headquarters, they took their partnership a significant step forward – and DaimlerChrysler was conceived. Day One for the merged company was November 17, 1998 with Eaton and Schrempp, the co-CEO's.

The last week of May, we went to our Boyne Mountain condo for a couple of days prior to attending the annual Regional Chamber of Conference at The Grand Hotel on Mackinac Island. We enjoyed being with

Kathy and Scott Heitmann, Nancy and Garry Carley and Patty and "Chip" Miller, representing Standard Federal Bank at the conference. The highlight of this meeting was an address by General Colin Powell. Mary Lou and I left for home early Sunday morning May 31, in order to attend my grandson Matthew's high school graduation ceremony at the Meadowbrook Pavillion at Oakland University that afternoon.

A Surprise Court of Honor

My oldest grandson, Matthew Robert Baker, also received his Eagle Scout award at a Court of Honor held at the Ortonville United Methodist Church on June 14. Matt's Eagle Scout project was a big one, as he completely rebuilt the steps and porch at the front entrance to this church. At the conclusion of Matt's ceremony, I was really surprised when my son Bob – the scoutmaster of Matt's troop and an Eagle Scout himself – called me to come to the front of the church so that I could have my Eagle Scout Award represented to me.

My mother had accepted my Eagle Scout Award for me when my ceremony was held, as

Photo by Doug Bauman

Three generations of Eagle Scouts on the steps of the Ortonville United Methodist Church that Matthew rebuilt as his service project to obtain his Eagle Scout rank. From left to right; Ernie Baker, my son scoutmaster Robert Baker, and my grandson Matthew Baker.

The team that took second place in the Detroit Newspaper's 1998 Tournament of Champions Pro-Am consisted of (left to right): Ernie Baker, Brian Campbell of Bruce Campbell Dodge in Redford; professional golfer Randy Kresnak; Teresa Lucido, senior advertising sales director for the Detroit Newspapers; and David Rothbart, president of Cattleman's Meat Company.

I was in the army, having enlisted on my 17th birthday. I was truly moved when I learned that my grandson Matt wanted to share his recognition day with me by having my Eagle Scout Award represented in a special ceremony following his. This was a special day for both of us.

The national Boy Scout organization arranged to have a picture taken of our three generations of Eagle Scouts with Governor Engler. This photo was taken for *Boys Life* and for *Scouting* magazine. My father was my first scoutmaster and, though he did not become an Eagle scout, he did receive the Silver Beaver award for his many years of service to the Boy Scouts of America.

In mid-June, my son Mike and his family came from Utah for a visit prior to their vacation in Germany and Italy. The big topic of conversation in the office was ISO training. Everyone in the office had started attending training sessions so that BBDO Detroit could become ISO 9001-certified before the year's end.

A Repeat of the Pro-Am Golf Tournament

The Detroit News invited me to play in the 1998 Michigan Pro-Am Golf Tournament at Boyne Mountain again in mid-July, and the team I played with came in second – a repeat of 1997.

This year, Randy Kresnak was the professional golfer that played with our foursome. Randy plays on the Nike Tour and his drives off the tees were awesome. In addition to me, the other members of our foursome were Teresa Lucido, senior advertising sales director for the Detroit News; Brian Campbell with Bruce Campbell Dodge, Inc.; and David Rothbart, President of the Cattleman's Meat Company.

Another Seminar For Our Clients

Six months of preparation and planning went into another seminar on "The Future of Media... Beginning Today" sponsored by PentaMark, along with the people at BBDO Detroit, PentaCom and Ross Roy. It was a half-day affair at Forest Lake Country Club in Bloomfield Hills on July 23. David Martin and several members of his staff arranged for all the speakers, while the planning details were handled by Debbie Jones, Jackie Rix and myself. The promotional materials and invitations were created and produced by the General Accounts Group, and Debbie Marshall handled the mailing list for the invitations.

The day started with a continental breakfast and the featured speakers made impressive presentations, making it a very successful seminar on the evolving world of media and the impact it has on advertising. Speakers included:

Tom Clark
President/CEO, PentaMark

Dave Martin
President, PentaCom

Teresa Rodriguez
Anchor/Executive Producer, Univision Network

Tom Evans
CEO, GeoCities

Neil S. Braun
President, NBC Television Network

Christopher Little
President, Merdith Publishing Group

Gary Bettman
NHL Commissioner, who was introduced by Michael Ilitch, owner of the Detroit Red Wings.

Dave Martin is president and CEO of PentaCom which is a full-service media planning and buying communications company that was developed in partnership by BBDO Detroit and DaimlerChrysler. It is unique to other media agencies since all media planning, buying, trafficking and invoice reconciliation are completed in one location for all Chrysler, Plymouth, Jeep and Dodge products, as well as media buying and trafficking for Mercedes-Benz, USA, Inc. which are part of the DaimlerChrysler AG organization.

Vacationing In France

Two days after the PentaMark-sponsored seminar, Mary Lou and I met my brother Joe and his wife Sue at Washington's Dulles Airport and the four of us flew to Paris, arriving early Sunday morning, July 26. By 10 a.m., we had checked into Hotel Saint Louis, near Notre

Dame Cathedral, and after breakfast at a nearby restaurant called Le Flore en L' Isle, we were ready to absorb Paris. We walked along the Seine to the Louvre Museum, where we spent the afternoon looking at some of the world's greatest art treasures. That evening, we had an outstanding dinner at the Pied Cochon restaurant.

On Tuesday morning, we took a bus tour of Paris, visited several famous stores, had lunch at Grand Hotel E Paix, and had dinner at the Champagne Province restaurant. The next day, we were up very early to go to Normandy – a five hour bus ride. On the way, the bus went through the tunnel in which Princess Diana died in a car crash. Our tour of Normandy began in the village of Arromanches, where the D-Day Landing Museum is located. A diorama, films, photos and exhibits help retrace the most historical moments of D-Day. We visited Omaha and Utah beaches, where the major assaults took place and where thousands of American soldiers and sailors died in June of 1944.

The remains of 9,386 servicemen and women are interred in the American Cemetery at Normandy, and I walked among the headstones reading their names and the states from which they came. A Star of David marks the grave of those of the Jewish faith and a Latin cross marks all the others. It is an emotional experience to visit this cemetery and think about all the young Americans who gave their lives for their country.

While we were in Paris we also visited the d'Orsay Museum, window shopped, and enjoyed dining at wonderful restaurants, but I particularly liked just sitting at a table in front of a restaurant while sipping coffee and soaking up the atmosphere.

On Saturday morning, July 30, we left Paris and traveled by train to Castlenaudry in Southern France. Our plans called for a seven day cruise down the Midi Canal. That evening, we enjoyed our first cassoulet dinner at a restaurant in town. This is a local specialty and, while there is no definitive recipe for cassoulet, it is usually a concoction of white haricot beans, garlic sausage, fat bacon, garlic, tomatoes, onions,

cloves, and parsley, all of which is cooked for a very long time.

We stayed overnight at a bed and breakfast called the Hotel du Canal. After breakfast on Friday morning, we checked in at the Crown Blue Lines headquarters, where I was issued a captain's license to pilot our boat. We then walked to a nearby store to buy groceries and, after a brief indoctrination and "check-out" on the boat, we headed down the Midi and soon encountered our first lock.

The Canal du Midi was the idea of Pierre Paul Riquet, who solved the problem of water supply for the canal by the creation of dams in the Black Mountains. The canal was filled with water in 1661 after 15 years of construction by 12,000 men and women. Riquet died October 1, 1660 without seeing his life's work completed, and the sea was only a league away when he died.

The Canal du Midi in France was filled with water in 1661 after 15 years of construction by 12,000 men and women. It was a shady cruise most of the way, due to the towering trees lining each side of the canal. We enjoyed the scenery and, late in the day, some wine and cheese while we cruised down the canal. Sue and Joe offer a toast to another delightful, successful day vacationing in France.

Rain early on Saturday turned into a drizzle lasting until late morning. We kept cruising after breakfast and, during the day, went through 23 locks. These locks were all manually operated and Sue helped each éclusier (lock keeper) crank the gates and close paddles after we entered the lock. Once the back gate was closed then the front paddles were cranked open, which allowed the water level to be adjusted.

This took about 20 minutes. As the water was being released from the lock the boat slowly dropped along with the water level in the lock. We lightly secured the boat with lines running to bollards at the bow and the stern that were let out as the boat lowered with the water level. When we reached the proper level the front gate was then cranked open and we proceeded downstream. We soon became very proficient at doing this, whether we were the only boat going through a lock or included with other boats.

At noon, we moored the boat to the shore of the canal with two steel stakes, unloaded the bicycles that we had on the front deck and rode some distance to a small village. We fortunately found a grocery store that would deliver our supplies to the boat, so we stocked up!

We arrived in Carcassonne early Sunday morning and had to anchor the boat to the shore of the "bassin," as the docking area was already full of boats. Joe, Sue and Mary Lou walked into town to find a laundromat. I stayed with the boat for a while, but later in the morning met them for lunch at the Bistro Florian. After lunch, we took a taxi to the Medieval Castle in the Old Walled City, the history of which dated from 300 B.C., and which is still inhabited to this day. It's built on a hill that rises 500 feet over the Aude Valley and has a profusion of turrets, towers and battlements. Late in the day we resumed our cruise down the Midi, stopping for the night just outside Trebes, where we again anchored to the shore with our steel posts.

On Monday, August 3, we arrived at Trebes just before lunch. We walked into the village to do some shopping then had lunch at a small restaurant right on the Midi Canal. After lunch we took a long taxi ride to La Grasse Abbe, a Benedictine Abbe founded in the 8th century. Fortunately, our taxi driver waited for us and took us back to Trebes, where we resumed our cruise. We stopped near Marsellette, where we anchored for the night.

At noon on Saturday, August 1, we moored the boat to the shore of the canal with two steel stakes, unloaded the bicycles and rode them to a small village for lunch. We ate our breakfast on the boat, but lunch or dinner was usually in a restaurant.

We were up and ready to go at 7:30 a.m. on Tuesday morning. We had a big breakfast on the boat, scrambled eggs with cheese and ham, and plenty of hot coffee. We had a good day cruising, enjoying the scenery. It was shady most of the way due to the towering trees lining each side of the canal. We managed to go through 17 locks on this day – all now operated mechanically – and stopped for the night near L'Somail.

On Wednesday, we started the day with breakfast on the boat, after which we left for Beziers, where we arrived at 4 p.m. We had to anchor at the top of a long series of locks as the lockkeeper closed the locks, for downstream traffic just as we arrived. We walked into town and had a cold beer sitting outside a restaurant on the main parkway in the town center. Then we had dinner at a small, old restaurant with interesting décor – the Restaurant Antiquaire.

Our last day cruising down the Canal Midi was Thursday, August 6. We had breakfast on our boat again and then waited our turn to go through a series of seven locks. We were with the first three boats to go through that day and after going through several more locks, we had a smooth cruise to Port Cassafieres, arriving in the late afternoon.

Early in the morning on Thursday, August 6, our boat was one of the first to go through a series of seven locks at Beziers. This was followed by several more locks in the afternoon to complete our seven day cruise down the Midi Canal. Quite an adventure!

Early on Friday morning, we turned our boat in at the Blue Line Reception office and took a taxi to the train station in Beziers. Our train to Nice didn't leave for several hours, so we took a taxi to St. Nazaire's Cathedral, built in the 14th and 15th centuries. It was very impressive, particularly its huge organ. Friday happened to be Market Day along the main street, les Allees Paul Riquet, and there were many stands selling flowers, produce, wine and other goods. In the afternoon, we took the train to Nice, a five-hour ride, much of it along the coast. We rented a car and drove along the Mediterranean sea to Le Cagnard, a 14th Century Provincial residence, where we stayed the next four nights. This hotel is perched on the ramparts of a medieval village on Rue Sous-Barri in Cagnes-Sur-Mer.

While in Southern France, we visited a number of small, old villages, went through both the Picasso and Renoir museums, and had some memorable lunches and dinners. I particularly liked a lunch I had at Le Jimmy's Brasserie – an unusual vegetable and bacon pizza with a fried egg in the middle of it. On Tuesday, August 11, we traveled across France from Nice to the De Gaulle airport outside Paris on the TGV (fast train) – a delightful way to travel.

We left Paris the next morning, arriving home late in the day, and I returned to the office on Thursday.

We're Up To Our Eyeballs In ISO

When I returned to the office, I was immediately immersed – along with everyone else in the office – in meetings to prepare BBDO Detroit to become ISO 9001-certified. Our sister companies, Ross Roy and PentaCom, were already at the audit stage and achieved certification ahead of BBDO.

The agency's Core team, headed by Dave Harrelson, led the agency in this all-out effort to not only improve the agency's business systems, but to also make them more efficient and effective. The entire staff had to learn new procedures by attending 34 training sessions for System Level Procedures (SLP's) and additional sessions on how to issue or revise Work Instructions (WI's). A great many people on the staff helped to write the new procedures as well as participate in the actual training. Everyone not only memorized BBDO Detroit's ISO 9001 Business System Quality Policy Statement but also learned how to apply it to their position in the agency:

"To be the foremost creative communications resource in helping clients develop their brands through our commitment to quality service and continuous improvement."

In the fall, BBDO Detroit did very well in its ISO 9001 preassessment and passed the audit with flying colors to become ISO 9001-certified. This was a huge achievement.

On Reaching 50 Years In The Advertising Business

My career in the advertising agency business began the third week of September 1948, so the 50 year milestone was passed in September 1998, and that's where this story will end.

I am proud to be in the advertising agency business; proud of the contributions advertising has made to our American economy; proud to be part of a craft that has helped to create a standard of living for us in America that is the highest in the world; and proud to be employed at BBDO, which has a great heritage of superlative advertising.

The past 50 years have been exciting and rewarding. There hasn't been a dull moment because very few professions have come so far so fast. Every year our level of professionalism has inched higher and higher.

And there has never been a dull moment because I have worked with bright, talented, adventurous men and women – people who refused to be satisfied, because there was always a better way and they were determined to find it.

I saw television revolutionize the advertising business and the development of websites as an advertising medium. But what unheard of media lay ahead for us to discover and conquer? What changes in the manners and mores of our nation are before us to anticipate and interpret?

The world is constantly speeding up. Yesterday's advanced methods are out of date even before your computer is delivered.

But no matter what the changes, the advertising agency will continue to be a business of people. It takes people to run this business and people must be motivated by it. And here, I think, is the challenge for the next 50 years.

The person who knows and understands people – as they constantly change, yet inherently remain the same – will have the key to success in the next century.

I am very grateful that my 50 years in advertising were spent doing something that I wanted to do, but I am also very grateful these years were so enjoyable and rewarding. That's due, in part, to the fact that I've taken time "to smell the roses," which I've described frequently in this book.

It's been said that, "one of the great secrets of life is to know what you want to get out of it!" So far as I'm concerned, though, the greatest secret of all is the know how to enjoy doing that.

All of us are in search of guidance, inspiration and reassurance. One of the best pieces of advice about how to live your life was given by Shakespeare in *Hamlet*. These incredible words of wisdom came from the mouth of a strange old man named Polonius: "This above all: to thine own self be true. And it must follow, as the night the day, thou canst not then be false to any man." (Hamlet, I 3:78).

To always be true to oneself is a very hard thing to do. What helps us to be true, I believe, is that we all have the capacity for love. Love is universal. This basic instinct is something we can share and relate to. And on whatever basis we express it to our fellow human beings, being ready and willing to love helps to propel us along on our life's journey.

As long as I enjoy every day, I plan to continue working in the advertising business. I am still living and loving my adventure – advertising.

Thank You, GOD!

Acknowledgements And An Apology

A great many people contributed in one way or another to this book. Although no attempt is made here to include everyone who either helped or influenced my thinking in writing this book, I am nevertheless grateful to ALL of them. The encouragement of Joe and Sue Baker, Kit King, George Pisani, and Mary Lou Vlasov was appreciated at times when I was ready to abandon this project.

I am especially grateful for the assistance of Dan Ewald in editing the book. He eliminated many pages where I wandered off on tangents and he significantly improved the text. Dan has authored or edited seven books and his experience and direction were most valuable.

And, I am particularly indebted to Vince Carducci, Dennis Goschka, and Carol Salsman who were kind enough to read the manuscript. The corrections, as well as the suggestions they made in the text, significantly improved this book.

To Michael Smith, archivist at the Walter P. Reuther Labor Library at Wayne State University, a sincere thanks for his encouragement and for locating and providing some of the photos.

I received assistance from a number of individuals who provided either background information or reference and to each of them I say "thank you." They include Cris Boulis, Ed Coosaia, Chet Craft, Bob Crewe, Leslye Davidson, Peter Farago, James P. Gallagher, Shiela Hoef, Sylvia Hoffman, Diane Lynch, Bob Machus, Andy Magnuson, Dan Meyvis, Karen Odenwald, Jack Sanders, Andy Schmittdiel, and Charlie VanBecelaere.

I owe a very special "thanks" to Linda Leinhos, Sarah Moberly, Linette Neumeyer and Matilda Prevost-Hart for typing the manuscript. I also want to recognize the invaluable assistance I received from Michele Gray, Laura Pizzo, Diane Shelby, and Laura Staats in the production of this book. And a big "thank you" to Kathy Canapini who typeset the book and Diane Schroeder for designing the jacket cover.

This book does not include all the clients that I served during my career in the advertising business as there are more than 25 companies that are not identified and reported for various reasons.

Nor does it include all the special dinners attended that were for some benefit, all the golf outings for some worthy cause in which I participated as well as other such activities that would have only added many, many more pages to this book. Enough of them were reported or described though to help present the experiences that were a part of my "50-Year Adventure in the Advertising Business."

And, there are some people who may read this book and wonder why they were they not included? If anyone is disappointed I apologize but it simply was not possible to include every client that I served over the years nor every individual with whom I had some interaction during the past 50 years.

INDEX

Burton, Rod, 179, 181, 192
Burton, Steve, 164, 171, 176, 178, 180
Bush, President George, 161
Busto, Dan, 202
Calvert, Harry, 1
Cameron, John, 25
Campbell, Brian, 249, 250
Canapini, Kathy (Grobbel), 210, 255
Cantor, Eddie, 25
Capone, Al, 101
Caponigro, Joe, 202
Caradi, Val, 160
Carducci, Sue, 246
Carducci, Vince, 202, 209, 246, 255
Carley, Garry, 193, 205, 218, 240, 248
Carley, Nancy, 205, 218, 245
Carlson, Richard, 25
Carmichael, Hoagy, 86
Carson, Johnnie, 86
Carter, President Jimmy, 96, 110, 111
Catallo, Tom, 183
Chapin, William, 212
Chase, Cochrane, 125
Chencharick, Diane, 137
Church, John, 198
Churchill, Winston, 223
Cipriano, Peter, 74
Clancy, Kathleen, 201
Clark, Chuck, 223
Clark, Karen, 220, 222
Clark, Linda, 198
Clark, Tom, 206, 207, 208, 217, 220, 222, 228, 230, 235, 244, 247, 250
Cline, Philip, 112
Clinton, Hillary, 224
Clinton, President Bill, 197
Collins, Cheryl, 109
Coogan, Jackie, 86
Coosaia, Ed, 255
Coraci, Jim, 181
Corby, Ellen, 97
Cosmopulos, Steve, 15, 17, 226
Costello, Jack, 82
Coward, Noel, 221
Craft, Chester "Chet," 120, 121, 255
Crawford, Tristan, 25
Crenshaw, Ursula, 173, 202, 212, 243, 246

Crewe, Bob, 255
Crooks, Lee, 41-43, 45
Crosby, Bing, 16
Cunningham, B (Tornow), 75, 78, 82, 105, 108, 161, 181, 245
Cunningham, Dwight, 225
Cunningham, Robert, 105, 108, 135, 141, 161, 181, 245
Cunningham, Russ, 217
Curwood, James O., 104
David, Ralph, 24, 42
David, Toby, 53
Davidson, Leslye, 255
Davis, James Vernor, 23, 60
Day, Doris, 220
Defechereux, Phillipe, 174, 175, 180, 183
DeLorean, John, 97
Deluise, Dom, 101
Demorotski, Dave, 110, 126
Denman, Phyllis, 42, 49
Denman, William, 13, 16, 18, 21, 22, 34, 42-46, 49
Denton, Karen, 78
DeVries, Henry, 136
Diana, Princess, 246, 250
Diles, Dave, 104
Diller, Barry, 150
Dillon, Tom, 203
Dingeman, Jim, 3
Diroff, Joe, 106, 107
Dixon, Walter, 94
Dole, Elizabeth, 232
Domergue, Faith, 86
Dorfman, Dr. Stanley, 155
Doyle, Kevin, 140
Drake, Ken, 64
Drew, Don, 149
Drier, Mr. and Mrs., 183
Duchin, Eddie, 16
Duff, Matt, 202, 203, 208, 210, 222
Duffy, Ben, 203
Duffey, Bruce, 174, 180, 182, 183, 200
Duika, Dennis, 70, 71
Duika, Mike, 70, 71
Duika, Paul, 70, 71
Dunaway, Craig, 194

Dunne, Walter, 152
Duronio, Liza (Vlasov), 199, 203
Duronio, Robert, 203
Durstine, Roy, 200, 201
Eaton, Robert, 232, 247, 248
Eberhard, Floyd, 195, 205, 227
Eberhard, Mark, 227
Eisenhower, President Dwight D., 18, 70
Elders, Dr. M. Joycelyn, 217
Eldridge, John, 24, 25
Elgin, Lord, 232
Ellis, Bobby, 24, 25
Emmert, John, 212
Enerson, Jim, 94
Engh, Sue, 170
Engh, Walter, 170
Engler, Governor John, 172, 212, 224, 232, 248, 249
Eubanks, Dayna, 154
Evans, Jeannette, 237
Evans, Keith, 60, 237
Evans, Tom, 250
Ewald, Dan, 63, 106, 159, 160, 172, 255
Ewing, J.R., 110
Fabio, Santa, 247
Farago, Peter, 164, 171, 174, 175, 180-182, 255
Fasules, James, 153
Feldmann, John, 125, 135, 162
Fenkell, Doc, 172
Fernstrum, F.O., 54
Fernstrum, Richard, 54
Field, Sally, 101
Fink, Peter, 84
Fitzpatrick, Sean Kevin, 146, 147
Foley, Ray, 90
Forbes, Jr. Malcom S., 224
Ford, Benson, 60
Ford, Capt. John B., 27
Ford, Cristina, 21
Ford, Edward, 27, 29
Ford, Emory M., 27, 29
Ford, Henry, 212
Ford, II Henry, 21
Ford, III John B., 27, 29, 49
Ford, President Gerald, 96